Lecture Notes in Computer Science 3549

Commenced Publication in 1973
Founding and Former Series Editors:
Gerhard Goos, Juris Hartmanis, and Jan van Leeuwen

Editorial Board

David Hutchison
  Lancaster University, UK
Takeo Kanade
  Carnegie Mellon University, Pittsburgh, PA, USA
Josef Kittler
  University of Surrey, Guildford, UK
Jon M. Kleinberg
  Cornell University, Ithaca, NY, USA
Friedemann Mattern
  ETH Zurich, Switzerland
John C. Mitchell
  Stanford University, CA, USA
Moni Naor
  Weizmann Institute of Science, Rehovot, Israel
Oscar Nierstrasz
  University of Bern, Switzerland
C. Pandu Rangan
  Indian Institute of Technology, Madras, India
Bernhard Steffen
  University of Dortmund, Germany
Madhu Sudan
  Massachusetts Institute of Technology, MA, USA
Demetri Terzopoulos
  New York University, NY, USA
Doug Tygar
  University of California, Berkeley, CA, USA
Moshe Y. Vardi
  Rice University, Houston, TX, USA
Gerhard Weikum
  Max-Planck Institute of Computer Science, Saarbruecken, Germany

Rogério de Lemos
Cristina Gacek
Alexander Romanovsky (Eds.)

Architecting Dependable Systems III

 Springer

Volume Editors

Rogério de Lemos
University of Kent, Computing Laboratory
Canterbury, Kent CT2 7NF, UK
E-mail: r.delemos@kent.ac.uk

Cristina Gacek
Alexander Romanovsky
University of Newcastle upon Tyne, School of Computing Science
Newcastle upon Tyne, NE1 7RU, UK
E-mail: {cristina.gacek, alexander.romanovsky}@ncl.ac.uk

Library of Congress Control Number: 2005932311

CR Subject Classification (1998): D.2, D.4

ISSN   0302-9743
ISBN-10   3-540-28968-2 Springer Berlin Heidelberg New York
ISBN-13   978-3-540-28968-5 Springer Berlin Heidelberg New York

This work is subject to copyright. All rights are reserved, whether the whole or part of the material is concerned, specifically the rights of translation, reprinting, re-use of illustrations, recitation, broadcasting, reproduction on microfilms or in any other way, and storage in data banks. Duplication of this publication or parts thereof is permitted only under the provisions of the German Copyright Law of September 9, 1965, in its current version, and permission for use must always be obtained from Springer. Violations are liable to prosecution under the German Copyright Law.

Springer is a part of Springer Science+Business Media

springeronline.com

© Springer-Verlag Berlin Heidelberg 2005
Printed in Germany

Typesetting: Camera-ready by author, data conversion by Scientific Publishing Services, Chennai, India
Printed on acid-free paper   SPIN: 11556169   06/3142   5 4 3 2 1 0

Foreword

Anyone reading this book very likely depends on software-intensive systems in his/her everyday life. We already know that we are vulnerable to significant personal and economic disruptions due to dependability problems with desktop application software and Web-based commerce applications. Failures of highly dependable systems such as telecommunication and medical applications, while unlikely for any particular system, in aggregate cause serious problems on a regular basis. There are also disturbing signs of increasing dependability problems with safety-critical software incorporated into automobiles and other applications. We live in a world where even car radios come with instructions on how to hold down multiple buttons to perform a system reboot in case of a software crash (the user manual assures us this is a "normal" occurrence and not a defect in the system). As our reliance on dependable computing systems grows, we must learn to do better than we have in the past.

Raising dependability to a first-class citizen in architectural approaches is perhaps the most promising way to improve overall system dependability. The key challenge and opportunity is to create ways to represent, evaluate, and improve dependability as an architectural attribute, rather than a property that is buried in the implementation details.

Historically, architecture-level dependability has meant brute force, statically allocated replication of hardware and software components. This approach was expensive, and was applicable only in the most critical systems. More recently, architectural dependability research has also embraced adaptation of systems so that the architecture itself changes to provide better dependability despite losses of components or changes in the operational environment. This can be accomplished in many ways, including cost-effective dynamic management of replicas, adaptive connectors between components, and even on-the-fly changes in system functionality. Evaluating and validating such approaches remains a challenge, but the opportunities for improving dependability offered by dynamic, changeable architectures is significant and worth pursuing.

This book is the third in a series of volumes presenting the latest results on architecting dependable systems. The series is unique in that it makes available the thinking of a unique collection of researchers that spans the areas of software engineering, fault tolerance, and system architecture. The contents of this volume show the fruits of the evolution and maturation of this area of research. Interest in the dependability of computing services has grown significantly, and is a major emphasis of the papers in this volume. So too has interest in using dynamic reconfiguration as an architecture-level approach to dependability. The ability to assess whether an architecture promotes or inhibits the creation of dependable systems remains an important topic of interest, as it has in previous years.

The papers in this volume are at the forefront of understanding dependability at the architectural level. Once requirements for a system are set, the biggest mistakes and the most beneficial system tradeoff decisions are made at the architectural level. Thus, the ideas presented in this volume are the latest progress in a vital research area for creating more dependable systems.

May 2005

Philip Koopman
Carnegie Mellon University

Preface

The structure of a system is what enables it to generate its behavior from the behaviors of its components. The architecture of a software system is an abstraction of the actual structure of that system. The identification of the system structure early in its development process allows us to abstract away from details of the system, thus assisting the understanding of broader system concerns. One of the benefits of a well-structured system is the reduction of its overall complexity, which in turn should lead to a more dependable system. System dependability is defined as reliance that can be justifiably placed on the service delivered by the system. It has become an essential aspect of computer systems as everyday life increasingly depends on software. It is therefore a matter for concern that dependability issues are usually left until too late in the process of system development.

The process of system structuring may occur at different stages of the development or at different levels of abstraction. Reasoning about dependability at the architectural level has lately grown in importance because of the complexity of emerging applications, and the trend of building trustworthy systems from existing untrustworthy components. There has been a drive from these new applications for dependability concerns to be considered at the architectural level, rather than late in the development process. From the perspective of software engineering, which strives to build software systems that are rid of faults, the architectural consideration of dependability compels the acceptance of faults, rather than their avoidance. Thus the need for novel notations, methods and techniques that provide the necessary support for reasoning about faults at the architectural level. For example, notations should be able to represent non-functional properties and failure assumptions, and techniques should be able to extract from the architectural representations the information that is relevant for evaluating the system architecture from a certain perspective.

This book comes as a result of an effort to bring together the research communities of software architectures and dependability. It was inspired by the Twin Workshops on Architecting Dependable Systems (WADS) organized during ICSE 2004 (International Conference on Software Engineering) and DSN 2004 (Dependable Systems and Networks Conference) where many interesting papers were presented and lively discussions took place. The book addresses issues that are currently relevant to improving the state of the art in architecting dependable systems. It presents a selection of peer-reviewed papers stemming from some original ICSE 2004 WADS and DSN 2004 WADS contributions and several invited ones. The book consists of five parts: Architectures for Dependable Services; Monitoring and Reconfiguration in Software Architectures; Dependability Support for Software Architectures; Architectural Evaluation; and Architectural Abstractions for Dependability.

The first part of the book, entitled *Architectures for Dependable Services*, includes five papers focusing on architectural approaches to ensure dependability for service-oriented computing. The paper "Semantics-Aware Services for the Mobile Computing Environment" by Georgantas, Mokhtar, Tartanoglu and Issarny introduces abstract semantic modelling of mobile services that allows both machine reasoning about service composability and enhanced interoperability at both middleware and application levels. The main motivation behind this work is that the existing service-oriented solutions restrict considerably the openness of dynamic mobile systems by assuming a specific middleware infrastructure for which the components are to be developed. The approach proposed combines software architecture modelling with the semantic reasoning provided by the Semantic Web paradigm. In particular, OWL-based ontologies are used to model mobile components and wireless connectors constituting mobile services and to express the conformance relations for checking composability and interoperability during composition of partially conforming services. The approach is demonstrated using composition of an e-shopping service with mobile customer components. The paper entitled "The Role of Agreements in IT Management Software" was written by Molina-Jimenez, Pruyne and van Moorsel. Various forms of agreements naturally arise in the service provider model as well as in multi-party computing models such as business-to-business, utility and grid computing. The authors argue that distributed computing infrastructures must incorporate agreements as first-class software building blocks to support automated adaptation and management in the presence of multiple (possibly competing) interests. The role of these agreements is twofold: they stipulate obligations and expectations of the involved parties, and they represent the goals to be met by the infrastructure. In order to automate run-time adaptation and management of systems and services, agreements should be encoded and integrated in management software platforms. The paper overviews the state of the art in software support for various forms of agreements, for all stages of their life cycle, as well as the platforms and technologies developed by standards bodies, industries and academia. Gaudel contributed to this part with the paper entitled "Toward Undoing in Composite Web Services". Cancelling or reversing the effect of a former action is a necessity in most interactive systems. The simplest and most frequent form of this activity is the undo command that is available in common text or graphic editors. In the context of collaborative work, undoing is more intricate since the notion of the last action is not always meaningful. Within this framework the so-called 'selective undo', which allows selecting and cancelling some of the former actions, has recently received a lot of attention. The paper builds on the similarities between cooperative work and composite Web services: component Web services are concurrently accessed and may be treated as shared documents for undoing former actions. Among the latest results on undoing in group editors, the transformational model has been found to be useful for generalization to other kinds of distributed systems because it completely avoids backward state recovery and allows the selection and cancellation of any former operation. The paper demonstrates how some aspects of the undo framework can be applied in the context of composite Web services. The next paper, on "Architecting Web Services Applications for Improving Availability", was written by de Lemos. This work introduces an architectural approach that incorporates a number of fault-tolerant techniques: self-checking, comparison, and dynamic reconfiguration. The first two techniques are associated with the detection and handling of faults detected at the component level, while the latter is associated with functionality conducted at the system level. The architectural pattern proposed improves the availability of the composite system by employing two core solutions: individual components, implementing crash-failure semantics, and the system supporting dynamic reconfiguration by switching the processing to a redundant component in case of component failures. The approach allows faults occurring in the services providers or in the communication channels to be tolerated. To demonstrate the applicability of this approach the paper uses a composite application offering dependable stock quotes from the Web by collecting quotes from different Web service providers. The system has been designed and implemented using the Web services core technologies. Some preliminary measurements have confirmed an improvement in the availability of the application. The last paper of the part, "Dependable Composite Web Services with Components Upgraded Online", was written by Gorbenko, Kharchenko, Popov and Romanovsky. The paper proposes solutions for achieving high dependability of composite Web services facing the component online upgrades. The solutions make use of the natural redundancy formed by the latest and the previous releases of a Web service being kept operational. The paper describes how 'confidence in correctness' can be systematically used as a measure of both the component's and the composite Web service's dependability. Architectural solutions are proposed for composing services in which the upgrade of the component service is managed by switching the composite service from using the old release of the component service to using its newer release only when the confidence is high enough, so that the composite service dependability does not deteriorate as a result of the switch. In particular, the solutions support parallel execution of releases for maximizing reliability and responsiveness and sequential execution of releases for minimizing server capacity. The effectiveness of the solutions is assessed by simulation. The paper discusses the implications of employing the proposed architectures, including ways of 'publishing' the confidence in Web services, in the context of relevant standard technologies.

The second part of this book is entitled *Monitoring and Reconfiguration in Software Architectures* and consists of four papers. In the first paper, "Adaptable Analysis of Dependable System Architectures Through Monitoring", Dias and Richardson present an architecture-based approach for software monitoring that allows adapting the analysis of dynamic evolvable dependable systems. As systems evolve the set of properties being monitored might change, as well as the type of analysis to be performed. The MonArch architectural approach described in this paper is configurable, service-oriented, and supported by tools. The second paper, entitled "Run-Time Verification of Statechart Implementations", by Pintér and Majzik, introduces a runtime verification framework for the concurrent supervision of UML statechart implementations. They propose a temporal logic variant for statecharts that enables the definition of dependability criteria in early phases of the development when only preliminary behavioral models are available, and a watchdog module for detecting the errors introduced during the implementation. The latter observes the application using an abstract, but fully elaborated behavioral model as reference information. These two aspects of the framework are integrated with the corresponding error-handling, which is based on the concept of exception events as error indication signals. Using these facilities the visual toolkit of UML is used not only for modelling the application under normal circumstances but also for specifying the behavior in exceptional situations and serves as reference information for error detection. The paper by Malek, Beckman, Mikic-Rakic and Medvidovic, entitled "A Framework for Ensuring and Improving Dependability in Highly

Distributed Systems", presents a framework for guiding the design and development of solutions for the deployment of distributed software systems. This framework enables the extension and reuse of existing solutions, and facilitates autonomic analysis and redeployment of a system's deployment architecture. For that, the framework provides a library of reusable, pluggable, and customizable components that can be leveraged in addressing a variety of distributed system deployment scenarios. A suite of integrated tools supports the framework. The final paper of this section, written by Zhang, Yang, Cheng and McKinley and entitled "Enabling Safe Dynamic Component-Based Software Adaptation", proposes an approach for dynamic adaptation that ensures safe structural and behavioral adaptation with respect to system consistency. The proposed approach takes into consideration dependency analysis for target components, specifically determining viable sequences of adaptive actions and those states in which an adaptive action may be applied safely. The solution is based on a centralized adaptation manager that schedules the adaptation process, which results in a globally minimum solution of adaptive actions. New added components are blocked until the system has reached a new safe state and thus avoiding unsafe adaptation. For dealing with possible failures during the adaptation process timeout and rollback mechanisms are employed to ensure atomicity in the adaptive actions.

Part three of the book is on *Dependability Support for Software Architectures* and includes two papers. The paper on "Architecting and Implementing Versatile Dependability" was authored by Dumitras, Srivastava and Narasimhan. The authors start by stating that distributed applications must often consider and select the appropriate trade-offs among three important aspects: fault-tolerance, performance and resources. The paper introduces the concept of versatile dependability that provides a framework for analyzing and reasoning about these trade-offs in dependable software architectures. The idea is demonstrated by presenting an architecture of a middleware framework that implements versatile dependability by providing the appropriate 'knobs' to tune and recalibrate the trade-offs. The framework can adjust the properties and the behavior of the system at development-time, at deployment-time, and throughout the whole application lifecycle. This renders the versatile dependability approach useful both to applications that require static fault-tolerance configurations supporting the loss/addition of resources and changing workloads, as well as to applications that evolve in terms of their dependability requirements. Through a couple of specific examples, one on adapting the replication style at runtime and the other on tuning the system scalability under given constraints, the paper demonstrates how versatile dependability can provide an extended coverage of the design space of dependable distributed systems. Sowell and Stirewalt contributed to the book with the paper entitled "A Feature-Oriented Alternative to Implementing Reliability Connector Wrappers". This work focuses on connectors and connector wrappers that explicitly specify the protocol of interaction among components and afford the reusable application of extra-functional behaviors, such as reliability policies. Often these specifications are used for modelling and analysis but in this paper the authors investigate how to use them in the design and implementation of the middleware substrate of a distributed system. More specifically the connectors and connector wrappers are elaborated as instantiations of a feature-oriented middleware framework called Theseus supporting the design of asynchronous distributed applications. The results of this study indicate that the relationship between specification features and implementation-level features is not one-to-one and that some specification features have complex, often subtle, manifestations in Theseus design. This work reports the lessons learned during development of these strategies and suggests techniques for designing middleware frameworks and composition tools that explicitly reify and expose the features specified by connectors and connector wrappers.

In the fourth part of this book, entitled *Architectural Evaluation*, there are three papers. In the first paper, entitled "Concerning Predictability in Dependable Component-Based Systems: Classification of Quality Attributes", Crnkovic, Larsson and Preiss analyze in the context of component-based software the relation between the quality attributes of components and those of their compositions. The types of relations are classified according to the possibility of predicting properties of compositions from the properties of the components and according to the influences of other factors such as software architecture or system environment. The classification is exemplified with particular cases of compositions of quality attributes, and its relation to dependability is discussed. Such a classification can indicate the efforts that would be required to predict the system attributes which are essential for system dependability, and in this way the feasibility of the component-based approach in developing dependable systems. In the next paper, entitled "Architecture-Based Reliability Prediction for Service-Oriented Computing", Grassi presents an approach for predicting the reliability of service-oriented computing based on the partial information published with each service. The methodology exploits ideas from the software architecture- and component-based approaches to software design. Different from other approaches, the proposed methodology exploits a "unified" service model that helps in the modelling and analyses of different architectural alternatives, where the characteristics of both "high level" services and "low level" services are explicitly taken into consideration. This model allows us to deal explicitly with the reliability impact of the infrastructure used to assemble the services and make them interact. Another issue that is discussed in this paper is how to automate the reliability prediction of a service assembly. In the last paper of this part, entitled "Fault Injection Approach Based on Architectural Dependencies", Moraes and Martins present a study on how the architectural representation of a system can guide fault injection. Fault injection can be a valuable approach to validate whether an architectural solution achieves the required reliability level. In the proposed approach a dependency analysis technique, based on the interactions through their provided and required interfaces, was applied to establish the relationships among components. Dependency analysis in fault injection can be used to determine the components that are worth injecting, that is, those components whose failures may have greater impact on the system. Dependency relationships can be used to determine the target components in which to inject the faults (or to observe) when a component of interest has low controllability (or observability). An advantage of the proposed approach is that it allows dependencies to be established even when the source code is not available, which can be the case when third-party components are used in a system.

The final part of this book, entitled *Architectural Abstractions for Dependability*, is a collection of two position papers that were based on presentations given during the panel organized at each of the Twin Workshops. The theme of the two panels was the same, as well as the questions that were given to the two sets of panellists. The aim of this exercise was to identify what would be the similarities and differences in the viewpoints of the two sets of panellists that would come predominantly from the software engineering and dependability communities. The two papers in this part of the book are essentially individual opinions taken from each of those panels. In the first position paper, "Problem Structure and Dependable Architecture", Jackson presents an approach to software development in which problem structuring is separated from software architecture. The problem is decomposed into subproblems of familiar classes that can be considered in isolation. Then the interactions among the subproblems are considered. The architectural task is seen as the task of composing the software machines associated with each subproblem and with the more complex interactions among them. This separation of concerns can contribute to achieving system dependability. In the second position paper, "The Lost Art of Abstraction", Hiltunen and Schlichting provide an overview of issues that arise when using abstractions in the area of architecting dependable distributed systems, and propose some approaches to addressing these issues. The latter include the use of translucent abstractions that expose some of the internal workings of the abstraction implementation, customizable abstractions that allow attributes to be matched to the application requirements and execution scenario, and an intrusion-stop process abstraction that potentially provides a basis for architecting survivable systems.

This book is the third book of a series that started two years ago, which includes expanded papers based on selected contributions to the ICSE 2002 and 2003 workshops on Architecting Dependable Systems, and a number of invited papers. We believe that the introduction of the topic of architecting dependable systems is very timely and that we should continue to promote cross-fertilization between the communities of software architectures and dependability.

As editors of this book, we are certain that its contents will prove valuable for researchers in the area and are genuinely grateful to the many people who made it possible. Our thanks go to the authors of the contributions for their excellent work, the ICSE 2004 WADS and DSN 2004 WADS participants for their active support and lively discussions, and Alfred Hofmann from Springer for believing in the idea of this book and helping us to get it published. Last but not least, we appreciate the time and effort our reviewers devoted to guaranteeing the high quality of the contributions. They are J. Burton, B. Cheng, N. Cook, I. Crnkovic, O. Das, F. Di Giandomenico, M. Dias, P. Ezhilchelvan, A.D.H. Farrell, N. Georgantas, C. Godart, P.A. de C. Guerra, H. Guiese, M. Jackson, M. Larsson, H. Madeira, I. Majzik, M. Malek, N. Medvidovic, M. Mikic-Rakic, C. Molina, P. Popov, J.F. Puett III, D. Richardson, C. Rubira, K. Saikoski, R. Schlichting, M. Sergot, E. Strunk, M. Tichy, E. Troubitsina, A. van Moorsel, P. Verbaeten, P. Gil Vicente, M. Zelkowitz, and several anonymous reviewers.

Rogério de Lemos
Cristina Gacek
Alexander Romanovsky

Table of Contents

Part 1. Architectures for Dependable Services

Semantics-Aware Services for the Mobile Computing Environment
*Nikolaos Georgantas, Sonia Ben Mokhtar, Ferda Tartanoglu,
Valérie Issarny* 1

The Role of Agreements in IT Management Software
Carlos Molina-Jimenez, Jim Pruyne, Aad van Moorsel 36

Toward Undoing in Composite Web Services
Marie-Claude Gaudel 59

Architecting Web Services Applications for Improving Availability
Rogério de Lemos 69

Dependable Composite Web Services with Components Upgraded
Online
*Anatoliy Gorbenko, Vyacheslav Kharchenko, Peter Popov,
Alexander Romanovsky* 92

Part 2. Monitoring and Reconfiguration in Software Architectures

Adaptable Analysis of Dependable System Architectures Through
Monitoring
Marcio S. Dias, Debra J. Richardson 122

Runtime Verification of Statechart Implementations
Gergely Pintér, István Majzik 148

A Framework for Ensuring and Improving Dependability in Highly
Distributed Systems
*Sam Malek, Nels Beckman, Marija Mikic-Rakic,
Nenad Medvidovic* 173

Enabling Safe Dynamic Component-Based Software Adaptation
*Ji Zhang, Betty H.C. Cheng, Zhenxiao Yang,
Philip K. McKinley* 194

Part 3. Dependability Support for Software Architectures

Architecting and Implementing Versatile Dependability
Tudor Dumitraş, Deepti Srivastava, Priya Narasimhan 212

A Feature-Oriented Alternative to Implementing Reliability Connector Wrappers
J.H. Sowell, R.E.K. Stirewalt 232

Part 4. Architectural Evaluation

Concerning Predictability in Dependable Component-Based Systems: Classification of Quality Attributes
Ivica Crnkovic, Magnus Larsson, Otto Preiss 257

Architecture-Based Reliability Prediction for Service-Oriented Computing
Vincenzo Grassi 279

Fault Injection Approach Based on Architectural Dependencies
Regina Lúcia de Oliveira Moraes, Eliane Martins 300

Part 5. Architectural Abstractions for Dependability

Problem Structure and Dependable Architecture
Michael Jackson 322

The Lost Art of Abstraction
Matti A. Hiltunen, Richard D. Schlichting 331

Author Index 343

Semantics-Aware Services for the Mobile Computing Environment

Nikolaos Georgantas, Sonia Ben Mokhtar, Ferda Tartanoglu, and Valérie Issarny

INRIA, UR Rocquencourt, Domaine de Voluceau, B.P. 105
78153 Le Chesnay Cedex, France
{Firstname.Lastname}@inria.fr
http://www-rocq.inria.fr/arles

Abstract. Today's wireless networks and devices support the dynamic composition of mobile distributed systems according to networked services and resources. This has in particular led to the introduction of a number of computing paradigms, among which the Service-Oriented Architecture (SOA) seems to best serve these objectives. However, common SOA solutions restrict considerably the openness of dynamic mobile systems in that they assume a specific middleware infrastructure, over which composed system components have been pre-developed to integrate. On the other hand, the Semantic Web introduces a promising approach towards the integration of heterogeneous components; current semantics-based approaches are, however, restricted to application-level interoperability. Combining the elegant properties of software architecture modeling with the semantic reasoning power of the Semantic Web paradigm, this paper introduces abstract semantic modeling of mobile services that allows both machine reasoning about service composability and enhanced interoperability at both middleware and application level.

1 Introduction

Mobile distributed systems cover a broad spectrum of software systems, by considering all the forms of mobility, i.e., personal, computer, and computational [9]. In this paper, we focus on the mobility of devices, as enabled by today's wireless devices. Then, most specifics of mobile distributed systems compared to their stationary counterpart follow from the features of the wireless infrastructure. Mobile software systems must in particular cope with the network's dynamics and quality of service (QoS) management; this is particularly challenging due to resource constraints of the wireless devices and varying bandwidth. A general approach to the management of the network's dynamics, following advances in wireless networks, lies in the automatic configuration and reconfiguration of networked devices and services. This is in particular supported by discovery protocols that provide proactive mechanisms for dynamically discovering, selecting and accessing reachable services and resources that meet a given specification [23]. This leads to building systems, in which (wireless) nodes advertise and consume networked resources according to their specific situation and requirements. This further leads to the design of mobile distributed systems as systems of systems, whose component systems are autonomous and hosted by networked nodes, either wireless or stationary. The systems' configuration then evolves and adapts according to the network connectivity of component systems.

Despite the above dynamics, composition of systems shall ensure the correctness of the system's behavior with respect to target functional and non-functional properties. With respect to the former, the composition must enforce selection of the appropriate component systems and coordination protocols that conform to the specification of the component systems. More specifically, coordination protocols shall be agreed upon by the component systems, i.e., the communication protocols to be followed and their behavior need to be understood and adhered to by all the composed parties, although the protocols implemented by the resulting composite system cannot be fixed at design time. With respect to the latter, it is mandatory to account for the quality of service delivered by component systems and their integration. Specifically, the dynamic composition of mobile distributed systems must both minimize resource consumption on mobile nodes and satisfy the users' requirements with respect to perceived QoS [11].

The dynamic composition of mobile distributed systems from component systems poses further the challenge of interoperability. The composed systems may be implemented and deployed on different software and hardware platforms and assume different network infrastructures. Many of the network interoperability aspects can be addressed by reliance on the ubiquitous Internet's network and transport protocols. However, at middleware and application level, the interoperability problem remains, concerning further both functional and non-functional properties. Considering the large number of players and technologies involved in realizing current mobile distributed systems, solutions to interoperability based on reaching agreements and enforcing compliance with interoperability standards cannot scale. Instead, component systems shall adapt at runtime their functional and non-functional behavior in order to be composed and interoperate with other component systems. Moreover, supporting composition and interoperation requires the definition of behavioral conformance relations to reason on the correctness of dynamically composed systems with respect to both functional and non-functional properties.

Various software technologies and development models have been proposed over the last 30 years for easing the development and deployment of distributed systems (e.g., middleware for distributed objects). However, the generalization of the Internet and the diversification of connected devices have led to the definition of a new computing paradigm: the *Service-Oriented Architecture (SOA)* [29], which allows developing software as services delivered and consumed on demand. The benefit of this approach lies in the looser coupling of the software components making up an application, hence the increased ability to making systems evolve as, e.g., application-level requirements change or the networked environment changes. The SOA approach appears to be a convenient architectural style enabling dynamic integration of application components deployed on the diverse devices of today's wireless networks. This paper provides an overview of SOA principles together with that of the most popular existing software technology complying with the SOA architectural style, which is the *Web Services Architecture*[1]. The Web Services paradigm has been successfully employed in elaborating mobile distributed systems [5]. However, the SOA paradigm

---

[1] http://www.w3.org/TR/ws-arch/

alone cannot meet the interoperability requirements for mobile distributed systems. Drawbacks include: (i) support of a specific core middleware platform to ensure integration at the communication level; (ii) interaction between services based on syntactic description, for which common understanding is hardly achievable in an open environment.

A promising approach towards addressing the interoperability issue relies on semantic modeling of information and functionality, that is, enriching them with machine-interpretable semantics. This concept originally emerged as the vehicle towards the *Semantic Web*[2][2]. The semantic representation of Web pages' content aims at enabling machines to understand and process this content, and to help users by supporting richer discovery, data integration, navigation, and automation of tasks. Semantic modeling is based on the use of ontologies and ontology languages that support formal description and reasoning on ontologies; the *Ontology Web Language (OWL)*[3] is a recent proposition by W3C. A natural evolution to this has been the combination of the Semantic Web and Web Services into *Semantic Web Services* [16]. This effort aims at the semantic specification of Web Services towards automating Web services discovery, invocation, composition and execution monitoring.

The Semantic Web and Semantic Web Services paradigms address application-level interoperability in terms of information and functionality [3,17]. However, interoperability requirements of mobile distributed systems are wider, concerning functional and non-functional interoperability that spans both middleware and application level; conformance relations enabling reasoning on interoperability are further required. In our previous work [6], building on software architecture principles, we elaborated base modeling of mobile software components, which integrates key features of the mobile environment and allows for reasoning on the correctness of dynamically composed systems with respect to both functional and non-functional properties. Building on this work as well as on SOA and Semantic Web principles, we introduce in this paper semantic modeling of mobile services to enable interoperability and dynamic composition of services. Specifically, we introduce OWL-based ontologies to model the behavior of mobile services, which allows both machine reasoning about service composability and enhanced interoperability. We note that our focus is on the functional behavior of services; specification of the non-functional behavior of services and definition of related ontologies is part of our future work, still based on [6]. We further point out that our approach to interoperability is generic, thus, it may as well apply to non-mobile systems. Nevertheless, the requirement for dynamic composition and interoperability is particularly evident in mobile systems, due to their high dynamics and, principally, heterogeneity. Specialization to mobile systems will get clearer when our solution will further address non-functional properties. Our work described in this paper is part of the effort of the IST Amigo[4] project, which elaborates a generic framework for integration of the mobile communications, personal computing, consumer electronics and home automation domains in the networked home environment.

---

[2] http://www.w3.org/2001/sw/
[3] http://www.w3.org/TR/owl-semantics/
[4] http://www.extra.research.philips.com/euprojects/amigo/

In the following, Section 2 provides an overview of the Service-Oriented Architecture paradigm, integrating the Web Services, Semantic Web and Semantic Web Services paradigms. Section 3 introduces our semantic modeling of mobile services. Based on this modeling, Section 4 presents our approach towards semantics-based interoperability. We discuss related work in Section 5 and conclude in Section 6.

2 Service-Oriented Architecture

Service-oriented computing aims at the development of highly autonomous, loosely coupled systems that are able to communicate, compose and evolve in an open, dynamic and heterogeneous environment. Enforcing autonomy with a high capability of adaptability to the changing environment where devices and resources move, components appear, disappear and evolve, and dealing with increasing requirements on quality of service guarantees raise a number of challenges, motivating the definition of new architectural principles, as surveyed below for the service-oriented architectural style. Key properties for service-orientation are further discussed in Section 2.2. Section 2.3, then, presents software technologies enabling service-orientation, focusing on the Web Services Architecture. Finally, an overview of Semantic Web standards and the Semantic Web Services is presented in Section 2.4.

2.1 Service-Oriented Architectural Style

A service-oriented system comprises autonomous software systems that interact with each other through well-defined interfaces. We distinguish *service requesters* that initiate interactions by sending service request messages and *service providers* that are the software systems delivering the service. An interaction is thus defined by the sum of all the communications (service requests and responses) between a service requester and a service provider, actually realizing some, possibly complex, interaction protocol.

Communications between service requesters and providers are realized by exchanging messages, formulated in a common structure processable by both interacting partners. The unique assumption on these interactions is that the service requester follows the terms of a *service contract* specified by the service provider for delivering the service with a certain guarantee on the quality of service. The service requester does not make any assumption on the way the service is actually implemented. In particular, neither the service name nor the message structure implies any specific implementation of the service instance. Indeed, the service implementation may actually be realized either by a simple software function or by a complex distributed system involving as well third party systems. Similarly, the service provider should not make any assumption about the implementation of the service requester side. The only visible behavior for interacting parties is the protocol implemented by the exchange of messages between them.

A *service-oriented architecture* is then defined as a *collection* of service requesters and providers, interacting with each other according to agreed *contracts*. Main characteristics of the service-oriented architecture are its support for the deployment and the interaction of *loosely coupled* software systems, which evolve in a *dynamic* and *open* environment and can be composed with other services. Service requesters usually locate service providers dynamically during their execution using some service discovery protocol.

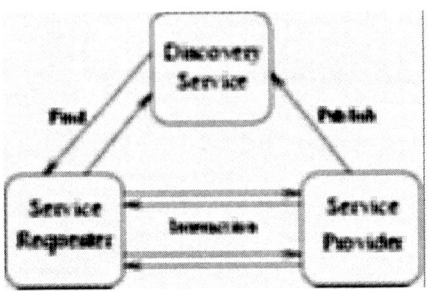

Fig. 1. Service-oriented architecture

A typical service-oriented architecture involving a service requester and a service provider is abstractly depicted in Figure 1. Localization of the service provider by the service requester is realized by querying a *discovery service*. Interactions are then as follows:

- The service provider deploys a service and publishes its description (the service contract) towards the discovery service.
- The service requester sends a query to the discovery service for locating a service satisfying its needs, which are defined with an abstract service contract, i.e., a service description that is not bound to any specific service instance.
- The discovery service returns to the service requester descriptions of available services, including their functional and non-functional interfaces. The requester then processes the description to get the messaging behavior supported by the service, that is, whether interactions should follow request-response, solicit-request, one-way messaging or even more complex interaction protocol, the structure of messages, as well as the concrete binding information such as the service's endpoint address.
- The service requester initiates interactions by sending a request message to the service.
- Interactions between the service requester and the service provider continue by exchanging messages following the agreed interaction protocol.

Note that the discovery service may be centralized (as depicted in Figure 1) or distributed (e.g., supported by all the service hosts), and may further adhere to either a passive (led by service provider) or active (led by service requester) discovery model. It is also important to note that the behavior of the interaction protocol between the service requester and provider may correspond to traditional communication protocols offered by middleware core brokers, but may as well realize a complex interaction protocol involving enhanced middleware-related services (e.g., replication, security, and transaction management) for the sake of quality of service.

The various refinements of the service-oriented software architectural style then lead to interoperability issue at the SOA level, possibly requiring interacting parties to compute and agree on the fly about a common discovery and communication protocol.

2.2 Key Properties of Service-Orientation

As previously stated, the benefit of service orientation for software system architectures lies in the looser coupling of the software components making up an application, hence the increased ability to making systems evolve as, e.g., application-level requirements change and the networked environment changes. Specifically, key properties of SOA with respect to openness include loose coupling, dynamicity and composability, as discussed below.

In a service-oriented architecture, services are provided by autonomously developed and deployed applications. In a dynamic and open system, designing tightly coupled services would compromise the services' respective autonomy, as they cannot evolve independently. Furthermore, failures would be more frequent in case of unavailability or failure of any of the composed applications. Instead, the service-oriented architecture focuses on loosely coupled services. Loosely coupled services depend neither on the implementation of another service (a requester or a third party constituent), nor on the communication infrastructure. To achieve interoperability among diversely designed and deployed systems, services expose a contract describing basically what the service provides, how a service requester should interact with the provider to get the service and the provided quality of service guarantees. Interactions between systems are done by message exchanges. This allows in particular defining asynchronous interactions as well as more complex message exchange patterns by grouping and ordering several one-way messages (e.g., RPC-like messaging by associating a request message with a response message). Moreover, the message structure should be independent of any programming language and communication protocol. A service requester willing to engage in an interaction with a service provider must be able – based solely on this contract – to decide if it can implement the requested interactions. The service contract comprises the functional interface and non-functional attributes describing the service, which is abstractly specified using a common declarative language processable by both parties. The service definition language should be standardized for increased interoperability among software systems that are autonomously developed and deployed. Indeed, the service definition language should not rely on any programming language used for implementing services, and the service being abstractly specified should be as independent as possible from the underlying implementation of the service. The service definition then describes functionalities offered by means of message exchanges, by providing the structure of each message and, optionally, ordering constraints that may be imposed on interactions involving multiple messages exchanges. Non-functional attributes may complement the functional interface by describing the provided support for QoS. Several non-functional properties may be here defined, such as security, availability, dependability, performance etc.

In a distributed open system, the system components and the environment evolve continuously and independently of each other. New services appear, existing services disappear permanently or get unavailable temporarily, services change their interfaces etc. Moreover, service requesters' functional or non-functional requirements may change over time depending on the context (i.e., both user-centric and computer-centric context). Adaptation to these changes is thus a key feature of the service-oriented architecture, which is supported thanks to service discovery and dynamic binding. To cope with the highly dynamic and unpredictable nature of service availability, services to be integrated in an application are defined using abstract service descriptions. Service requesters locate available services conforming to abstract service descriptions using a service discovery protocol, in general by querying a service registry. On the other hand, service providers make available their offered services by publishing them using the service discovery protocol. The published service descriptions contain the functional and non-functional interfaces of services, and provide as well concrete binding information for accessing the service such as the service's URI and the underlying communication protocol that should be used. Service discovery and integration of available concrete services are done either at runtime, or before the execution of interactions. Each interaction initiated by a service requester in a service-oriented architecture may thus involve different services or service providers, as long as the contract between the service provider and the service requester is implementable by both parties, i.e., the service description complies with the requirements of the service requester, which can in turn implement supported interactions of the service provider.

An advantage of describing services through well-defined interfaces is the possibility to compose them in order to build new services based on their interfaces, irrespective of technical details regarding their underlying platform and their implementation. A service built using service composition is called a composite service, and can in its turn, be part of a larger composition. The composition process is a complex task requiring integrating and coordinating diversely implemented services in a heterogeneous environment. It further requires dealing with the composition of QoS properties of individual services in order to provide a certain degree of QoS at the level of the composite service.

2.3 Software Technologies Enabling Service-Orientation

Compared to existing software technologies in the area of distributed computing, concepts introduced with the service-oriented architectural style are not new and can be implemented using various technologies. However, none of existing computing models or technologies do provide a complete solution. Furthermore, they often make assumptions that are not fully compatible with service-oriented computing concepts. A standardized model is also crucial to achieve the vision of service-oriented computing for providing full interoperability among autonomous components.

Object-oriented computing promotes the distinction between the implementation of a class and its public interface. However, there is a tight coupling between the interface of a class and its implementation. On the other hand, object-orientation tends to build fine-grained classes with strong dependencies between them. Component-based systems do provide means for building composite systems out of independent building blocks that hide their implementation. However, component-based system integration is not appropriate for building dynamic systems, because of the strong dependencies upon available components at design time and of the interoperability issues between diversely implemented systems on heterogeneous platforms. Furthermore, interaction of components is often done using specific communication protocols, which is not always implementable by all parties. Distributed computing models such as CORBA[5] tried to fill this gap by enforcing interoperability by providing implementation-independent interfaces, standard communication protocols and a dynamic discovery service. However, strong assumptions made on related standards, like the specific communication protocol that is not easily implementable in all environments and the interface definition language that is tightly coupled with the type system of the service implementation, caused different vendors and developers to adopt custom and not standardized implementation decisions. While CORBA is widely used within single administrated domains, it failed to be adopted in the large scale.

The Web Services Architecture appears as the most compliant architecture to SOA principles, essentially due to its support for machine-readable, platform-neutral description languages using XML (eXtensible Markup Language), message-based communication that supports both synchronous and asynchronous invocations, and its adaptation to standard Internet transport protocols. According to the working definition of the W3C, a Web service is a software system identified by a URI, whose public interfaces and concrete details on how to interact with are described using XML-based languages. Using standardized specifications for defining Web services enforces interoperability among diversely implemented and deployed systems. In particular, Web service descriptions may be published and discovered by other software systems by querying common Web service registries. Systems may then interact in a manner prescribed by the service description, using XML-based messages conveyed by standard Internet transport protocols like HTTP. Web services can be implemented using any programming language and executed on heterogeneous platforms, as long as they provide the above features. This allows Web services owned by distinct entities to interoperate through message exchange. By providing standardized platform-neutral interface description languages, message-oriented communications using standard Internet protocols, and service discovery support, Web Services enable building service-oriented systems on the Internet. Although the definition of the overall Web Services Architecture is still incomplete, the base standards have already emerged from standardization consortiums such as W3C and Oasis[6], which define a core middleware for Web Services, partly building upon results from object-based and component-based middleware technologies. These standards relate to the specification of Web services and of supporting interaction protocols, referred to as conversation, choreography[7] or orchestration (see Figure 2).

---

[5] OMG Common Object Request Broker Architecture. http://www.corba.org.
[6] http://www.oasis-open.org/
[7] http://www.w3.org/2002/ws/chor

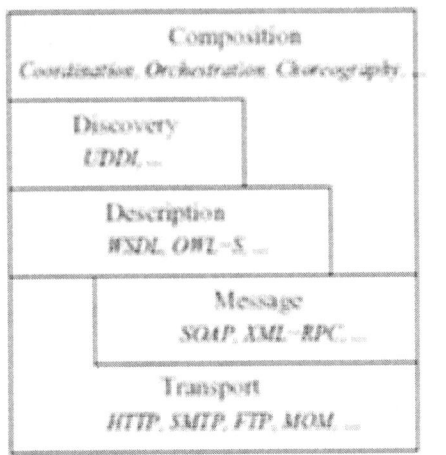

Fig. 2. Web Services Architecture

There is no single implementation of the Web Services Architecture. As Web Services refer to a group of related, emerging technologies aiming at turning the pervasive Web into a collection of computational resources, each with well-defined interfaces for their invocation, a number of implementation of these technologies are being introduced. Furthermore, Web Services are designed to be language and platform-independent, which leads to the implementation of a number of software tools and libraries easing the integration of popular software platforms into the Web Services Architecture and/or easing the development and enabling deployment of Web services in various environments. The interested reader is referred to Web sites keeping track of relevant implementations for an exhaustive list, and in particular the Xmethods site at http://www.xmethods.com/.

2.4 Semantic Modeling of Services

The World Wide Web contains a huge amount of information, created by multiple organizations, communities and individuals, with different purposes in mind. Web users specify URI addresses and follow links to browse this information. Such a simple access method explains the popularity of the Web. However, this comes at a price, as it is very easy to get lost when looking for information. The root of the problem is that today's Web is mainly syntactic. Documents structures are well defined but their content is not machine-processable. The Semantic Web specifically aims at overcoming this constraint. The "Semantic Web" expression, attributed to Tim Berners-Lee, envisages the future Web as a large data exchange space between humans and machines, allowing an efficient exploitation of huge amounts of data and various services. The semantic representation of Web pages' content will allow machines to understand and process this content, and to help users by supporting richer discovery, data integration, navigation, and automation of tasks.

To achieve the Semantic Web objectives, many Web standards are being used, and new ones are being defined. These standards may be organized in layers representing the Semantic Web structure, as shown in Figure 3. The *Unicode* and *URI* layers are the basic layers of the Semantic Web; they enforce the use of international characters, and provide means for object identification. The layer constituted of *XML*, *XML namespace* and *XML schema* allows a uniform structure representation for documents. By using *RDF* and *RDF Schema*, it is further possible to link Web resources with pre-defined vocabularies. The *ontology* layer is then based on RDF (Resource Description Framework) and RDF Schema, and allows the definition of more complex vocabularies, and relations between different concepts of these vocabularies. Finally, the *logic* and *proof* layers allow the definition of formal rules and the reasoning based on these rules.

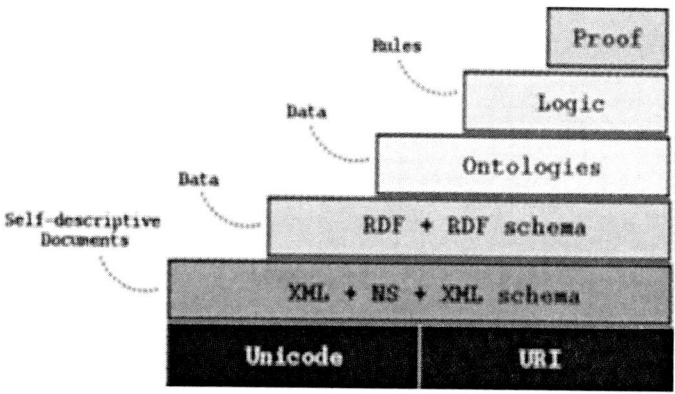

Fig. 3. Semantic Web structure

Specifically, RDF is a simple language allowing the semantic description of Web resources. This semantic description is specified as a triple in RDF. Such a triple is constituted of a subject, a predicate and an object. The subject is a link to the described resource. The predicate describes an aspect, a characteristic, an attribute, or a specific relation used to describe the resource. The object is an instance of a specific predicate used to describe a specific resource. Each piece of information in a triple is represented by a URI. The use of URIs ensures that the concepts that are used are not just structures stored in documents, but references to unique definitions accessible everywhere via the Web. For example, if one wants to access several databases storing persons' names and their addresses, and gets a list of the persons living in a specific district by using the postal code of the district, it is necessary to know for each database what are the fields representing the names and the postal codes. RDF allows specifying that: "(the field 5 of the database A)(is of type)(postal code)", by using URIs for each term. RDF Schema is then a standard describing how to use RDF to define vocabularies, by adding to RDF the ability to define hierarchies, in terms of classes and properties. In RDF Schema, a class is a set of resources having similar characteristics, and the properties are relations that link the subject resources to the object ones.

In its origin, the term ontology is a philosophic term that means "the science of being". This term has been reused in computer science to express knowledge representation and the definition of categories. Ontologies describe structured vocabularies, containing useful concepts for a community that wants to organize and exchange information in a non-ambiguous manner. Thus, an ontology is a structured and coherent representation of concepts, classes, and relations between these concepts and classes pertaining to a vision of the world of a specific community. One of the most common goals in developing ontologies is for "sharing common understanding of the structure of information among people or software agents". According to the description given in [24], an ontology is a formal explicit description of concepts in a domain of discourse (classes, sometimes called concepts), properties of each concept describing various features and attributes of the concept (slots, sometimes called roles or properties), and restrictions on slots (facets, sometimes called role restrictions). An ontology together with a set of individual instances of classes constitutes a knowledge base.

One of the most widely used languages for specifying ontologies is the DAML+OIL language. DAML+OIL is the result of the fusion of two languages: DAML (Darpa Agent Markup Language) by the DARPA organization and OIL (Ontology Inference Layer) by European projects. Based on the DAML+OIL specification, the W3C has recently proposed the *Ontology Web Language (OWL)*, which has been used in introducing *Semantic Web Services*, as surveyed below. OWL is a one of the W3C recommendations related to the Semantic Web. More expressive than RDF Schema, it adds more vocabulary for describing properties and classes (such as disjointness, cardinality, equivalence). There are three sublanguages of OWL: OWL Lite, OWL DL and OWL Full. OWL Lite is the simplest one; it supports the basic classification hierarchy and simple constraints. OWL DL is named so, due to its correspondence with Description Logics[8]; it provides the maximum of OWL expressiveness, while guaranteeing completeness and decidability. OWL Full also provides the maximum of OWL expressiveness, but without computational guarantees. Thus, due to its syntactic freedom, reasoning support on OWL Full ontologies is less predictable compared to OWL DL.

OWL-S[9] (previously named DAML-S) is an OWL-based Web service ontology to describe Web services properties and capabilities, resulting from the work of many industrial and research organisms such as BBN Technologies, CMU, Nokia, Stanford University, SRI International and Yale University. OWL-S specifies a model for Web services semantic description, by separating the description of a Web services' capabilities from its external behavior and from its access details. Figure 4 abstractly depicts the model used in OWL-S. In this figure, we can see that a service description is composed of three parts: the service profile, the process model and the service grounding. The service profile describes the capabilities of the service, the process model describes the external behavior of the service, and the service grounding describes how to use the service.

---

[8] A field of research concerning logics that form the formal foundation of OWL.
[9] http://www.daml.org/services/

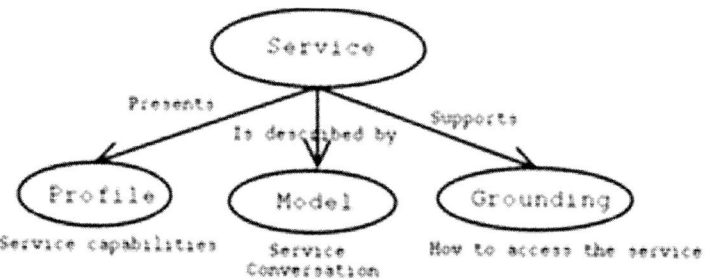

Fig. 4. OWL-S model

The service profile gives a high level description of a service and its provider. It is generally used for service publication and discovery. The service profile is composed of three parts:

- An informal description of the service oriented towards a human user; it contains information about the origin of the service, the name of the service, as well as a textual description of the service.
- A description of the services' capabilities, in terms of Inputs, Outputs, Preconditions and Effects (IOPE). The inputs and outputs are those exchanged by the service; they represent the information transformation produced by the execution of a service. The pre-conditions are those necessary to the execution of the service and the effects are those caused by the execution of the service; in combination, they represent the state change produced to the world by the execution of a service. Preconditions and effects are represented as logical formulas in an appropriate language.
- A set of attributes describing complementary information about the service, such as the service type, category, etc.

The process model is a representation of the external behavior – termed conversation – of the service as a process; it introduces a self-contained notation for describing process workflows. This description contains a specification of a set of sub-processes that are coordinated by a set of control constructs, such as a *sequence* or a *parallel* construct; these sub-processes are atomic or composite. The atomic processes correspond to WSDL operations. The composite processes are decomposable into other atomic or composite processes by using a control construct.

The service grounding specifies the information that is necessary for service invocation, such as the protocol, message formats, serialization, transport and addressing information. It is a mapping between the abstract description of the service and the concrete information necessary to communicate with the service. The OWL-S service grounding is based on WSDL. Thus, it introduces a mapping between high-level OWL classes and low-level WSDL abstract types that are defined by XML Schema.

3 Modeling Services for Mobile Computing

As already discussed, interoperability requirements of mobile distributed systems concern functional and non-functional interoperability that spans both middleware and application level; conformance relations enabling reasoning on interoperability are further required. As inferred from the survey of the previous section, the Service-Oriented Architecture with Web Services as its main representative, semantically enhanced by Semantic Web principles into Semantic Web Services, only partially address the interoperability requirements of mobile distributed systems.

On the other hand, mobile services may be conveniently modeled using concepts from the software architecture field: architectural components abstract mobile services and connectors abstract interaction protocols above the wireless network. Based on these concepts, we have addressed in [6] the composition of mobile distributed systems at both middleware and application level by modeling functional and non-functional properties of services and introducing conformance relations for reasoning on composability. Building on this work, we introduce in this section semantic modeling of mobile services so as to offer enhanced support to the interoperability requirements of mobile distributed systems. We focus on the functional behavior of services; semantic modeling of the non-functional behavior of services is part of our future work. Specifically, we introduce OWL-based ontologies to model mobile components and wireless connectors constituting mobile services. The reasoning capacity of OWL enables conformance relations for checking composability and interoperability methods for composing partially conforming services, as further detailed in Section 4. In our modeling, we have adopted some existing results from the OWL-S community [20]. Nevertheless, our approach is wider and treats in a comprehensive way the interoperability requirements of mobile distributed systems. In Section 5, we point out the enhanced features of our approach, comparing with OWL-S approaches.

In order to illustrate the exploitation of our model, we consider the example of an *e-shopping* service selling a specific type of goods, provided by a *vendor* component, which is normally stationary, hosted by some server. Mobile *customer* components hosted by wireless devices may access the vendor component over the wireless Internet to purchase goods on behalf of a human client.

3.1 Mobile Services

In traditional software architecture modeling, a service specifies the *operations* that it provides to and requires from the environment. The dynamic composition of the mobile service with peer networked services further requires enriching the service's functional specification so as to ensure adherence to the coordination protocols to be satisfied for ensuring correct service delivery despite the dynamics of the networks, i.e., the interaction protocols that must be atomic. The specification of coordination protocols among mobile services relates to the one of conversation or choreography in the context of Web Services. Such a specification also relates to the one of interaction protocols associated with component ports to ensure conformance with connector roles, as, e.g., supported by the Wright architecture description language [25].

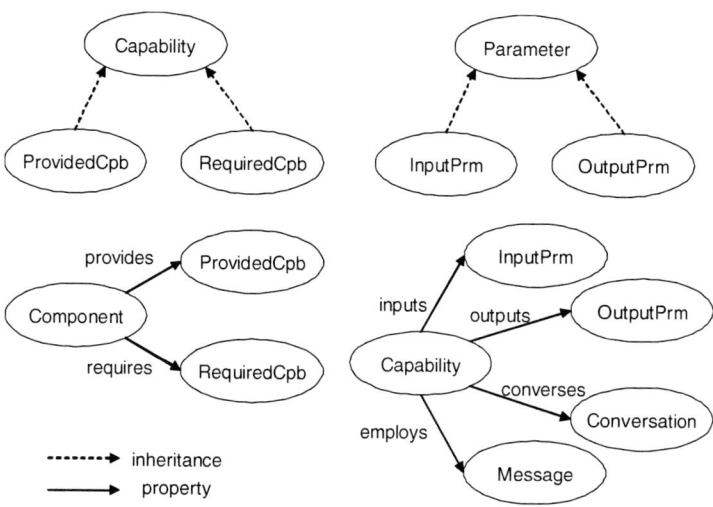

Fig. 5. Basic elements of the mobile service ontology

Building on the above fundamentals, we introduce a *mobile service* ontology to model the functional behavior of mobile services. The basic elements of this ontology are depicted in Figure 5. Component is the central class of the ontology representing the component realizing a mobile service. We introduce the notion of Capability for a component, which is a high-level functionality provided or required by the component, thus, refined as ProvidedCpb and RequiredCpb. A capability specifies a number of inputs and outputs, modeled as classes InputPrm and OutputPrm, which are derived from the parent class Parameter. We associate capabilities to distinct conversations supported by a component. Thus, Capability is related to Conversation, which contains the specification of the related conversation. Capability is further related to a set of messages employed in the related conversation; class Message is used to represent such messages. Conversations are specified as processes in the π-calculus [4], as introduced in [6].

We model communication between service components as exchange of one-way messages. This is most generic and assumes no specific interaction model, such as RPC or event-based, which is realized by the underlying connector. For example, in the case of RPC, communication between two peer components is based on the execution of operations that are provided by one peer and invoked by the other peer. Such an operation may be represented as the exchange of two messages, the first being the invocation of the operation and the second being the return of the result. Hence, we enrich our ontology to represent messages in a detailed manner, as depicted in Figure 6. Class Message is related to class Parameter, which represents all parameters carried by the message; members of the same class are the inputs and outputs of a capability, as defined above. As capability is a high-level functionality of the component, the inputs and outputs of a capability are a subset of all parameters of the messages employed within this capability. Parameter is associated to classes PrmType, PrmValue and PrmPosition; the latter denotes the position of the parameter within the message. This representation of messages is most generic. A special parameter commonly carried by a message is an identifier of its function, i.e., what the message does. In the case of RPC, for example, this identifier is the name of the operation. We represent this identifier with the derived class MsgFunction.

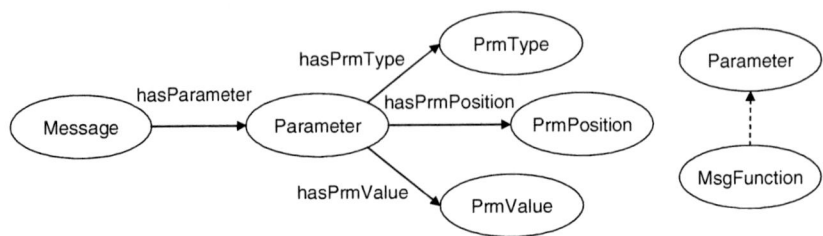

Fig. 6. Message modeling in the mobile service ontology

Based on the introduced mobile service ontology, a mobile service specification is as follows. For simplicity and space economy, we use – instead of the OWL notation – a simplified notation, only listing related OWL classes and their properties. Classes and instances of classes – termed *individuals* in OWL – are denoted by their first letter in uppercase, while properties are written in lowercase.

```
Component
    provides ProvidedCpb
    requires RequiredCpb
ProvidedCpb or RequiredCpb
    inputs InputPrm
    outputs OutputPrm
    converses Conversation
    employs Message
Message
    hasParameter MsgFunction
    hasParameter Parameter
MsgFunction or Parameter
    hasPrmType PrmType
    hasPrmPosition PrmPosition
    hasPrmValue PrmValue
```

Example. We now employ the elaborated mobile service ontology to model the vendor component involved in the e-shopping service of the example introduced above. We refine the mobile service ontology to produce the vendor ontology. Each class of the mobile service ontology is instantiated; the produced individuals constitute the vendor ontology. We assume that the vendor component supports the operations *browse()*, *book()* and *buy()*, which shall be realized as synchronous two-way interactions. From these operations we derive the messages supported by the vendor component, which we define as individuals of the class Message. For example, operation *browse()* produces the following listed messages, where parameters (MsgFunction and `Parameter` individuals) of the messages are also specified. In our simplified notation, we use braces to denote that a class or individual is associated through a property to more than one other classes or individuals.

```
Message BrowseReq
    hasParameter BrowseReqFunc
    hasParameter ArticleInfo
Message BrowseRes
    hasParameter BrowseResFunc
    hasParameter {ArticleInfo, ArticleId, Ack}
```

`BrowseReq` is the input request message and `BrowseRes` is the output response message of the synchronous two-way interaction. The other two operations produce the following messages, where `MsgFunction` parameters have been omitted:

```
Message BookReq
    hasParameter ArticleId
Message BookRes
    hasParameter {ReservationId, Ack}

Message BuyReq
    hasParameter {ReservationId, CreditCardInfo, ShippingInfo}
Message BuyRes
    hasParameter {ReceiptId, Ack}
```

Operation *browse()* allows browsing for an article by providing – possibly incomplete – information on the article; if this article is available, complete information is returned, along with the article identifier and a positive acknowledgement. Operation *book()* allows booking an article; a reservation identifier is returned. Operation *buy()* allows buying an article by providing credit card information and shipping information; a receipt identifier is returned. The vendor component supports further the operations *register_for_availability()* and *notify_of_availability()*, which shall be grouped in an asynchronous two-way interaction. These operations are encoded as follows:

```
Message RegisterForAvailabilityIn
    hasParameter {ArticleInfo, ReplyAddress}
Message NotifyOfAvailabilityOut
    hasParameter {ArticleInfo, SourceAddress}
```

The suffixes *in* and *out* have been added to these message names just to make clear the direction of the messages. The first operation or message allows registering for a specific article. When this article becomes available, a notification is sent back to the registered entity by means of the second operation or message. The vendor component and a peer customer component take care of correlating the two operations by including appropriate identifiers in the operations. Furthermore, we specify syntactic characteristics of the produced messages. For example, for message `BrowseReq`:

```
MsgFunction BrowseReqFunc
   hasPrmType string
   hasPrmPosition 1
   hasPrmValue "browse_req"
Parameter ArticleInfo
   hasPrmType some complex type
   hasPrmPosition 2
```

The supported messages are incorporated into the following specified two capabilities (`ProvidedCpb` individuals) provided by the vendor component. We specify the inputs (`InputPrm` individuals) and outputs (`OutputPrm` individuals) of these capabilities, as well as the associated conversations (`Conversation` individuals) described in the π-calculus. In the conversation specifications the following listed notation is used. For simplicity, we omit message parameters in the conversation specifications.

$P, Q ::=$		Processes
	$P.Q$	Sequence
	$P\|Q$	Parallel composition
	$P+Q$	Choice
	$!P$	Replication
	$v(x)$	Input communication
	$v[X]$	Output communication

```
Component Vendor
   provides {Buy, Available}
ProvidedCpb Buy
   inputs {ArticleInfo, CreditCardInfo, ShippingInfo}
   outputs {ArticleInfo, ReceiptId, Ack}
   converses "
       BrowseReq().BrowseRes[].
       (
         !(BrowseReq().BrowseRes[]) +
         !(BrowseReq().BrowseRes[]).BookReq().BookRes[].BuyReq().BuyRes[]
       ) "
ProvidedCpb Available
   inputs ArticleInfo
   outputs ArticleInfo
   converses "RegisterForAvailabilityIn().NotifyOfAvailabilityOut[]"
```

An entity using capability `Buy` may either browse for articles several times, or browse several times and then book and buy an article. The inputs and outputs of `Buy` are a subset of all the parameters involved in the three included operations. A number of intermediate parameters, such as `ArticleId` and `ReservationId`, are further involved in the conversation; these are not visible at the level of capability `Buy`. An entity using capability `Available` registers and gets notified asynchronously of a newly available article.

It is clear from the example that most of the introduced classes of our ontology represent a semantic value that expresses the meaning of the specific class. For example, giving the value Buy to ProvidedCpb, we define the semantics of the specific capability provided by the vendor component, as long as we can understand the meaning of Buy. The only classes that do not represent a semantic – according to the above definition – value are Conversation, which is a *string* listing the π-calculus description of the related conversation; PrmPosition, which is an *integer* denoting the position of the related parameter within the message; and PrmValue, which is the actual value of the parameter. Incorporating these non-semantic elements into our ontology allows an integrated modeling of mobile services with minimum resorting to external formal syntactic notations, as the π-calculus.

3.2 Wireless Connectors

In the mobile environment, connectors specify the interaction protocols that are implemented over the wireless network. This characterizes message exchanges over the transport layer to realize the higher-level protocol offered by the middleware, on top of which the mobile component executes. In addition, the dynamic composition of mobile services leads to the dynamic instantiation of connectors. Hence, the specification of wireless connectors is integrated with the one of mobile services (actually specifying the behavior of connector roles), given that the connectors associated with two interacting mobile services must compose.

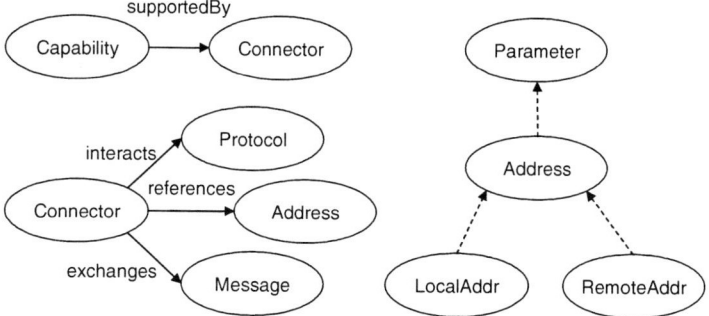

Fig. 7. Connector modeling in the mobile service ontology

To integrate connectors in the so far elaborated mobile service model, we extend the mobile service ontology with a number of new classes, as depicted in Figure 7. Capability is related to class Connector, which represents the specific connector used for a capability; we assume that a capability relies on a single connector, which is a reasonable assumption. A connector realizes a specific interaction protocol; this is captured in the relation of Connector to class Protocol, which contains the specification of the related interaction protocol. Interaction protocols are specified as processes in the π-calculus.

An interaction protocol realizes a specific interaction model for the overlying component, such as RPC or event-based. This interaction model is implicitly specified in the π-calculus description of the interaction protocol. Nevertheless, the interaction model may additionally be semantically represented by class `Connector`. As there is a large variety of connectors and associated interaction models [21], there is no meaning in enriching the generic mobile service ontology with a taxonomy of connectors. Class `Connector` may be associated to external ontologies on a case by case basis to represent the interaction model supported by a specific connector.

Furthermore, a connector supports an addressing scheme for identifying itself as well as its associated component over a network realized by the underlying transport layer. A number of different approaches are allowed here, depending on the addressing functionality already supported by the transport layer and on the multiplexing capability of the connector, i.e., its capability to support multiple components. The latter further relates to a connector acting as a container for components, e.g., a Web server being a container for Web applications. Thus, considering the Web Services example, we may distinguish the following addressing levels:

- The TCP/IP transport layer supports IP or name addressing of host machines.
- A Web Services SOAP/HTTP connector binds to a specific TCP port; in this case the transport layer specifies an addressing scheme for the overlying connectors.
- The SOAP/HTTP connector supports addressing of multiple Web service components, treating Web services as Web resources; thus, incorporating the underlying IP address & port number addressing scheme, the SOAP/HTTP connector supports URI addressing.

To be most generic, we enable a connector addressing scheme without assuming any connector addressing pre-specified by the transport layer. This scheme shall incorporate the established transport layer addressing. Moreover, this scheme shall integrate component identifiers for distinguishing among multiple components supported by a single connector, when this is the case. The introduced generic scheme is represented by the relation of `Connector` to class `Address`. Thus, `Address` represents a reference of a mobile service component accessible through a specific connector and underlying transport layer. `Address` is a subclass of `Parameter`.

`Connector` is further related to a set of messages exchanged in the related interaction protocol, which are members of the class `Message`. This is the same generic class used for component-level messages, as it also applies very well to connector-level messages. Communication between connectors can naturally be modeled as exchange of one-way messages; this takes place on top of the underlying transport layer. To enable component addressing, connector-level messages integrate addressing information. To be most generic, we enable connector-level messages to carry complete addressing information, assuming no addressing information added by the transport layer; certainly, this scheme may easily be adapted according to the addressing capabilities of the transport layer. We introduce two subclasses of `Address`, named `LocalAddr` and `RemoteAddr`, which represent the local address and remote address information included in a connector-level message exchanged between two peer connectors. Remote address information is used to route the message to its destination, while local address information identifies the sender and may be used to route back a possible response message.

According to the distinction introduced in the previous section, only `Protocol` does not represent a semantic value among the new classes of our ontology. Based on the extended mobile service ontology, a mobile service specification is extended as follows to integrate connectors:

```
ProvidedCpb or RequiredCpb
   supportedBy Connector
Connector
   interacts Protocol
   references Address
   exchanges Message
Message
   hasParameter LocalAddr
   hasParameter RemoteAddr
```

Example. We now complete the modeling of the vendor component based on the extended mobile service ontology. As specified in the previous section, the vendor component relies on two connectors, one supporting synchronous two-way interactions and one supporting asynchronous two-way interactions. By properly instantiating class Connector and its associated classes, we can model the two required connectors, thus completing the vendor ontology. We define two individuals of Connector:

```
Connector VConn1
   interacts "vreq(vreq_prm).vres[VRES_PRM]"
   references VAddr
   exchanges {VReq, VRes}
Connector VConn2
   interacts "vreq(vreq_prm)" , "vres[VRES_PRM]"
   references VAddr
   exchanges {VReq, VRes}
Address VAddr
   hasPrmType URL
   hasPrmValue "http://www.e-shopping.com:8080/vendor"
```

Both connectors exchange a request and a response message. For connector VConn1, the emission of the response message is synchronous, following the reception of the request message; while for connector VConn2, the emission of the response message is asynchronous, not coupled with the reception of the request message. Both connectors enable addressing the vendor component with a URL address following the scheme *http://<host>:<port>/<path>*. Each connector supports a specific capability of the vendor component:

```
ProvidedCpb Buy
   supportedBy VConn1
ProvidedCpb Available
   supportedBy VConn2
```

Furthermore, we specify the characteristics of messages VReq and VRes. For example, for message VReq, which is input by the vendor component:

```
Message VReq
   hasParameter VReqFunc
   hasParameter {VLocalAddr, VRemoteAddr}
   hasParameter VReqPrm
MsgFunction VReqFunc
   hasPrmType byte
   hasPrmPosition 1
   hasPrmValue 7Ah
RemoteAddr VRemoteAddr
   hasPrmType URL
   hasPrmPosition 3
   hasPrmValue "http://www.e-shopping.com:8080/vendor"
LocalAddr VLocalAddr
   hasPrmType URL
   hasPrmPosition 2
Parameter VReqPrm
   hasPrmType hex
   hasPrmPosition 4
```

PrmValue for VLocalAddr will be determined by the peer connector – supporting a customer component – sending the request message. PrmType hex of VReqPrm determines the encoding of the component-level message (e.g., an invocation of a remote operation) carried by the connector-level request message. This further corresponds to the serialization of remote method invocations performed by a middleware platform.

4 Semantics-Based Interoperability

Given the above functional specification of mobile services and related wireless connectors, functional integration and composition of mobile services in a way that ensures correctness of the mobile distributed system may be addressed in terms of conformance of respective functional specifications. Conformance shall be checked both at component and at connector level; for two services to compose, conformance shall be verified at both levels. To this end, we introduce a conformance relation for each level. To allow for the composition of heterogeneous mobile services, our conformance relations enable identifying partial conformance between components and between connectors. Then, we employ appropriate interoperability methods at each level to ensure composition of heterogeneous components and connectors; for two services to compose, interoperability must be established at both levels.

Our conformance relations and interoperability methods exploit our ontology-based modeling of mobile services. As detailed in Section 3, the introduced mobile service ontology enables representing semantics of components and connectors. Nevertheless, to enable a common understanding of these semantics, their specification shall build upon possibly existing globally shared ontologies. Incorporating external commonly shared ontologies serve two purposes: (i) these ontologies are used as common vocabulary for interpreting mobile services' semantics; and (ii) these ontologies may be used to extend the mobile service ontology to enable a more precise representation of mobile services' semantics. OWL targeting the semantic Web provides inherent support to the distribution of ontologies enabling the incremental refinement of ontologies based on other imported ontologies. Further, employing OWL to formally describe semantics allows for automated interpretation and reasoning on them, thus enabling conformance checking and interoperability.

In the following, we introduce our solution to interoperability at connector and at component level, specifying conformance relation and interoperability method for each level. We first address connector level, as this constitutes the base for service interoperability.

4.1 Interoperability at Connector Level

Based on our functional modeling of wireless connectors, a connector (`Connector`), realizes an interaction protocol (`Protocol`) specified as a process in the π-calculus, establishes an addressing scheme (`Address`) described by a complex data structure (`Parameter`), and employs a number of messages (`Message`) described as complex data structures (`Parameter`). These classes are complementary or may even overlap in specifying a connector. For example, we may associate class `Connector` to external ontologies representing some features not, partially or even fully specified by the other classes; in this way, we may, for example, represent with `Connector` the interaction model realized by the connector, such as RPC or event-based. This redundancy may be desirable in order to facilitate the conformance relation or the interoperability method described in the following.

Conformance relation. We introduce a conformance relation for connectors based on the above classes. As already discussed, we specify a connector by instantiating these classes into individuals specific to this connector. Two connectors may be composed if they (at least partially) conform to each other in terms of their corresponding individuals for all the above classes. The definition of partial conformance depends on the capacity to deploy an adequate interoperability method to compensate for the non-conforming part.

Conformance in terms of interaction protocols is checked over the associated π-calculus processes, as detailed in [6]; this implicitly includes the realized interaction models. For interaction models, conformance may alternatively be asserted by semantic reasoning on the related individuals of class `Connector`. In the same way, for addressing schemes, exchanged messages, parameters of messages and types of parameters, conformance may be asserted by semantic reasoning on the related individuals of classes `Address`, `Message`, `Parameter` and `PrmType`. Finally, to ensure syntactic conformance in exchanged messages, the specific values of `PrmPosition` and `PrmValue` shall be the same for the two connectors.

Interoperability method. To compose non-absolutely conforming connectors, an appropriate interoperability method shall be employed. We employ a *connector customizer* that serves as an intermediate for the message exchange between the two connectors. The customizer has access to the ontologies of the two connectors, and from there to the parent mobile service ontology and the possibly incorporated external ontologies. The customizer shall take all appropriate action to remedy the incompatibilities between the two connectors. For example, upon reception of a message, the customizer shall interpret it and perform all necessary conversions to make it comprehensible to the other peer. The connector customizer may be collocated with one of the two peers or be located on an intermediate network node, depending on architectural requirements; for example, for wireless ad hoc computing environments the former solution is more appropriate.

Example. We now concretize the above outlined conformance relation and interoperability method for the e-shopping service example. In Section 3, we specified the vendor ontology defining the vendor component and its associated connectors. The vendor component provides its services to customer components.

To enable a more precise representation of connector semantics for the vendor and customer components, we assume the existence of an external *remote operation connector* ontology, which defines a simple taxonomy of connectors supporting remote operation invocation. This ontology provides a common vocabulary for connectors of this type. This ontology is outlined in the following:

```
RemoteOperationConn
    hasLegs {OneWay, TwoWay}
    hasSynchronicity {Sync, Async}
    keepsState {State, NoState}
```

Class `RemoteOperationConn` is related to three other classes, which are defined above by enumeration of their individuals. Property `hasLegs` determines whether a connector supports one-way or two-way operations; `hasSynchronicity` determines whether a connector supports synchronous or asynchronous operations; finally, `keepsState` determines whether a connector maintains state during the realization of an operation, e.g., for correlating the request and response messages of an asynchronous operation. We additionally pose the restriction that each one of the three above properties has cardinality *exactly one*, which means that any `RemoteOperationConn` individual has exactly one value for each of the three properties.

We further refine the remote operation connector ontology to identify a number of allowed combinations of the above properties, which produces a number of feasible connector types specified by the ontology. Hence, the following subclasses of `RemoteOperationConn` are defined:

```
SyncConn
    hasLegs TwoWay
    hasSynchronicity Sync
    keepsState State
```

```
AsyncStateConn
    hasLegs TwoWay
    hasSynchronicity Async
    keepsState State

AsyncNoStateConn
    hasSynchronicity Async
    keepsState NoState
```

In the above definitions, properties in boldface are set to be a *necessary and sufficient condition* for identifying the associated connector class. For example, a synchronous connector has synchronicity Sync, and synchronicity Sync is sufficient to identify a synchronous connector. NoState for an asynchronous connector means that the communicating components take care of correlating the request and response messages of an asynchronous operation. In this case, it makes no difference whether an asynchronous connector is one-way or two-way. Thus, hasLegs is left undefined in AsyncNoStateConn; it may take any of the two values OneWay or TwoWay.

We now exploit the above ontology to specify interaction model semantics for the two connectors supporting communication between the vendor component and a specific customer component. To this end, the two connectors inherit from both the mobile service and remote operation connector ontologies. More specifically, the two connectors are represented by two classes that are subclasses of both Connector and RemoteOperationConn, which means that they inherit properties of both classes:

```
VendorConn
    hasLegs TwoWay
    hasSynchronicity Async
    keepsState NoState

CustomerConn
    hasLegs OneWay
```

These two connector classes are defined independently, each one by the designer of the related connector, and make part of the vendor and customer ontologies, correspondingly, which are normally local to the related components and connectors. Here, the two designers have opted not to reuse any of the specialized connector classes, pre-defined in the remote operation connector ontology; they have instead defined two new connector classes. We can see that class VendorConn represents the features required by the Connector individual VConn2 defined in Section 3.2. Employing an OWL reasoning tool, an inference about conformance between VendorConn and CustomerConn may be drawn as follows:

VendorConn has both property values Async and NoState, which makes it necessarily an AsyncNoStateConn. CustomerConn must have exactly one value for each of the two undefined properties. Its synchronicity cannot be Sync, because this would make CustomerConn necessarily a SyncConn, which, however, is two-way, while CustomerConn is one-way. Thus, CustomerConn has property value Async. In the same way, its state property cannot be State, because this together with `Async` would make it necessarily an `AsyncStateConn`, which also is two-way. Thus, `CustomerConn` has property value `NoState`. Property values `Async` and `NoState` make `CustomerConn` necessarily an `Async-NoStateConn`. Thus, `VendorConn` and `CustomerConn` belong to the same connector class within the remote operation connector ontology, which makes them conforming in terms of their supported interaction models.

In the above, interaction model conformance was asserted by comparing semantics co-represented by class `Connector` of the mobile service ontology (together with class `RemoteOperationConn` of the remote operation connector ontology). Conformance between `VendorConn` and `CustomerConn` shall be further checked in terms of all the other classes of the mobile service ontology. We instantiate `Vendor-Conn` and `CustomerConn` to define the rest of their characteristics according to this ontology:

```
VendorConn VConn2
```
(as specified in Section 3.2)

```
CustomerConn CConn2
   interacts "cout[COUT_PRM]" , "cin(cin_prm)"
   references CAddr
   exchanges {COut, CIn}
Address CAddr
    hasPrmType URL
    hasPrmValue some URL
Message COut
    hasParameter COutFunc
    hasParameter {CLocalAddr, CRemoteAddr}
    hasParameter COutPrm
MsgFunction COutFunc
    hasPrmType word
    hasPrmPosition 1
    hasPrmValue 3FEDh
RemoteAddr CRemoteAddr
    hasPrmType URL
    hasPrmPosition 2
    hasPrmValue "http://www.e-shopping.com:8080/vendor"
LocalAddr CLocalAddr
    hasPrmType URL
    hasPrmPosition 3
Parameter COutPrm
    hasPrmType bin
    hasPrmPosition 4
```

Interaction protocol conformance for VConn2 and CConn2 is checked over the associated π-calculus processes, which are obviously complementary (see [6]); however, different names are used for messages VReq-COut, VRes-CIn and for message parameters VReqPrm-COutPrm, VResPrm-CInPrm. Semantic conformance between corresponding messages and parameters is asserted by using external ontologies, as already done for semantic conformance between interaction models. In the same way, semantic conformance is asserted between addressing schemes (`VAddr`-`CAddr`).

Thus, the conformance relation applied to the current example requires: (i) semantic conformance between interaction models, addressing schemes, messages and message parameters; and (ii) workflow conformance between interaction protocols.

Nevertheless, there are still incompatibilities between `VConn2` and `CConn2` in terms of types of parameters (e.g., between `VReqPrm` and `COutPrm`), position of parameters within messages (e.g., between `VRemoteAddr` and `CRemoteAddr` within `VReq` and `COut`), and values of parameters (e.g., between `VReqFunc` and `COutFunc`). Further, referenced types such as *URL*, *byte*, *word*, *hex* and *bin* may not belong to the same type system. Thus, we employ a connector customizer which resolves these incompatibilities by (i) converting between types by accessing some external type ontology; if different type systems are used, external ontologies can help in converting between type systems; (ii) modifying position of parameters; and (iii) modifying values of parameters. This customizer exploits the semantic conformance established above to identify the semantically corresponding messages and message parameters of `VConn2` and `CConn2`.

A weaker conformance relation than the one applied to this example would require a more competent interoperability method, e.g. a connector customizer capable of resolving incompatibilities in addressing schemes or even in interaction models and workflows of interaction protocols. The feasibility of such cases depends on the nature of addressing schemes or interaction protocols and the degree of heterogeneity, and shall be treated on a case-by-case basis. Enabling automated, dynamic configuration or even generation of the appropriate interoperability method from some persistent registry of generic interoperability methods is then a challenging objective. Ontologies could then be used to represent generic interoperability methods and to guide the automated generation or configuration of these methods based on the concrete ontologies of the two incompatible connectors.

4.2 Interoperability at Component Level

Based on our functional modeling of mobile components, a component provides or requires a number of capabilities (`ProvidedCpb`, `RequiredCpb`). Each capability has a number of inputs (`InputPrm`) and outputs (`OutputPrm`) described as complex data structures (`Parameter`), realizes a conversation (`Conversation`) specified as a process in the π-calculus, and employs a number of messages (`Message`) described as complex data structures (`Parameter`). Based on the similarity of capability `Conversation` to connector `Protocol` and on the common use of `Message` by both capabilities and connectors, we could introduce a conformance relation and associated interoperability method for component capabilities similar to the ones elaborated for connectors. Nevertheless, considering the diversity of component capabilities and conversations, requiring workflow conformance between component conversations and semantic conformance for each single message and message parameter

– as for the two connectors in the example above – is too restrictive. Moreover, the introduced connector-level interoperability method, based on communication interworking, cannot deal with the high heterogeneity of components, e.g., it cannot resolve highly incompatible component conversations. Therefore, we introduce a more flexible, coarse-grained approach for component conformance and interoperability based on component capabilities.

Conformance relation. Our high-level conformance relation for components states that two components may be composed if they require and provide in a complementary way semantically conforming capabilities. We model a capability by instantiating classes ProvidedCpb or RequiredCpb, InputPrm and OutputPrm into individuals specific to this capability. Semantic conformance between two capabilities is asserted by reasoning on their corresponding individuals. As already detailed for connectors, these individuals shall as well inherit from external ontologies; this allows a rich representation of capabilities based on common vocabularies, which enable their interpretation and conformance checking.

Depending on the existence of external ontologies, capabilities may be directly provided with semantics (class ProvidedCpb or RequiredCpb). Alternatively, capabilities may be semantically characterized by the semantics of their inputs and outputs (classes InputPrm and OutputPrm). As discussed in [26] for Semantic Web Services capabilities, the latter approach requires a reduced set of ontologies, as inputs and outputs may be combined in many diverse ways to produce an indefinite number of capabilities. However, semantically characterizing a capability based only on its inputs and outputs may produce ambiguity and erroneous assertions, e.g., when checking conformance between capabilities. We opt for a hybrid approach, where, depending on the availability of related ontologies, both capability semantics and input/output semantics are used. As presented in Section 2.4, OWL-S identifies Web services by their inputs and outputs, enhanced by preconditions and effects. This enables a more precise representation of a service. We consider integrating preconditions and effects into our model as part of our future work.

Our conformance relation adopts the approach presented in [10] for matching Semantic Web services' capabilities, which identifies several degrees of matching: (i) *exact*; (ii) *plug in*, where the provided capability is more general than the requested one, thus it can be used; (iii) *subsume*, where the provided capability is more specific than the requested one, thus it may be used in combination with another Web service complementing the missing part; and (iv) *fail*. As we are assessing conformance between two peer components, we exclude case (iii). Our conformance relation requires that inputs of a required capability be a superset of inputs of the associated provided capability, while outputs of a required capability be a subset of outputs of the associated provided capability. This refers to both the number of equivalent inputs and outputs and to subsumption relations between mapped inputs and outputs. Equivalence and subsumption are asserted by semantic reasoning, where the degree of similarity may be measured as the distance between concepts in an ontology hierarchy. This approach ensures that a service is fed at least with all the needed input and produces at least all the required output.

Interoperability method. To compose the high-level-conforming components resulting from the introduced conformance relation, an appropriate interoperability method shall be employed. To this end, we intervene in the execution properties of the component requiring the specific capability. First, the component providing the specific capability is a normal component, the executable of which integrates the hard-coded implementation of the conversation and messages associated to the capability. Thus, this component exposes a normal specific functional interface. Regarding the component requiring the specific capability, its executable is built around this capability, which may be represented as a high-level local function call. This component integrates further an *execution engine* able to execute on the fly the specific conversation associated to this capability and supported by its peer component. Thus, this component comprises a specific part implementing the component logic that uses this capability, and a generic part constituting a generic interface capable of being composed with diverse peer interfaces. The execution engine shall be capable of:

- Executing the declarative descriptions of conversations; to this end, execution semantics of the π-calculus descriptions are employed;
- Parsing the incoming messages and synthesizing the outgoing messages of the conversation based on the syntactic information provided by classes `PrmType`, `PrmPosition` and `PrmValue`; access to an external type ontology may be necessary if the type system of the peer is different to the native type system;
- Associating the inputs and outputs of the required capability to their corresponding message parameters; this is based on semantic mapping with the inputs and outputs of the remote capability, which are directly associated to message parameters; conversion between different types or between different type systems may be required.

It is clear from the above that for components it is not necessary to provide messages and message parameters – at least parameters that are not capability inputs or outputs – with semantics.

The introduced component-level interoperability method shall be employed in combination with the connector-level interoperability method discussed above to ensure service interoperability. It is apparent from the above that the component-level method is more adaptive and can resolve higher heterogeneity than the connector-level one, which is appropriate for components, considering their diversity. On the other hand, the connector-level method permits lower heterogeneity, which is normal for connectors, which shall not be allowed to deviate significantly from the behavior expected by the overlying component. By locating the connector customizer on the side of the component requiring a specific capability, this component becomes capable of adapting itself at both component and connector level to the component providing the specific capability. Employing dynamic schemes for the instantiation of connectors as the one outlined in the previous section would make this adaptation totally dynamic and ad hoc.

Example. We will now complete the e-shopping service example by applying the introduced component-level conformance relation and interoperability method. In Section 4.1, we specified connector CConn2 within the customer ontology. We complete the customer ontology by defining capabilities for the customer component and a second connector. As discussed above, the customer component will be specified only at capability level. We assume that the customer component requires the capabilities Get and NewRelease, which also concern buying an article and registering for notification of new releases of articles.

```
Component Customer
    requires {Get, NewRelease}
RequiredCpb Get
    inputs {ArticleData, Address, PaymentData, Customer-
Profile}
    outputs {ArticleData, Ack}
RequiredCpb NewRelease
    inputs ArticleData
    outputs ArticleData
```

To assert conformance between the customer and the vendor component with respect to capabilities Get and Buy or NewRelease and Available, semantic matching shall be sought for the compared capabilities and their inputs and outputs.

We discuss the case of Get and Buy. We assume that there exists a *commerce* ontology specifying among other the class Purchase, as one of the activities included in commerce. Furthermore, we assume the existence of a specialized ontology describing the specific articles being sold by the vendor component and possibly sought by the customer component. Finally, a *payment information* ontology – describing payment methods, such as by credit card, by bank transfer, etc. – and a *location information* ontology are available. Having – independently – defined capabilities Get and Buy as direct or less direct descendants of class Purchase enables the assertion of their conformance. In the same way, ArticleData may be mapped to ArticleInfo if the vendor component sells what the customer component seeks to buy; the same for the couple Address-ShippingInfo. PaymentData can be found to be more general than CreditCardInfo in the payment information ontology. This means that the customer component is capable of managing as well other payment methods than by credit card, which is required by the vendor component. This is in accordance with our conformance relation. We may further see that Get additionally inputs CustomerProfile, which is not required by Buy, and Buy additionally outputs ReceiptId, which is not required by Get. This, too, is in accordance with our conformance relation.

To be able to use the remote capability Buy, the customer component shall have a connector (e.g., CConn1) conforming to VConn1. Then, the customer component will execute the declarative conversation associated to Buy in the way detailed above.

5 Related Work

In the last couple of years there has been extensive research towards semantic modeling of services. This research has mostly been focused on adding semantics to Web Services, which, as presented in Section 2.3, is the dominant paradigm for service-oriented architectures on the Web. Hence, there are a number of efforts towards Semantic Web Services. The most complete effort concerns OWL-S, which was outlined in Section 2.4. In this section, we compare our approach with OWL-S and discuss OWL-S-based and non-OWL-S-based efforts.

OWL-S defines an ontology for semantically describing Web Services in order to enable their automated discovery, invocation, composition and execution monitoring. From our standpoint, this may be regarded as enabling application-level interoperability. Our work has aimed at introducing semantic modeling of mobile services in order to deal with the interoperability requirements of mobile distributed systems. This has led us to elaborate a comprehensive modeling approach that spans both the application and middleware level. Furthermore, our modeling considers services from a software architecture point of view, where services are architecturally described in terms of components and connectors. This abstracts any reliance on a specific technology, as on Web Services in the OWL-S case. We compare further our approach with OWL-S in the following.

Our modeling of provided capabilities along with their inputs and outputs may be mapped to the OWL-S service profile. Both describe the high-level functionalities of services and may be used for discovering services, thus, for matching or conformance verification. We additionally explicitly model required capabilities for a component, which is done implicitly in OWL-S, e.g., for an agent contacting Web services. As further discussed in Section 4.2, OWL-S enhances the description of capabilities with preconditions and effects, which we consider integrating into our approach.

Our modeling of conversation and component-level messages may be mapped to the OWL-S process model. We have opted for a well-established process algebra, such as the π-calculus, which allows dealing with dynamic architectures [27] and provides well-established execution semantics. The OWL-S process model provides a declarative, not directly executable specification of the conversation supported by a service. One has to provide external execution semantics for executing a process model, which has been done, for example, in [22]. The OWL-S process model decomposes to atomic processes, which correspond to WSDL operations. Our modeling employs component-level messages, which make no assumption of the underlying connector. The types of the inputs and outputs of an OWL-S atomic process are made to correspond to WSDL types, which are XML Schema types. This restricts the employed type system to the XML Schema type system. Our approach enables using different type systems, and, further, heterogeneous type systems for the two peer components.

Our modeling of connectors may be mapped to the OWL-S grounding. The OWL-S grounding is restricted to the connector types specified by Web Services, which comprise an interaction model prescribed by WSDL on top of the SOAP messaging protocol, commonly over HTTP. As WSDL 2.0 has not yet been finalized, the current version of OWL-S relies on WSDL 1.1, which supports only two-way synchronous operations and one-way operations. The WSDL 1.1 interaction model does not support, for example, two-way asynchronous interactions or event-based interactions, as has been indicated in [1]. WSDL 2.0 will allow greater flexibility in its interaction model. Nevertheless, our approach enables the use of any connector type, which is modeled by the connector-level part of our mobile service ontology; this allows any interaction model, interaction protocol and addressing scheme. Finally, our approach enables using different type systems for connectors and, further, heterogeneous type systems for the two peer connectors, while WSDL and SOAP rely on the XML Schema type system.

Work by Carnegie Mellon University described in [26] is the most complete effort up to now in the OWL-S community; the authors have realized an OWL-S based architecture for automated discovery and interaction between autonomous Web services [19]. Discovery is based on the matching algorithm detailed in [10], which has been adopted by several other efforts in the literature. The main features of this algorithm were discussed in Section 4.2; as stated there, our component-level conformance relation incorporates some of the principles of this work. However, this matching algorithm does not exploit the full OWL-S representation of services in terms of inputs, outputs, preconditions and effects; preconditions and effects are not employed. Interaction between autonomous Web services is based on an OWL-S (formerly DAML-S) virtual machine [28], which is capable of executing OWL-S process model descriptions. As mentioned above, execution is based on the execution semantics defined by the authors in [22]. The virtual machine integrates OWL reasoning functionality to be able to interpret and synthesize messages. Its implementation is based on the DAML-Jess-KB [14], an implementation of the DAML (a predecessor of OWL) axiomatic semantics that relies on the Jess theorem prover [13] and the Jena parser [15] to parse ontologies and assert them as new facts in the Jess Knowledge Base. Our component-level interoperability method employing an execution engine capable of executing the π-calculus descriptions of service conversations can certainly build upon tools and experience coming from this work. Nevertheless, as it realizes a more general conceptual model, our approach addresses also connector-level interoperability.

In the work presented in [18], the authors elaborate an ontology-based framework for the automatic composition of Web Services. They define an ontology for describing Web services and specify it using the DAML+OIL language (a predecessor of OWL). They further propose a composability model based on their service ontology, for comparing the syntactic and semantic features of Web services to determine whether two services are composable. They identify two sets of composability rules. Syntactic rules include: (i) *mode composability*, which compares operation modes as imposed by WSDL, that is, two-way synchronous operations and one-way operations; and (ii) *binding composability*, which compares the interaction protocols of communicating services, e.g., SOAP. Semantic rules include (i) *message composability*, which compares the number of message parameters, their data types, business roles, and units, where business roles and units represent semantics of parameters; (ii) *operation semantics composability*, which compares the semantics of service operations; (iii) *qualitative composability*, which compares quality of service properties of Web services; and (iv) *composition soundness*, which semantically assesses whether combining Web services in a specific way is worthwhile. The introduced service ontology resembles our mobile service ontology, while it additionally represents quality of service features of services. However, what is lacking is representation of service conversations; actually, in this approach, services are implicitly considered to support elementary conversations comprising a single operation. These operations are employed into an external workflow to provide a composite service produced with a development time procedure. Additionally, there is no attempt to provide interoperability in case that the composability rules identify incompatibilities. Composability rules are actually used for matching existing services to requirements of the composite service. Same as the other approaches adding semantics to Web services, this approach treats only application-level composability.

6 Conclusion

Mobile distributed systems are characterized by a number of features, such as the highly dynamic character of the computing and networking environment due to the intense use of the wireless medium and the mobility of devices; the resource constraints of mobile devices; and the high heterogeneity of integrated technologies in terms of networks, devices and software infrastructures. To deal with high dynamics, mobile distributed systems tend to be dynamically composed according to the networking of mobile services. Nevertheless, such a composition must be addressed in a way that enforces correctness of the composite systems with respect to both functional and non-functional properties and deals with the interoperability issue resulting from the high heterogeneity of integrated components. The Semantic Web paradigm has emerged as a decisive factor towards interoperability, which up to then was being pursued based on agreements on common syntactic standards; such agreements cannot scale in the open, highly diverse mobile environment. Related efforts elaborating semantic approaches are addressing application-level interoperability in terms of information and functionality. However, interoperability requirements of mobile distributed systems are wider, concerning functional and non-functional interoperability that spans both middleware and application level.

Towards this goal, we have introduced semantic modeling of mobile services based on ontologies, addressing functional properties of mobile components and associated wireless connectors. We have further elaborated conformance relations over component and connector models so as to be able to reason on the correctness of the composition of peer mobile services with respect to offered functional properties. Our conformance relations enable identifying partial conformance between components and between connectors, thus reasoning on interoperability. Based on these conformance relations, we have further specified appropriate interoperability methods to realize composition and interoperation of heterogeneous mobile services. Nevertheless, our modeling needs to be complemented with specification of the non-functional behavior of services and definition of related ontologies. We plan to do this building on our previous work described in [6], which has identified key non-functional features of the mobile environment.

As discussed and demonstrated in this paper, ontologies enable a rich representation of services and a common understanding about their features. As discussed in the

OWL specification[10] and in [17], there are two advantages of ontologies over simple XML schemas. First, an ontology is a knowledge representation backed up by enhanced reasoning supported by the OWL axiomatic semantics. Second, OWL ontologies may benefit from the availability of generic tools that can reason about them. By contrast, if one built a system capable of reasoning about a specific industry-standard XML schema, this would inevitably be specific to the particular subject domain. Building a sound and useful reasoning system is not a simple effort, while constructing an ontology is much more manageable. The complex reasoning employed in the example of Section 4.1 to assert conformance between connector interaction models would not be easy to implement based simply on XML schemas.

OWL reasoning tools shall be employed by the introduced conformance relations and interoperability methods. A number of such tools already exist, such as the ones discussed in the previous section. Conformance verification needs to be integrated with the runtime system, i.e., the middleware, and be carried out online. Interoperability methods further involve processing and communication cost upon their functioning, but also upon their dynamic instantiation, as discussed in Section 4.1; they shall as well function with an acceptable runtime overhead. These requirements are even more challenging if we take into account the resource constraints of wireless devices. A number of techniques need to be combined in this context, including effective tools for checking conformance relations and lightweight interoperability mechanisms in the wireless environment, possibly exploiting the capabilities of resource-rich devices in the area so as to effectively distribute the load associated with the dynamic composition of mobile services. We are thus currently investigating base online tools and techniques to support open, dynamic system composition, while keeping the runtime overhead acceptable for wireless, resource-constrained devices.

In the spirit of the general principles identified for connector modeling and connector interoperability, we have already elaborated preliminary work towards middleware interoperability. Specifically, we have studied service discovery protocol interoperability in the open mobile environment [12]. This solution employs a mapping of several standard service discovery protocols (SLP [7], UPnP[11], Jini [8]) on semantic events. This approach includes dynamic instantiation of the appropriate connector customizer, as discussed in Section 4.1. This work is currently being extended to interoperability between standard middleware communication protocols (SOAP, RMI).

References

1. Curbera, F., Mukhi, N., Weerawarana, S. On the Emergence of a Web Services Component Model. In *Proceedings of the WCOP 2001 workshop at ECOOP 2001*, Budapest, Hungary, June 2001.
2. Tim Berners-Lee, James Hendler, Ora Lassila. The Semantic Web. *Scientific American*, May 2001

---

[10] http://www.w3.org/TR/owl-guide/
[11] http://www.upnp.org/

3. A. Tsounis, C. Anagnostopoulos, and S. Hadjiefthymiades. The Role of Semantic Web and Ontologies in Pervasive Computing Environments. In *Proceedings of Mobile and Ubiquitous Information Access Workshop, Mobile HCI '04*, Glasgow, UK, Sept. 2004.
4. R. Milner. *Communicating and Mobile Systems: The π-Calculus*. Cambridge University Press, 1999.
5. Valerie Issarny, Daniele Sacchetti, Ferda Tartanoglu, Francoise Sailhan, Rafik Chibout, Nicole Levy, Angel Talamona. Developing Ambient Intelligence Systems: A Solution based on Web Services. In *Journal of Automated Software Engineering*, Vol. 12(1), January 2005.
6. V. Issarny, F. Tartanoglu, J. Liu, F. Sailhan. Software Architecture for Mobile Distributed Computing. In *Proceedings of 4th Working IEEE/IFIP Conference on Software Architecture* (WICSA'04). 12-15 June 2004. Oslo, Norway. To appear.
7. E. Guttman, C. Perkins, J. Veizades, and M. Day. Service Location Protocol, version 2. IETF RFC 2608, June 1999.
8. Waldo, J. (1999). The Jini Architecture for Network-centric Computing. In *Communications of the ACM*, July 1999, pp. 76-82.
9. G.-C. Roman, G. Picco, and A. Murphy. Software Engineering for Mobility: A Roadmap. In *Proceedings of the 22nd International Conference on Software Engineering (ICSE'22)*, 2000.
10. Paolucci, M. et al. Semantic Matching of Web Services Capabilities. In *Proceedings of the 1st International Semantic Web Conference (ISWC 02)*, 2002.
11. Jinshan Liu, Valerie Issarny. QoS-aware Service Location in Mobile Ad Hoc Networks. In *Proceedings of the 5th IEEE International Conference on Mobile Data Management (MDM'2004)*, January 2004.
12. Yerom-David Bromberg, Valerie Issarny. Service Discovery Protocols Interoperability in the Mobile Environment. In *Proceedings of the International Workshop Software Engineering and Middleware (SEM)*. September 2004.
13. E. Friedman-Hill. *Jess: Java Expert System Shell*.
14. J. Kopena and W. C. Regli. DAMLJessKB: A Tool for Reasoning with the Semantic Web. In *ISWC 2003*, 2003.
15. B. McBride. Jena: Implementing the RDF Model and Syntax Specification. In *Semantic Web Workshop, WWW 2001*, 2001.
16. S. McIlraith, D. Martin. Bringing Semantics to Web Services, *IEEE Intell. Syst.*, 18 (1) (2003), 90–93.
17. Declan O'Sullivan and David Lewis. Semantically Driven Service Interoperability for Pervasive Computing. In *Proceedings of the Third ACM International Workshop on Data Engineering for Wireless and Mobile Access, MobiDE 2003*, September 19, 2003, San Diego, California, USA.
18. B. Medjahed, A. Bouguettaya, and A. Elmagarmid. Composing Web Services on the Semantic Web. *The VLDB Journal*, 12(4):333-351, November 2003.
19. M. Paolucci and K. Sycara, Autonomous Semantic Web Services, *IEEE Internet Computing*, vol. 7, no. 5, September/October 2003.
20. D. Martin, M. Paolucci, S. McIlraith, M. Burstein, D. McDermott, D. McGuinness, B. Parsia, T. Payne, M. Sabou, M. Solanki, N. Srinivasan, K. Sycara. Bringing Semantics to Web Services: The OWL-S Approach. In *Proceedings of the First International Workshop on Semantic Web Services and Web Process Composition (SWSWPC 2004)*, July 6-9, 2004, San Diego, California, USA.
21. N. Mehta, N. Medvidovic, and S. Phadke. Towards a taxonomy of software connectors. In *21st International Conference on Software Engineering*, November 1999.

22. Anupriya Ankolekar, Frank Huch and Katia Sycara. Concurrent Execution Semantics for DAML-S with Subtypes. In *Proceedings of The First International Semantic Web Conference (ISWC)*, 2002.
23. C. Bettstetter and C. Renner. A Comparison of Service Discovery Protocols and Implementation of the Service Location Protocol. In *Proceedings of the 6th EUNICE Open European Summer School: Innovative Internet Applications*, 2000.
24. Natalya F. Noy and Deborah L. McGuinness. *Ontology Development 101: A Guide to Creating Your First Ontology*. Stanford University.
25. R. Allen and D. Garlan. A Formal Basis for Architectural Connection. *ACM Transactions on Software Engineering and Methodology*, 6(3):213-249, 1997.
26. Sycara, Katia; Paolucci, Massimo; Ankolekar, Anupriya; Srinivasan, Naveen. Automated Discovery, Interaction and Composition of Semantic Web Services. *Journal of Web Semantics*, Volume 1, Issue 1, December 2003.
27. J. Magee and J. Kramer. Dynamic Structure in Software Architecture. In *Proceedings of the ACM SIGSOFT'96 Symposium on Foundations of Software Engineering*, pages 3-14, 1996.
28. Massimo Paolucci, Anupriya Ankolekar, Naveen Srinivasan and Katia Sycara. The DAML-S Virtual Machine. In *Proceedings of the Second International Semantic Web Conference (ISWC)*, 2003, Sandial Island, Fl, USA, October 2003, pp 290-305.
29. M. P. Papazoglou, D. Georgakopoulos (Eds.). Service-oriented computing. *Special section in Communications of the ACM*, Volume 46, Issue 10, October 2003.

The Role of Agreements in IT Management Software

Carlos Molina-Jimenez[1], Jim Pruyne[2], and Aad van Moorsel[1]

[1] University of Newcastle Upon Tyne, School of Computing Science,
Newcastle upon Tyne, NE1 7RU, United Kingdom
{carlos.molina, aad.vanmoorsel}@ncl.ac.uk
[2] Hewlett-Packard Laboratories, 1501 Page Mill Rd., Palo Alto, CA 94304
jim.pruyne@hp.com

Abstract. Various forms of agreements naturally arise in the service provider model as well as in multi-party computing models such as business-to-business, utility and grid computing. The role of these agreements is twofold: they stipulate obligations and expectations of the involved parties, and they represent the goals to be met by the infrastructure. As a consequence of this latter point, in order to automate run-time adaptation and management of systems and services, agreements should be encoded and integrated in management software platforms. In this paper, we review the state of the art in software support for various forms of agreements, for all stages of their life-cycle. We also review emerging platforms and technologies in standard bodies, industries and academia.

1 Introduction

We will argue and illustrate in this paper that distributed computing infrastructures must incorporate *agreements* as first-class software building blocks to support automated adaptation and management in the presence of multiple (possibly competing) interests. These agreements represent expectations and obligations of various partners about the functionality and performance of systems and services. Additionally, these agreements are means to set the objectives for automated decision-making in system adaptation and management. It can therefore be useful for an IT operator to formulate objectives in the form of agreements even if no other parties are exposed to this information.

Modern-day and emerging computing infrastructures are increasingly flexible in their support of computational and business models, as witnessed by the developments of adaptive and on-demand computing solutions advocated by HP, IBM, Oracle, SUN and others. These solutions typically envision a service provider model for various aspects of computing, such as CPU use, network use, application hosting, etc. As software platform, such solutions are often tied to the grid [20], which supports resource sharing across multiple parties using open software. This software virtualises resources and applications, thus shielding the customer from the complexities of the underlying infrastructure and providing the operator with tools to adapt the system gracefully at run-time.

To enable the mentioned multi-party computing models the supporting software infrastructure should make use and keep track of the agreements established between parties. Therefore, it should embody these agreements in software. Such *run-time agreements* can come in various shapes or forms (at times we will use the adjective 'run-time' to stress that we discuss software embodiments of agreements, used at run-time to manage the execution of services). For instance, a run-time agreement can be defined by an operator to represent aspects of a hard-copy contract signed between provider and customers. Alternatively, the run-time agreement represents agreed-upon service levels automatically negotiated by software agents of the provider and customer. Irrespective, the information in the agreement can be used throughout the platform as needed, e.g., to adapt the system to meet service levels while optimising profits. Agreements thus naturally fit the service provider model, but also provide the necessary information to allow for automated decision-making by management software and self-managing components and services.

Since this article has been prepared for the series of books on architectures for dependable systems, it is opportune to address the relation of agreements with both dependability and architectures. The notion of architecture used in this paper relates to the structure of software platforms (middleware). These architectures will be heavily influenced by the emergence of the service provider computing model (including utility or on-demand computing), and by an increased pressure to automate system operation and hence save operational cost. We foresee a prominent role for agreements, which will be integrated in such architectures and will be represented as objects, services or other software components. Once these are in place, they define the objectives to be used in the algorithms that adapt systems and services.

With respect to dependability, run-time agreements play a double role, as indicated above. On the one hand, agreements must be available in system operations software to determine how to adapt the system, also in response to failures. This entails further automation of the processes traditionally involved in fault management. On the other hand, agreements are a way of providing trust in the system, by allowing customers to express their interests, and by providing them with information about whether the agreements are met (possibly through a trusted third party).

There are many open issues in the technologies required to support run-time agreements. The emphasis in this paper is on a survey of existing and ongoing work related to software architectures, with pointers to remaining research issues. The survey is extensive, but arguably not exhaustive because of the vastness of the area we want to cover. In Section 3 we discuss technologies in (1) specification, (2) provision, (3) monitoring, (4) adaptation and (5) resolution, roughly following the life cycle of typical agreements. Table 1 summarizes our findings. In Section 4 we then discuss representative solutions proposed by standards bodies (WS-Agreement in the Global Grid Forum), industries (Hewlett Packard and IBM enterprise IT) and academia (TAPAS, an EU research project). To set the stage, we first discuss terminology used in this paper and in the literature.

2 Definition and Terminology

In this paper we research the software embodiment of contracts or other types of agreement or objectives. As mentioned above, at times we will use the term *run-time agreement* to stress we are concerned about utilising these agreements during service execution. We define run-time agreement as follows.

> A *run-time agreement* is a machine interpretable representation of agreed-upon service characteristics or objectives, established between two (logical) parties. These run-time agreements are used as the goals that drive some form of automation. For this purpose, multiple run-time agreements may be combined to establish the overall objective.

Software embodiments of agreements have been proposed and implicitly used in various places, predominantly in the area of policy-based management. For instance, in the Gallifrey project at Bell Labs [7], goals bound to policy rules form first class objects in the software architecture. However, most policy work (see [35] for a survey in network management) focuses on the rules instead of goals [8].

With the emergence of the service provider model, the distinction between goals and rules becomes much more important. It does not make sense for a customer of a utility computing data centre to set policy rules that manage the system. Instead, this is the responsibility of the service provider, and as a consequence policy rules and agreed-upon objectives must be decoupled. It also is not appropriate to assume that written documents can be used to define the service level agreements, and that operators manually adapt policies based on these documents. Utility computing or other service provider operations can be expected to be much too dynamic to allow such slow processes.

The consequence of the above is that open software and standards are emerging that allow run-time agreements to be exchanged between parties. The utility system is then managed and adapted based on these run-time agreements. Eventually, we expect system management to be so intimately tied to run-time agreement that operators and administrators will introduce additional agreements in the system, to modify the goals driving the management system. In this process, system operators move more and more from defining and refining policy rules to defining and refining goals (as advocated in [8], among others).

It may be good to compare our definition of agreement with existing related terms and definitions, for instance the definition of service level agreement (SLA) in IETF RFC 3198 [61]. There, a service level agreement is defined as "the documented result of a negotiation between a customer and a provider of a service, that specifies levels of Quality of Service or other attributes of the service." A service level objective is "a set of parameters and their value." This is a very natural definition, although the explicit requirement that parties negotiate is not always valid in our setting.

More important is the fact that in the current paper, we consider machine-interpretable agreements, and focus on run-time software components representing agreements. This was not the objective behind RFC 3198. Note furthermore that the RFC 3198 definition also points to QoS, which is a typical connotation when SLAs are concerned. In this paper we do not restrict the contents of run-time agreements to QoS. For a good understanding, it is important to realise that (service level) agreements are not synonymous to QoS. QoS is about metrics (performance, up-time, throughput), which may or may not be used in an agreement or SLA to specify expected values, associated penalties, etc.

It is also of interest to clarify the relationship between policies and agreements, since both are often used in system management. The term policy usually refers to "a plan of actions" [31], while agreements are used to denote a set of goals. Ideally, the goals represented in run-time agreements should determine (or be used to parameterise) the actions suggested by the policies (see [8] for a further discussion of this topic). However, it is important to note that agreements can also be used for adaptation of a system by other means than policies, e.g., using games, auctions or run-time mathematical optimisation algorithms (see Section 3.4).

3 Software Infrastructure Requirements

We discuss requirements for software support of agreements in five groups, roughly corresponding to stages in the life-cycle of an agreement.

1. **Specification.** Languages and formalisms for expressing the agreement, choice of metrics, negotiation, run-time embodiment.
2. **Provision.** Automated and customised deployment of resources and monitoring tools, dealing with resource scarceness.
3. **Monitoring.** Techniques and tools for collecting performance metrics, algorithms for evaluation of performance, violation detection, third-party involvement, data exchange protocols.
4. **Adaptation.** Decision-making about new requests and adapting resource allocations, automated response to changes, business-driven adaptation, alarm handling, self-management and autonomic management.
5. **Resolution.** Auditing and non-repudiation, validity of and changes in agreements, conflict resolution.

Within each item, we touch on a diverse range of issues, from dependability requirements and automation needs to standardisation and third-party solutions. Table 1 summarizes our findings.

3.1 Specification

There is a large body of literature available on the specification of service level agreements, but far less on the formatting of a run-time agreement as a software building block, for instance through the definition of interfaces. The latter is of particular interest to us, since it determines the information the software platform makes available for automation. The obvious exception is WS-Agreement, which we discuss in Section 4.1.

Table 1. State of the art and open issues

	Status	Open or Underdeveloped Issues
Specification	-threshold SLAs in commercial management software [15,18] -QoS languages [2,17,19,21] [28,31,53,55] -WSLA [15,33] adopted in WS-Agreement [3] -WSOL extension to WSDL [57]	-practical mix of expressiveness and simplicity -tool support to define agreements [34] -penalties and rewards [16,62] -business metrics and business-driven management [9,11,36,62] -(domain-specific) ontologies -(automated) negotiation [27,30]
Provision	-job and workload scheduling [11] -resource provision [2,5,22,19] -monitoring provision [15,53]	-mapping (business) metrics on resource needs [16,36] -inclusion of QoS concerns [2,5,18] -domain or product-specific deployment templates [22]
Monitoring	-automatic monitor ignition [15,39,53] -third-party monitoring [16] -threshold alarms [45]	-measurement exchange protocols [37] -business-driven monitoring [9,11] -performance assessment [11] -scaling to very large scale networks -techniques to enhance trust
Adaptation	-(on-line) optimisation algorithms [12,54] -dynamic resource allocation [5,13,44] -domain-specific research prototypes [12,50,51]	-guaranteed end-to-end QoS [47,51] -signalling protocols [18,37] -aggregated objective from multiple agreements -secure sharing of agreements within and across platforms -service definition extension with adaptations [24,32] -self-management, emerging behaviour [6,23,26,59]
Resolution	-customer credits [46] -non-repudiation with trusted third party [44]	-changing and terminating agreements -resolution protocols -enhanced trust solutions

We envision many run-time agreements to be present at any point in time, representing agreements with different customers and possibly additional provider objectives. In software terms, each run-time agreement may be represented by an object or a service, or they will be aggregated into one software component to make them simpler to track. Irrespective, to be useful for automation run-time agreements must contain enough information to facilitate decision-making: sufficiently detailed statements about expected functionality, exact enough quality-of-service parameters and values, and reward and penalty information for met and missed objectives. The latter is particularly important: without rewards and penalties a decision-making unit can not make trade-off decisions in times of scarcity. A serious shortcoming in many current agreement specification efforts (WS-Agreement is an exception) is the lack of attention paid to rewards and penalties, possibly expressed in monetary values [9,11,36]. This ultimately will result in suboptimal decisions during the adaptation phase (discussed below).

In the web services area service descriptions and workflow-style service definitions are commonplace through the Web Service Description Language (WSDL), Business Process Execution Language, and similar efforts [1]. For every client of the web service, the web service run-time system maintains information to manage the interactions with the client. Arguably, this corresponds to maintaining a run-time agreement, as we defined in Section 2. Two approaches can be thought of to populate such run-time agreements with sufficient information for system management. First, one can leave it to the operator to provide the management system with additional information about priorities across customers, QoS guarantees for customers, rewards and penalties for meeting and missing objectives, etc. This will require operator tools to facilitate inputting such information. It is not impossible that commercial software vendors are thinking in this direction, although we are not aware of other efforts than the WS-Agreement related research demo Cremona [34].

Alternatively, one can extend the service definition with additional information, as is done in Web Service Offering Language (WSOL) [57]. WSOL is fully compatible with the WSDL description language and extends WSDL with capabilities relevant to service offerings. A key concept in WSOL is that of classes of services, which are defined as services of the same functionality but with different constraints. The goal behind this concept is to cater for customers with different budgets and needs. Thus WSOL envisions that a web service offers a service S as a set of classes $c_1, c_2, ..., c_m$, where c_i and c_j offer the same functionality but differ in terms of constraint parameters.

Other related work has been focused predominantly on unambiguous representation of QoS metrics [21,33,53,55], sometimes through the application of formal methods [19,39]. For a recent overview of QoS definition technologies we refer to [17,28]. Of course, no matter which formal approach is used, the problem of semantic meaning of objectives will remain, and it may therefore be that intricate or complete languages will lose out in practice to descriptions with succinct but sufficient expressiveness. Furthermore, it may be needed to invest in domain-specific ontologies for agreements, scoped such that one can achieve a reasonably precise and widely-accepted understanding of terms in the domain of concern.

3.2 Provision

In this section we consider the first phase in run-time use of agreements, namely the provision of the service specified in the agreement as well as the provision of the monitoring software to verify if an agreement is being met.

In terms of the software architecture we can identify a range of possible approaches to standardisation of provision software. On one end, the specification of a service interaction, or of resource usage, is given in the form of a file, typically human readable for reasons of convenience. Examples of this are typical usage scenarios for the grid job submission description language [4], or utility computing definitions in the SmartFrog language [22]. Alternatively, the agreement is represented by a first-class software object (or service) with standardised interfaces. This leaves a more powerful interaction paradigm and is the idea behind WS-Agreement, which we discuss in detail in Section 4.1. Of course, independent of the chosen approach, the provision system needs to keep track of the various agreements in its software.

Provision systems such as SmartFrog predominantly focus on core tasks behind service provision, such as loading, initialising and starting software components, in prescribed order. Many challenges exist when one needs to provide for additional agreement parameters such as QoS, although research attempts exist in various domains [2,5,18,50]. When we review the technologies of HP and IBM in Section 4, we see these are driven by utility or on-demand computing opportunities [29]. The key enabler of utility computing is software for automated provision, such as SmartFrog [22] and Oceano [5]. Enrichment of such software to be governed by agreements is needed to deliver on the promise of fully automated management in multi-party setting.

Monitoring provision. Much of industry research in the area of monitoring has been concerned with automatically igniting monitor activities, that is, with automated provision of monitoring. This emphasis is understandable, since one of the major barriers in using monitoring software is the effort required to instrument systems and initiate the monitoring. A well-specified agreement is an excellent tool to determine what monitoring is needed. The challenge is not to specify the required monitoring, but to infer from the agreements which monitoring software should be started up, who is in charge of the monitoring, when alarms should be generated and when SLA breaches occur. This idea is described in [37,53] in the context of web services.

3.3 Monitoring

When run-time agreements are used to guide system or service management, the issue of monitoring can be dealt with in straightforward manner. An abundance of monitoring tools is available to collect metrics from almost all elements in the infrastructure, both commercial, e.g., [10], and Open Source [60]. As we indicated above, the challenge lies in automatically igniting the correct monitoring software based on the specification of the present run-time agreements [37,53].

When multiple parties are interested in the monitored data, matters immediately become much more intricate. Each metric in the agreement will be monitored at one of the two parties, and the results will be reported to the other. The question then is why the second party should believe the reported results. All present solutions to this problem rely on a trusted third party [14]. At some level, a trusted third party is unavoidable, but trust-enhancing techniques for non-repudiation, privacy and authenticity remain of prime interest.

Especially when relying on trusted third parties it is desirable to allow agreements to be dynamically initiated, without cumbersome set-up procedures involving the third party. This implies that protocols must be in place to exchange the needed set-up information and credentials, disseminate data to the right parties, and issue actions to adapt the monitoring software to the new agreements. A possible solution to the problem is the introduction of a signalling network overlay, such as the ones proposed in the context of differentiated IP services [18] and web services [37].

One step beyond monitoring is the inference of agreement violations using the measured data [45]. Based on this inference, corrective actions can be triggered and remaining disputes can be dealt with. Potentially, one can build such a full-blown agreement violation management system as a service, which retrieves metrics from the databases of the measurement service, performs computation on them, compares the results of the computation against high or low thresholds and sends notifications of violations to the interested parties when violations of agreements are detected. This service then acts as a trusted third party, as we will discuss in Section 3.5 when we discuss resolution.

3.4 Adaptation

To be useful at the adaptation stage the agreements must provide management software with the necessary information for system adaptation. The ability to adapt a system based on the existing agreements is the key behind the autonomic and adaptive infrastructure proposals from IBM and HP, as we will discuss in Section 4. However, in reality, current research and developments rarely consider automated adaptation as the goal for agreements, and it can therefore be expected that the current specification languages need to be modified to appropriately specify all elements needed for automated management. As an example, trade-off decisions require an understanding of rewards and penalties, but many agreement specifications ignore such aspects.

We envision automated management at the service provider site to be effectively hidden from the customer. However, one could take a different perspective and assume that the service or workflow description of the service includes a specification of adaptations, and are thus visible to and possibly parameterisable by the customer. Technologies based on such an approach have been proposed in [24,32].

There is a rich body of literature on adaptive middleware to guarantee QoS properties (e.g., [12,50], a survey can be found in [51]). For various application areas interesting result are available from these projects. The current paper takes a more generic view at adaptive systems, targeting open software platforms for general-purpose computing.

Mathematical optimisation algorithms can be used on-line and at run-time to optimise the actions taken by the adaptive system. The use of such algorithms has been considered by many authors, sometimes based on SLA specifications, e.g., [2,7,13,54,58]. However, none of this work has been concerned with how to integrate such techniques in an open standardised software architecture. Such a software architecture for mathematical decision making algorithms would have to deal with reliability, scalability, privacy and many other issues. It is therefore of particular interest to study the implications of distributing the optimisation algorithms. An interesting first step to approach the mathematical and system issues can be found in [42].

Mathematical optimisation modules as mentioned above provide an infrastructure for run-time adaptation of systems, but provide no protocols or message exchange mechanisms to let adaptation 'emerge' in the system. Instead, it provides optimisation outside the system, aiming at a global optimum. In [26] it is argued that this is not true self-management, and does not resolve the scalability issues we will face in the management of truly large-scale systems. Indeed, as discussed at length in [59], none of the architectures discussed in Section 4 achieves management based on emerging behaviour. If this lack of self-management indeed turns out to hurt scalability, research in biologically or socially inspired emerging behaviour in computing systems may be of interest, e.g., [6].

3.5 Resolution

The final stage of agreement-based management is the termination and after care of the agreement. Obviously, this is particularly important if there are disputes to settle between parties. But also in case of undisputed agreements, dismantling of the monitoring and adaptation software needs to be taken care of, without introducing security and privacy vulnerabilities. To the best of our knowledge, no research about dismantling agreements exists, but it is an important issue.

Related is the issue of introducing changes to existing agreements, realised to be very challenging but not yet much researched. Issues arise about when exactly the new agreement is considered to be agreed upon, since it is not always possible to specify a time instant or unambiguously specify the event that determines the instance the agreement holds. Similar, at what exact moment does the old agreement terminate, and when and how does one dismantle the monitoring and adaptation software? A substantial amount of research will be needed to find practical solutions for these problems.

In practice, a trusted third party is often considered the appropriate approach to determine if agreements have been met [46]. The term 'trusted' implies that all parties involved believe monitoring conducted by a trusted third party is done correctly, consequently, they consider outcomes coming from the trusted third party to be authoritative. Based on this idea, one can imagine business models around trusted third parties that monitor, report and discover violations (compare this with similar monitoring products and services for traditional web sites from companies like Keynote and AlertSite.com).

A property one would like to establish when information is being exchanged between customers and providers is that of non-repudiation. Non-repudiation ensures that the party distributing the information can not successfully deny at a later stage knowing about this information. Of particular interest is the recent work of Cook *et. al.* [14], which introduces trusted interceptors to achieve non-repudiation. These interceptors insert signatures, and have a protocol for all parties to agree in non-repudiable way on information updates (e.g., monitoring data).

If future systems exhibit the amount of dynamism we envision in this paper, agreements come and go at fast pace and in large numbers. When third parties are involved additional protocols are needed to deploy the monitoring software from the third party, exchange data and pass on warnings and other information to the interested party [37]. Hence, as for all other stages, also for the resolution stage one can imagine protocols to be developed that take care of issues that involve multiple parties. For instance, these protocols could report violations and distribute credits to customers if agreements are not met. Such scenarios are speculative, but open up interesting research opportunities.

4 Existing and Emerging Architectures

Service level agreements are already main stay for IP back bone service providers. For example, Sprint openly publishes SLAs as well as measured past performance and availability on the world wide web [56], as do other backbone providers. The used metrics concern delay, jitter, packet loss and data delivery percentage. Backbone providers are willing and able to guarantee, measure and expose service levels because the service they deliver is under their control, not requiring a third party for networking (but of course relying on power supply, hardware and software reliability, etc.). Also when acquiring a virtual private network (VPN) an SLA is commonly agreed upon between customer and provider [46]. GTE Networks reportedly uses a third party for monitoring, and provides 'credits' to customers when SLAs are not met [46]. All contracts signed between customers and providers contain caveats related to dependency on other parties in the service delivery. A staggering amount of metrics and disclaimers can for instance be found in JANET's SLAs for the UK's higher education network [25].

A recent study suggests that SLAs are becoming increasingly prevalent in outsourcing deals, some bigger companies reporting to have more than one thousand SLAs closed for their outsourced IT [52]. Remarkable enough, SLA monitoring is still in its infancy and some times non-existing [52], but that apparently does not negate the value of agreeing on an SLA. In general, one would expect that the service provider model will provide a further push for deployment of SLAs.

All the above has had relatively little influence on the software architectures on which services are build. This must change when the services become more complex and the service usage becomes more dynamic. If customers come and go continuously (for instance when using computing equipment for scientific computations) or when the application is extremely intricate (for instance when customers are load balanced across application servers), integration of agreements in the software architecture becomes necessary. In what follows we discuss some important existing and emerging software solutions that aim at that vision.

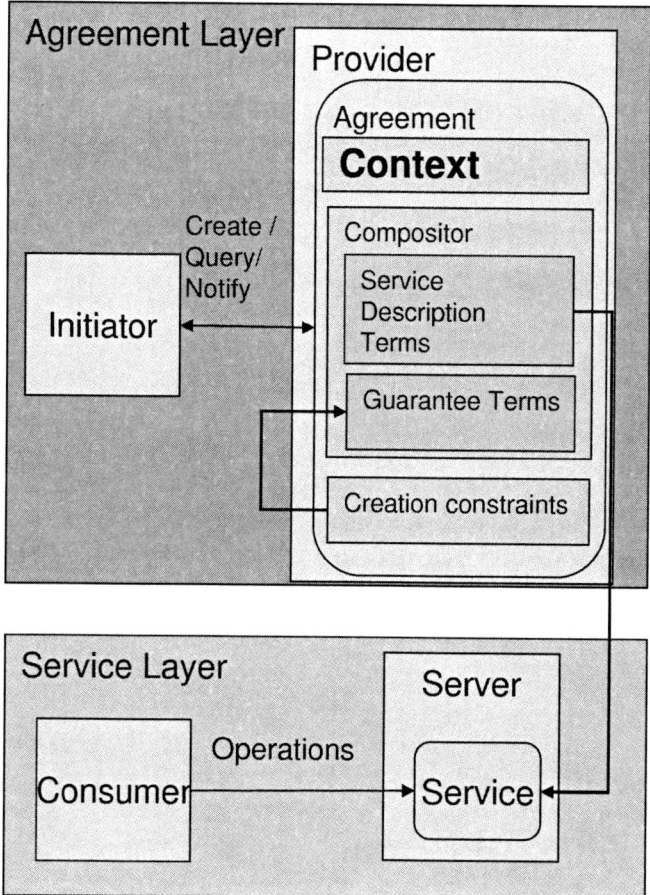

Fig. 1. View of WS-Agreement contents and layering

4.1 Global Grid Forum

Web services are becoming a popular infrastructure for developing distributed systems, particularly in Internet and Intranet setting. One of the distinguishing features of web services is the large number of activities hosted in standards bodies defining specific functions which can be combined to create an extremely rich environment. Agreements have become a part of this suite via the WS-Agreement specification [3], which has been developed within the Global Grid Forum (GGF).

WS-Agreement defines a structure into which an arbitrary set of agreement terms may be placed. The key point is that agreements need not be about any specific type of service (such as a web service), and so can be created and maintained independently of other services. This, in turn, implies that existing service infrastructures need not be changed to introduce agreements. This imposes the layered model shown in Fig. 1. The service layer on the bottom represents the service which is the subject of the agreement. The WS-Agreement model does not change this interaction because the agreement is created, managed, and monitored at a separate logical-layer. One can view an agreement in two ways: as a document or as a service. In the document view, WS-Agreement defines an XML Schema which specifies the components of an agreement. In the service view, an agreement is itself a service which can be monitored and managed in the same way that other services interact with one another.

WS-Agreement Contents. The agreement document contains the following sub-sections which are also shown in Fig. 1.

- A *Context* contains immutable properties of the agreement as a whole. These include who the provider and consumer of the agreement are, a completion time for the agreement, and references to other agreements which may be related to this one. Related agreements can be used in many ways. One use is to refer to other agreements that are held simultaneously with this agreement to define a larger aggregate agreement. Another is to allow parties to form a long standing agreement with shorter term, sub-agreements defined for a specific interaction at a particular point in time. WS-Agreement currently does not provide any specifics for how these multi-agreement relationships are formed, specified or monitored.
- *Service Description Terms* describe the service to which the agreement refers. WS-Agreement does not specify the content of them, so they can contain any arbitrary XML schema. In the simplest case, a description term may contain only a reference to an existing service to which the agreement applies. In other cases, these terms could provide detailed specifications of the functional properties for the service to which the agreement will apply. In these cases, it will be common for a new service to be created which conforms to these property definitions.
- *Guarantee Terms* define the non-functional properties of the agreement. Like the service description terms, WS-Agreement does not specify what the contents of the guarantee terms are, but it is expected that they contain enough information that a monitoring system could be configured to enforce the properties of the agreement. In addition to the non-functional properties, guarantee terms may also contain clauses referred to as 'business value' that contain rewards or penalties based on a service provider succeeding or failing in meeting the guarantees.
- *Constraints* are used to narrow the possible values for either the service description or guarantee terms. These are placed into an agreement document called a *template* which can be published to define a providers agreement options. The use of templates is described in more detail below.
- All of the terms are grouped by a *compositor*. The compositor groups the terms, and provides a logical relationship for those terms. The relationships are: "all of," "exactly one of," or "at least one of." Compositors therefore allow for alternative choices within the agreement document. When paired

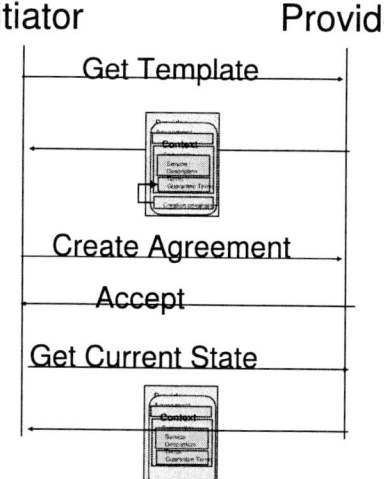

Fig. 2. Message exchanges in WS-Agreement

with guarantee terms and business values, this allows a single agreement document to define multiple, acceptable service levels with corresponding rewards. Compositors can be nested within one another providing an extremely rich structure of alternative and required service description or guarantee terms.

WS-Agreement Workflow. The WS-Agreement specification defines a simple workflow for the advertisement, creation and monitoring of agreements. It is anticipated that these basic functions could be combined to perform more complex interactions such as brokering or negotiation though no specific protocols are presently defined. The basic message exchanges are shown in Fig 2.

The interchange begins when an initiator requests a template document from an agreement provider. This template effectively defines the structure of the agreement it supports by defining the terms and their compositor structure. The template also gives hints to the initiator about acceptable values for those terms via the constraints described previously. In some cases, this template could be generated in response to each request, so the constraints could be used to reflect the current state of the provider.

Upon receiving the template, it is up to the initiator to fill in values for the terms which describe the desired agreement. It then sends the proposed agreement document to the provider as a *create* request. The provider can then accept the agreement in which case it returns a positive acknowledgement which also contains a handle to the agreement for use in monitoring. This handle provides a means of interacting with the agreement as a first-class service in a web services environment. If the agreement cannot be reached, an error is returned.

The initiator can use the handle for the agreement to monitor its state. This may be through requests to get an updated version of the agreement document where term values are filled in to represent the current state of the agreement. For example, a guarantee term that specifies the performance level may be filled in with the most recently measured performance observation.

Status. The first version of the WS-Agreement specification is complete. It has been authored by participants from Globus, HP, IBM and Platform Computing, and has entered the public comment period at the Global Grid Forum at the time of this writing. The GGF working group which developed WS-Agreement is presently working toward defining higher-levels of functionality on top of WS-Agreement such as more complex negotiation protocols, definition of basic guarantee terms which are widely reusable, and possibly profiles for specific interaction models such as brokering or auctioning.

4.2 Industrial Developments: HP and IBM

As we mentioned above, network providers are using SLAs extensively, but this has had limited influence on software architectures. Instead, the recent flurry of research and development related to agreements and software architectures is driven by enterprise IT industry. We discuss this by reviewing the technology strategy of two major enterprise IT companies, namely Hewlett-Packard and IBM.

Hewlett-Packard. Since the early nineties, Hewlett-Packard has been a leading management software vendor through its OpenView products [40]. OpenView predominantly focuses on monitoring and visualisation of IT operations. Over the years, the software has consistently moved 'up the stack,' expanding the network monitoring functionality to include system and service monitoring. The primary user target for this software are IT administrators and data center operators.

Service level agreements [45] have always been part of monitoring software such as OpenView and that from its competitors Computer Associates, IBM Tivoli, BMC Software, etc. In a typical setting, an administrator uses SLA thresholds to trigger alarms when performance deteriorates. If the metrics are chosen wisely (that is, based on service or even business considerations [9]), the SLAs assist in assuring higher level management goals. These ideas are illustrated well by the NetGather enhancements of OpenView from software vendor ProdexNet [48]. However, in reality the use of SLAs is often restricted to some of the more obvious metrics, such as basic performance and reliability metrics. Moreover, the level of automation to deal with SLA violations is limited, mainly targeted to triggering alarms.

Such use of SLAs is widespread in all existing management software but is of limited consequences to the exploited software architecture. Powerfully expressive SLA languages are not needed if the metrics differ little across customers, nor are highly effective adaptation algorithms needed if the main objective is to alarm the administrator. For HP, this has dramatically changed with the introduction of its adaptive infrastructure software strategy.

HP's adaptive infrastructure envisions that future IT is flexible enough to adapt to any form of change, from newly arriving customers to failing equipment, from changing business demands to sharing resource ownership. To allow for such flexibility, the proposed software architecture has three main characteristics: virtualisation, service-orientation and automation [59]. Virtualisation enables adaptation by substituting hardware-implemented and hard coded behaviour with software implemented adaptive solutions. Service-orientation based on web services is needed for standards-based interoperability, hiding of heterogeneity, scalability and software reuse. Automation is needed to deliver on the promises of the adaptive infrastructure vision without requiring prohibitively many highly-educated technicians.

One can read more about these ideas in [9,59], or in the many web pages published by HP. HP has chosen to pursue grid and web service standards as underpinning of the adaptive infrastructure and is leading research and working groups in GGF [3], chairs the organisation itself, and was instrumental in creating the link between web services and grid standards through their introduction of GGF recommendations in the OASIS web services distributed management working group [43]. Recently, HP moved from their monolithic and sizable utility data center product (discontinued in 2004) to new lighter weight adaptive infrastructure offerings based on acquired start-up technologies [44] and research efforts [29].

Within the context of the adaptive enterprise, the main focus with respect to agreements is on the work in the WS-Agreement working group, co-chaired by HP, see Section 4.1.

IBM. IBM's technology strategy is centred on the notion of autonomic computing [10,23]. Autonomic computing suggests that computing systems exhibit capabilities to recover from failures in ways not unlike the human body's immune system: locally initiated and emergent (that is, not dictated by a 'big brother' style decision maker). The main driver for autonomic computing is to limit the amount of personnel needed to run the infrastructure, since human involvement in IT management is expensive and often a source for failures. Part of the autonomic computing strategy is a focus on on-demand computing and federation through open, standardised web services.

The technology push from IBM is very similar to that from HP. HP's adaptive infrastructure is in spirit and in fact similar to IBM's autonomic computing, and utility computing is largely identical to on-demand computing. Also the business models of the two companies align: from a traditional product focus, the attention is increasingly on services for IT operations, delivered by consultants, very often through 'outsourcing' deals. Also from this business perspective the push for automation and on-demand computing fits nicely, since it makes IT management less expensive.

IBM product technologies around self-healing storage equipment and web server load balancing have made autonomic computing tangible. Research prototypes such as Oceano [5] have provided an emphasis on software for highly adaptive systems. With respect to software architectures, IBM focuses on web services and GGF grid technologies, implemented through open source prototypes or on top of IBM's Websphere J2EE compliant application server. The work described in Section 4.1 on WS-Agreement is heavily influenced by IBM's involvement. In particular, the proposed web service level agreement specification language WSLA [15,33] has been modified to be incorporated in the WS-Agreement proposals.

4.3 Academic Research: TAPAS

We discuss one academic project we have been involved in since it contributes some interesting technologies to agreement-driven service management [14,38,39,55]. The project is called TAPAS, which stands for Trusted and QoS–Aware Provision of Application Services, which has as one aim to develop QoS enabled middleware capable of meeting SLAs between pairs of interacting parties. It is representative for a range of adaptive middlewares, such as those surveyed in [51], but is of particular interest because of its focus on the service provider model.

In a typical TAPAS scenario a service provider provides its services to several consumers whose access to the service might overlap. The services required by each client are not necessarily the same and neither are the SLAs that they

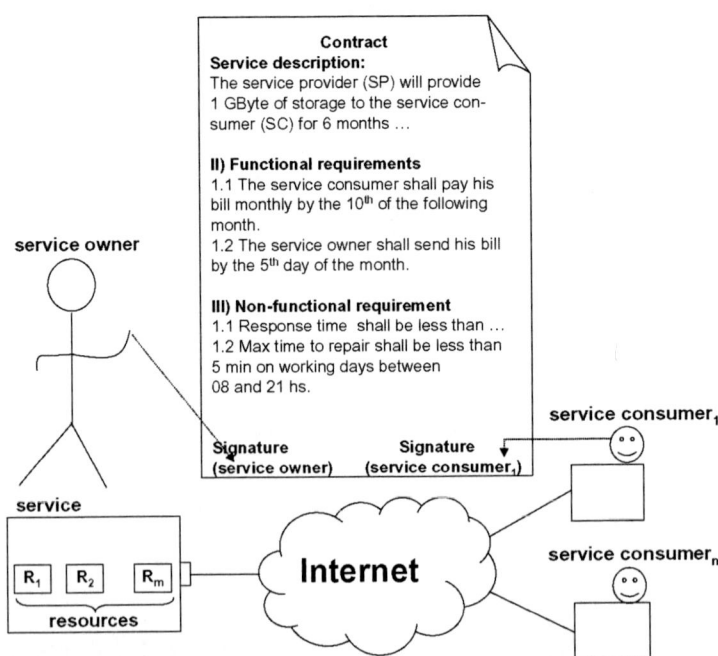

Fig. 3. TAPAS scenario showing provider, consumers and contract

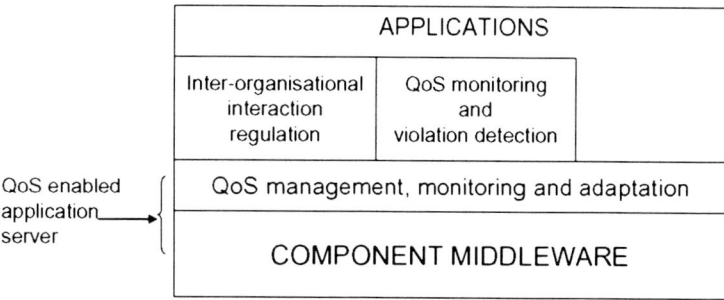

Fig. 4. TAPAS architecture showing its main building components

require. As shown in Fig. 3. TAPAS assumes that the service owner is in control of a pool of resources ($R_1, R_2, \ldots, R_m$) used to build the services that its consumers require. Examples of these resources are cpu, disks, database, servers, etc. Though not explicitly shown in the figure, it is assumed that some of the resources are owned by the service provider, whereas others are hired from other providers over the Internet.

In TAPAS interacting parties are mutually suspicious and reluctant to engage in business interactions unguarded. Because of this, interactions are regulated by legal contracts signed by the interacting parties. For the sake of simplicity only one contract is shown in Fig 3, but it should be assumed that the service provider is involved in multiple contracts, one with each consumer. As shown in the figure, legal contracts contain, in addition to conventional contract headers, a list of functional and a list of non functional requirements, that describe in conventional English prose, the rights and the obligations that the interacting parties are expected to honour. SLAs are considered useful if their compliance is monitored and enforced by computer means at run time. This requirement has a significant impact in TAPAS middleware. The challenge for the service provider is to manage his resources in order to guarantee that the contracted SLAs with his customers are met.

A module architecture of the TAPAS platform is shown in Fig. 4. Without the three shaded entities a fairly 'standard' application hosting environment would emerge, that is, an application server constructed using component middleware (e.g., J2EE application server). It is the inclusion of the TAPAS specific entities that makes all the difference, as we describe.

Inter organisation interaction regulation. This module represents the middleware that guarantees that the functional SLAs between two interacting parties are monitored and, possibly, enforced when a violation is detected. For example, for auction applications, it guarantees that bidders place bids only when bid rounds are declared open. The current version of TAPAS realises this module as finite state machines that model the functional SLAs of the original legal contract [39]. Conceptually speaking, this module is located between the two interacting parties to intercept messages exchanged between the interacting parties and prevent the ones that divert from the expected sequence from reaching the receiving business partner.

QoS monitoring and violation detection. This module represents the middleware that guarantees that the non–functional SLAs between two interacting parties are monitored and notifications are sent to the interested parties when a violation is detected [38]. For example, for auction applications, it guarantees that the time a response to a 'PlaceBid' operation takes is less or equal to what is stipulated in the original legal contract. In the current version of TAPAS, this module is realised as (logical) trusted third parties, which periodically probe the provider to collect metrics about its performance [14]. TAPAS also proposes the SLAng language for precise specification of SLAs [55] to reduce the level of ambiguity.

QoS management, monitoring and adaptation. This module represents the middleware to convert conventional application services into QoS enabled ones. For example, this module contains all the necessary logic to locally monitor the performance that the application service delivers to each customer and the performance of the resource used for building the service. Likewise, it contains algorithms for comparison, tuning, optimisation and adaptation. The current version of TAPAS implements this module as an adaptive clustering mechanism that incorporates QoS awareness into the application service. The current environment consists of a set of Linux computers running instances of the JBoss application server.

It is worth emphasising that the three modules discussed above are fairly independent in the sense that a given application does not necessarily need to implement the three modules together. For example, it is conceivable that, to save costs, in an auction application a bidder prefers to exclude non-functional SLAs from his contract. Similarly, it is quite possible that a provider in possession of a large number of resources might opt for over provisioning rather than paying for the cost of implementing and running the QoS monitoring and violation detection module.

5 Conclusion

This paper surveys the state of the art in technologies for agreements, with an emphasis on the implications for IT management software platforms. Agreements form the basis for a variety of advanced forms of automated management, enabling functionalities such as adapting systems to optimise business objectives, resolving conflicts resulting from agreement violations, and gathering non-repudiable evidence about agreement breaches. As we point out in the paper, many pieces must come together to achieve such advanced functionality, requiring technological advances in five categories: agreement specification, automated provision of resources, monitoring, adaptation, and resolution of conflicts. We reviewed recent advances in all these areas, summarizing both state of the art and open problems. We also discussed in more detail the technologies emerging from industry (HP and IBM), and the software platform support being developed in standards bodies (WS-Agreement) and academia (TAPAS). The recent flurry of attention for software support for agreements is encouraging. However, as can be seen in the overview table (Table 1), many challenges remain to be addressed on the road to comprehensive automated agreement-based system and service management solutions.

Acknowledgement

The work in this paper has been funded in part by the UK Engineering and Physical Sciences Research Council, under e-Science Grant No. GR/S63199/01 (Trusted Coordination in Dynamic Virtual Organisations), and by the European Union under Projects IST-2001-34069: TAPAS (Trusted and QoS-Aware Provision of Application Ser-vices), and IST-2001-37126: ADAPT (Middleware Technologies for Adaptive and Composable Distributed Components).

References

1. G. Alonso, F. Casati, H. Kuno and V. Machiraju, *Web Services: Concepts, Techniques and Applications,* Springer, 2004.
2. G. Alvarez, E. Borowsky, S. Go, T. Romer, R. Becker-Szendy, R. Golding, A. Merchant, M. Spasojevic, A. Veitch, J. Wilkes, "Minerva: an automated resource provisioning tool for large-scale storage systems," *ACM Transactions on Computer Systems,* ACM, vol. 19, no. 4, pp. 483–518, 2001.
3. A. Andrieux, K. Czajkowski, A. Dan, K. Keahey, H. Ludwig, J. Pruyne, J. Rofrano, S. Tuecke and M. Xu, *Web-Services Agreement Specification (WS-Agreement),* Recommendation track document of the Global Grid Forum, 2004.
4. A. Anjomshoaa, F. Brisard, A. Ly, S. McGough, D. Pulsipher and A. Savva, *Job Submission Description Language (JSDL),* pre-release draft for the Global Grid Forum, 2005.
5. K. Appleby, S. Fakhouri, L. Fong, G. Goldszmidt, M. Kalanter, S. Krishnakumar, D. Pazel, J. Pershing and B. Rochwerger, "Oceano-SLA Based Management of a Computing Utility," *IFIP/IEEE International Symposium on Integrated Network Management,* IEEE Computer Society Press, pp. 855–868, 2001.
6. O. Babaoglu, M. Jelasity, A. Montresor, C. Fetzer, S. Leonardi, A. van Moorsel and M. van Steen (Eds.), *Self-Star Properties in Complex Information Systems,* Springer, LNCS vol. 3460, 2005.
7. M. Bearden, S. Garg, A. van Moorsel and W. Lee, "Gallifrey: A Component-Based Framework for Building Policy-Based Management Applications," *Bell Labs Research, Technical Memorandum BL011356-000120-01,* Lucent Technologies, Bell Laboratories, 2000.
8. M. Bearden, S. Garg, W. Lee and A. van Moorsel, "User-Centric QoS Policies, or Saying What and How," *IFIP/IEEE International Workshop on Distributed Systems: Operations and Management,* work-in-progress report, 2000.

9. C. Bartolini, A. Boulmakoul, A. Christodoulou, A. Farrell, M. Salle and D. Trastour, "Management by Contract: IT Management Driven by Business Objectives," *HP Labs Technical Report, HPL-2004-184*, HP Laboratories, 2004.
10. Bloor Research, *The Grid Report: The Commercial Implications of the Convergence of Grid Computing, Web Services, and Self-Managing Systems*, Bloor Research North America, 2002.
11. M. Buco, R. Chang, L. Luan, C. Ward, J. Wolf and P. Yu "Utility Computing SLA Management Based Upon Business Objectives," *IBM Systems Journal*, IBM, vol. 43, no. 1, 2004.
12. W. Chen, M. Hiltunen and R. Schlichting, "Constructing Adaptive Software in Distributed Systems," *International Conference on Distributed Computing Systems*, IEEE Computer Society Press, pp. 635–643, 2001.
13. L. Cherkasova, W. Tang and S. Singhal, "An SLA-Oriented Capacity Planning Tool for Streaming Media Services," *IEEE Conference on Dependable Systems and Networks*, IEEE Computer Society, pp. 743–752, 2004.
14. N. Cook, P. Robinson and S. Shrivastava, "Component Middleware to Support Non-Repudiable Service Interactions," *IEEE Conference on Dependable Systems and Networks*, IEEE Computer Society, pp. 605–614, 2004
15. A. Dan, D. Davis, R. Kearney, A. Keller, R. King, D. Kuebler, H. Ludwig, M. Polan, M. Spreitzer and A. Youssef, "Web Services On Demand: WSLA-Driven Automated Management," IBM Systems Journal, vol. 43, no. 1, pp. 136–158, 2004.
16. Y. Diao, F. Eskesen, S. Froehlich, J. Hellerstein, A. Keller, L. Spainhower and M. Surendra, "Generic On-Line Discovery of Quantitative Models for Service Level Management," *IFIP International Symposium on Integrated Network Management*, G. Goldszmidt and J. Schönwälder (Eds.), Kluwer, pp. 157–170, 2003.
17. G. Dobson, "Quality-of-Service in Service-Oriented Architectures," *Dependability Infrastructure for Grid Services Project*, http://digs.sourceforge.net/papers/qos.html, 2004.
18. G. Fankhauser and D. Schweikert "Service Level Agreement Trading," ETH Computer Engineering and Networks Lab Technical Reports, ETH Zurich, no. 59, 1999.
19. A. Farrell, D. Trastour and A. Christodoulou, "Performance Monitoring of Service Level Agreements for Utility Computing using the Event Calculus," *HP Labs Technical Report, HPL-2004-20*, HP Laboratories, 2004.
20. I. Foster, C. Kesselman and S. Tuecke, "The Anatomy of the Grid: Enabling Scalable Virtual Organizations," *International Journal of High Performance Computing Applications*, SAGE Publications, vol. 15, no. 3, pp. 200–222, 2001.
21. S. Frølund and J. Koistinen, "Quality-of-Service Specification in Distributed Object Systems", *Distributed Systems Engineering Journal*, Institute of Physics, vol. 5, no. 4, 1998.
22. P. Goldsack, J. Guijarro, A. Lain, G. Mecheneau, P. Murray and P. Toft, "SmartFrog: Configuration and Automatic Ignition of Distributed Applications," *10th OpenView University Association workshop*, June 2003.
23. P. Horn, *Autonomic Computing: IBMs Perspective on the State of Information Technology*, IBM, 2002.
24. S. Hwang and C. Kesselman, "Grid Workflow: A Flexible Failure Handling Framework for the Grid," *IEEE International Symposium on High Performance Distributed Computing*, IEEE Computer Society Press, pp. 126–137, 2003.
25. JANET/UKERNA, *JANET/UKERNA Service Level Agreements*, http://www.ja.net/documents/sla.html.

26. M. Jelasity, A. Montresor and O. Babaoglu, "Grassroot Self-Management: A Modular Approach," in *Workshop on Self-* Properties in Complex Information Systems*, University of Bologna, O. Babaoglu, M. Jelasity, A. Montresor, C. Fetzer, S. Leonardi, A. van Moorsel and M. van Steen (Eds.), pp. 85–88, 2004.
27. N. R. Jennings, P. Faratin, A. R. Lomuscio, S. Parsons, C. Sierra and M. Wooldridge, "Automated Negotiation: Prospects, Methods and Challenges," *Group Decision and Negotiation*, Springer, vol. 10, no. 2, pp. 199-215, 2001.
28. J. Jin and K. Nahrstedt, "QoS Specification Languages for Distributed Multimedia Applications: A Survey and Taxonomy," *IEEE Multimedia Magazine*, vol. 11, no. 3, pp. 74-87, 2004.
29. M. Kallahalla, M. Uysal, R. Swaminathan, D. Lowell, M. Wray, T. Christian, N. Edwards, C. Dalton and F. Gittler, "SoftUDC: A Software-Based Data Center for Utility Computing", *IEEE Computer*, vol. 37, no. 11, pp. 38–47, 2004.
30. K. Keahey, T. Araki, P. Lane "Agreement-Based Interactions for Experimental Science", *IFIP/ACM/IEEE Euro-Par*, M. Danelutto, M. Vanneschi and D. Laforenza (Eds.), Springer, LNCS vol. 3149, pp. 399–408, 2004.
31. J. Lobo, R. Bhatia and S. Naqvi, "A Policy Description Language," *AAAI Innovative Applications of Artificial Intelligence*, AAAI Press, pp. 291-298, 1999.
32. Y. Long, H. Lam and S. Su, "Adaptive Grid Service Flow Management: Framework and Model," *IEEE International Conference on Web Services*, IEEE Computer Society Press, pp. 558-565, 2004.
33. H. Ludwig, A. Keller, A. Dan, R. King and R. Franck, *Web Service Level Agreement (WSLA) Language Specification, Version 1.0, Revision wsla–2003/01/28*, http://www.research.ibm.com/wsla/documents.html, 2003.
34. H. Ludwig, A. Dan and B. Kearney, "Cremona: An Architecture and Library for Creation and Monitoring of WS-Agreements," *ACM International Conference on Service Oriented Computing*, M. Aiello, M. Aoyama, F. Curbera and M. Papazoglou (Eds.), ACM Press, pp. 65–74, 2004.
35. L. Lymberopoulos, E. Lupu and M. Sloman "An Adaptive Policy-Based Framework for Network Services Management," *Journal of Network and Systems Management*, Plenum Publishing Corporation, vol. 11, no. 3, pp. 277-303, 2003
36. V. Machiraju, J. Rolia and A. van Moorsel, "Quality of Business Driven Service Composition and Utility Computing," *HP Labs Technical Report HPL-2002-66*, Hewlett Packard Laboratories, 2002.
37. V. Machiraju, A. Sahai and A. van Moorsel, "Web Services Management Network: An Overlay Network for Federated Service Management," *IFIP International Symposium on Integrated Network Management*, G. Goldszmidt and J. Schönwälder (Eds.), Kluwer, pp. 351–364, 2003.
38. C. Molina-Jimenez, S. Shrivastava, J. Crowcroft and P. Gevros, "On the Monitoring of Contractual Service Level Agreements," *IEEE International Workshop on Electronic Contracting*, IEEE Computer Society, pp. 1–8, 2004.
39. C. Molina-Jimenez, S. Shrivastava, E. Solaiman and J. Warne, "Run-time Monitoring and Enforcement of Electronic Contracts," *Electronic Commerce Research and Applications*, Elsevier, vol. 3, no. 2, pp. 108–125, 2004.
40. N. Muller, *Focus on OpenView: A Guide to Hewlett-Packard's Network and Systems Management Platform*, CBM Books, 1996.

41. G. Nudd and S. Jarvis, "Performance-based Middleware for Grid Computing," *Concurrency and Computation: Practice and Experience*, John Wiley and Sons, vol. 17, pp. 215–234, 2005.
42. T. Nowicki, M. Squillante and C. Wu, "Fundamentals of Dynamic Decentralized Optimization in Autonomic Computing Systems," *Self-Star Properties in Complex Information Systems*, O. Babaoglu, M. Jelasity, A. Montresor, C. Fetzer, S. Leonardi, A. van Moorsel and M. van Steen (Eds.), Springer, LNCS vol. 3460, to appear, 2005.
43. *OASIS Web Services Distributed Management Technical Committee*, http://www.oasis-open.org/committees/tc_home.php?wg_abbrev=wsdm.
44. *OpenView Automation Manager*, http://managementsoftware.hp.com/solutions/server/demo_0001_transcript.html.
45. *OpenView Service Desk SLA*, http://www.managementsoftware.hp.com/products/sdesk
46. L. Phifer, "SLAs Meet Managed VPNs," *isp-planet.com*, http://www.isp-planet.com/business/slas_for_vpns1.html, 2000.
47. P. Pongpaibool and H. Kim, "Providing End-to-End Service Level Agreements Across Multiple ISP Networks," *Computer Networks*, Elsevier, vol. 46, no. 1, pp.3–18, 2004.
48. *ProdexNet*, independent software vendor, http://www.prodexnet.com.
49. J. Pruyne and V. Machiraju, "Quartermaster: Grid Services for Data Center Resource Reservation," *HP Labs Technical Report, HPL-2003-228*, HP Laboratories, 2003.
50. Y. Ren, D. Bakken, T. Courtney, M. Cukier, D. Karr, P. Rubel, C. Sabnis, W. Sanders, R. Schantz and M. Seri. "AQuA: An Adaptive Architecture that Provides Dependable Distributed Objects," *IEEE Transactions on Computers*, IEEE Computer Press, vol. 52, no. 1, pp. 31-50, 2003.
51. A. Robinson and D. Lounsbury, "Measuring and Managing End-To-End Quality of Service Provided by Linked Chains of Application and Communication Services," *Workshop on Evaluating and Architecting System Dependability*, 2002.
52. B. Rosenthal, "A Surprising New Study: SLAs Now Have Teeth," *OutsourcingSLA.com*, http://www.outsourcing-sla.com/surprising.html.
53. A. Sahai, V. Machiraju, M. Sayal, A. van Moorsel and F. Casati, "Automated SLA Monitoring for Web Services," *IFIP/IEEE Workshop on Distributed Systems: Operations and Management: Management Technologies for E-Commerce and E-Business Applications*, Springer, pp. 28–41, 2002.
54. C. Santos, X. Zhu and H. Crowder, "A Mathematical Optimization Approach for Resource Allocation in Large Scale Data Centers," *HP Labs Technical Report, HPL-2002-64R1*, HP Laboratories, 2002.
55. J. Skene, D. Lamanna and W. Emmerich, "Precise Service Level Agreements," *International Conference on Software Engineering*, IEEE Computer Society, pp. 179–188, 2004.
56. *Sprint Back Bone SLAs and Measured Metrics*, http://www.sprint.com/business/support/serviceLevelAgreements.jsp.
57. V. Tosic, B. Pagurek, K. Patel, B. Esfandiari and W. Ma, "Management Applications of the Web Service Offerings Language (WSOL)," *Information Systems*, Elsevier, to appear, 2005.

58. A. van Moorsel, "The 'QoS Query Service' for Improved Quality-of-Service Decision Making in CORBA," *IEEE Symposium on Reliable Distributed Systems,* IEEE Computer Society, pp. 274–285, 1999.
59. A. van Moorsel, "Grid, Management and Self-Management," *The Computer Journal*, Oxford University Press, to appear, 2005.
60. R. West, "Open-Source Network Monitoring Software," *PC Network Advisor*, www.itp-journal.com, no. 124, pp. 3–6, 2000.
61. A. Westerinen, J. Schnizlein, J. Strassner, M. Scherling, B. Quinn, S. Herzog, A. Huynh, M. Carlson, J. Perry and S. Waldbusser, *IETF Request for Comments RFC 3198,* 2001.
62. L. Zhang and D. Ardagna, "SLA-Based Profit Optimization in Web Systems," *ACM International Conference on World-Wide Web*, ACM Press, alternate track paper, pp. 462–463, 2004.

Toward Undoing in Composite Web Services

Marie-Claude Gaudel

LRI, Paris-Sud University & CNRS, Orsay, France
mcg@lri.fr

Abstract. Cancelling or reversing the effect of a former action is a necessity in most interactive systems. The simplest and most frequent form of this facility is the "undo" command that is available in usual, individual, text or graphic editors. As soon as collaborative work is considered, undoing is more intricate since the notion of a last action is not always meaningful. Within this framework, the so-called "selective undo", which allows selecting and cancelling any (or rather some...) former action, has received lot of attention. There are some similarities between cooperative work and composite web services: Component web services are concurrently accessed; they may be treated as shared documents for undoing former actions. Among the latest results on undoing in group editors, the transformational model seems suitable for generalization to other kinds of distributed systems. It completely avoids backward state recovery and allows the selection and cancellation of any former operation. We present some relevant aspects of this model, and then some hints on how to transpose it into the framework of composite web services.

1 Introduction

Dependable composition of web services, and web services architecture, are likely to play a major role in developing the next generation of distributed systems. Reusing solutions from distributed systems techniques seems a natural perspective. However, most solutions will not be reusable directly, mainly because of the openness of the Internet. For instance: every component web service is used and shared by a very large and a priori unknown class of users (persons or other web services); component web services may appear or disappear, etc.

This paper brings in some contribution to the dependable composition of web services, by studying how some aspects of dependability could be addressed in web services architecture. Dependability, in closed distributed systems, often relies on the concept of transaction, which solves both issues of concurrency control and failure occurrences [Gray 1993]. In an open environment the concept of transaction is no more suitable. Transactions may be long lasting, and locking a service for a long time is not acceptable. Another issue is backward recovery: Recovery or cancellation of operation is necessary for every involved component when a composed operation fails for some reason (site crash or user-initiated cancellation). Backward recovery is hardly acceptable in the presence of cooperation-based mechanisms over autonomous component systems such as web services.

One solution to this concern lies in forward recovery: It makes it possible to address dependable service composition in a way that neither undermines the web service's autonomy nor increases their individual access latency [Tartanoglu et al. 2003 a]. It comes to cancelling, or reversing, or compensating the effect of a former action. In interactive systems, the simplest and most frequent form of this facility is the "undo" command that is available in our usual, individual, text or graphic editors. It provides a way of performing the so-called "linear undo": Only the last action is undoable, and then the previous one, and so on; Moreover, there are cases where it is impossible to undo this last action. The implementation of linear undo is based on some history buffer coupled with a "redo stack" (the history buffer behaving as a stack, as well). The "undoing" itself is realized either via state recovery or via the relevant reverse action.

As soon as collaborative work is considered, as it is the case for distributed group editors, linear undo is no more suitable since the notion of a last action is not always meaningful. Within this framework, the so-called "selective undo", which allows selecting and cancelling any (or rather some...) former action, has received a lot of attention [Karsenty and Beaudouin-Lafon 1993, Berlage 1994, Prakash and Knister 1994, Dix et al. 1997, Sun et al. 1998, Ressel and Gunzenhäuser 1999, Sun 2000].

There are some similarities between cooperative work and composite web services: Component web services are concurrently accessed and modified. They may be treated as shared documents when undoing former actions, as discussed above.

Among the latest results on undoing in group editors, the transformational model presented in [Sun 2000] seems suitable for generalization to other kinds of distributed systems since it avoids completely backward state recovery and allows the selection and cancellation of any former operation in the history buffer, under the condition that there exists a reverse operation.

We present some relevant aspects of this model, and then we give some hints on how to transpose it into the framework of composite web services.

2 Doing and Undoing in Collaborative Work

The transformational model considers three meta-commands, namely *do(O)*, *undo(O)* and *redo(O)*, where *O* is an instance of any operation of the collaborative environment. We briefly present the way *do(O)* is dealt with, since it is a necessary introduction to the way *undo(O)* is realised. The way *redo(O)* is performed is not addressed here because currently it does not seem to be of general interest for composite web services.

There is a distinction between the site where an operation *O* is generated and immediately executed, and the other sites where the *do(O)* command is received later on, very likely in a different context (i.e. a different history).

The principle of the transformational model is that operations received from other sites are transformed, according to the local history, before being executed.

The classical example for introducing operation transformation considers the same initial state "abc" for two users [Sun 2000]. User 1 generates *O1 = insert[2,X]*. His or her intention is to insert X between "a" and "bc". Concurrently, user 2 generates *O2 =*

insert[3, Y]. His or her intention is to insert Y between "ab" and "c". The execution of the command *do(O2)* when received by user 1 must transform *O2* into *O'2* = *insert[4, Y]*, including in *O2* the impact of *O1*, before executing it.

The management of transformations and executions must ensure the three following properties: convergence, causality preservation and intention preservation.

Convergence. Convergence requires that when the same set of operations has been executed at all sites, all copies of the shared document are identical.

Causal ordering preservation. It is a classical notion in distributed systems. Let operation O_a generated at site i, and operation O_b generated at site j, $O_a \rightarrow O_b$ (read O_b is *causally dependent* on O_a) if and only if:

- $i = j$ and O_a was generated before O_b
- $i \neq j$ and the execution of O_a at site j happened before the generation of O_b

Causality preservation requires that for any dependent pair $O_a \rightarrow O_b$, O_a is executed before O_b on all sites. An operation O_x is said to be *causally ready* at site k if it has been received and not yet executed at this site, and all the operations O_y such that $O_y \rightarrow O_x$ were already executed on this site.

A related relation is that two operations O_a and O_b are said to be independent (noted $O_a \parallel O_b$) if and only if neither $O_a \rightarrow O_b$ nor $O_b \rightarrow O_a$.

Intention preservation. Intention preservation requires that the effect of the execution of *do(O)* in a remote site must achieve the same effect as executing *O* at its original site, at the time of its generation; moreover, the execution effects of independent operations do not interfere.

Convergence and causal ordering preservation are classical properties. They can be ensured by well-known techniques [Lamport 1978, Raynal and Singhal 1996] by associating some vector time stamp to every operation when generated. The innovative and specific notion is intention preservation. It is the key to avoid long lasting blocking, and roll back or backward recovery. Intention preservation is realized by some transformations of the parameters of *O* in order to take into account the difference of context, which is due to the fact that different operations may have been done at the receiving site. A history buffer must be maintained on every site in order to keep the information necessary to the determination of the right transformations when doing a remote operation.

2.1 Transformations

Let us come back to the example above. Operations *O1* and *O2* are independent. The transformation of *O2* = *insert[3, Y]* into *O'2* = *insert[4, Y]* is achieved by the so-called "inclusion transformation" *IT*: *O'2* = *IT(O2, O1)*. In this precise case:

IT(insert[i1, c1], insert[i2, c2]) = *insert[i1, c1]* when $i1 < i2$ and *insert[i1+1, c1]* otherwise.

Remark. Note that this approach has no pretension to solve conflicts. In the example, if $i1 = i2$ and $c1 \neq c2$, there is a conflict that must be detected and solved in some way. Even if this method can help at detecting conflicts [Molli et al. 2003], solving them is out of its scope.

Conversely, in some cases it is necessary to exclude from the operation O_x to be done the impact of some other operation O_y via the "exclusion transformation" $ET(O_x, O_y)$. It is the case when independent operations are generated from different document states, for instance: Operations O_1 and O_2 are generated independently, respectively by user 1 and user 2, and then, just after O_2, before the propagation of O_1, user 2 generates O_3. When received by user 1, (after O_2, because of causality preservation), the impact of O_2 on the parameters of O_3 must be excluded before including the effect of O_1.

It is worth noting that very often *IT* and *ET* come to identity, as it is the case in the example for couples of *insert* operations.

IT and *ET* are supposed to be defined for every couple of operations of the collaborative system.

2.2 A Generic Schema for Controlling Operation Transformations

The general schema for applying operation transformations is generic. It is independent from the application and the operations. In [Sun et al. 1998], the authors give a general algorithm that can be (rather drastically) summarized as follows:

- When a causally ready operation has its original history being the same as the current history of the receiving site, it can be executed as it is;
- When a causally ready operation has its original history being different from the current history (due to preceding executions of independent operations), this operation needs to be transformed.

To determine the transformation to be applied to a new operation, the algorithm only uses its vector time stamp and the local history. The state vectors time stamping of the operations make it possible to know whether two operations are independent. Moreover, there is in every site a so-called "minimum state vector table" (one state vector by site) that is used to know if an operation is causally ready, to compare its local history with the current history and to perform some kind of garbage collection in the history buffer. This last point avoids keeping the whole history by eliminating operations that cannot be involved in future transformations (see [Sun et al. 1998] for more details and discussion on compatibility with undoing).

2.3 Undoing

Undo is realised on the basis of the transformations above, under the assumption that for any operation O a reverse operation noted $\underline{O}$ is available. Let us consider the case where $Undo(O_i)$ is generated or received at site k, with history buffer $HB_k = O_1...O_iO_{i+1}...O_n$. $Undo(O_i)$ will be performed by the execution of $\underline{O}'_i$ obtained by transformation of $\underline{O}_i$ such that: $O_1...O_iO_{i+1}...O_n\underline{O}'_i$ has the same effect as $O_1...O_i\underline{O}_i O'_{i+1}...O'_n$. Thus there is no rollback.

The transformation of $\underline{O}_i$ into $\underline{O}'_i$ includes the impacts of $O_{i+1}...O_n$, and, in the history buffer, the transformation of $O_{i+1}...O_n$ into $O'_{i+1}...O'_n$ excludes the impact of O_i.

$\underline{O}_i$ is not kept in the history buffer, but the fact that O_i was done and undone is, for making possible some $Redo(O_i)$.

More precisely, using two straightforward generalizations of *IT* and *ET* to lists *L* of operations whose impacts must be included *(LIT(O,L))* or excluded *(LET(O,L))* before doing operation *O*, the following treatments are performed at run-time:

- $\underline{O}'_i$ is computed and executed, with $\underline{O}'_i = LIT(\underline{O}_i, HB_k[i+1, n])$
- The new history buffer is computed, namely: $O_1...O_i\checkmark O'_{i+1}...O'_n$, with $O'_x = ET(O_x, O_i)$ for $i+1 \leq x \leq n$. O_i is still present, but marked by some symbol (here $\checkmark$) as a "do-undo pair". This allows an efficient treatment of some possible subsequent *Redo(O_i)*.

Note that it is equivalent to doing $\underline{O}_i$, with $O_x \to \underline{O}_i$ for $1 \leq x \leq i$, and $\underline{O}_i \parallel O_x$ for $i+1 \leq x \leq n$.

This approach has been implemented for various applications where it is necessary to maintain the consistency of shared data: group editors, graphic ones [Sun and Chen 2002] or textual ones [Sun et al. 2004], file synchronizer [Molli et al. 2003]. Here we suggest to use it for slightly different purpose, namely to develop adequate transactional attitudes for web services.

3 Undoing in Composite Web Services via Operational Transformations

In composite Web services, doing and undoing operations of component services is easier because there is no distributed common document to maintain in a consistent state. However, the problem remains that some operations requested by other sources than the composite web service can be performed by the component service. These operations must be taken into account when undoing even the last operation previously requested to a component service.

In the example of Figure 1, a composite Web service, *CWS*, sends operations O^c_1 and then O^c_2 to the *WS* Web service. Between the executions of O^c_1 and O^c_2 by *WS*, *WS* performs operations O^w_1 and then O^w_2 requested by some other sources than *CWS*. Moreover, after O^c_2, it performs O^w_3. Then it receives some Undo command from CWS.

Let us consider the case of *Undo(O^c_2)*. The history buffer of *WS* is $O^c_1\ O^w_1\ O^w_2\ O^c_2\ O^w_3$. Following the transformational approach, if we assume that *WS* provide a reverse operation $\underline{O}^c_2$ for O^c_2 and the *IT* and *ET* transformations, the undo command can be realised by

- Execution of *IT($\underline{O}^c_2, O^w_3$)*, including the impact of O^w_3 and
- Transformation of the history buffer into $O^c_1\ O^w_1\ O^w_2\ O^c_2\checkmark ET(O^w_3, O^c_2)$

Similarly, the command *Undo(O^c_1)* from *CWS*, with the same history buffer of WS, is realised by

- Execution of *LIT($\underline{O}^c_1$, <$O^w_1\ O^w_2\ O^c_2\ O^w_3$>)* and
- Transformation of the history buffer into $O^c_1\checkmark ET(O^w_1, O^c_1)\ ET(O^w_2, O^c_1)\ ET(O^c_2, O^c_1)\ ET(O^w_3, O^c_1)$

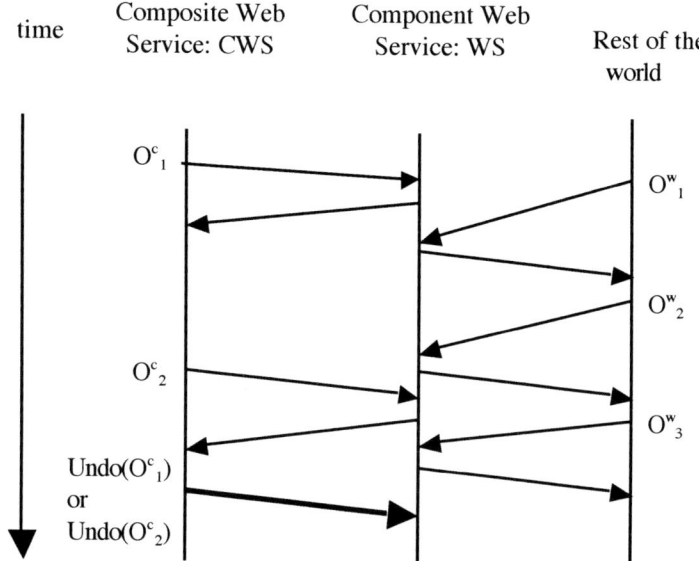

Fig. 1. Example of a scenario when undoing in composite web services

In the general case, let $HB = HB_{pre}.O.HB_{post}$ the history buffer of a web service that receives the $Undo(O)$ command, this command is realised by:

- Execution of $LIT(O, HB_{post})$
- Transformation of HB into $HB' = HB_{pre}.O\downarrow.LET(O, HB_{post})$

It turns out that in the context of composite web services, the algorithm for applying operation transformations is much simpler than in the case of collaborative work. When some *Undo* command is received by a component web service, only the local state of this web service is concerned. Causal ordering is no more an issue since the only order to be considered is the local total order of execution of the component web service that is registered in the history buffer.

However, the operations of web services are of a different nature than the operations of group editors. It turns out that *IT* and *ET* may require a bit more than modifications of parameters.

3.1 Transformations in the Case of Web Services

Let us consider an example from the classical travel agent case study [Mikalsen et al. 2002, Tartanoglu et al. 2003a]. The travel agent service assists the user in booking complete trips according to his/her requests and is built by composing several existing web services (e.g., accommodation and flight booking, and car rental web services) located through a public web services registry. Each web service is an autonomous component, which is not aware of its participation into a composition process.

We consider one of the airline reservation systems that the travel agent uses.

Let O^c_2 be a successful flight reservation, and O^w_3 another reservation for the same flight. If O^w_3 has been successful, then $IT(O^c_2, O^w_3) = O^c_2$ and $ET(O^w_3, O^c_2)$ is just O^w_3. If O^w_3 has not been successful, then $IT(O^c_2, O^w_3)$ must remove the pending reservation from the waiting list and satisfy it, in order to get a result similar as if O^c_2 was never executed. In this case $ET(O^w_3, O^c_2)$ consists in modifying the indication that O^w_3 was not satisfied. It turns out that the history buffer changes of type of content. It needs to keep more than a simple list of executed operations: for instance, indications on the success or failure of the reservation operations.

The transformations are dependent on the application, but they also depend on an adequate definition of "has the same effect as" in the sentence: $O_1...O_iO_{i+1}...O_n\,Q'_i$ has the same effect as $O_1...O_i\,Q_i\,O'_{i+1}...O'_n$ (cf. Section 2.3). It would be unrealistic to require the system to be exactly in the same state as if O_i never happened. Thus the transformations must be designed in function of some weaker state equivalence: for instance that the same set of travellers has got reservations on the flight.

However, in some cases this is not obtainable. In the example, if the waiting list of the flight was full, O^w_3 will not be satisfied, even if O_2 is undone. Thus some approximation of state equivalence must be considered.

Defining such a notion and the corresponding operation transformations is a major design activity: depending of the underlying application of the web service, the designer must decide what approximation is acceptable and thus, what are the transformations required, and what kind of information must be kept in the history buffer.

But the simplified version of the transformational approach that we propose here provides a framework and some guidelines for this activity. Even more, it gives some possibilities of formal verification [Imine et al. 2003].

IT and ET must satisfy some reversibility properties. In [Sun 200] they are summarised as:

$$O'_a = IT(O_a, O_b) \Rightarrow O_a = ET(O'_a, O_b)$$

It simply means that including the effect of O_b in the parameters of O_a, and then excluding this effect yields O_a again.

In our case, it is possible to weaken this property by taking into account that it is only required in equivalent states. Let us note $\equiv_s$ the relation between states discussed above. Let HB_a (resp. HB_b) the history buffer when Op_a (resp. Op_b) was generated, and $[HB_a]$ and $[HB_b]$ the corresponding states. Then IT and ET must satisfy the following properties:

$$[HB_a] \equiv_s [HB_b] \Rightarrow [HB_a . O_a] \equiv_s [HB_a . ET(IT(O_a, O_b), O_b)]$$

$$[HB_b] \equiv_s [HB_a . O_a] \Rightarrow [HB_a . O_a] \equiv_s [HB_a . IT(ET(O_a, O_b), O_b)]$$

In [Imine et al. 2003] the authors report how they used the SPIKE theorem prover to check these properties on various existing sets of transformation functions, discovering several incorrections or over-specifications. They are currently modifying the SPIKE theorem prover in order to build an integrated development environment for transformation functions. Such an environment would provide a highly valuable assistance for the design of web services with Undo possibilities.

3.2 Transactional Attitudes of Component Web Services

This model provides an elegant solution for undoing in distributed systems without backward recovery. It is applicable under the following conditions:

- For any operation, there is a reverse one
- Every site manages a history buffer
- For every site there are definitions of *IT* and *ET* for all couples of basic operations.

The local algorithm for computing and managing the operation transformations and the history buffer is much simpler than in the case of group editors: there is no problem of causal ordering preservation, since only the local order of execution matters; there is no problem of convergence of different versions of the state of the web services since the only state to be modified is the local one.

This approach is practicable if the vocabulary of operations of each web service is not too large, otherwise the work required for the definition of *IT* and *ET* becomes too important. Besides, there is a significant constraint of efficiency: the web service must be locked during the computation of the transformations of the reverse operation and of the history buffer. Thus these computations must not take too much time. Actually, very often no transformations are needed as it has been observed for group editors [Sun and Chen 2002], [Sun et al. 2004].

For a given web service, the statement of the set of transformations and of the control algorithm corresponds to the definition of a so-called "transactional attitude". Such transactional attitudes are presented as some essential ingredients for the composition of autonomous web services by several authors, for instance [Mikalsen et al. 2002, Pires et al. 2002].

Such a transactional attitude leads to some relaxed notions of transactions based on the "run and then compensate if needed" strategy, where backward recovery is never required. It is compatible with the coordinated forward recovery solution presented in [Tartanoglu et al. 2003 b] for designing dependable composite web services.

It is an interesting alternative to other possible transactional attitudes, such as "pre-commit and wait for a commit or an abort". Both kinds of attitudes could coexist in a composite web service, depending on the context (how frequent are compensations?) and the application behind the component web services (what is easier: to pre-commit or to undo?).

A point in favour of this model is that, as soon as the underlying application of a web service provides reverse operations, it is possible to implement it as a wrapper of the web service [Fabre et al. 2003]. The role of the wrapper is to receive the requested operations, to transform them when needed, and to manage the history buffer. An example of the adaptation of a single-user editor (namely MS Word) to the operational transformation technique is reported in [Xia et al. 2004].

4 Conclusion and Perspectives

In this article, we show how to transpose techniques developed for collaborative work and group editors to composite web services. The so-called Operational Transformation approach provides an elegant general model for undoing operations in multi-user applications avoiding backward recovery.

This approach can be simplified and adapted into an "optimistic" transactional attitude: we call it optimistic because it is based on a "run and then compensate if needed" strategy. It is an interesting alternative to other more classical transactional attitudes, such as "pre-commit and wait for commit or abort". As soon as the underlying application of the web site provides reverse operations, this transactional attitude can be implemented without modifying it, as a front-end or a wrapper.

It is possible to formalise this approach and to formally verify the correction of the transformations, thus of the compensation strategy.

This model and the corresponding transactional attitude seem worth to explore.

Acknowledgement

The beginning of this work was motivated and briefly supported by the IST-1999-11585 DSoS project. I am indebted to many members of the project, especially Valérie Issarny and Nicole Levy, for several discussions. I thank warmly Michel Beaudouin-Lafon and Stéphane Conversy who directed my attention to the operational transformation approach in collaborative work.

References

[Berlage 1994] Berlage, Th.: A Selective Undo Mechanism for Graphical User Interfaces Based on Command Objects. ACM Trans. on Computer-Human Interaction, 1(3), 269-294, 1994

[Dix et al. 1997] Dix, A., Mancini, R., Levialdi, S.: The Cube Extending Systems for Undo. DSVIS'97, Granada1997

[Fabre et al. 2003] Fabre, J-C., de Lemos, R., Gacek, C., Gaudel, M-C., Georgantas, N., Issarny, V., Levy, N., Romanovsky, A., Tartanoglu, F.: Final Results on Architectures and Dependable Mechanisms for Dependable SoSs. Deliverable DSC1 of the DsoS IST Project, April 2003, http://www.newcastle.research.ec.org/dsos/

[Gray 1993] Gray, J., Reuter, A.: Transaction Processing: Concepts and Techniques. Morgan Kaufmann, 1993

[Imine et al. 2002] Imine, A., Molli, P., Oster, G., Rusinowitch, M.: Development of Transformation Functions Assisted by Theorem Prover. 4th International Workshop on Collaborative Editing (ACM CSCW 2002), New Orleans, Louisiana, USA, November 2002

[Imine et al. 2003] Imine, A., Molli, P., Oster, G., Rusinowitch, M.: Proving Correctness of Transformation Functions in Real-time Groupware. Proceedings of the 8th European Conference on Computer Supported Cooperative Work, 14-18 September 2003, Helsinki, Finland, pages 277-293, Kluwer, 2003

[Karsenty and Beaudouin-Lafon 1993] Karsenty, A., Beaudouin-Lafon, M.: An Algorithm for Distributed Groupware Applications. IEEE ICDS'93 Conference, 193-202, 1993

[Mikalsen et al. 2002] Mikalsen, T., Tai, S., Rouvellou, I.: Transactional Attitudes: Reliable Composition of Autonomous Web Services, DSN 2002 Workshop on Dependable Middleware-based Systems (WDMS 2002), 2002

[Molli et al. 2003] Molli, P., Oster, G., Skaf-Molli, H., Imine, A.: Using the Transformational Approach to Build a Safe and Generic Data Synchronizer. Proceedings of GROUP 2003, ACM 2003 International Conference on Supporting Group Work, November 9-12, 2003, Sanibel Island, Florida, USA. ACM, 2003

[Pires et al. 2002] Pires, P. F., Benevides, M. R. F., Mattoso, M.: Building Reliable Web Services Compositions. International Workshop on Web Services Research, Standardization, and Deployment - WS-RSD'02, 551-562, 2002

[Prakash and Knister 1994] Prakash, A., Knisler, M.: A Framework for Undoing Actions in Collaborative Systems. ACM Trans. on Computer-Human Interaction, 4(1), 295-315, 1994

[Raynal and Singhal 1996] Raynal, M., Singhal, M.: Logical Time: Capturing Causality in Distributed Systems. IEEE Computer Magazine 29(2), 49-56, 1996

[Ressel and Gunzenhäuser 1999] Ressel, M., Gunzenhäuser, R.: Reducing the Problem of Group Undo. ACM conf. on Supporting Group Work, 131-139, 1999

[Sun 2000] Sun, C.: Undo any Operation at any time in Group Editors, Proc. of ACM conf. on Computer-Supported Cooperative Work, 2000

[Sun et al. 1998] Sun, C., Jia, X., Zhang, Y., Yang, Y., Chen, D.: Achieving Convergence, Causality-preservation, and Intention-preservation in Real-time Cooperative Editing Systems. ACM Trans. on Computer-Human Interaction, 5(1), 63-108, 1998

[Sun and Chen 2002] Sun, C., Chen, D.: Consistency maintenance in real-time collaborative graphics editing systems. ACM Transactions on Computer-Human Interaction, 9(1), 1-41, 2002

[Sun et al. 2004] Sun, D., Xia, S., Sun, C., Chen, D.: Operational transformation for collaborative word processing. Proceedings of ACM 2004 Conference on Computer Supported Cooperative Work, Nov 6-10, Chicago, 2004

[Tartanoglu et al. 2003 a] F. Tartanoglu, V. Issarny, A. Romanovsky, N. Lévy : Dependability in the Web Service Architecture, Proc. of ICSE 2002 Workshop on Architecting Dependable Systems, Orlando, Florida. LNCS 2677, 89-108, Springer-Verlag, 2003

[Tartanoglu et al. 2003 b] F. Tartanoglu, V. Issarny, A. Romanovsky, N. Lévy : Coordinated Forward Recovery for Composite Web Services, 22nd IEEE Symposium on Reliable Distributed Systems, Florence, 2003

[Xia et al. 2004] Xia S., Sun D, Sun C., Chen D., Shen H. : Leveraging Single-user Applications for Muti-user Collaboration : the CoWord Approach, CSCW'04, 162-171, November 6-10, 2004

Architecting Web Services Applications for Improving Availability

Rogério de Lemos

Computing Laboratory,
University of Kent,
Canterbury, Kent CT2 7NF, UK
r.delemos@kent.ac.uk

Abstract. In this paper, we address the problem of improving the availability and correctness of Web Services. An architectural approach is proposed that incorporates fault-tolerant techniques, such as, self-checking, comparison, and dynamic reconfiguration. The first two techniques are associated with the detection and handling of faults at the component level, while the latter is associated with the system. To demonstrate its applicability, a distributed application was designed and implemented that addresses the problem of obtaining dependable stock quotes from the Web. The system was implemented using Web Services core technologies, and preliminary measurements confirmed the improved availability of the whole application.

1 Introduction

This paper deals with the dependability of systems that are built from existing systems. In these systems, characterised as open distributed systems, such as the Internet, the sources of information are not necessarily under the controlling domain of the developer, and thus cannot be trusted. In this paper, we present an approach that incorporates fault tolerant techniques at the architectural level of the system, rather than at the lower levels of abstraction. Most of the architectural solutions proposed for improving the dependability of systems have relied on means for avoiding the introduction of faults, instead of their acceptance. The architectural focus for incorporating fault tolerant techniques is justified since it is the architecture that provides the ability of a system to respond to faults. If a system is not well structured, it tends to become more complex, thus defeating the initial efforts of improving its dependability. Moreover, the architecture of a system tends to abstract away from the system details, but assist the understanding broader system-level concerns [27], and this is fundamental when building systems out of existing systems.

The proposed architectural approach for improving the dependability of systems, defined in the paper, is a pattern consisting of architectural elements for the elimination of mismatches that might exist between the required and provided services, and the provision and management of redundancies. The identified architectural pattern could be instantiated into a wide range of applications, mainly those that rely on data. For this type of systems, it is assumed that the sources of data, i.e. those system components that are outside the controlling domain of the developers, can fail arbitrarily, while the components of the pattern will tolerate these failures by imposing crash-failure semantics when inconsistencies are detected in the data, and by reconfiguring the system when handling component failures. In order to show the effectiveness of the architectural approach being proposed, a distributed application was built that addresses the problem of providing uninterrupted stock quotes that are obtained from several unreliable sources from the Web. This case study is illustrative of the kind of system that the proposed architectural pattern is ideal for, which are those systems that contain an abundance of ready available redundancies – this is the case of the Internet. To show the feasibility of the proposed architectural pattern in the context of an Internet application, the whole stock quotes system was implemented using Web Services technologies [21]. In a previous work, the implementation of the architectural solution being proposed was done in Jini [22], a set of API's and network protocols that help to build and deploy distributed systems that are organized as federations of services [13].

The essential motivation for this work is to show that, depending on the type of system, application independent fault tolerant techniques can be easily incorporated in the architectural modelling of systems, like the notion of multi-versioning connectors (MVC) [25], which was proposed for the evolution of software systems, but derived from concepts associated with N-version programming (NVP) [1]. On the other hand, application dependent techniques, such as exceptional handling, might be more costly to incorporate because more care must be taken at every stage of software development [27]. The rest of the paper is structured as follows. In the next section, we discuss the architectural pattern being proposed for improving availability and correctness of Web Services. In section 3, a system that collects stock quotes from different Web Services providers is presented as an illustrative case study. In section 4, we present some evaluation results that were obtained from the implementation of the case study. Section 5 provides a background on crash-failures, giving special emphasis to fail-stop processor and crash-only components. Finally, section 6 presents the concluding remarks and provides directions for future work.

2 Structuring Systems

The structure of a system is what enables it to generate the system's behaviour, from the behaviour of its components [12]. The architecture of a software system is an abstraction of the actual structure of that system. The identification of the system structure early in the development process allows abstracting away from details of the system, thus assisting the understanding of broader system concerns [27]. From the perspective of fault-tolerance, system structuring should ensure that the extra software involved in detecting and recovering errors provides effective means for error confinement [1], does not add to the complexity of the system, and improves the overall system dependability [26].

2.1 Architectural Representation

The architectural representation of a system exposes its organization in terms of a collection of interacting components. For representing the architecture of systems, the following three basic concepts will be adopted [11][19]:

- *Components* represent the computational elements and data stores of a system.
- *Connectors* represent the interactions among components. They have interfaces that define the *roles* played by the participant components in the interactions.
- *Configurations* characterize the topology of the system in terms of the interconnection of components via connectors.

Components have multiple interfaces, called *ports*, each one defining a point of interaction with its environment. Interfaces are sets of operations and events that define the services *provided* or *required* by the component. The former are related to the services that the component offers, while the latter describes the services used by the component.

Patterns, in general, allow codifying solutions of specific problems as interactions between components [20]. The notion of an architectural pattern adopted in this paper is that of a architectural configuration that fulfils a particular purpose, and which can be instantiated into several applications.

2.2 Architectural Pattern

The architectural pattern being proposed aims to improve the availability and correctness of systems that provide a service based on information sources that reside outside the developers control domain. In particular, we are looking into services that essentially consist of data. The pattern relies on two principles: components that implement crash-failure semantics, and systems that support dynamic reconfiguration. Crash-failure semantics relies on the halt-on-failure property, in which processing of a component halts before produces an incorrect outcome [30]. Dynamic reconfiguration is a fault tolerant technique to avoid the re-activation of a faulty component by switching the processing to a redundant component [2]. The types of faults that the proposed architectural pattern aims to tolerate are faults in the value and time domains that might occur in the information sources or communication channels.

In order to increase the correctness of the service data, multiple information sources are used. The data provided by the sources, before it reaches the end service interface, is checked in both time and value for correctness. The component performing the checks implements crash-failure semantics by comparing the data from two or more information sources, and in case of discrepancy, the component crashes itself. The number of sources used to perform comparison depends on the number of faults the system can tolerate. Crash-failure components are also replicated in the system for increasing the availability of the end service, since the architectural pattern incorporates the ability to dynamically reconfigure itself when reacting to failures. When a crash-failure component fails, the system reconfigures to another available component in order to mask the failure. This responsibility is assigned to the component providing the end service. This architectural pattern resembles the N Self-

Checking Programming (NSCP) technique for software fault tolerance [16], however it does not employs two levels of comparison since we are not dealing with design flaws.

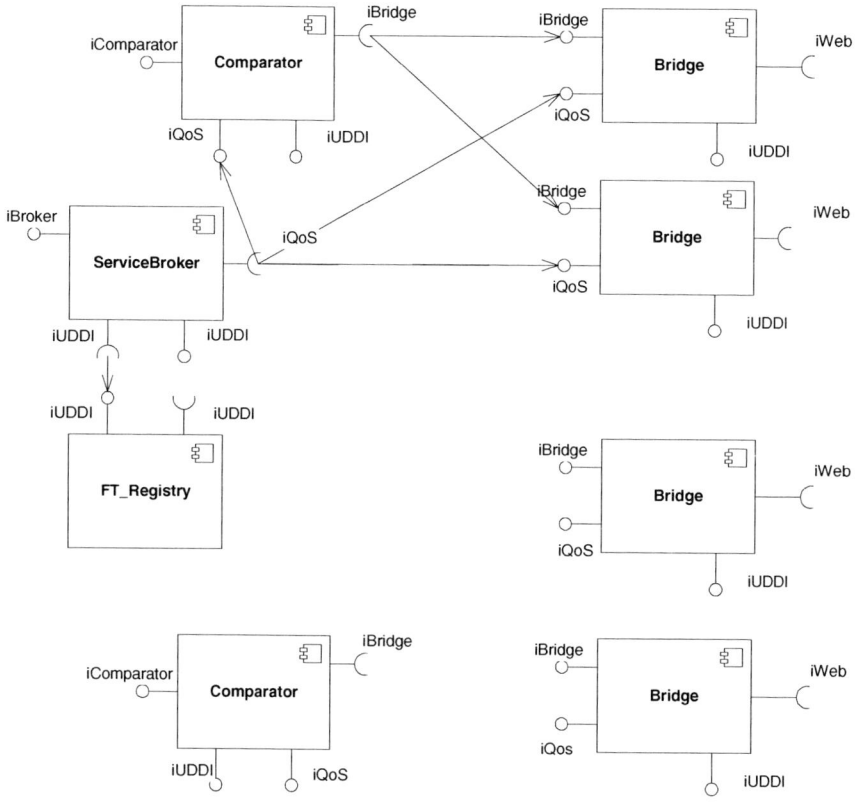

Fig. 1. Overall architectural pattern

The architectural pattern is presented in figure 1, in terms of an UML diagram representing its basic components, their required and provided interfaces, and the connections between these interfaces. In the following, we present very briefly each of the basic components, in the next section each of these components will be presented in more detail. The use of diverse sources of information introduces packaging mismatches, and one way for resolving these mismatches is by using the on-line bridge technique [8]. This technique was referential in the design of the **Bridge** component for eliminating potential mismatches that might exist between information sources and the **Comparator**. The component **Comparator** implements the crash-failure semantics by comparing two sources of information, assuming a single fault should be tolerated. In case there is a discrepancy between two sources, the **Comparator** crashes itself, and forces the **Bridges** also to crash. The provision for the continuous delivery of the specified services to the client is based on architectural reconfiguration, which relies on a fault tolerant **FT_Registry** for finding alternative **Comparators** and **Bridges**. In this case, the client of the services enquiries the **FT_Registry** for alternative **Comparators**, while the **Comparator** enquiries the **FT_Registry** for alternative **Bridges**. In order to select the most appropriate service provider, the concept of a service **Broker** is introduced, which is responsible for collecting information concerning the quality of the services been provided by the different **Comparators** and **Bridges** which are the basic building blocks of this architectural pattern. This information might be related to issues like, response time, availability and correctness of the different services.

In order to analyse the applicability of the proposed architectural pattern, we discuss in the following its instantiation into a Web Services application.

3 Architectural Components: Design and Implementation

Several technologies have been recently introduced for developing Web Services. The requirements for those technologies are the ability to provide seamless business integration, which is obtained by a layer of abstraction above existing software systems, operating system, and any hardware or programming platform [21][19].

XML (Extensible Markup Language) is a well-formed textual document, which is basically the foundation of the Web Services. It provides a standard language for defining data and how to process it. Since XML is plain text data, programs on various platforms should be able to process it. Three primary technologies have been accepted for developing Web Services, which are all based on XML. The technologies are [6][21]: SOAP (Simple Object Access Protocol), which provides a standard packaging structure for transporting XML documents over a number of different standard Internet technologies, such as HTTP and SMTP; WSDL (Web Services Description Language), which is using XML to describe the interface of a Web Service in a standardised way; and UDDI (Universal Description, Discovery and Integration), which provides a worldwide registry of Web Services for advertisement, discovery, and integration purpose. One of the promises of Web Services is to enable dynamic business integration through a standard infrastructure. For example, a business that might require a service would inquiry a UDDI to find an appropriate provider of that service. Once the service is identified, the business downloads and processes the provider's WSDL, so that the business can automatically generate a client that is able to interface with the discovered service.

3.1 Case Study

The suitability of the architectural pattern being proposed is demonstrated in the context of a distributed application that deals with the continuous provision of correct stock quotes. For that, our system employs several providers of stock quotes for guaranteeing the delivery of an uninterrupted and correct service[1].

---

[1] We abstract from the fact that there might exist a single point of failure from the system that is responsible for disseminating stock prices [15].

The service interface allows a client to specify the stock quote that he/she is interested, and the interval that he/she wishes to receive updates on its price. The system backend implements the proposed architectural pattern, utilising four **Bridge** components, which are connected to four different online sources. Those **Bridges** collect the required data from the online sources, and translate them to an object representation that contains the price of a stock at a given time along with that time. The **Comparator** component performs the comparison on the data produced by the **Bridges**, in terms of the value of the stock price and its respective timestamp. In this case, the comparison in the value domain is only meaningful if the stock quotes have the same timestamp. In case of discrepancies in the value or time domains, the **Comparator** and its respective **Bridges** are crashed, and alternative ones are sought through the **FT_Registry** for the continuous provision of services. In the context of this application, the crash-failure semantics is appropriate because after a crash, the loss of its internal state should not have major impact since its state can be easily recovered on future readings. Outside this architectural pattern, it is assumed there exists a component, which is responsible for detecting a **Comparator** failure, starting system reconfiguration, and providing the final service to the client.

For this case study, all the components of the architectural were implemented using Web Services technologies: SOAP messages are exchanged between components, WSDL interfaces define the services associated with a particular component, and for the registry, the UDDI standard was employed. In the following, we describe each of the components in more detail.

3.2 Design and Implementation

In this section, we present a design of the main components of the architectural pattern, in terms of their structure and internal behaviours. When necessary, their implementation in the context of the Web Services architecture will be also discussed.

3.2.1 Bridge

The **Bridge** component, shown in more detail in figure 2, is responsible for collecting information from a single Web source, in HTML format, and translating it to a compatible format, a SOAP message. It does so by providing, respectively, an interface with the Web source for the collection of information (**iWeb**), an interface with the rest of the architectural pattern (**iBridge**), and the means for resolving any mismatch between these interfaces. The packaging mismatch that the **Bridge** might be required to resolve is that of data representation, transport protocol, data transfer, and control transfer.

The online Web server provides the data, and for standardising its collection by the **Bridge**, a required interface is introduced (**iWeb**) together with a component (**Collector**) responsible for the collection of the data. This component provides methods for collecting data, and setting the type of data to be collected. By introducing this interface, we attempt to make the **Bridge** as flexible as possible without binding it to a particular collection method. After performing the first step in resolving any packaging mismatch, the **Bridge** has to extract the required data. In order to do that, the **Bridge** needs to parse the information it receives (**Parser**).

Unfortunately, the diversity of data representation among the online sources makes it difficult to design a generic parser with a well-defined grammar (this will cease to exist once all the information is encoded in XML, for example). Instead, we introduce an interface (iParser) that can be implemented by classes wishing to provide parsing functionality.

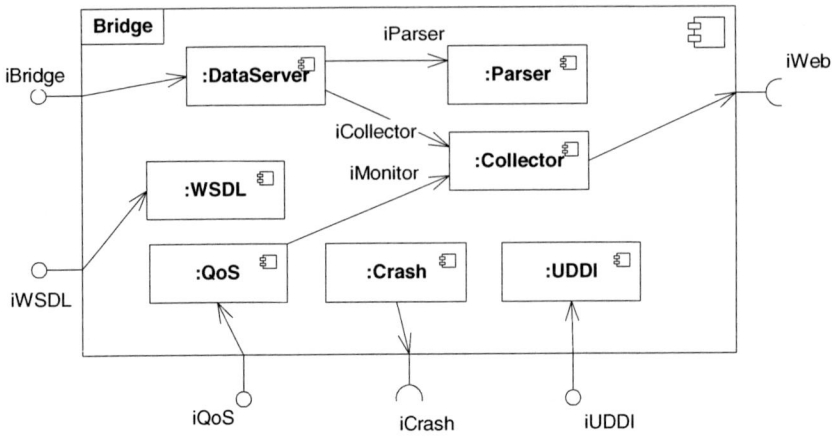

Fig. 2. Design of the Bridge component

The Bridge is also responsible for providing a service interface (iBridge) that performs data and control transfer in a way compatible with the rest of the architectural pattern. The Bridge receives HTTP requests from the Comparator, and forwards these requests to the online Web server. Then it should accept the HTTP responses from the Web server, and return them to the Comparator. In case the transfer protocol used by the Web server is HTTP, which is the same employed by the rest of the architectural pattern, the only packaging mismatch to be solved is that of data representation. The bridge component is responsible for translating the data representation from HTML document to SOAP message. The basic functionality of the Bridge is described in the sequence diagram of figure 3.

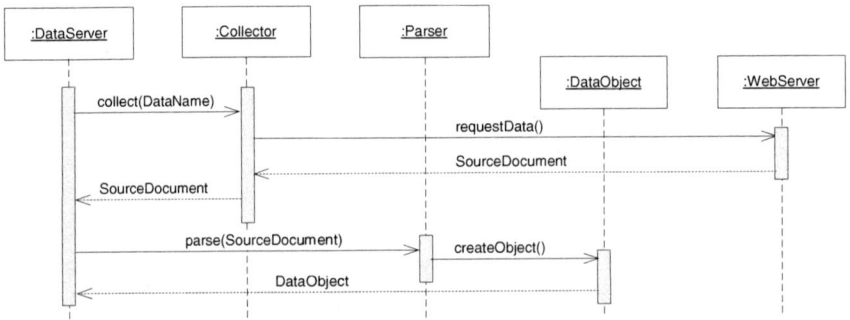

Fig. 3. Sequence diagram of the Bridge

There are two other interfaces that are associated with the Bridge component. A required interface (iCrash) that the Comparator uses for crashing the Bridge in case there is a discrepancy in the data provided by two different Bridges, and this is executed by the component Crash. A provided interface (iQoS) responsible for monitoring the performance of the Bridge for the purpose of obtaining its operational profile that will be fed into the services Broker, and implemented by the by the QoS component.

In addition of solving the packaging mismatch problem, the Bridge is also required to provide a WSDL interface to describe the services it provides (iWSDL). The WSDL interface includes a description of the interaction pattern, required parameter, provided response and transport protocol. In order to allow the interested parties to search for the Web service provided by a particular Bridge, the Bridge needs to refresh at regular time intervals its entry on a UDDI server, otherwise the UDDI server will consider that the Bridge has failed, and stops publishing its services. This refreshing time interval is associated with the leasing time mechanism of the UDDI, which is a mechanism that rids the UDDI of services that cease to be available (this leasing time mechanism was addition to the UDDI standard, and it will be discussed in more detail later on). From the perspective of the Comparator, no assumption is made how the Bridge component might fail.

3.2.2 Comparator

The role of the Comparator is to decide on the integrity of the data that is provided by the Bridges. The sources of data can come from two or more distinct Bridges, depending on the number of failures that has to handle. The Comparator assumes arbitrary failures for the Bridges, and to detect these failures the Comparator is a self-checking component that monitors both the behaviour of the connected Bridges, and its internal behaviour. In order to achieve this, the Comparator relies on two techniques: timeout based inter-component communication and comparison of data. The Comparator together with the associated Bridges forms a component that enforces crash-failure semantics. The design of a Comparator is shown in figure 4.

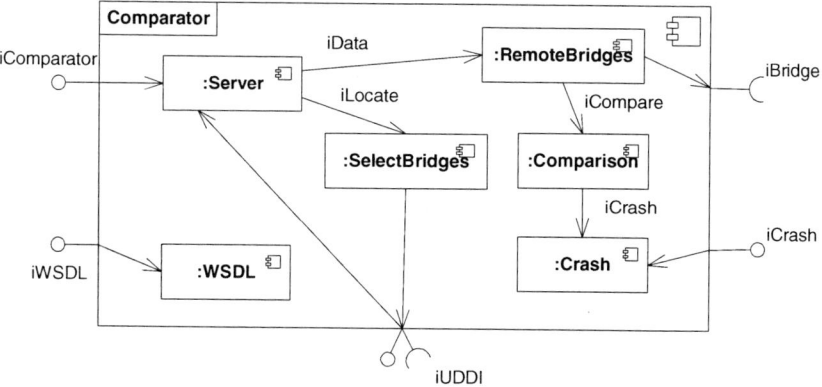

Fig. 4. Design of the Comparator component

In this paper, we consider a configuration in which there are two online **Bridges** per **Comparator**. The comparison of data from the **Bridges** is performed both in the value and time domains. For the comparison of the value of two data items to be meaningful, their timestamps must be equal. In case that either the timestamps or the values are different, the **Comparator** causes the two connected **Bridges** to crash (iCrash), and then crashes itself.

In addition to the required (iBridge) and provided (iComparator) interfaces, which are related to the **Comparator** functionality, the specification of the **Comparator** also includes a WSDL interface (iWSDL), which exposes the operations that the **Comparator** provides, and a UDDI interface (iUDDI) for publishing the services it provides, and for discovery services that it requires, i.e., services provided by **Bridges**.

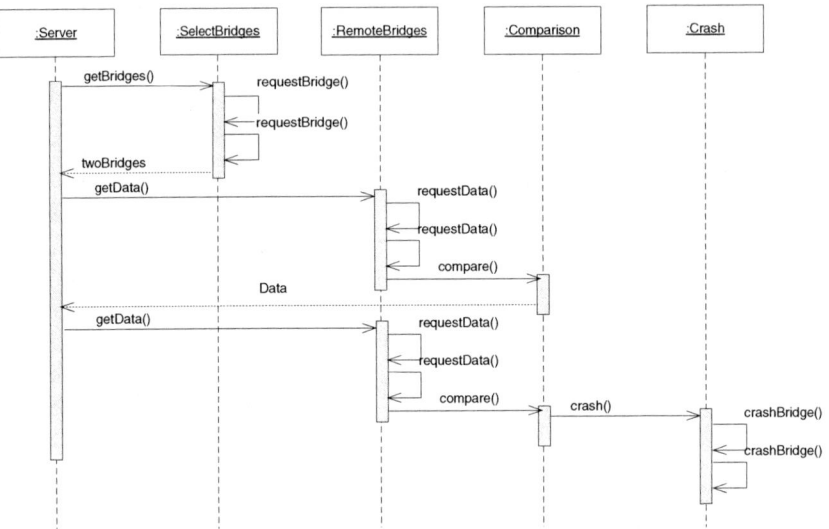

Fig. 5. Sequence diagram of the Comparator

When a **Comparator** is instantiated, the first step is to obtain two **Bridge** components from the UDDI registry from which can obtain stock quotes. The request for the stock quotes is made in the form of a SOAP message. The **Quote** objects, which are returned from the **Bridges**, are also in the form of SOAP XML documents. The two **Quote** objects received from the two **Bridges** are compared in terms of their timestamp and value. The timestamps of the two **Quote** objects must be equal in order for the comparison of the stock prices to be meaningful. In the event that the two timestamps are not equal, the **Comparator** causes the two online **Bridges** to crash, and then crashes itself. The same crash procedure will also be followed in the eventuality there is a discrepancy in the two stock prices. The comparison between two **Quote** objects is implemented by the **Comparison** interface. The **Comparator** component is also crashed if there are any communication faults occurring between itself and the **Bridges**. The communication protocol in Web Services is HTTP, which has got a default timeout facility that is used by the **Comparator** to detect response failures in any of the two bridges. If such failures are detected, the **Comparator** crashes both **Bridges** and then crashes itself. The basic functionality of the **Comparator** is described in the sequence diagram of figure 5.

3.2.3 Fault Tolerant Registry

In Web Services, the UDDI (Universal Description, Discovery and Integration) registry supports advertisement, discovery, and integration of services: a component can register and publish its services, and discover other registered services to build new services. The role of the registry in the context of the proposed architectural pattern is to support architectural reconfiguration when a **Comparator** crash-fails. When this happens, the client interface, external to the pattern, inquiries the UDDI about alternative services, and once another **Comparator** is instantiated and activated, the **Comparator** can inquiry the UDDI registry for other services that it will require, that is, the **Bridges**. In order to avoid being repetitive with material already available in the literature about UDDI [3][21], in the following, we describe only those additions that have been made to the standard UDDI that enables the provision of fault tolerance.

In order to enforce that the information of the UDDI is always updated concerning the availability of services, a leasing time was added to the UDDI standard. Otherwise, it would be difficult to identify which resources are available since the UDDI standard does not present a mechanism for eliminating from its records services that cease to exist. The leasing time technique, borrowed from Jini [13], requires every registered service to refresh periodically its records, otherwise the service will be considered unavailable. During the refresh process, each registered service is required to supply its `uuid_key`, which enables the registry to determine whether it is a new service. If the key is omitted, the service is assumed to be a new service, and a new record is created in the registry's data store. Records of expired services will not be removed from the registry, so that they can still use the old key when resuming service following a failure. This approach maintains a certain compatibility with the UDDI standard, though it is different from Jini, which completely removes the expired records.

For the provision of fault tolerance, UDDI registry was replicated using the semi-passive replication technique [7][24]. In this technique only one replica (master/primary) handles requests, provides replies, and sends messages to update the internal states of the other replicas (slaves/backups). For an efficient recovery, in case the master replica crashes, this technique ranks all slaves in order, so that the top ranked slave will automatically take over the master's job. In order to implement the semi-passive technique for the fault tolerant UDDI registry, a client stub was introduced for switching from a failed master to the top ranked slave. This ensures a dynamic system recovery when the master UDDI registry fails.

The design of a fault tolerant UDDI **Registry** is shown in figure 6. The main types of components of this design are: **Processor**, which communicates with clients or client stub in XML; **Function**, which is used to process the requests and provide replies; **DataStore**, which is responsible for storing all the information related to the UDDI **Registry**.

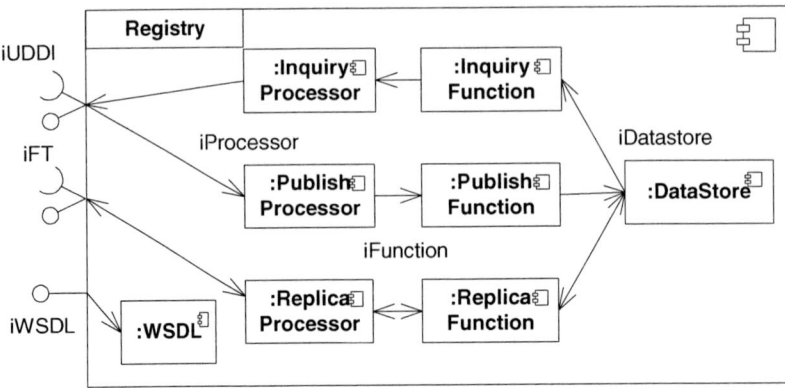

Fig. 6. Design of the Registry component

The internal services of the fault tolerant Registry are transparent to the client, and this is enforced by the client stub, implemented by the ReplicaUDDIProxy. The ReplicaUDDIProxy is also responsible for dynamically recovering the system. This component extends the UDDIProxy class from IBM's UDDI4J package [32]. It still provides all ordinary tasks (such as, retrieving registered services) for interaction between the registries and clients, but additionally introduces the support for fault treatment. Except for the master, all slaves will be given a unique ID by the master, which will ensure that all slaves are ranked in order. During the initialisation of the ReplicaUDDIProxy, this ordered list of slaves is downloaded from the master. If the master crashes, all ReplicaUDDIProxys, one for each client, know which is the next candidate to become master. Each ReplicaUDDIProxy will notify this slave to upgrade to master. The new master upgrades its state and notifies all other slaves.

In the semi-passive mechanism employed to replicate the UDDI Registry, the master ensures that all the other replicas' internal states are consistent. For instance, a registered service must be referred to using an identical uuid_key in each of the replicas, which is the responsibility of the master Registry for issuing and maintaining the keys. Any requests that modify the master's internal state should be forwarded to all registered slaves. However, a problem may arise if the master Registry crashes after replying to a publishing request and the component involved is a newly joined component. From this point the component will start to use the issued uuid_key from the reply to refresh its service, and then the ReplicaUDDIProxy will upgrade one slave to become master since the master has crashed. However, the master has not notified the slaves about this new record. Finally, the new master will reject this refresh request. To solve this problem, the master will firstly notify all slaves about any successful modifications. Once the master has received acknowledgements from slaves, it will then return the result to the clients. If the master crashes during this process, then it will not return anything to the client. Hence, the ReplicaUDDIProxy will resend the message to the new master and receive a reply including a uuid_key from it. The sequence diagram of figure 7 shows the process of replication backup. If any slave crashes during the duplication, the master removes it from the slave list and notifies all other slaves to make this change.

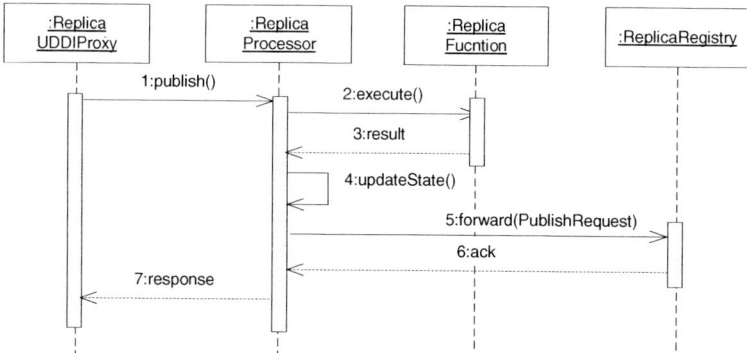

Fig. 7. Sequence diagram of the Registry replica management

On the master **Registry**'s side, if a **ReplicaUDDIProxy** is making an enquiry for the registered slaves, the master retrieves registered slaves from its **DataStore**. The data of a replica **Registry** consists of the five elements of Replica_UDDI_ID, Name, Inquiry_URL, Publish_URL and Description. The Replica_UDDI_ID field is the primary key of the table that ensures the uniqueness of records. The Inquiry_URL and Publish_URL must also be unique as well. The slave list returned to the **ReplicaUDDIProxy** will always be in ascending Replica_UDDI_ID order, so that the **ReplicaUDDIProxy** knows which slave is the next candidate to replace the failed master. Figure 8 shows the process of retrieving registered slave replicas.

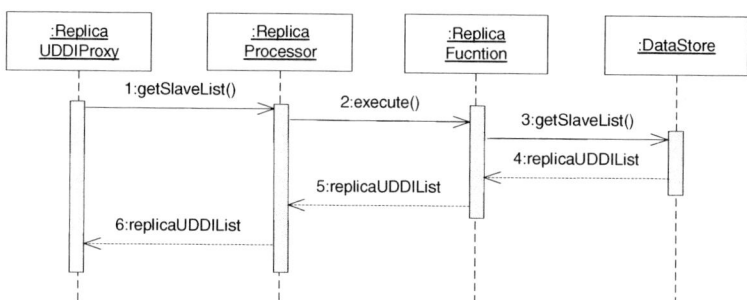

Fig. 8. Sequence diagram of the Registry when requesting replica slaves

During execution, new **Registry** replicas may join. A new replica should automatically send a join request including its access points (inquiry and publish URLs) to the master **Registry**. The master will then respond to this new replica with all records (including expired records) it holds before inserting this replica into its data store. The new replica will insert all records into its data store and send an acknowledgement message back. After receiving the acknowledgement message, the master knows the new replica is alive and their internal states are consistent, which allows the master to insert this replica in the list of registered slaves. Finally, this join

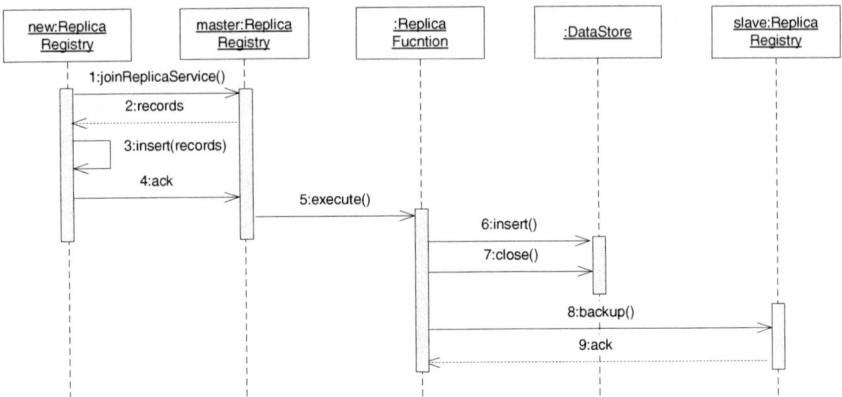

Fig. 9. Sequence diagram of the Registry when replicas join

message will also be forwarded to all registered slaves. Figure 9 illustrates sequence diagram of this process.

As soon as the ReplicaUDDIProxys notices the failure of the master Registry, they will notify the first available slave to be the master. This involves sending a message that contains information about the replica to the chosen replica. The message receiver will check if the inquiry and publish URLs received in the message are identical to its own, and it will upgrade itself to master only if this condition is satisfied. If it has been upgraded to master, it will forward this message to other slaves. The other slaves will update their internal states to reflect the change. When the former master recovers from failure, it sends a join message to the new master and resumes service as a slave.

3.2.4 Services Broker

The role of the ServiceBroker is to evaluate and compare the quality of alternative Web Services, when choosing a service. The motivation for introducing this component is to provide the means for a system to select a particular service provider based on the quality of its services. The current specification of the UDDI does not support this facility when multiple alternative services are available. When the client is presented with several options of services, the selection of a particular Web Service usually does not rely on concrete criteria. The existence of a ServiceBroker allows clients to make informative choices in the selection of Web Services based on operating profiles associated with quality of their services. In the proposed architectural pattern the ServiceBroker is an intermediary component between a client and the Web Services, and its purpose is to collect information and measurements from the different Web Services. In the context of the stock quote application, if some of the parameters being measured are response time, availability of the Web server, and the correctness of the stock prices being provided, then a more dependable system configuration can be obtained by selecting the most appropriate servers. The design of the ServiceBroker is shown in figure 10.

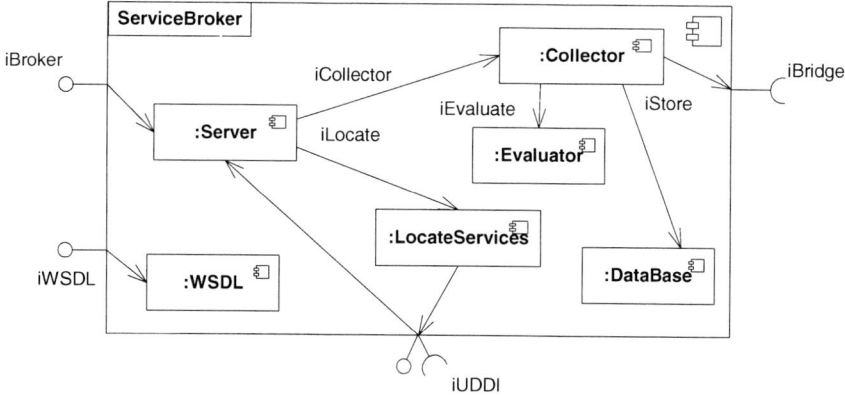

Fig. 10. Design of the SeviceBroker component

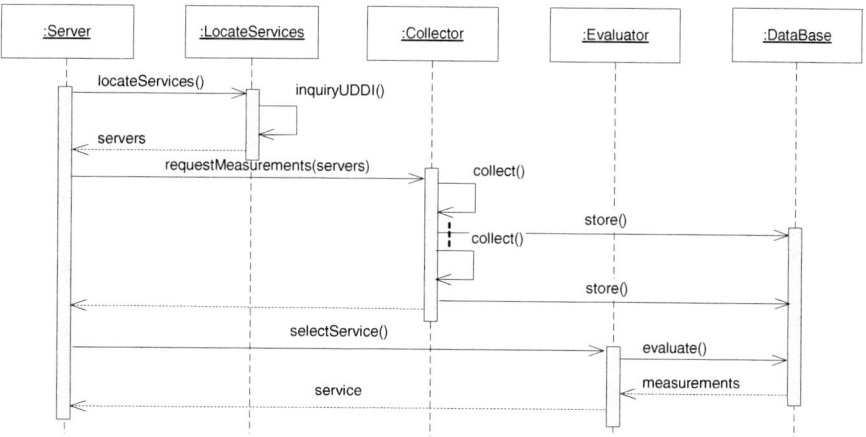

Fig. 11. Sequence diagram of the ServiceBroker

When a client requires a particular service, it contacts the ServiceBroker, which then contacts the registry (UDDI) to obtain a list of Web servers currently providing that particular service. After obtaining this information, the ServiceBroker is responsible for collecting measurements about the quality of services of the different Web servers, and this can be performed in two distinct ways. First, the ServiceBroker obtains these measurements either from a Web server or through a third party that would be responsible for monitoring the services of a Web server (in our case, that monitoring could be performed by the Bridges). Second, the ServiceBroker performs itself the measurements after receiving a client's request. In either case, the measurements collected are stored in a DataBase from which an evaluation can be made. When the ServiceBroker relies on a component like the Bridge to collect the measurements, guarantees have to be in place that those measurements are stored in a stable storage [29] for avoiding them to be lost in the eventuality of a crash. After collecting the measurements related to the operating profile of the different Web servers, the ServiceBroker selects a particular Web service for the delivery of the requested service according to the criteria identified by the client. The basic functionality of the ServiceBroker is described in the sequence diagram of figure 11.

4 Evaluation

The evaluation of the architectural pattern has been performed on a Dell Laptop PC Pentium III with 640Kbytes of memory on Win XP platform. The network connection was a dial-up modem connection with 56K bandwidth, and all measurements were performed during the opening hours of the U.S. stock market. The whole architectural pattern was evaluated, except for the ServiceBroker, according to the following measures [9][10][18]:

1. *Response time*: this measure is defined by the time elapsed from the request submission to the arrival of the first byte of the sequence.
2. *Availability*: this measure is defined as the ratio between the amount of time the system is available and the total duration of the run (or the experiment).
3. *Accuracy*: this measure is defined as the error rate in the service provided by the system, essentially, is a measure for correctness. This measure is computed as follows: Accuracy = 100 - (Number of requests with errors / Number of total requests) x 100.

Although the service can be available, errors may exist in the information being provided, hence the difference between availability and accuracy. Availability measures the quality of services from the perspective of the server. In other words, the only concern is whether the service is delivered (there is no need to evaluate whether the service being provided is correct or not - the major concern is with failures that can affect the server or the communications between the server and the client). Accuracy is a measure of the quality of services from the client perspective. The concern is to evaluate whether the service being provided is correct. The accuracy measure is stricter than the availability one.

4.1 Evaluation of the Bridges

The response time of each of the Bridges was measured as the time spam between the arrival of a request for a stock quote at the Bridge, and the time the Bridge provides the required information. The results of these measurements are shown at **Table 1.**

The availability measure of the four Bridges was based on whether the specified service, in terms of stock quote values, was delivered or not: if the bridge did not produce this service then it was regarded as unavailable. The results of these measurements are shown at **Table 2.**

Table 1. Response times for the Bridges

	MSN	Lycos	PCQuote	Yahoo
Response Times (ms)	6235±52.51	8264±40.12	5504±36.40	1799±47.38

Table 2. Availability for the Bridges

	MSN	Lycos	PCQuote	Yahoo
Availability (%)	97.60	97.93	99.77	99.98

For measuring the accuracy of the **Bridges**, these were placed in groups of three together with a voting algorithm. A **Bridge** was recorded as accurate when the timestamp and the value of a stock quote agreed with at least one other **Bridge**. If there was any discrepancy with the other two **Bridges**, the **Bridge** being evaluated was recorded as inaccurate. When stock quotes were not delivered due to omission, accuracy was not measured. The results of the accuracy measurements are shown at **Table 3**.

Table 3. Accuracy for the Bridges

	MSN	Lycos	PCQuote	Yahoo
Accuracy (%)	74.40	75.69	94.29	93.00

4.2 Evaluation of the Comparator

A preliminary evaluation of the **Comparator** was performed without considering the reconfiguration of the architecture. Under these conditions, the response time of the **Comparator** is almost the same as that of the **Bridges**.

For measuring the availability and accuracy of the **Comparator** a fixed time interval between requests was assumed, and these measures were performed at the interface of the **Comparator**. The measurements were performed during a period of three hours, and a total 390 requests were made.

The results for the availability measurements are shown in **Table 4**. This lower value compared with the value obtained by the individual **Bridges** was expected since a stock quote would not be delivered if either the timestamps or values produced by two **Bridges** were different.

Table 4. Availability of the Comparator

Number of failures	35
Availability (%)	91.02

For measuring the accuracy of a **Comparator**, a second **Comparator** was used. If there was a discrepancy between either the timestamps or the stock quote values of the two **Comparators**, the **Comparator** being evaluated was deemed to have failed. The results for accuracy measurement are shown in **Table 5**. This higher value compared with the value obtained by the individual **Bridges** was expected since the **Comparator** is able to eliminate stock quotes that might be erroneous. However, if higher levels of accuracy are sought then the failure assumptions have to be revised.

Table 5. Accuracy of the Comparator

	Comparator	
	Timestamp Failures	Value Failures
Number of failures	1	7
Accuracy (%)	97.94	

4.3 Evaluation of the Reconfiguration

For evaluating the reconfiguration of the architectural solution a different experimental setup was establish in which different types of faults were injected at the **Bridges**: incorrect timestamps and stock quote values, and the crash of **Bridges**. The objective was to analyse the impact that architectural reconfiguration would have on the response time and the accuracy of the system. Once a **Comparator** has crashed, the system reconfiguration would involve the search for new **Comparator**, and two new **Bridges**.

The responsive time is significantly affected since an architectural reconfiguration based on the UDDI registry requires that an alternative **Comparator**, and its two **Bridges**, have to be found, deployed and initialised. The response time was measured as the elapsed time between the submission of a request and the arrival of the first byte after the reconfiguration. The worst response time associated with the reconfiguration of the system was associated with the fact that new **Comparator** and **Bridge** components were not available when required because they might had not yet recovered from a previous crash. The load on the system may have contributed to delay in restarting each of the components. The data obtained for the responsive times are shown in **Table 6**.

Table 6. Response times considering architectural reconfiguration

	Normal Response Time	Reconfiguration Response Time
Response time (ms)	7021±2243	26635±16419

For measuring the availability of the architectural solution, the worst case response time, associated with the architectural reconfiguration, was taken into account. The system was given a maximum response time of 43 seconds in which to provide a stock quote, if the system took longer than this, then it was considered to be unavailable. The results for the availability measurements are shown in **Table 7**.

Table 7. Availability of the Comparator during reconfiguration

Number of failures	9
Availability (%)	97.69

For the sake of completeness, accuracy measures were also performed when considering system reconfiguration. These were not expected to change, however as it can be observed from the results shown in **Table 8**, there was a slight improvement in the results perhaps due to the inconsistency of the quality of the data.

Table 8. Accuracy of the Comparator during reconfiguration

	Comparator	
	Timestamp Failures	Value Failures
Number of failures	0	4
Accuracy (%)	98.97	

4.4 Evaluation of the Fault Tolerant Registry

The UDDI registry service has been tested on a UNIX server (Sun Microsystems Solaris 5.8), and a personal PC (a laptop running Microsoft Windows XP Professional, with an Intel Pentium III 1.0 GHz CPU and 512Mb memory). The UNIX server is responsible for running the master registry and the client, whereas the PC's role is to run a slave registry. The network between the client and server has 10Mbps bandwidth. The measurements were performed in normal office hours, and there was an unknown network load produced by other users of the university network. This is similar to the real deployment scenario, where the server could be running on a network that is connected to a number of components.

The measurement for the reliability of the UDDI registry service was not performed, since it depends upon the reliability of the host running the UDDI, and these measurements were not available. The measurements were obtained by comparing the data published into the UDDI, related to a particular service, and the data subsequently retrieved from it. Since the UDDI did not produce any corrupted data during the evaluation trials, it is assumed that no failures occur that significantly affect both the accuracy and availability. Consequently, the remaining measurements left to be made was the response times between the clients and the registry.

The most frequent usage of the UDDI registry service is related to service inquiries. However, this does not affect this UDDI modification since it has employed the leasing time mechanism. This mechanism requires the registered services to periodically refresh their services, so that the internal states of system are frequently updated. The major difference between the two types of registry is the fault-tolerant UDDI requires its client stubs (ReplicaUDDIProxy) to download first the registered slave registries from the master registry. The time taken (553 milliseconds average) to download slaves has not been included, because this is only done the first time the ReplicaUDDIProxy is loaded.

Table 9. Average times for the UDDI services (milliseconds)

	Non-Fault-Tolerant Registry	Fault-Tolerant Registry
Average response time	65	90
Shortest response time	20	27
Longest response time	1537	5321
Inquiry time	27	30
Publish time	80	120
Recovery time	N/A	4201
Backup time	N/A	25

From the data shown on **Table 9**, the average response time in the fault-tolerant UDDI is usually longer than the non-fault-tolerant UDDI. The difference is especially noticeable in the process of publishing requests and in the case when the master crashes. In the first case, the master has to wait for the slaves' acknowledgement messages before sending back a reply to the clients. In the latter case, the long response time is due to the time taken on average for:

- The network socket to timeout (2 seconds);
- An available slave to be found (30 milliseconds);
- The slave to be upgraded to become master including obtaining a new authToken (1021 milliseconds);
- The message to be resent to the new master (151 milliseconds).

In the fault-tolerant UDDI, the inquiry requests generally take less time (average 30 milliseconds) than publish requests (average 120 milliseconds). The response time in this worst case could overall take up to 5321 milliseconds. This is because publish requests involve checking the validity of the authToken and include more transactions with databases. The result was estimated using the mixed requests with both inquiries and publishes. The final average response time is 90 milliseconds by testing 1,000 times.

The system recovery time was measured from the time the service clients send requests to the client stub (ReplicaUDDIProxy), to the time the clients receive a reply from the client stub. The average time is 4201 milliseconds.

The backup time was the time taken for the master to backup its latest internal state to registered slaves. This could be affected by the bandwidth of the network and the processing power of the master and slaves involved. The average time is 25 milliseconds.

The actual response time can vary depending on the processing power of the computers, the number of records in the database and the bandwidth of the network. Furthermore, it usually takes longer the first time the registry performs the task. This directly affects the recovery time, in the case when the upgraded slave has not been used before.

4.5 Discussion

The evaluation performed on the architectural pattern has confirmed that the crash-failure semantics improved the accuracy of the overall system, while the dynamic reconfiguration improved its availability. The only measure that has degraded it was the response time of the system, mainly when architectural reconfiguration was involved. This was an expected outcome, since provision of fault tolerance has the tendency of decreasing the performance of a system.

The accuracy was improved by removing all the ambiguities from both the value and time domain of the data. Any discrepancy between two stock quotes would cause the data to be discarded, and part of the components of the architectural pattern would be forced to crash. For the continue provision of services the architectural pattern relies on its reconfiguration, which uses the registry for identifying alternative services.

In our understanding, the overall evaluation figures could be improved if the criteria for correctness could be weakened by performing the comparison of stock quotes in terms of acceptable ranges, instead of strict equalities. Under the current setting, it was noticed that the architectural pattern is constantly reconfiguring itself, which degrades the overall performance of the system.

5 Related Work

An advantage of a component that suffers a crash-failure is that there is no uncertainty about its state: it either works correctly or halts. Schlichting and Schneider proposed a methodology for designing fault-tolerant computing systems based on the notion of fail-stop processors [29]. They defined a fail-stop processor as one that halts automatically in response to any internal failure and does so before the effects of the failure become visible. Candea and Fox [4], proposed a design based on the *crash-only* semantics in which a component can be stopped only by crashing it, and started only by initiating recovery. This approach aims to support micro-recovery of system components for improving the availability of the whole systems, an idea that has already been applied to processors [23]. The main difference between crash-failure and crash-only semantics is that, while the former enforces crash through internal mechanisms, the latter relies on external mechanisms for crashing the component.

As already mentioned, the proposed architectural pattern presented in this paper is very similar to N Self-Checking Programming (NSCP), which is a diverse technique for software fault tolerance [16][15]. NSCP consists of four components grouped into two pairs in hot standby redundancy. The two variants compare between themselves, and after the two pairs are compared with each other. Distinct from this technique, the proposed architectural pattern only tolerates node and communication faults, and because of that the second pair of replicas is actually not needed for a second level of comparison. When the first pair fails, the system reconfigures itself based on the availability of resources, which are identified through a look up services.

The work presented by Tichy and Giese proposes an architectural solution, built on the Jini infrastructure, for improving the availability for application services. The architecture relies on principles, such as, service registry, leasing time of services, and smart proxies [17]. The latter runs as part of the client application for performing reconfiguration between replicas.

6 Conclusions

In this paper, we have identified an architectural approach for improving the availability and correctness of Web Services by using fault-tolerance techniques, such as, enforcement of crash-failure and dynamic reconfiguration. However, there are applications other than data oriented that require more sophisticated solutions for maintaining the integrity of systems. In particular, those applications in which the state of the system cannot be lost, for these cases alternative architectures that exploit the redundancy and diversity of Internet services have to be investigated if the delivery of dependable services is paramount.

The feasibility of the proposed architectural pattern was evaluated in the context of a Web Services application. The objective of the case study was to obtain, with minimal interruption, correct stock quotes. Considering Web Services and aiming to improve the overall dependability of the system, we have also proposed a fault tolerant UDDI registry and a Web Services broker. The provision of redundancies for the registry eliminates the existence of a single point of failure in the architectural solution, while the broker allows services to be selected according to their historical record, thus supporting the delivery of more dependable services. As part of the evaluation, a thorough analysis of the architectural implementation of the stock quote case study was performed adopting as evaluation criteria response time, availability and accuracy. Although the experimental setting might not be viewed as ideal for the kind of evaluation to be performed, new and thorough evaluations are planned in a more stable setting.

As already mentioned, the focus of this paper was on the architectural modelling of systems that incorporate techniques for tolerating general class of faults. However, particularly in the context of Web Services, other techniques, such as exception handling, should be considered for dealing with specific types of faults that might occur either at the application level, or at the Web Services technologies, such as, SOAP messages or WSDL interfaces. Although, there have been some initiatives that deal with exceptions at SOAP level, nothing significant has been proposed at the WSDL level, which from the perspective of structuring systems should be the most relevant.

Acknowledgements

I would like to thank the following students from the University of Kent that have contributed directly or indirectly to this work: Evangelos Parchas, Nan Chen, Yang Yu, Shy Long Chyan, Sheldon Spencer, and Stelios Georgiou. I would like to thank the anonymous referees for their useful comments.

References

[1] Avizienis. The N-Version Approach to Fault Tolerant Software. *IEEE Transactions on Software Engineering*, 11(2). December 1995. pp. 1491-1501.
[2] Avizienis, J.-C. Laprie, B. Randell, C. Landwehr. "Basic Concepts and Taxonomy of Dependable and Secure Computing". *IEEE Transactions on Dependable and Secure Computing 1(1)*. January-March 2004. pp. 11-33.
[3] N. Apte, T. Mehta. *UDDI: Building Registry-Based Web Services Solutions*. Prentice Hall. 2003.
[4] G. Candea, A. B. Brown, A. Fox, D. Patterson. "Recovery-Oriented Computing: Building Multitier Dependability. *Computer 37(11)*. November 2004. pp. 60-67.
[5] G. Candea, A. Fox. "Crash-Only Software". *Proceedings of the 9th Workshop on Hot Topics in Operating Systems (HotOS-IX)*. May 2003.
[6] D. A. Chappell, T. Jewell. *Java Web Services*. O'Reilly. March 2002.
[7] X. Defago, A. Schiper. *Specification of Replication Techniques, Semi-Passive Replication, and Lazy Consensus*. Research Report KS-RR-2002-001, JAIST, Ishikawa, Japan, February 2002.
[8] R. DeLine. "A Catalogue of Techniques for Resolving Packaging Mismatch". *Proceedings of the 5th Symposium on Software Reusability (SSR'99)*. Los Angeles, CA. May 1999. pp. 44-53.
[9] J. Durães, H. Madeira. "Web-server Availability from the End-user Viewpoint: a Comparative Study (Fast Abstract)". *IEEE/IFIP International Conference on Dependable Systems and Networks (DSN 2004)*. Florence, Italy. June 2004.
[10] J. Durães, M. Vieira, H. Madeira. "Dependability Benchmarking of Web-Servers". *The 23rd International Conference of Computer Safety, Reliability and Security (SAFECOMP 2004)*. Potsdam, Germany. September 2004.
[11] D. Garlan, S.-W. Cheng, A. J. Kompanek. "Reconciling the Needs of Architectural Description with Object-Modeling Notations". *Science of Computer Programming Journal (Special UML Edition)*. Elsevier Science. 2001.
[12] P. A. de C. Guerra, C. M. F. Rubira, A. Romanovsky, R. de Lemos. "A Dependable Architecture for COTS-Based Software Systems using Protective Wrappers". R. de Lemos, C. Gacek, A. Romanovsky (Eds.). *Architecting Dependable Systems II*. Lecture Notes in Computer Science 3069. Springer. Berlin, Germany. 2004. pp. 144-166.
[13] *Jini TM Architecture Specification Version 1.2*. Sun Microsystems. December 2001.
[14] Jones, B. Randell. "Dependability – the Role of Structure". 2004. (Manuscript in preparation)
[15] J. Kumagai. "London Exchange Vanishes for 8 Hours". *IEEE Spectrum*. June 2000. pp. 30-32.
[16] J.-C. Laprie, et al. "Hardware and Software Fault Tolerance: Definition and Analysis of Architectural Solutions". *Proceedings of the 17th International Symposium on Fault Tolerant Computer Systems (FTCS-17)*. Pittsburgh, PA. 1987. pp. 116-121.

[17] P. Ledru. "Smart Proxies for Jini Services". *ACM SIGPLAN Notices 37*. 2002. pp. 57–61.
[18] M. Merzbacher, Dan Patterson. "Measuring End-User Availability on the Web: Practical Experience". *Proceedings of the International Performance and Dependability Symposium.* Washington DC, USA. June 2002.
[19] R. Monge, C. Alves, A. Vallecillo. "A Graphical Representation of COTS-based Software Architectures". *Proceedings. of IDEAS 2002.* La Habana, Cuba, April 2002. pp. 126-137.
[20] R. T. Monroe, A. Kompanek, R. Melton, D. Garlan. "Architectural Styles, Design Patterns, and Objects". *IEEE Software 14(1)*. January 1997. pp. 43-52.
[21] E. Newcomer. *Understanding Web Services.* Addison-Wesley. September 2002.
[22] E. Parchas, R. de Lemos. "An Architectural Approach for Improving Availability in Web Services". *Proceedings of ICSE 2004 Workshop on Architecting Dependable Systems (WADS).* Edinburgh, Scotland, UK. May 2004.
[23] M. Pflanz. *On-line Error Detection and Fast Recover Techniques for Dependable Embedded Processors.* Lecture Notes in Computer Science 2270. Springer. Berlin, Germany. 1998.
[24] Powell. "Distributed Fault Tolerance: Lessons from Delta-4". *IEEE Micro.* February 1994. pp. 42 – 43.
[25] M. Rakic, N. Medvidovic. "Increasing the Confidence in Off-the-Shelf Components: A Software Connector-based Approach". *Proceedings of the 2001 Symposium on Software Reusability (SSR'01).* May 2001. pp. 11-18.
[26] Randell. "System Structure for Software Fault Tolerance". *IEEE Transactions on Software Engineering SE 1(2).* June 1975. pp. 220-232.
[27] M. F. Rubira, R. de Lemos, G. R. M. Ferreira, F. Castor Filho. "Exception Handling in the Development of Dependable Component-Based Systems". *Software-Practice and Experience. Volume 35(3).* March 2005. pp. 195-236.
[28] M. Shaw. "Moving from Qualities to Architecture: Architecture Styles". *Software Architecture in Practice.* L. Bass, P. Clements, R. Kazman (Eds.). Addison-Wesley. 1998. pp. 93-122.
[29] R. D. Schlichting, F. B. Schneider. "Fail-Stop Processors: An Approach to Designing Fault-Tolerant Computing Systems". *ACM Transactions on Computer Systems 1(3).* August 1983. pp. 222-238.
[30] F. B. Schneider. "Byzantine Generals in Action: Implementing Fail-Stop Processors". *ACM Transactions on Computer Systems 2(2).* May 1984. pp. 145-154.
[31] M. Tichy, H. Giese, "An Architecture for Configurable Dependability of Application Services". *Architecting Dependable Systems II.* R. de Lemos, C. Gacek, A. Romanovsky (Eds.). Lecture Notes in Computer Science 3069. Springer. Berlin, Germany. 2004.
[32] *UDDI4J.* IBM UDDI4J Project. IBM. http://www-124.ibm.com/ developerworks/oss/uddi4j/ [September 2004].

Dependable Composite Web Services with Components Upgraded Online

Anatoliy Gorbenko[1], Vyacheslav Kharchenko[1], Peter Popov[2], and Alexander Romanovsky[3]

[1] Department of Computer Systems and Networks, National Aerospace University, Kharkiv, Ukraine
A.Gorbenko@csac.khai.edu, V.Kharchenko@khai.edu
[2] Centre for Software Reliability, City University, London, UK
ptp@csr.city.ac.uk
[3] School of Computing Science, University of Newcastle, Newcastle upon Tyne, UK
alexander.romanovsky@ncl.ac.uk

Abstract. Achieving high dependability of Web Services (WSs) dynamically composed from component WSs is an open problem. One of the main difficulties here is due to the fact that the component WSs can and will be upgraded online, which will affect the dependability of the composite WS. The paper introduces the problem of component WS upgrade and proposes solutions for dependable upgrading in which natural redundancy, formed by the latest and the previous releases of a WS being kept operational, is used. The paper describes how 'confidence in correctness' can be systematically used as a measure of dependability of both the component and the composite WSs. We discuss architectures for a composite WS in which the upgrade of the component WS is managed by switching the composite WS from using the old release of the component WS to using its newer release only when the confidence is high enough, so that the composite service dependability will not deteriorate as a result of the switch. The effectiveness of the proposed solutions is assessed by simulation. We discuss the implications of the proposed architectures, including ways of 'publishing' the confidence in WSs, in the context of relevant standard technologies, such as WSDL, UDDI and SOAP.

1 Introduction

The Web Service architecture [1] is rapidly becoming the de facto standard technology for achieving interoperability between different software applications running on a variety of platforms. This architecture supports development and deployment of open systems in which component discovery and system integration can be postponed until the systems are executed. Individual components (i.e. Web Services – WSs) advertise their services via a registry (typically developed using the UDDI standard[1]) in which their descriptions, given in a standard XML-based language called Web Service Definition Language (WSDL[2]), can be looked up. After

---

[1] http://www.uddi.org/
[2] http://www.w3.org/TR/wsdl

a WS capable of delivering the required service has been found it can be used or even dynamically integrated into a composite WS.

The WS architecture is in effect a further step in the evolution of the well-known component-based system development with off-the-shelf (OTS) components. The main advances enabling this architecture have been made by the standardisation of the integration process (a set of interrelated standards such as SOAP[3], WSDL, UDDI[4], etc.). WSs are the OTS components for which a standard way of advertising their functionality has been widely adopted.

The problem of dealing with online system upgrades is well known and a number of solutions have been proposed (see, for example [2]). The main reasons for upgrading the systems are improving/adding functionality or correction of bugs. The difficulties in dealing with upgrades of COTS components in a dependable way are well recognised and a number of solutions have been proposed. The WS architecture poses a new set of problems mainly caused by its openness and by the fact that the component WSs are executed in different management domains and are outside of the control of the composite WS. Moreover, switching such systems off or inflicting any serious interruptions in the service they provide is not acceptable, so all upgrades have to be dealt with seamlessly and online. One of the motivations for our work is that ensuring and assessing dependability of complex WSs is complicated when any component can be replaced online by a new one with unknown dependability characteristics.

There is clearly a need to develop solutions making use of natural redundancy which exists in such systems and guaranteeing that the overall dependability of the composite system is improving rather than deteriorating. Note that the idea of using the old and the new releases of a program side by side to improve its dependability is far from new: it was first mentioned by B. Randell in his work on recovery blocks in which the earlier releases of the primary alternate are seen as a source of secondary alternates [3].

The rest of the paper is organised as follows. Section 2 gives an overview of the Web Service dependability and shows how it can be assessed using measures such as "confidence in WS correctness". In section 3 we introduce the problem of a component WS upgrade. Section 4 discusses how keeping several releases of a component WS available can affect the composite WS. In section 5 we provide a brief description of the Bayesian inference and show how it can be applied in the context of WS for assessing the confidence in their correctness. Some simulation results are also presented to illustrate the effectiveness of the proposed architectural solutions. Finally, in section 6 we briefly outline the on-going work on building a test harness for managed WS upgrade together with several ways of 'publishing' the confidence in a WS, compatible with relevant standards, such as WSDL, UDDI and SOAP.

2 Web Services Dependability

The WS architecture is now extensively used in developing various critical applications with high dependability requirements, such as banking, auctions, Internet shopping,

---

[3] http://www.w3.org/TR/soap12-part0/
[4] http://www.oasis-open.org/committees/uddi-spec/

hotel/car/flight/train reservation and booking, e-business, e-science, business account management, which in turn demands adequate mechanisms for dependability assurance and dependability assessment in the new context of WSs (see [4], [5]). In [1] the idea of 'Service Management' is advocated as a way of providing the users of a WS with information about its dependability. Such a service is achieved via a set of capabilities, such as monitoring, controlling, and reporting on the use of the deployed WS.

Dependability of a computing system is the ability to deliver service that can be justifiably trusted [6]. Dependability of the Web Services is a system property that integrates several attributes, the most important of which are availability (including responsiveness), reliability (correctness), and security. For many applications it would be desirable if the service requester (consumer) could quantify these attributes by either assessing them independently or relying for the assessment on a third party, e.g. a trusted independent dependability broker or even the WS provider.

We recognise that security is a very important dependability attribute, especially in the context of WSs. However, since the techniques for security assessment are still at an embryonic stage, security is not addressed in this paper. Whether the ideas presented here, e.g. confidence in security, are applicable, is to be seen when security assessment techniques mature.

2.1 Web Services Failures

A system failure is an event that occurs when the delivered service deviates from system specification.

A number of approaches has been used to analyse failures, their modes, effects and causes in the context of Web Services [7], system software [8] and a computer system as a whole [6], [9]. In this paper we focus on the following failure modes.

Transient failure – a failure triggered by transient conditions which can be tolerated by using generic recovery techniques such as rollback and retry even if the same code is used.

Non-transient failure – a deterministic failure. To tolerate such failure the diverse redundancy should be used. Such redundancy naturally exists during WS upgrading when the old (one or more) and new releases of the same WS are available.

Evident failure – a failure that needs *no special means* to be detected. It may be, for example, an exception, denial of service or absence of response during a predefined period of time, which will be detected by a general-purpose mechanism such as timeout.

Non-evident failure – a failure that can be detected only by using the existing redundancy at the application level (e.g. in the form of diversity). It is clear, that the non-evident failures can have more dramatic consequence than the evident failures.

This understanding of possible failure modes will be taken into account while building dependable Web Services and will affect the choice of the error detection mechanisms and fault-tolerance techniques employing several WS releases available online.

2.2 Confidence in the Web Services

WSs, as any other complex software may contain faults which may manifest themselves in operation. In many cases the consumers of the WSs may benefit from knowing how confident they can be in the availability, responsiveness and correctness of the information processing provided by the WSs. This issue may seem new in the context of WSs but is not new for some well-established domains with high dependability needs such as safety critical applications for which it is not unusual to state dependability requirements in probabilistic terms, e.g. as probability of failure of software on demand [10].

This fits nicely in the context of WSs, which can be seen as successive invocations of the operations published by a WS. It may be very difficult (or impossible) to guarantee that software behind a WS interface is flawless, but the confidence of the consumers will, no doubt, be affected by knowing for how long the service has been in operation and by how many failures have been observed. Informally, we will be much more confident in the results we get from a piece of software after we have seen it in operation for a long period of time without a failure than if we have not seen it in operation at all. How long software has been used is no guarantee that we will have high confidence in its dependability. Clearly, if we have seen it fail many times in the past we will take with doubt the next result that we get from this piece of software.

Building confidence measures to assess the correctness, the availability and the responsiveness can be formalised. Bayesian inference [11] is a mathematically sound way of expressing the confidence combining the knowledge about how good or poor the service is prior to deployment with the empirical evidence which becomes available after deployment. A priori knowledge can be gained by the WS provider using standard techniques for reliability assessment, e.g. the quality of the development process or other techniques such as those described in [12].

The confidence in the dependability of the composite Web Service will be affected by the confidence in the dependability of the component WSs it depends upon and by the confidence in the dependability of the composition (the design of the composition and its implementation, i.e. the 'glue' code held in the composite WS itself). The confidence naturally links two important aspects – the value of the dependability attribute, e.g. probability of failure on demand, with the risk that the particular WS delivers this attribute (e.g. its probability of failure is better than the specific value). For instance, we may want to compare two WSs, A and B, for which the confidence is expressed as follows:

- For WS A we have confidence 99% that its probability of failure on demand (*pfd*) is lower than 10^{-3}, 70% that the *pfd* is less than 10^{-4}, etc.
- For WS B we have confidence 95% that its probability of failure on demand (*pfd*) is lower than 10^{-3}, 90% that the *pfd* is less than 10^{-4}, etc.

Now which of the two WSs will be chosen depends on the dependability requirements, i.e. the particular dependability context: A will be used if the targeted pfd is 10-3, because the confidence that this target is satisfied with WS A is higher (99% vs. 95% with WS B). However, if a more stringent target is set, e.g. 10-4, then WS B should be preferred to WS A, because the confidence that it meets the target is higher (90% vs. 70% with WS A). In the context of this – on-line upgrade management of a component

WS – confidence is particularly relevant. The key idea behind an upgrade managed online is that the composite WS does not switch to the newest release of the component WS as soon as this new release becomes available since its dependability may suffer as a result. The new release may provide better functionality but it also brings in the increased risk that new faults may have arisen in the new release, which did not exist in the old release. A prudent policy of switching would be for the composite WS to wait until it gains sufficiently high confidence that the new release will not lead to deterioration of dependability.

In section 5 we show how the Bayesian inference can be applied in the context of WSs for calculating the confidence of a component WS.

3 The Web Service Upgrade Problem

A well-known problem for any component-based software development with OTS components is the upgrade of the OTS components. When a new release of an OTS component is made available the system integrator has two options:

1. Change their 'integrated' solution[5] so that it can use the new release of the OTS component. This may cause problems for the integrated solution and significant effort to rectify.
2. Stick to the old version of the OTS component and take the risk to face the consequences if the vendor of the OTS component ceases to support the old releases of the OTS component.

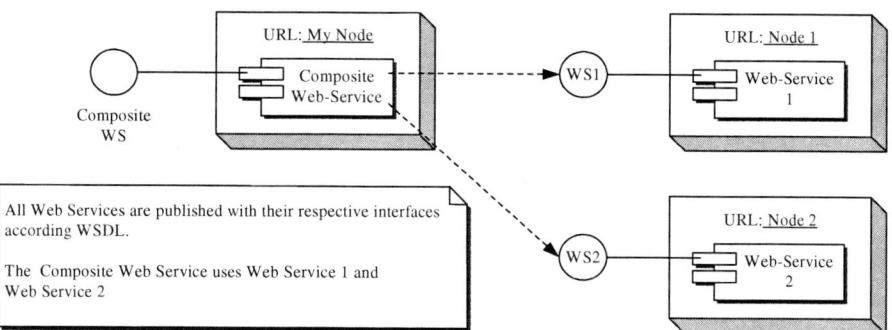

Fig. 1. A UML Deployment diagram of a composite WS, Composite Web-Service, which depends on two other component WSs provided by third parties, Web-Service 1 and Web-Service 2, respectively

The situation with a composite WS is very similar. Indeed, WS 1 and WS 2 in Fig. 1 are two component WSs used by a composite WS; conceptually this is equivalent to integrating any other OTS software component in an integrated solution. There may, however, be a difference from the maintenance point of view between a composite WS and an integrated solution in which OTS components are used. In the latter case, as indicated above, the integrator has a choice whether to update the integrated

---

[5] A term used by ECUA: http://www.esi.es/en/Projects/ecua/ecua.htm

solution with every new release of the OTS components or not. Such a choice may not exist in the former case of composite WSs. The deployment of a composite WS assumes that the component WSs (Web-Service 1 and Web-Service 2 in our example in Fig. 1) used by the composite WS have been deployed by their respective providers. If the providers decide to bring down their WSs the composite WS may become unavailable, too. What seems more interesting is that when the provider of a component WS, on which the composite WS depends upon, decides to update their WS the provider of the composite WS may not be even notified about the update. The composite service may be affected without its provider being able to do anything to prevent this from happening. Thus, the provider of the composite WS is automatically locked-in by the very decision to depend on another WS.

Are there ways out of the lock-in? If not, can the provider of the composite WS do something at least to make the consumers of the composite WS aware of the potential problems as a result of the update(s) which are beyond their control? Below we discuss two plausible alternatives.

3.1 Third-Party Component WS Upgrade with Several Operational Releases

This scenario is depicted in Fig. 2. The choice of whether to switch to a new release of a WS used by the composite WS is with the provider of the composite WS. They may use whatever methods are available to them to assess the dependability of the new release before deciding whether or not to move to the upgraded version(s) of the used component WS.

The designer of the composite service may even make provisions at design stage of the composite WS which facilitate the assessment of the new releases of the services the composite service depends upon when these become available. An example of such a design would be making it possible to run 'back-to-back' the old and the new releases of the component WS used in the composite WS.

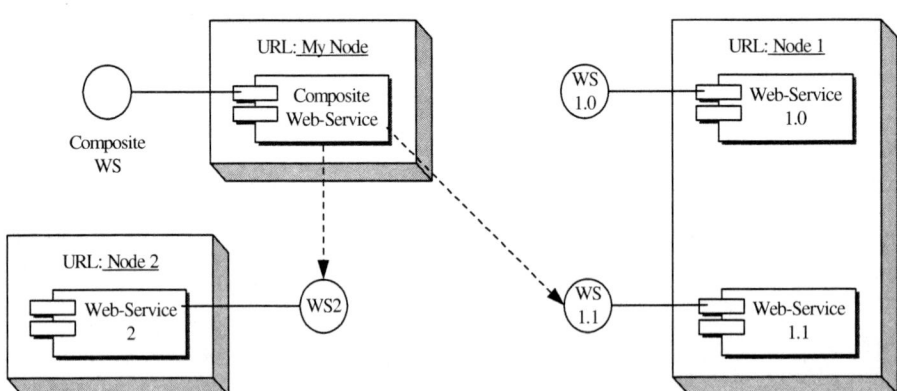

Fig. 2. A new release, Web-Service1.1, of a component WS is released, but the old version, Web-Service1.0, is also kept operational. The new release has no effect on the composite service, Composite Web-Service, as long as it continues to use the old release, Web-Service1.0, of the component WS. Eventually, the composite service is 'upgraded' to use the newer version, Web-Service 1.1.

During the transitional period (i.e. after the new release, WS 1.1 in Fig. 2, becomes available) the old version of the component WS will continue to be the version used by the composite WS, but by comparing the responses coming from the old and the new release, WS 1.0 and WS 1.1 respectively, the provider of the composite WS will gain empirical evidence about how good the new release, WS 1.1, is. Once the composite service gains sufficient confidence in WS 1.1 it may switch to using it and cease using WS 1.0.

Essentially, the composite service will have to run its own 'testing campaign' against the new release of the WS and may use the old release as an 'oracle' in judging if WS 1.1 returns correct responses.

3.2 Third-Party Component WS Upgrade with a Single Operational Release

Under this scenario Fig. 1 remains applicable: the most recent release of Web Service 1 will be deployed behind the interface WS 1. The options left to the provider of the composite WS are very limited. If the new release is at least distinguishable from the previous release, e.g. the release carries the release number, the provider of the composite WS will be able to detect the upgrade of the component WS and try to 'adjust' the confidence in the quality of the composite WS which may be caused by the upgrade and publish it to its consumers. A conservative view when calculating the impact of the upgrade on the dependability of the composite WS would be treating the upgraded component WS as if it were no better than the old release, i.e. the confidence in its dependability is no higher than the confidence in the old release as suggested in [12].

3.3 Own Component WS Upgrade with Several Operational Releases

In some cases a composite WS may use the component WS maintained by the same vendor. In this case the upgraded component WS will be deployed in a way which reflects the vendor's view on whether the upgraded component WS may have detrimental impact on the dependability of the own composite WSs which depends on the upgraded component WS.

We expect that even in this case, when the vendor has access to the internal details of the upgraded component WS, that prudence may dictate deployment of the new release of the component WS side by side with the old release in a special environment which has features for transparent upgrade including: interactive features for monitoring the dependability of old and new versions (including typical adjudicator functionality for comparing their results), support for several modes of operations (using the old release only, running the old and the new releases in parallel and adjudication of their responses, switching to the new release only and phasing out the old release from the composite WS) and a standard interface (i.e. using the WSDL description of the component WS). The component WS provider should be able to monitor the way the new release of the WS is operating and choose the best way of ensuring the dependability of the service. The main difference between this form of the upgrade and the upgrade of the third-party component WS is that here the extra information that might be available about the component WS may affect the way the dependability is measured. For instance, an extensive validation and verification (e.g. regression testing and testing the bugs of the previous release on the new release or the introduction of sophisticated mechanisms of fault-tolerance in the new release of the component WS) prior to deployment may justify placing high confidence in the dependability of the new release than has been achieved in the old release. This, in theory, may justify the immediate switch of the composite WSs developed by the same vendor to using the latest release of the component WS or at least configuring the environment responsible to manage the upgrade in a way, which will require a very limited amount of operational evidence before the composite WS switches s to using the upgraded component WS.

4 Solutions for Dependable WS Upgrading

In this section we describe several architectures which allow for a managed upgrade of a WS. The architecture can be deployed as part of a composite WS in which the WS in question is used as component WS or deployed by a dependability-conscious consumer of the WS aware of the inevitable upgrade of the WS. The architecture can also be deployed by the vendor of the WS if they want to provide high dependability guarantees to the consumers of the WS. In either case the impact of the upgrade on the consumers of the WS will be minimised.

4.1 General Architecture

The general architecture for a managed WS upgrade consists of:

- a specialised middleware which runs several releases of the WS. The middleware intercepts the consumer requests coming through the WS interface, relays them to all the releases and collects the responses from the releases. It is also responsible for 'publishing' the confidence associated with the WS (or its releases);
- a subsystem which monitors the behaviour of the releases and assess their dependability including confidence;
- a management subsystem which adjudicates the responses from the replicas and returns an adjudicated response to the consumer of the WS. This subsystem is also responsible for reconfiguration (switching the releases on or off), recovery of the failed releases and for logging the information which may be needed for further analysis.

The architecture can be used to implement the forms of upgrade discussed above: third-party WSs (Fig.3, 4) and own component WSs (Fig.5).

The architecture for managed upgrade of third-party WS can be deployed either as part of the consumer of the WS (Fig.3) or as a composite WS solely dedicated to the management of the upgrade (Fig.4). The architecture shown in Fig 5 which is deployed by the WS provider and which makes the upgrade transparent for any service subscriber is particularly relevant in practice since it allows for optimal management of the upgrade based on full knowledge about the design and implementation of the releases available to the vendor of the WS.

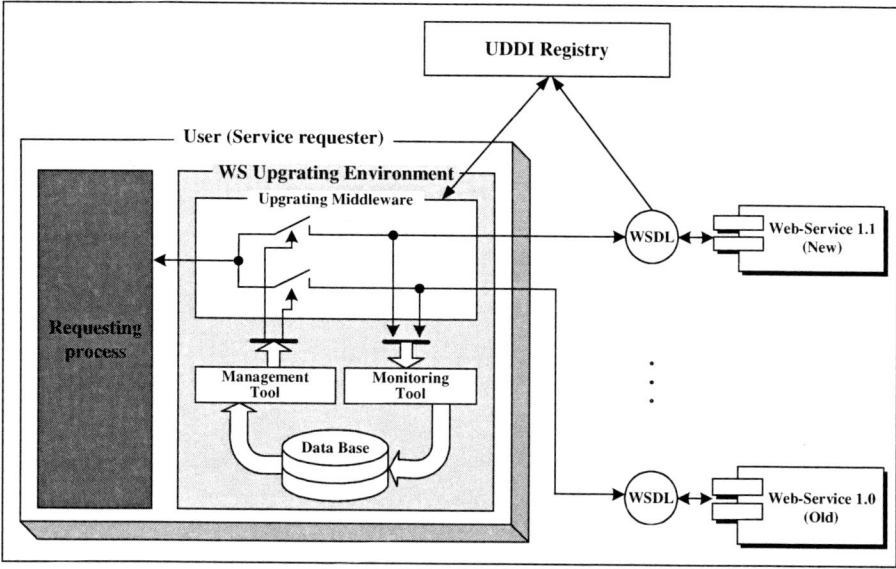

Fig. 3. Architecture for managed upgrade of third-party Web Service deployed by the consumer of the WS

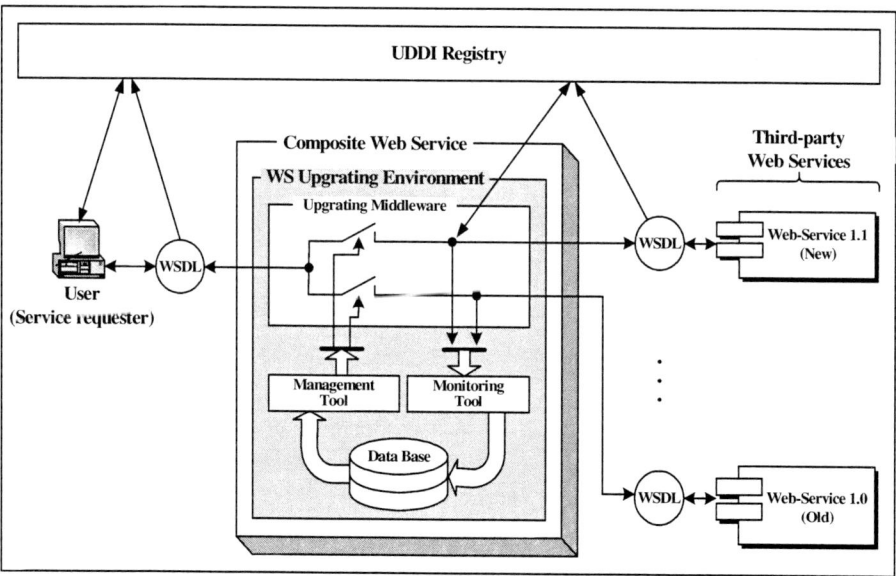

Fig. 4. Architecture for managed upgrade of third-party WS deployed as a composite WS

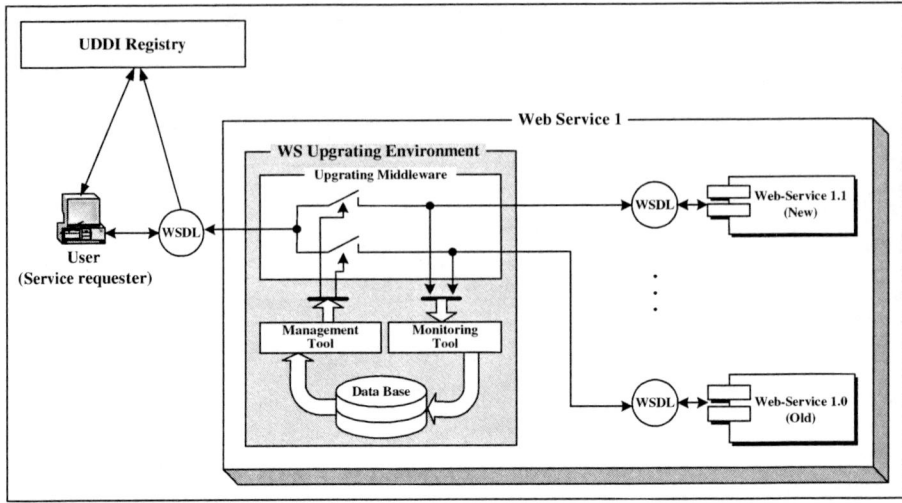

Fig. 5. Architecture for managed upgrade of a WS deployed by the vendor of the WS

4.2 Operating Modes with Several WS Releases

There are some possible operating modes of the web services with several operational releases:

1. *Parallel execution for maximum reliability.* All available releases of the WS are executed concurrently and their responses are used by the middleware to produce an adjudicated response to the consumer of the WS. Various adjudication mechanisms can be used which range from tolerating evident failures only to detecting and tolerating non-evident failures. In the latter case some form of self-checking may be need which will allow for diagnosing which of the releases has produced a (non-evidently) incorrect response before the adjudicated response can be determined.
2. *Parallel execution for maximum responsiveness.* All available releases of the WS are executed concurrently and the fastest non-evidently incorrect response is returned to the consumer of the service as an adjudicated response.
3. *Parallel execution with dynamically changed reliability/responsiveness.* It is a generalised parallel execution mode. All available releases of the WS are executed concurrently. The middleware may be configured to wait for up to a certain number of responses to be collected from the deployed releases, but no longer than a pre-defined timeout. The actual responses collected are then adjudicated to define the response returned to the consumer of the WS. The number of responses and the timeout can be changed dynamically so that different configurations for the adjudicated response can be defined.
4. *Sequential execution for minimal server capacity.* The releases of the WS are executed sequentially (the order of execution can be chosen randomly or can be predefined). The subsequent releases are only executed if the responses received from the previous releases are evidently incorrect. A variation of this mode would

be to collect more than one non-evidently incorrect responses and adjudicate them using an appropriate rule.

4.3 Monitoring and Measurement

The monitoring subsystem conducts measurement of the dependability characteristics including the confidence associated with them of the deployed releases of the WS, compares their responses.

Every time the consumer invokes the WS this subsystem monitors the availability (timeout can be used to detect if the service is down), execution time and the correctness of the responses for each releases of the WS and stores these parameters in a database. Detecting non-evident failures and diagnosing the release which has returned a non-evidently incorrect response is far from trivial. The implications of using imperfect detection/diagnosis for the confidence are scrutinised in section 5.1.

4.4 Management

The main functions of this subsystem are controlling several operational releases and choosing the current operational mode, which is based on dependability assessment conducted by the monitoring subsystem. Adjudicating the responses collected from the deployed releases and returning a response to the consumer of the WS is also a responsibility of this subsystem. The adjudication mechanisms have already been discussed together with the operating modes in section 4.2.

5 Assessment and Modelling

5.1 Bayesian Approach to Assessment of Confidence in Web-Service

In this section we illustrate how the Bayesian approach is normally applied to assessing the confidence associated with a single dependability attribute, e.g. the probability of failure on demand (*pfd*).

If the WS is treated as a black box, i.e. one can only distinguish between failures or successes (Fig. 6), the Bayesian assessment proceeds as follows.

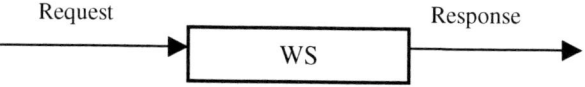

Fig. 6. Black-box model of a WS. The internal structure of the WS is unknown. Only correctness of the response (success or failure) is recorded on each request and used in the inference of the WS's *pfd*

On every request the WS may succeed, i.e. return a correct response, or fail, i.e. return an incorrect response or not return any response at all. The failure behaviour of the WS is characterised by the probability of failure (*pfd*). Let us denote it as p. This probability will vary between the environments in which the WS is used. The various factors, which affect the *pfd* may be unknown with certainty, thus the value of *pfd* may be uncertain. This uncertainty is captured by a (prior) probability distribution $f_p(\bullet)$, which characterises the assessor's knowledge about the system *pfd prior* to observing the WS in operation. This distribution quantifies the assessor's perception that some values of *pfd* are more likely than some other values.

Assume further that the WS is subjected to n requests, a sample of demands drawn from a 'realistic' operational environment (profile), and r failures are observed[6]. Presented with the *new evidence* the assessor may change their a priori uncertainty about the *pfd* of the WS. Now it will be represented by a posterior distribution, $f_p(\bullet | r, n)$, of p after the observations, which is defined as:

$$f_p(x | r, n) \propto L(n, r | x) f_p(x), \qquad (1)$$

where $L(n, r | x)$ is the *likelihood* of observing r failures in n demands *if* the *pfd* were exactly x, which in this case of independent demands is given by the *binomial distribution*, $L(n, r | x) = \binom{n}{r} x^r (1-x)^{n-r}$.

(1) is the general form of the Bayes's formula, applicable to any form of likelihood and any prior distribution.

Now assume that the WS is implemented as shown in Fig. 5, i.e. two releases of the WS are deployed in parallel, which see and process 'independently' a request from a consumer of the WS. On each demand (request) there are 4 possible outcomes which can be observed, given in Table 1 below. The four probabilities given in the last column of Table 1 sum up to 1. Even if these probabilities are not known with certainty, i.e. they are treated as *random variables*, their sum will be always 1. Thus, a joint probability distribution of any three (out of the four listed in Table 1) of these probabilities, e.g. $f_{p_{01}, p_{10}, p_{11}}(\bullet, \bullet, \bullet)$, gives an exhaustive description of the uncertainty associated with the failure behaviour of the system, which in this cases consists of WS1.0 and WS1.1. In statistical terms, the model has three degrees of freedom.

The probabilities that WS 1.0 will fail, let us denote it p_A, and that WS 1.1 will fail, p_B, respectively, can be derived from the probabilities used in Table 1 as follows:

$p_A = p_{10} + p_{11}$ and $p_B = p_{01} + p_{11}$.

Table 1. A joint probability distribution

Event	WS 1.0	WS 1.1	Observed in n tests	Probability
α	Fails	Fails	r_1	p_{11}
β	Fails	Succeeds	r_2	p_{10}
γ	Succeeds	Fails	r_3	p_{01}
δ	Succeeds	Succeeds	r_4	p_{00}

---

[6] The number of observed failures can be 0

p_{11} represents the probability that both releases of the WS fail, hence the notation $p_{AB} \equiv p_{11}$ captures well the intuitive meaning of the event it is assigned to.

Instead of using $f_{p_{10}, p_{01}, p_{11}}(\bullet, \bullet, \bullet)$ we can use any other distribution, which can be derived from it through functional transformation. In this section we will use $f_{p_A, p_B, p_{AB}}(\bullet, \bullet, \bullet)$.

It can be shown that for a given observation (r_1, r_2, and r_3 in N demands) the joint posterior distribution, $f_{p_A, p_B, p_{AB}}(\bullet, \bullet, \bullet \mid N, r_1, r_2, r_3)$, can be calculated as:

$$f_{p_A, p_B, p_{AB}}(x, y, z \mid N, r_1, r_2, r_3) = \frac{f_{p_A, p_B, p_{AB}}(x, y, z) L(N, r_1, r_2, r_3 \mid p_A, p_B, p_{AB})}{\iiint\limits_{p_A, p_B, p_{AB}} f_{p_A, p_B, p_{AB}}(x, y, z) L(N, r_1, r_2, r_3 \mid p_A, p_B, p_{AB}) dx dy dz}, \quad (2)$$

where $L(N, r_1, r_2, r_3 \mid p_A, p_B, p_{AB})$ is the likelihood of the observation [13].

The posterior distribution, $f_{p_A, p_B, p_{AB}}(\bullet, \bullet, \bullet \mid N, r_1, r_2, r_3)$, represents the updated uncertainty about the system failure behaviour *consistent with the prior and the observations*. From this distribution one can derive the marginal uncertainties associated with the probabilities of failure of each of the releases, $f_{p_A}(\bullet \mid observation)$, $f_{p_B}(\bullet \mid observation)$ and of the probability of coincident failure of both releases, $f_{p_{AB}}(\bullet \mid observation)$. For instance the distribution of the probability of coincident failure, $f_{p_{AB}}(\bullet \mid observation)$, can be derived from $f_{p_A, p_B, p_{AB}}(\bullet, \bullet, \bullet \mid N, r_1, r_2, r_3)$ by integrating out the 'nuisance parameters' P_A and P_B:

$$f_{P_{AB}}(x \mid r_1, r_2, r_3, n) = \int\limits_{P_A} \int\limits_{P_B} f_{P_{AB}, P_A, P_B}(x, y, z \mid r_1, r_2, r_3, n) dP_A dP_B \quad (3)$$

Similarly the marginal posteriors, $f_{p_A}(\bullet \mid observation)$ and $f_{p_B}(\bullet \mid observation)$, can be expressed as:

$$f_{P_A}(x \mid r_1, r_2, r_3, n) = \int\limits_{P_B} \int\limits_{P_{AB}} f_{P_{AB}, P_A, P_B}(x, y, z \mid r_1, r_2, r_3, n) dP_B dP_{AB} \quad (4)$$

$$f_{P_B}(x \mid r_1, r_2, r_3, n) = \int\limits_{P_A} \int\limits_{P_{AB}} f_{P_{AB}, P_A, P_B}(x, y, z \mid r_1, r_2, r_3, n) dP_A dP_{AB} \quad (5)$$

The expressions (3-5) can be used to calculate the confidence that the pair or each of the channels meet a specific reliability target. For instance, the confidence that the probability of failure of the old release is smaller than a given target, T, will be:

$$P(P_A \mid observation \leq T) = \int_0^T f_{P_A}(x \mid observation) dP_A \qquad (6)$$

Using (6) we can calculate a set of *percentiles* for a set of confidence values, e.g. {90%, 95%, 99%,...}. For instance, the 99% percentile of channel A, $T_{A99\%}$, is a value of the P_A such that $\int_0^{T_{A99\%}} f_{P_A}(x \mid observation) dP_A = 99\%$.

5.1.1 Examples

We will illustrate how the Bayesian inference can be used to determine the duration of the WS managed upgrade (Fig. 5), i.e. when the old release can be replaced by the new one. We will use for this purpose several contrived but plausible scenarios.

5.1.1.1 Scenarios

Scenario 1

In this scenario we assume that the old release has been used for a very long time and, as a result, its reliability has been measured accurately: its *pfd* is believed to be 10^{-3}, and the uncertainty associated with this is *very low*. The new release has been significantly changed, compared with the old release. It is believed that the new release is an improvement, i.e. that its *pfd* is lower than the *pfd* of the old release, but since it has not seen a significant operational use there is a significant level of uncertainty about how good the new release actually is. We parameterise this scenario using the following prior distribution:

- The distribution of the *pfd* of the old release, P_A, is a Beta(α_A, β_A) distribution, $f_{P_A}(\bullet)$, defined in the range [0, 0.002] with parameters $\alpha_A = 20$, $\beta_A = 20$, i.e. the expected value of P_A is indeed 10^{-3}, consistent with the prior measurements. The parameters are chosen such that the distribution mass is concentrated in a very narrow interval, which adequately represent the low level of uncertainty about the 'true' *pfd* of the old release.
- The distribution of *pfd* of the new release, P_B, is also a Beta(α_B, β_B) distribution, $f_{P_B}(\bullet)$, defined in the same range [0, 002], with parameters $\alpha_B = 2$, $\beta_B = 3$, chosen such that the expected value of P_B is 0.8×10^{-3}, i.e. slightly better than the expected value of P_A, but the level of uncertainty about the true *pfd* of the new release is significant.
- We assumed that P_A and P_B are independently distributed, i.e. $f_{P_A, P_B}(\bullet, \bullet) = f_{P_A}(\bullet) f_{P_B}(\bullet)$.
- We assume uniform distribution of the conditional probability $P_{AB} \mid P_A, P_B$ in the range [0, min(P_A, P_B)], which represents the assessor being 'indifferent' about the values of the probability of coincident failure. This, in fact, is a very conservative assumption, since the expected value is 1/2 of min(P_A, P_B), i.e. the system is expected to tolerate only 50% of the failures, which seems justified given the fact that we are dealing with two releases of the same product.

Scenario 2
In this scenario we assume that the old release has been only used for a short time without a failure. The uncertainty associated with the *pfd* of the release, therefore, is significant. The new release has been produced following a very thorough development process. However since this process has never been applied in the context of WS there is a significant level of uncertainty about the *pfd* of the new release, too.

The new release is conservatively considered to be worse than the old release. This scenario is parameterised with the following prior distribution:

- The distribution of *pfd* of the old release, P_A, is a Beta(α_A, β_A) distribution, $f_{P_A}(\bullet)$, in the range [0, 0.01] with parameters $\alpha_A = 1$, $\beta_A = 10$, i.e. the expected value of P_A is ~10^{-3}, but a significant level of uncertainty is built-in this prior.
- The distribution of *pfd* of the new release, P_B, is also a Beta(α_B, β_B) distribution, $f_{P_B}(\bullet)$, with parameters as in the first scenario $\alpha_B = 2$, $\beta_B = 3$. The level of uncertainty about the true *pfd* of the new release is significant.
- We assumed, again, that P_A and P_B are independently distributed, i.e. $f_{P_A,P_B}(\bullet,\bullet) = f_{P_A}(\bullet)f_{P_B}(\bullet)$.
- As in the previous scenario, we assume uniform distribution of the conditional probability $P_{AB}|P_A,P_B$ in the range $[0,\min(P_A, P_B)]$.

50,000 observations used with the two scenarios have been Monte-Carlo simulated using the following parameters:

Scenario 1: $P_A = 10^{-3}$, $P_B|A$ failed $= 0.3$, $P_B|A$ did not fail $= 0.5\times10^{-3}$. The chosen parameters define a marginal probability of failure for the new release $P_B = 0.8\times10^{-3}$. Thus the marginal *pfd* of both channels are equal to the expected values of their respective distributions. The chance of coincident failure of the releases is significant: every 3 out of 10 failures of the old release will coincide with failures of the new release. This is, however, less frequent than assumed in the prior (every other failure of the less reliable channel was assumed to coincide with a failure of the more reliable channel).

Scenario 2: $P_A = 5\times10^{-3}$, i.e. the actual *pfd* is significantly worse than assumed in the prior (the mean of the prior distribution is 10^{-3}), $P_B|A$ failed $= 0.1$, $P_B|A$ did not fail $= 0$ (i.e. never failed on its own). The chosen parameters define a marginal probability of failure for the new release $P_B = 0.5\times10^{-3}$, an order of magnitude better than the old release.

5.1.1.2 Upgrade Criteria (Switching from Managed Upgrade to WS 1.1)
We will apply a few plausible alternatives of switching from the old to the new release as follows:

- *Criterion 1*: the new release, WS 1.1, reaches the dependability level offered by the old release, WS 1.0, *at the time of deploying the managed upgrade*, i.e. as defined by the prior distribution, $f_{P_A}(\bullet)$. For instance, if prior to the upgrade there $P(P_A \leq X) = 99\%$, then the managed upgrade should last until $P(P_B \leq X) = 99\%$, i.e. the same confidence, 99%, is build that WS 1.1 is better than X. This scenario does not

address the possibility that during the managed upgrade the knowledge about WS 1.0 may also change: it may turn out to be worse or better than thought prior to deploying the managed upgrade.
- *Criterion 2*: the new release, WS 1.1, reaches a predefined level of dependability with a predefined level of confidence, e.g. $P(P_B \leq 10^{-3}) = 99\%$. Under this criterion the dependability of the old release, WS 1.0, prior or during the managed upgrade is irrelevant.
- *Criterion 3*: With a given confidence, e.g. 99%, the new release, WS 1.1, is better than the old release, WS 1.0. In other words, for the 99% percentiles of the releases the following inequality holds: $T_{B99\%} \leq T_{A99\%}$. Clearly, this criterion takes into account the possibility that the priors of both WS 1.0 and WS 1.1 may be 'inaccurate' and may evolve to different distributions during the managed upgrade.

5.1.1.3 Imperfection of Failure Detection
As described above, Bayesian inference depends on the observations and, thus, imperfection in detecting failures of WS releases will, inevitably, affect the posteriors, hence the decisions when to switch to using the new release. We simulated *omission failures* only, i.e. such that some demands on which the releases did fail were counted as being correct. This type of failure may have dangerous consequences. First, because incorrect responses may have been returned to the consumers of the WSs, and, second, because the inference may produce optimistic predictions, which, in turn, may lead to premature decisions to switch to the new release before the required confidence has been achieved. The following omission failures have been simulated:

- omission failure of the 'oracles' judging the correctness of the responses from each of the releases;
- back-to-back testing under the *pessimistic assumption* that all coincident failures will be identical and non- evident.

The first kind on failure will lead to changes of the scores on a demand of a release from '1' (failure) to '0' (success). The greater the likelihood of such a failure the more optimistic the observations become – in the extreme case when the omission failure takes place with probability 1 – the inference will be supplied with observations 'No failure' no matter how many times the release in question has failed.

The effect of the second kind of failure on the observations will be limited to those demands on which both releases fail. In this case the scores '11' (coincident failure of both releases) will be replaced by '00' (success of both). Clearly, in real operation there may be coincident but *different failures*, which will be detected by back-to-back testing and there is a good chance that on this demand the score of at least one of the releases will be correctly counted as a failure.

We did not include in our study the 'false alarm' type of failure of the failure detection mechanisms, i.e. when an 'oracle' flags out as a failure a valid response from a release. Although in practical systems this may be a concern, its implications are not dangerous: the consumers may be required to ignore valid responses and the inference will produce *pessimistic predictions*. As a result the decision to switch to the new release may be delayed beyond the sufficient evidence that the new release has met the set dependability target.

5.1.1.4 Inference Results

The results of the study are summarised below in Table 2, in which we show for the 3 criteria specified in 5.1.1.2 how long the managed upgrade (Fig. 5) should last before switching from WS 1.0 to WS 1.1. For Criterion 2 we used $P(P_B \leq 10^{-3})=99\%$ as the target for the switch.

Table 2. Duration of managed upgrade

		Criterion 1	Criterion 2	Criterion 3
Scenario 1	Perfect 'oracles'	35,500 demands	Not attainable (> 50,000)	40,000 demands
	Omission, $P_{omit} = 0.15$	22,000 (oscillates till 26,000)	50,000 demands	35,000 demands
	Back-to-back testing	20,000	40,000	34,000 demands
Scenario 2	Perfect 'oracles'	1,400 demands	10,000 demands	1,100 demands
	Omission, $P_{omit} = 0.15$	1,400 demands	7,000	1,100 demands
	Back-to-back testing	1,400 demands	6,000 demands	1,100 demands

One can see from Table 2 that the effect of the detection coverage upon the duration of the managed upgrade is significant, which is hardly surprising. We further use 90% and 99% percentiles to illustrate the relationship between the failure detection coverage and the confidence. Fig. 7, clearly indicates, however, the link that exists between the imperfection of the detection mechanism deployed and the confidence in having achieved the specified target, Criterion 1 in this case. For instance, consider the 90% percentile that the new release is as reliable as the old release was prior to the upgrade (the solid thin curve in Fig. 1). This percentile remains always lower not only than the 99% percentile with perfect oracle (which is always the case), but also than the 99% percentile with imperfect oracles which miss a failure with probability 0.15. In other words, using imperfect oracles with detection coverage of 85% (which is often seen as achievable, e.g. [14]) and using Bayesian inference in this case means that the confidence error caused by the imperfection of the oracles is no greater than 9%. At any stage of the inference what the assessor would consider to be a 99% percentile on the *pfd* of the new release will actually be no worse than 90% percentile.

The difference between the inference with perfect detection and back-to-back testing is slightly different – the error up to ~20,000 demands does not exceed 9% and then becomes greater than 9%. Incidentally, it is 20,000 demands when the decision will be taken to switch to the new release (Table 2), i.e. the actual confidence achieved at this time will be no worse than 90%.

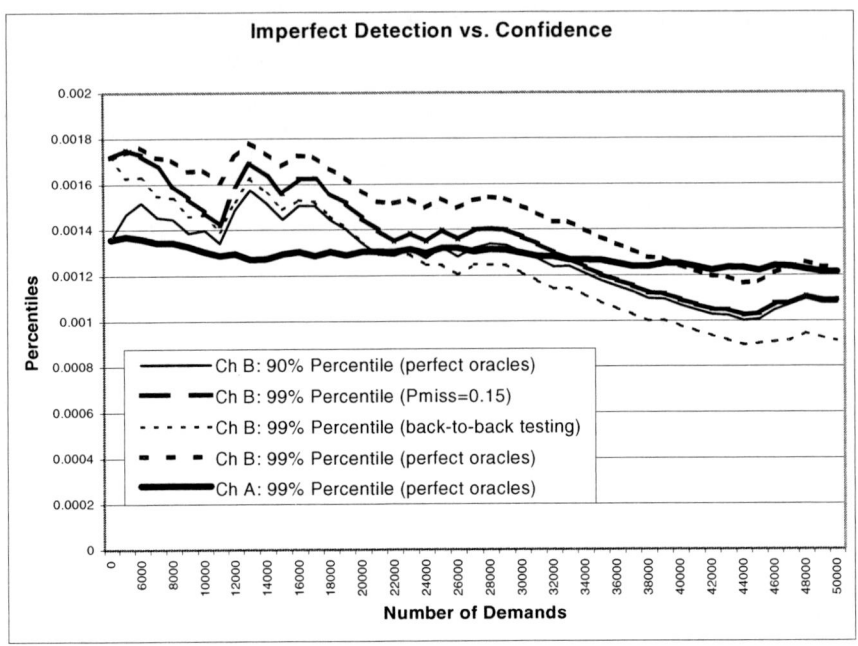

Fig. 7. Scenario 1: percentiles for perfect and imperfect failure detection

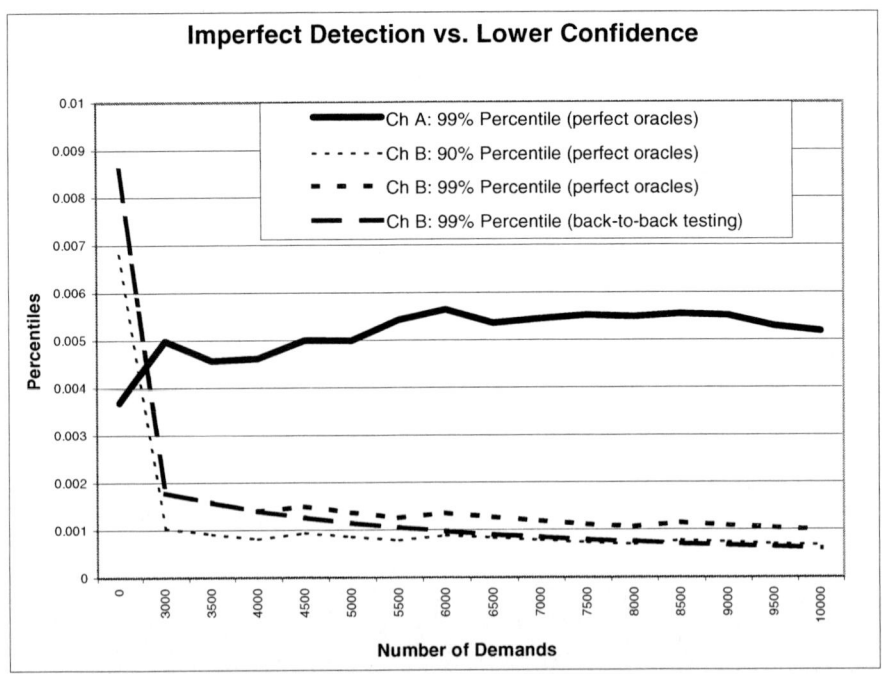

Fig. 8. Scenario 2: percentiles for perfect and imperfect failure detection

It is worth mentioning that the number of demands needed in order to get the required level of confidence under Scenario 1 are significant. This is a consequence of the *pfd* targets being very close to what the real reliability of the new release is (the explicitly stated target of 10^{-3} remains unattainable with perfect detection even after 50,000 demands). A significant number of failures is observed which does not allow the assessor to build quickly the required confidence.

Scenario 2 in this respect is very different – the targets to be met by the new release are significantly worse than what the 'true' *pfd* of this release is. Under this scenario the prior confidence in the old release was also low due to the minimal operation exposure of this release. As a result, meeting the set targets (with all 3 criteria) requires significantly fewer demands. The effect of imperfect detection on the decision to switch to the new release under this scenario is illustrated in Fig. 8. The 90% percentile with perfect failure detection remains lower than the 99% percentile with imperfect detection throughout the entire range of demands of interest, including the values when a decision to switch to the new release will be taken (up to 7000 demands). Thus, again, the effect imperfect of the failure detection on the confidence is relatively modest – the error is less than 9%.

5.1.2 Realism of Bayesian Inference in the Context of Web-Services

Two important aspects of using Bayesian assessment in the context of Web-services are worth mentioning:

1. The choice of a prior is important, as it is for Bayesian inference in any other context. In the context of a managed upgrade we use a white-box inference, which requires a trivariate distribution, $f_{p_A, p_B, p_{AB}}(\bullet, \bullet, \bullet)$ to be defined. This is far from trivial. It is reasonable to expect that the marginal distributions, $f_{p_A}(\bullet)$ and $f_{p_B}(\bullet)$, will be available in some form. The old release will have seen some (in some cases long) operational exposure, which is relatively straightforward to translate into confidence using a black-box inference. The new release will have been subjected to some level of testing, but the prior will be largely based on *expert judgement*, and thus will leave significant uncertainty about the true value of the *pfd*. The real difficulty is in defining the third variate of the distribution, which characterises how likely the two releases of the WS are to fail together. Since we are dealing with two releases of the same service it is plausible to assume high level of correlation between their failures[7]. The 'indifference' assumption, which we used in our examples, seems a safe option. Even if the prior is inaccurate we leave it 'open to quick changes' as new empirical evidence becomes available ('data will speak for itself'). The downside of the safe option is that it will take some time for the error in the prior to be compensated, which will delay the decision to switch to the new release. This is, however, the inevitable price to be

---

[7] This plausible view is counterbalanced by the empirical fact that in many cases the new releases of software products may fail in circumstances where the old releases do not. Thus, even if the new release fixes faults in the old release(s) it is far from clear whether the new release is always an improvement and what might be a plausible expectation regarding the coincident failures.

paid for the extra assurance that the WS dependability *will not deteriorate* as a result of the upgrade.
2. Coverage of the deployed failure detection mechanism. We have only touched upon this aspect due to the limited space and further studies are needed in order to get further insight into the relationship between the detection coverage and the confidence achieved. The results presented here seem to suggest that this problem can be tackled relatively simply. In our examples we saw a consistent picture that ~10% imperfection of failure detection translates into error in predicted confidence less than 10%. If this is consistent across many systems a relatively simple engineering *rule of thumb* can be defined so that despite the errors the needed confidence is *actually achieved* and one can proceed with the switch to the new release. In fact the limited coverage of failure detection is not necessarily a problem! It is clearly a problem when an explicit dependability target for the new release is stated (Criterion 2), but we doubt that this criterion is appropriate for the context of the WS upgrade. Indeed, it seems always worth deploying the more dependable release, even if it does not meet an explicitly stated higher target. Making a decision to switch to the new release based on comparison of the two releases (i.e. Criterion 1 or 3 defined above) seems much more plausible than wait until the new release meets an explicit target. Under these circumstances both releases will have been affected by the limited coverage of the deployed detection mechanisms. It seems reasonable to assume that the imperfect detection will affect *both releases similarly*, hence the decision to switch even based on inaccurate measurements will be justified.

Despite these problems, it seems clear that Bayesian inference can be used to assess the confidence in dependability of WS releases and control the managed upgrade of WSs.

5.2 Simulation Modelling of the Dependable WS Upgrading

5.2.1 Model Description

An event-driven simulation model, executed in the MATLAB 6.0 environment, was developed to analyse the effectiveness, both in terms of improved dependability and performance, of the managed WS upgrade. Below we present the simulation results obtained for running concurrently two releases of a WS. The middleware for managed upgrade implements the following rules:

1. A request from a consumer is forwarded to both releases;
2. The middleware waits to collect responses from the releases, but no longer than a predefined *Timeout*. The collected responses are adjudicated and the consumer of the WS is presented with the adjudicated response. The implemented adjudication rules are as follows:
   - if all collected responses are evidently incorrect then the middleware raises an exception (i.e. the adjudicated response itself is evidently incorrect);
   - if all releases return the same response (correct or non-evidently incorrect) then this response is returned to the consumer of the Web Service, too;
   - if all the responses collected from the releases are valid (i.e. none is evidently incorrect), then the middleware returns to the consumer of the Web service a

response, selected at random from the ones collected. Clearly, even if a correct response exists among the collected ones a possibility still exists that the consumer of the Web service gets an incorrect response, when the middleware picks at random an incorrect response from those collected;
- if the TimeOut expires and a single valid response is collected this response is returned to the consumer of the Web service, which may turn out to be non-evidently incorrect.
- if no response has been collected the middleware returns a response 'Web Service unavailable'.

It takes each release some time (execution time) to respond to a request. The execution times of the releases may be affected by various factors. The execution time is modelled as a sum of two components as follows:

$$\text{Ex. Time}(\text{Release}(i)) = T1 + T2(i) \tag{7}$$

where $T1$ – is the same for both releases and models the computational difficulty of the demand, which is common for both releases, while $T2(i)$ may differ for the two replicas and may be due to differences between the releases. Both $T1$ and $T2$ are simulated as exponentially distributed random variables, $\exp(T1\text{Mean})$, $\exp(T2\text{Mean}_1)$ and $\exp(T2\text{Mean}_2)$, respectively, with different parameters.

The overall execution time of the *system* with several operational releases of the WS is calculated as:

$$\text{Ex. time}(WS) = \min(\text{TimeOut}, \max(\text{Ex. time}(\text{Release}(i)))) + dT \tag{8}$$

where dT is the time taken by the middleware to adjudicate the release responses.

The behaviour of the releases is simulated under the assumption that a degree of correlation between the types of responses exists which is modelled through a set of conditional probabilities:

$$P(\text{slower response is X | faster response is Y}) \tag{9}$$

Where the types of responses (X and Y) are:
- correct (CR);
- evident failure (ER);
- non-evident failure (NER).

A special case would be independence of the behaviour of the releases (i.e. the type of response they returns on demand), which is included in our results for reference, although it is clearly unrealistic.

5.2.2 Simulation Settings

The execution times were simulated with the following parameters:
- T1Mean=0.7 sec;
- $T2\text{Mean}_1 = T2\text{Mean}_2 = 0.7$ sec;
- dT=0.1 sec.

The choice of simulation parameters was dictated by us trying to cover realistic scenarios. In particular we varied widely the degree of correlation between the behaviour of the simulated channels both in terms of correct and different types of incorrect responses.

Table 3. Marginal probabilities associated with the responses of the releases

Run	Independent probabilities for different outcomes					
	Release 1 (Rel_1)			Release 2 (Rel_2)		
	CR	ER	NER	CR	ER	NER
1	0.70	0.15	0.15	0.70	0.15	0.15
2	0.70	0.15	0.15	0.60	0.20	0.20
3	0.70	0.15	0.15	0.50	0.25	0.25
4	0.60	0.20	0.20	0.40	0.30	0.30

Table 4. Conditional probabilities associated with the response from the slower release (10)

Run	Condition		Probabilities: P(outcome Rel_2 | outcome Rel_1)		
			CR	ER	NER
1	Outcome of Release 1	CR	0.90	0.05	0.05
		ER	0.05	0.90	0.05
		NER	0.05	0.05	0.90
2	Outcome of Release 1	CR	0.80	0.10	0.10
		ER	0.10	0.80	0.10
		NER	0.10	0.10	0.80
3	Outcome of Release 1	CR	0.70	0.15	0.15
		ER	0.15	0.70	0.15
		NER	0.15	0.15	0.70
4	Outcome of Release 1	CR	0.40	0.30	0.30
		ER	0.30	0.40	0.30
		NER	0.30	0.30	0.40

5.2.3 Simulation Results

The simulation results – mean execution time and number of responses of different types - are presented in Tables 4 and 5 obtained on 10,000 requests processed under different regimes, as defined in section 5.2.2.

The simulation results can be summarised as follows:

1. The system availability offered by the architecture for managed upgrade is higher than the availability of each of the versions. This is to be expected since the system is a 1-out-of-2 system. This observation is important because it reduces the pressure of having to switch to the new release quickly. From the point of view of dependability the managed upgrade is the best alternative – the 1-out-of-2 by definition is no worse than the more reliable channel. Thus we can prolong the switch to the new release as long as necessary without any negative implications for the dependability of the service.

Table 5. Simulation results assuming positive correlation between release failures

Run	Observations		TimeOut = 1.5 sec			TimeOut = 2.0 sec			TimeOut = 3.0 sec		
			Rel_1	Rel_2	System	Rel_1	Rel_2	System	Rel_1	Rel_2	System
1	MET[8]		1.0077	1.0054	**1.2194**	1.0077	1.0054	**1.2290**	1.0077	1.0054	**1.2357**
	Outcomes	CR	6709	6230	**6762**	6785	6301	**6815**	6840	6348	**6851**
		EER	1443	1668	**1449**	1460	1690	**1470**	1470	1706	**1475**
		NER	1412	1664	**1463**	1428	1676	**1472**	1437	1686	**1480**
		Total	9564	9562	**9674**	9673	9667	**9757**	9747	9740	**9806**
	NRDT[9]		436	438	**326**	327	333	**243**	253	260	**194**
	Total requests		10000	10000	**10000**	10000	10000	**10000**	10000	10000	**10000**
2	MET		0.9955	0.9912	**1.2052**	0.9955	0.9912	**1.2148**	0.9955	0.9912	**1.2214**
	Outcomes	CR	6733	5706	**6683**	6819	5764	**6755**	6866	5802	**6780**
		EER	1420	1944	**1502**	1436	1964	**1506**	1452	1982	**1529**
		NER	1414	1941	**1504**	1434	1962	**1514**	1447	1983	**1522**
		Total	9567	9591	**9689**	9689	9690	**9775**	9765	9767	**9831**
	NRDT		433	409	**311**	311	310	**225**	235	233	**169**
	Total requests		10000	10000	**10000**	10000	10000	**10000**	10000	10000	**10000**
3	MET		0.9870	0.9949	**1.2153**	0.9870	0.9949	**1.2153**	0.9870	0.9949	**1.2213**
	Outcomes	CR	6777	5231	**6661**	6777	5231	**6672**	6823	5268	**6702**
		EER	1438	2217	**1530**	1438	2217	**1521**	1449	2230	**1526**
		NER	1492	2269	**1611**	1492	2269	**1609**	1503	2283	**1618**
		Total	9707	9717	**9802**	9707	9717	**9802**	9775	9781	**9846**
	NRDT		293	283	**198**	293	283	**198**	225	219	**154**
	Total req.		10000	10000	**10000**	10000	10000	**10000**	10000	10000	**10000**
4	MET		0.9966	0.9925	**1.2097**	0.9966	0.9925	**1.2183**	0.9966	0.9925	**1.2246**
	Outcomes	CR	6744	3519	**6395**	6808	3559	**6462**	6845	3581	**6491**
		EER	1434	3016	**1635**	1444	3042	**1629**	1457	3065	**1631**
		NER	1436	3076	**1679**	1456	3106	**1689**	1467	3134	**1705**
		Total	9614	9611	**9709**	9708	9707	**9780**	9769	9780	**9827**
	NRDT		386	389	**291**	292	293	**220**	231	220	**173**
	Total requests		10000	10000	**10000**	10000	10000	**10000**	10000	10000	**10000**

2. The mean execution time recorded for the system is greater than for the individual releases. This is the price for the improved dependability assurance provided by the fault-tolerant architecture – it waits for the second (i.e. slower) response before adjudicating the responses. Some improvement can be achieved by returning to the consumer the fastest response as soon it is received. dT is inherent for the chosen architecture and cannot be eliminated. The performance penalty inevitable with the managed upgrade is the real reason for us to try to minimise its duration.

---

[8] MET – mean execution time, in sec.
[9] NRDT – no response received within TimeOut

Table 6. Simulation results assuming independence of release failures

Run	Observations		TimeOut = 1.5 sec			TimeOut = 2.0 sec			TimeOut = 3.0 sec		
			Rel_1	Rel_2	System	Rel_1	Rel_2	System	Rel_1	Rel_2	System
1	Outcomes	MET	0.9995	0.9959	**1.2095**	0.9995	0.9959	**1.2191**	0.9995	0.9959	**1.2267**
		CR	6729	6647	**7759**	6794	6709	**7812**	6852	6770	**7853**
		EER	1406	1447	**755**	1424	1458	**758**	1432	1473	**768**
		NER	1453	1481	**1177**	1471	1496	**1194**	1483	1514	**1201**
		Total	9588	9575	**9691**	9689	9663	**9764**	9767	9757	**9822**
	NRDT		412	425	**309**	311	337	**236**	233	243	**178**
	Total requests		10000	10000	**10000**	10000	10000	**10000**	10000	10000	**10000**
2	Outcomes	MET	1.0086	1.0081	**1.2239**	1.0086	1.0081	**1.2327**	1.0086	1.0081	**1.2386**
		CR	6730	5712	**7396**	6805	5780	**7470**	6856	5824	**7509**
		EER	1428	1928	**1021**	1443	1947	**1017**	1454	1956	**1013**
		NER	1424	1949	**1286**	1446	1971	**1292**	1455	1992	**1309**
		Total	9582	9589	**9703**	9694	9698	**9779**	9765	9772	**9831**
	NRDT		418	411	**297**	306	302	**221**	235	228	**169**
	Total requests		10000	10000	**10000**	10000	10000	**10000**	10000	10000	**10000**
3	Outcomes	MET	0.9856	0.9894	**1.2013**	0.9856	0.9894	**1.2107**	0.9856	0.9894	**1.2175**
		CR	6700	4816	**6982**	6775	4869	**7039**	6834	4904	**7079**
		EER	1432	2400	**1203**	1446	2424	**1226**	1459	2445	**1245**
		NER	1458	2378	**1510**	1471	2404	**1515**	1483	2436	**1519**
		Total	9590	9594	**9695**	9692	9697	**9780**	9776	9785	**9843**
	NRDT		410	406	**305**	308	303	**220**	224	215	**157**
	Total requests		10000	10000	**10000**	10000	10000	**10000**	10000	10000	**10000**
4	Outcomes	MET	0.9884	0.9926	**1.2031**	0.9884	0.9926	**1.2126**	0.9884	0.9926	**1.2193**
		CR	6687	3855	**6624**	6762	3887	**6680**	6813	3917	**6704**
		EER	1419	2823	**1416**	1434	2865	**1429**	1444	2885	**1444**
		NER	1484	2886	**1656**	1504	2928	**1672**	1518	2955	**1687**
		Total	9590	9564	**9696**	9700	9680	**9781**	9775	9757	**9835**
	NRDT		410	436	**304**	300	320	**219**	225	243	**165**
	Total requests		10000	10000	**10000**	10000	10000	**10000**	10000	10000	**10000**

3 Somewhat unexpected result from this simulation is the fact that when the releases are assumed highly correlated (the first run in Table 5 with correlation between the releases 0.9) the reliability of the system is higher than the reliability of either of the two releases. When the correlation between the releases goes down (runs 2-4 in Table 5 with correlation 0.8 – 0.4) the system reliability remains better than the less reliable release (normally the old release) but is now worse than the reliability of the better release (normally the new release). This observation, true with respect to all types of responses - correct and incorrect – may be due to the specific way the correlation between the releases has been parameterised (Table 4). A more detailed study with a wider variety of values and different combinations of the conditional probabilities will provide further details about the interplay between the properties of the individual releases and of the chosen architecture for managed upgrade.

116   A. Gorbenko et al.

4 For the second set of simulation runs (Table 6) under the assumption that the responses of the releases are independent, the system reliability is better than the reliability of both releases. This observation is good news – fault-tolerance works. However, the result does not seem particularly useful because the assumption of independence is implausible: after all the two releases are likely to be very similar (significant portion of the code will be reused in the newer release). Software faults present in the older release and not fixed in the newer release will lead to identical failures.

The obtained results provide indications of the potential usefulness of the architecture and of its limitation. Through extensive simulation one can identify the range of possibilities which can be encountered in practice. The particular parameters of a real life-system, e.g. which set of conditional probabilities describes best the concrete system at hand, of course, is unknowable. However, the simulation results may help in shaping the 'prior' for a Bayesian assessment of the chosen architecture for a managed upgrade, as described in section 5.1 above.

6 Implementation

6.1 Test Harness

A test harness is under development for experimenting with the architecture for a managed upgrade of a third-party WS deployed as a composite WS (Fig. 4). It allows the requests to the WS to be forwarded to the deployed releases of the WS transparently for the consumers of the WS. When responses from the releases are collected, the test harness adjudicates them and returns a response to the respective consumer.

The test harness monitors the responses, using the calculated confidence in their dependability and adjusts the adjudication accordingly. The consumers of the WS will be offered a set of operations for changing the configuration of the test harness according to their preferences:

- users can add new or remove some of the old releases of the WS (add or remove URI to the WSDL description of the WS releases)
- users can specify the operational modes of the composite WS (serial or concurrent execution of the deployed releases)
- users can explicitly specify the adjudication mechanism they would like applied to their own requests to the WS (e.g. majority voter or other plans)
- the user can read back the confidence associated with each of the deployed releases of the WS and calculated by the harness for different dependability attributes (e.g. confidence in correctness, confidence in availability, etc.).

The test harness is being developed in Java using IBM WebSphere SDK for Web Services[10] (WSDK). Currently under development is the visual environment for the managed upgrade of own and third-party WS, for which the Eclipse IDE[11] will be extended with a specialised plug-in, also under development.

---

[10] http://www-106.ibm.com/developerworks/webservices/wsdk/
[11] www.eclipse.org

6.2 'Publishing' the Confidence in Dependability of Web Services

In this section we discuss some practical ways of 'publishing' the confidence (or indeed any other dependability related measure) using the adopted standards for WSs. The confidence is a probability and can be accurately represented by a floating point number. To illustrate the idea of publishing the confidence let us consider a contrived example of WS with the following fragment of its WSDL description:

```
<types>
  <s:schema ... >
    <s:element name="Operation1Request">
      <s:complexType>
        <s:sequence>
          <s:element minOccurs="0" maxOccurs="1"
            name="param1" type="s:int">
          <s:element minOccurs="0" maxOccurs="1"
            name="param2" type="s:string">
        </s:sequence>
      </s:complexType>
    </s:element>
    <s:element name="Operation1Response">
      <s:complexType>
        <s:sequence>
          <s:element minOccurs="0" maxOccurs="1"
            name="Op1Result" type="s:string">
        </s:sequence>
      </s:complexType>
    </s:element>
    ...
</types>
```

In other words, the WS interface publishes an operation "operation1" which requires two parameters when invoked, "param1" of type int and "param2" of type string, and returns a result "Op1Result" of type string.[12] Now assume that the WS provider wishes to 'publish' the calculated confidence in the correctness of "operation1".

There are two ways of doing it:

- The response to a consumer invoking "operation1" can be changed as follows:

```
<s:element name="Operation1Response">
  <s:complexType>
    <s:sequence>
      <s:element minOccurs="0" maxOccurs="1"
        name="Op1Result" type="s:string">
      <s:element minOccurs="0" maxOccurs="1"
        name="Op1Conf" type="s:double">
    </s:sequence>
  </s:complexType>
</s:element>
```

---

[12] For the sake of brevity the fragments of the WSDL description related to messages, parts and the service are not shown.

- A new operation is defined which takes as a parameter the name of an operation (for which the consumer seeks confidence) and returns the confidence in the quality of the operation:

```
<s:element name="OperationConfRequest">
   <s:complexType>
     <s:sequence>
       <s:element minOccurs="0" maxOccurs="1"
          name="operation" type="s:string">
     </s:sequence>
   </s:complexType>
</s:element>
<s:element name="OperationConfResponse">
   <s:complexType>
     <s:sequence>
       <s:element minOccurs="0" maxOccurs="1"
          name="Op1Conf" type="s:double">
     </s:sequence>
   </s:complexType>
</s:element>
```

The advantage of the first implementation is that the confidence is associated with every execution of "operation1". The obvious disadvantage is that the new WSDL description is not backward compatible with the old one, which is not acceptable for the existing WS but may be OK for newly deployed services.

The advantage of the second solution is that the new WSDL is backward compatible with the old WSDL. The disadvantage is that the confidence will have to be extracted in a separate invocation of a different operation published by the service ("OperationConf" in the example above), which may lead to complications.

Finally, a third option exists, which combines the advantages of both solutions given above. It consists of defining a new operation, e.g. "operation1Conf", in which the response is extended by a number providing the confidence in the correctness of the operation. This approach allows the 'confidence conscious' consumers to switch to using "operation1Conf", while it does not break the existing client applications which can continue to use "operation1", i.e. backward compatibility is achieved.

The confidence will have to be updated when necessary (e.g. by the service provider). The clients will be able to get this information directly from the UDDI archive. Both the clients and the provider will be able to keep this up to date. This will, for example, allow the clients to collect and publicise information about the confidence in the service, which in many situations is the most appropriate way of collecting information about confidence as only the clients know exactly if the service provided is correct. However, an architectural solution in which the WSDL description of a WS is extended with additional information reflecting confidence in this service, as was shown above, is more static.

Another two solutions are possible. The first one, which uses protocol handlers on the service and client sides to transparently add/remove additional information describing confidence to/from each XML message sent between the WS and clients, is more structured and transparent. The protocol handlers should be able to understand the additional information in the same way on both sides. This architectural solution completely separates the application functionality from dealing with the confidence-related issues and ensures compatibility in that when there is no handler on the client side it keeps functioning.

The Web Service architecture allows us to develop another solution, which consists of a dedicated trusted confidence service functioning as a mediator for all messages sent to and from the WS. This mediator can monitor all messages and express the confidence in a convenient way; an example of such an intermediary is given in section 4.1 (Fig. 4). The advantage of this solution is a complete separation of confidence from the client and service functionality. Moreover, it may be beneficial to use such mediators as trusted-third parties in online negotiations between clients and services. A disadvantage of this solution, clearly, is that the operational 'evidence' about how good the WS is will be generated by the traffic produced by the consumers connected to the intermediary. In case significant traffic bypasses the intermediary, i.e. many consumers interact directly with the WS, the confidence reported by the intermediary may be out of date.

7 Discussion and Conclusions

7.1 Related Work

Paper [15] discusses an architectural framework that allows a WS to be distributed into a number of nodes. The specific focus is on supporting uninterrupted service when a service migrates from one node to another. This approach cannot be directly used for WS upgrading when we want to make use of natural redundancy and diversity existing in the system with old and new releases and when we want to make decisions by measuring confidence in the old and new releases of an WS. Moreover, our solution guarantees uninterrupted service. The approach proposed in [15] does not explicitly work with any dependability-related characteristics of the WS (such as confidence).

The Hercules framework [16] relies on the same idea [3] of ensuring reliability of upgrading by employing old and new releases. But the main focus of this work is on formal specification of specific subdomains on which different releases of a component work correctly. Our approach uses confidence in service as the main characteristics used to reasoning about its dependability. Moreover, our technique is oriented towards the Web Service architecture with a special emphasis on service specification description and using service registries to publicize services.

7.2 Outstanding Issues

Due to space limitations we could not address several practical aspects of implementing the proposed managed upgrade. A few are discussed in this section, while others will be covered in our future work.

One of the reasons for introducing the managed upgrade is the lack of notification of consumers when an WS is upgraded, which may be useful in the context of the managed upgrade, e.g. if the managed upgrade is deployed by consumers. Here we explicitly discuss various ways for implementing such notification. It could be used to initiate the managed upgrade from the old to the new release. There are several degrees of notification and various ways of implementing it. One possibility is to use the existing registry mechanism and extend the WSDL description of a WS by adding a reference to a new release of a WS; this would allow a consumer to detect this with both releases staying operational. Another possibility is to use a WS notification service[13] as a separate mechanism to inform all the consumers of a WS about a new release. A similar approach would be to explicitly notify subscribers (consumers) using some form of "callback" function to consumers of a WS.

Another problem with the proposed approach to using the confidence in the dependability of the releases is defining a plausible 'prior' about the dependability of the new release. A related issue, which affects the accuracy of the confidence in the dependability of the releases and the effectiveness of the managed upgrade, is the perfection of the 'oracles' (adjudicators) of the responses from the releases. We touched upon these problems in section 5.1 and provided some initial assessment of the impact of imperfect detection on the predicted confidence. However, further extensive studies are needed, e.g. via simulation, to assess how severe the problem of imperfect detection is. More importantly, such studies may allow for measures to be found which, if put in place, e.g. implemented in the middleware for the managed upgrade, will reduce the problem to an acceptable level.

7.3 Conclusion

We have addressed various aspects of a dependable on-line upgrade of a WS. We concentrated on the managed upgrade in which two releases of the service can be deployed and discussed the implications of using a standard fault-tolerant architecture in which the releases are used as 'independent' channels. We argued that the confidence in dependability can be calculated and used to make a decision when to switch the consumers of the WS from the old to the new release: when the confidence in the dependability of the new release becomes 'sufficiently' high. Through simulation we confirmed that the managed upgrade can deliver some improvement compared with the situations when either of the releases is used.

Finally, we discussed the advantages and disadvantages of various alternative ways of deploying the managed upgrade: i) by the consumers of the service, ii) by the provider or iii) by an independent broker.

Acknowledgements

This work is partially supported by the Royal Society grant (RS 16114) and by the UK Engineering and Physical Sciences Research council (EPSRC) (DOTS Project). A. Romanovsky is partially supported by IST RODIN project (IST 511599).

---

[13] http://www-106.ibm.com/developerworks/webservices/library/specification/ws-notification/

References

1. W3C Working Group, Web Services Architecture. 2004. http://www.w3.org/TR/2004/NOTE-ws-arch-20040211/
2. Romanovsky, A. and I. Smith. Dependable On-line Upgrading of Distributed Systems COMPSAC'2002. 2002. Oxford. p. 975-976.
3. Randell, B., System Structure for Software Fault Tolerance. IEEE Transactions on Software Engineering, 1975. SE-1(2): p. 220-232.
4. Ferguson, D.F., T. Storey, et al., Secure, Reliable, Transacted Web Services: Architecture and Composition. 2003, Microsoft and IBM.
5. Tartanoglu, F., V. Issarny, et al., Dependability in the Web Service Architecture, in Architecting Depndable Systems. 2003, Springer-Verlag. p. 89-108.
6. Avizienis, A., J.-C. Laprie, et al., Basic Concepts and Taxonomy of Dependable and Secure Computing. IEEE Transactions on Dependable and Secure Computing, 2004. 1(1): p. 11-33.
7. AmperPoint, Managing Exceptions in Web Services Environment. 2003. http://www.eaiindustry.org/docs/member%20docs/amberpoint/AmberPoint_Managing_Exceptions.pdf
8. Chandra, S., Chen, P. M. Whither Generic Recovery from Application Faults? A Fault Study using Open-Source Software International Conference on Dependable Systems and Networks (DSN'2000). 2000, June. NY, USA. p. 97-106.
9. Deswarte, Y., K. Kanoun and J.-C. Laprie. Diversity against Accidental and Deliberate Faults Computer Security, Dependability and Assurance: From Needs to Solutions. 1998. York, England and Washington, D.C., USA: IEEE Computer Society Press.
10. Kharchenko, V., P. Popov and A. Romanovsky. On Dependability of Composite Web Services with Components Upgraded Online. In Supplemental Volume Workshop on Architecting Dependable Systems (WADS-DSN'2004). 2004. Florence, Italy. p. 287-291.
11. Box, G.E.P. and G.C. Tiao, Bayesian Inference in Statistical Analysis. 1973: Addison-Wesley Inc. 588.
12. Littlewood, B. and D. Wright, Some conservative stopping rules for the operational testing of safety-critical software. IEEE Transactions on Software Engineering, 1997. 23(11): p. 673-683.
13. Littlewood, B., P. Popov and L. Strigini, Assessing the Reliability of Diverse Fault-Tolerant Software-Based Systems. Safety Science, 2002. 40: p. 781-796.
14. Cukier, M., D. Powell and J. Arlat, Coverage Estimation Methods for Stratified Fault-Injection. IEEE Transactions on Computers, 1999. 48(7): p. 707-723.
15. Alwagait, E. and S. Ghandeharizadeh. DeW: A Dependable Web Services Framework 14th International Workshop on Research Issues on Data Engineering: Web Services for E-Commerce and E-Government Applications (RIDE'04). 2004. Boston, Massachusetts. p. 111-118.
16. Cook, J.E. and J.A. Dage. Highly Reliable Upgrading of Components The 21st International Conference on Software Engineering (ICSE 1999). 1999. p. 203-212.

Adaptable Analysis of Dependable System Architectures Through Monitoring

Marcio S. Dias[1,2] and Debra J. Richardson[1]

[1] Department of Informatics, Donald Bren School of Information and Computer Science,
University of California at Irvine, Irvine, CA, 92697, USA
{mdias,djr}@ics.uci.edu

[2] Department of Computer Science, e-Science Research Institute, University of Durham,
Durham, DH1 3LE, UK
{marcio.dias@dur.ac.uk}

Abstract. Every day, our society becomes more dependent on complex software systems with high availability requirements, such as those present in telecommunications, air traffic control, power plants and distribution lines, among others. In order to facilitate the task of maintaining and evolving such systems, dynamic software architecture infrastructures have recently been in the research agenda. However, complexity and dynamic evolution of dependable systems bring some challenges for verification. Some of these challenges are associated to modifications in the set of properties being verified and also in the types of analysis being performed during system operation. In this work, we present a multiple specification and architectural-based approach for software monitoring that allows the adaptation of analysis tasks in order to properly handle the challenges mentioned above.

1 Introduction

Every day, our society becomes more dependent on complex software systems with high availability requirements. These systems are present in many different businesses and operations, such as telecommunication, power plants and distribution lines, air traffic control, global markets, and financial institutes. Some of these systems run on distributed environments and heterogeneous (hardware and software) platforms, and need to be online 24/7. Sometimes, these systems are the result of integrating independent subsystems, where different technologies and processes might have been applied during their development. All these factors contribute to the complexity of such systems.

In addition to the inherent complexity of dependable systems, and in order to attend the demands of a fast pace society, many of these systems suffer from rushed development processes or rely on legacy systems, which were not initially developed to attend current demands. In this scenario, activities of maintenance and evolution become imperative and a hard task to accomplish, given that they have to be performed over systems that cannot have their services interrupted.

A critical challenge faced during maintenance and evolution of dependable systems is to verify, measure, and ensure their quality. The high availability requirement of such systems demands maintenance and evolution being performed at runtime. The dynamic evolution on such systems imposes some problems for system analysis. For example, dynamic changes can bring the system to global states that would be unreachable if those changes were performed statically (e.g., dynamic changes may not guarantee new parts of the system to be aware of the history of events that occurred previously to that change); and, properties of interest for analysis and verification may have to be redefined (and some new properties to be defined) in order to reflect the changes in the system configuration [5].

Moreover, since maintenance and evolution of dependable systems may raise new conditions and properties for analysis and verification, such analysis should be able to dynamically and accordingly adapt to changes, and the verification should be performed over heterogeneous properties. Heterogeneous properties are properties described for different analysis purposes, and multiple specification languages may be required for their description.

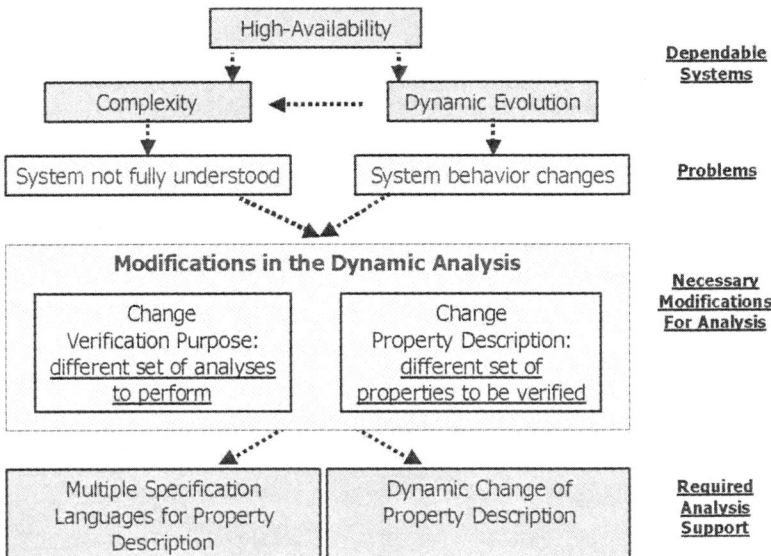

Fig. 1. Modification in the dynamic analysis due to high-availability requirement, system complexity and dynamic evolution

Therefore, we need to identify and understand how analysis of heterogeneous properties can be performed over dependable and evolvable systems, considering that properties of interest may also change during system execution. In order to deal with this problem, dynamic analysis techniques are required (such as those supported by monitoring systems [4,11]), but these techniques should be prepared for: (1) handling heterogeneous properties (multiple specification languages for their description) and; (2) dynamic adaptation of the analysis (see Fig. 1.). Although applying only dynamic analysis and monitoring on dependable systems may not be sufficient to avoid failures, it can identify conditions, alert and even take some actions before failures happen, similarly to the airplane collision avoidance analysis performed in air traffic control systems.

2 Example

In the real world, elevator systems are structurally static, have some limited level of complexity, and are not commonly reconfigured at runtime. However, through simulation, we can show how dynamic recofiguration can increase the complexity of such systems.. We decided to use a simulator for the elevator application domain in our example because of three simple reasons: (1) everyone is familiar with elevator systems, and can easily understand the commonalities and variabilities on this application domain; (2) these systems contain stateful components and timing requirements, what give them a level of complexity that is interesting for verification purposes, and; (3) we can easily identify the components of these systems and describe their structural architectures, on which elements the dynamic system reconfiguration will take place.

After understanding the reason for such example of dependable system and dynamic system reconfiguration, it is also worth to mention that we are making no claims that the design decisions taken here are neither the best nor a good solution for this application domain. Other design decisions could have been taken, and some of the problems we discuss here might not occur on these other solutions. However, this design is purposely taken to demonstrate common problems we face when analyzing dynamic system reconfiguration.

2.1 Elevator Application Domain

For the elevator domain, we can find some commonalities and variabilities we can explore here. As common components to all elevator systems, we have:

- *ElevatorADT*. This component maintains the information about the elevator car state, such as: motion and direction. In addition to state information, the ElevatorADT (Elevator Abstract Data Type) keeps a list of all the calls it needs to attend. If a call is not in its list, the elevator will not attend it.
- *ElevatorPanel*: This component represents the internal panel of an elevator car. After entering the elevator, the passenger can request calls through it, and see the current floor.
- *BuildingPanel*: This component represents all the elevator call panels of the building. Through this component, users in different floors can request a call to the elevator system, indicating the desired direction.

A basic architecture for the elevator system is presented in Fig. 2 using only these components and following the C2 architectural style [10,14]. In C2 style, components are connected through directed broadcast buses, which broadcast incoming event requests (from the bottom) to all the components above the bus, and incoming notifications (from the top) to all the components connected below the bus. In Fig. 3, some different variations of the basic architecture are presented, with modified architecture and additional components, such as *Scheduler* and *Call Generator*. Three possible points for variation are shown: V1 represents addition or removal of new elevators components (ADT+Panel+Bus); V2 represents addition of a Scheduler component and an extra bus between *BuildingPanel* component and the main bus; and V3 represents the addition of a *Call-Generator* component for simulation.

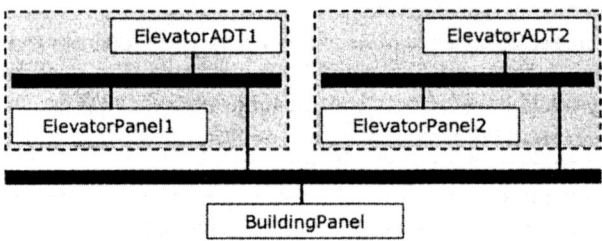

Fig. 2. Basic architecture configuration for elevator system commonalities. Black rectangles represent broadcast buses that interconnect system components (C2 style).

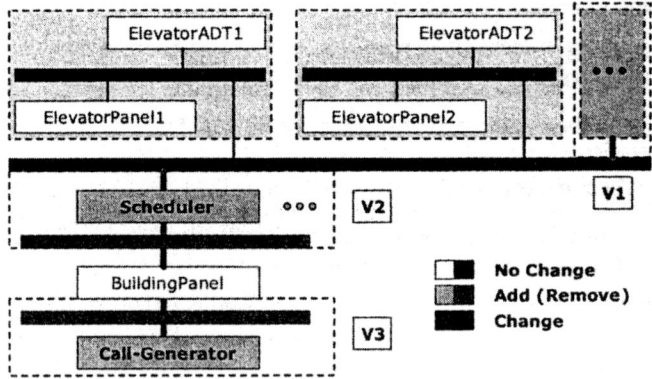

Fig. 3. Variations from the basic architecture configuration for the elevator system

2.2 Challenges for Dynamic Analysis in the Example

Dynamic software analysis, or more specifically software monitoring, can be applied to different purposes [11]. As the system evolves dynamically, different and new analysis may be needed during the system operation.

Challenge #1: As different purposes for dynamic analysis may be required during system evolution, different methods to specify the properties for verification are necessary.

In the example, let's consider three different purposes for verification: (1) behavior conformance verification, (2) functional correctness verification, and (3) performance evaluation. In order to be able to perform such different analysis, there is a need to handle different (heterogeneous) property descriptions:

- *Behavioral conformance verification*. The properties to be analyzed are related to the behavior of the elements of the system. Component level verification would require a description of the expected behavior of the components, and this could be provided as finite state machines or statecharts, for example. In other words, we may have the property for behavior conformance of the ElevatorADT component described using finite state machines. On the other hand, a system level verification would require a behavioral description of the system, such as activity or sequence diagrams, for example.

- *Functional correctness verification*. In this case, the properties to be analyzed are related to the functionality provided by the system. The description of system functionality could be done with specification methods such as, for example: use-case, activity, sequence diagrams; event-based regular expressions; etc. An example of a property for functional correctness verification could be "no elevator should pass by a floor with a pending call, in the same direction, without stopping to attend it". This property could be described as a regular expression.
- *Performance verification*. Timing, throughput and other measurements are described in properties for performance evaluation. In general, specification languages used in this context are either based on classical temporal logics or linear temporal logics.

Therefore, in this context, it is required from the dynamic analysis the ability to allow multiple, different and possibly new specification languages.

Challenge #2: As the system evolves, some previously defined (described) properties may either become obsolete or require modifications in their description, and new properties may become necessary for verification.

To illustrate the problems mentioned above, consider that we have the following set of properties being verified before the dynamic evolution of the elevator system.

P1: No elevator should be idle while there still is an unattended call in the building.
P2: An elevator should not miss a call when moving in the same direction and passing at the same floor of the call.
P3: The time between a call being placed and one elevator being assigned to attend that call should be less than 1 sec.
P4: The time between a call being placed and one elevator attending the call should be less than 45s.

After suffering dynamic modifications according to variation V2 (the addition of a Scheduler component), some of these properties may become inadequate or need redefinition. For example, by adding a Scheduler component:

P1 becomes inadequate because the scheduler will assign a call to one elevator, while the other ones may be in idle state.
P2 may become inadequate depending on the scheduling policy.
P3 may either become inadequate or need to be redefined, depending on the scheduling policy and how it was described before.
P4 would still be valid, unless the addition of the Scheduler component had the purpose to reduce the waiting time (a requirement change).

Therefore, it is also required from the dynamic analysis the ability to support dynamic definition (and modification) of the properties of interest for verification.

3 MonArch Approach

In this section, we describe our approach, discussing:
- the concepts supporting our approach,
- the difference of our approach to current approaches,
- how analysis are described in our approach, and
- the MonArch supporting tools.

3.1 Conceptual Basis

In order to address the problems of necessary modifications of dynamic analysis in order to verify dependable systems (described before), our approach relies on four main points:

A. Configurable Monitoring Systems

Many monitors are developed with the intention to be generic for multiple purposes, but they fail because they are not adaptable, for instance, to situations or purposes that would require new specification languages for property description. Therefore, instead of proposing a generic monitor system, the approach encourages configurable monitor systems, with increased reuse of common monitoring services (see Fig. 4) and the support for development and adaptation of specialized services. More details can be found in [6] about each monitoring services presented in Fig. 4 (as well as information and example of how to develop new monitoring services for MonArch.)

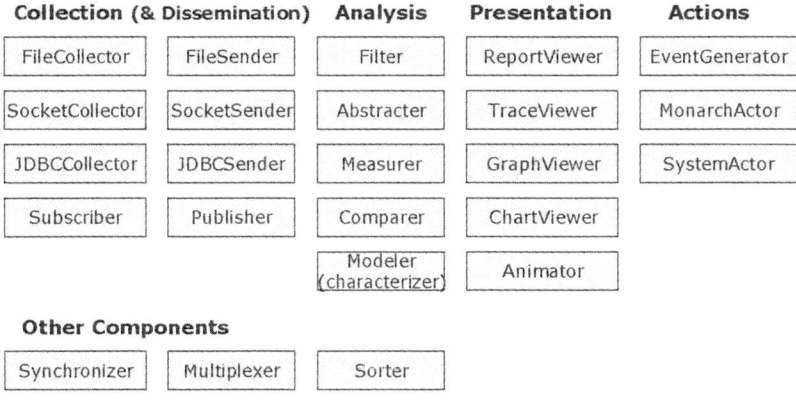

Fig. 4. Examples of common monitoring services

B. Service-Oriented Monitoring Systems

Instead of making the services provided by the monitor based on a (global) specification language (language oriented monitors), the approach uses the "service" as the element of composition. In other words, a specification language does not limit the types of services a monitor can offer. A monitor can be composed from a collection of services, including not only common services, but also extensible and "pluggable" services.

We have identified not only what are the common services of monitor systems, but we define a classification to organize them. The analysis of a monitor system can be broken into these smaller services, and these services can be associated to independent and different specification languages. For example, while one abstracter service may be associated to regular expression specifications, another abstracter may be associated to DAG, binary tree, or another specification method. The combination of different services will define the monitor.

C. Software-Architecture Based Monitors

Instead of developing a monitor system by first designing an algorithm to process the services, the approach is based on an appropriate architectural style where dynamic (re)configuration and evolution are feasible. Figures 5 and 6 present examples of different monitors and their configuration based on the monitoring service oriented components.

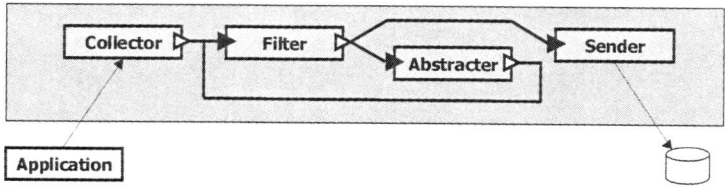

Fig. 5. Example of a very simple monitor system with four service-oriented components

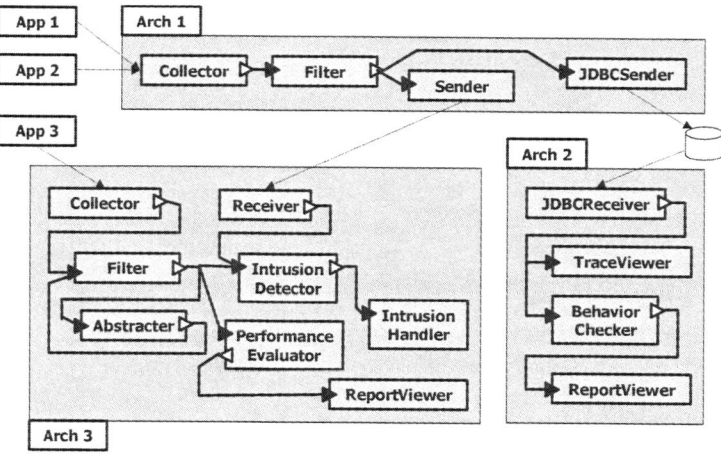

Fig. 6. Example of distributed monitoring performed by three different monitors.

D. Configuration Before and During Operation

Provide the ability to modify analysis (and other monitor services) given the changes on the properties of interest and system evolution, instead of having the entire configuration performed before system operation. By configuration we mean not only configuration in the set of properties being verified (which would represent modification in the description of properties being analyzed), but also modification on the set of analyses being performed (new purposes for verification may require new analysis techniques to be included during runtime in the set of dynamic analyses being performed.)

3.2 Comparing the MonArch Approach to Current Approaches

These following points characterize the main differences of our approach in relation to current monitoring system approaches (see Fig. 7):

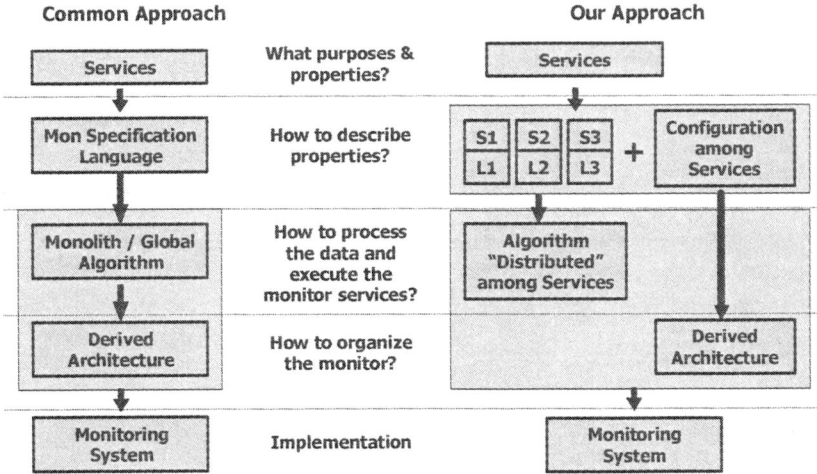

Fig. 7. Differences between how current monitors are developed and our approach to develop them

- **Purpose and Properties**. Similarly, our approach starts with the set of services the monitor should support. The set of services is related with the purpose for monitor, and also to what types of properties should be analyzed. However, instead of supporting only the initial set of services, our approach allows any other service to be added after the monitor is ready and even in operation.

- **Property Specification**. Instead of defining a specification language that will be used to specify the properties for analysis and describe all the services the monitor should provide, in our approach each service (Si) can be based on an independent specification language (Li). In addition, different services can share specification languages to describe the properties they are going to analyses (useful when different types of analysis can be performed over a single model, for example).

- **Monitor Execution**. Instead of defining a global algorithm and the architecture that will process and perform analysis accordingly to a single specification language, in our approach, the configuration of the service-oriented components and the topology of the architecture define a distributed processing algorithm for the monitor system.

- **Implementation**. Instead of having a single monitor as the result of the development, in our approach, a monitor consists simply of a composition of services, composition that can be derived from the architecture of the monitor, and the configuration for these services described in possibly different specification languages. Therefore, our approach facilitates the creation of multiple monitors by modifying the set of service components or simply the topology of the monitor architecture.

The characteristics of our approach address the initial problem of verifying systems that are dependable, complex, highly available and dynamically reconfigurable.

3.3 Describing the Dynamic Analysis in MonArch Approach

In our approach, the description of the monitor is divided into two parts: (A) monitor architecture and (B) monitor services. Once described the monitor architecture and the configuration of the monitor services, we need to define the links between the monitor architecture and the services described for a specific target application. These links are maintained in a project.

A. Specifying the Monitor Architecture

The architecture description for the monitor system contains basically the same type of information supported by ADLs (architecture description languages): the set of components (and types), the connectors and the configuration of the architecture of the monitor system.

The monitor architecture defines what set of services the monitor offer, and contains the structure of the monitor system, and it can be independent of the target application that will be observed by the monitor. In other words, the monitor architecture contains the information about what analysis and services will be provided, independently of what events and definitions that will be used for processing.

B. Specifying the Monitoring Services

In order to monitor the target application, it is necessary to describe the types of events that occur in this application, as well as how these events can be composed into others, what type of events or information should be presented, etc. The description of the services is specific to the target application. And although a service description is going to be associated to a component of the monitor system, it can be defined independently of the monitor system and its architecture.

Although specification of monitor architecture and the monitoring services are kept independently, they are interconnected (linked) in a project. Once they are linked and the monitor is in operation, the architecture of the monitor can change (architectural evolution, by replacing, adding or removing service-oriented components or connectors), as well as the description of the properties for each service (modification in the specification of the properties being analyzed by each service-oriented component).

By existing different specifications for the monitor architecture and for the monitor services, it is possible to reuse the monitor (purpose) with different applications, as well as reuse the application description for multiple monitor purposes (Fig. 8)

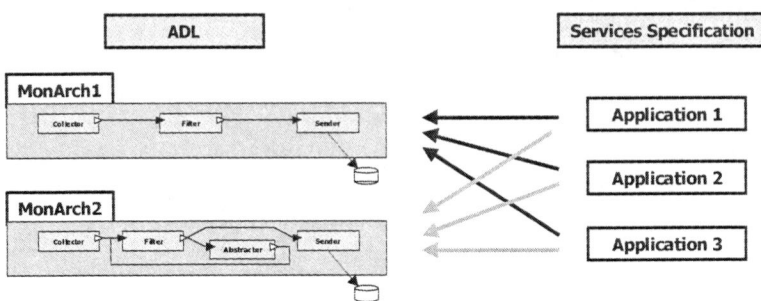

Fig. 8. Monitor Architecture and Monitor Services being described separatedly. While the monitor architecture specification dictates the services available, the monitor services specification contains the information regarding the target application being monitored. One monitor architecture can be used for multiple target applications, and an application service description can be used by multiple monitors.

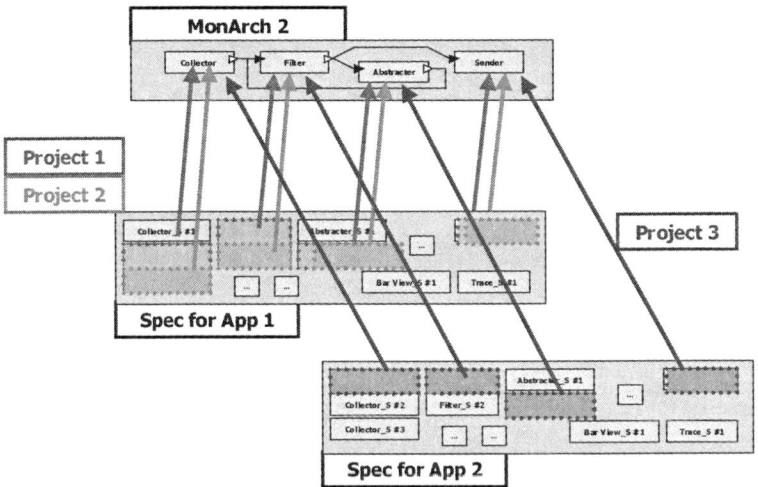

Fig. 9. Projects associate monitor architecture description with service description

C. Project

To instantiate or initialize a monitor system, it is necessary to link service descriptions to monitor components of one architecture. In our approach, these links are defined in a project. The project associates a monitor architecture to the service specification for one application, defining what service description is associated to each service (or component) of the monitor architecture (see Fig. 9). Defining these links, the monitor can be instantiated and executed.

Once a monitor is in operation for a specific project, changes in the architecture or in the service description may be reflected or not in the initial descriptions. For example, if during the monitor operation, a modification in the service description is required or simply performed, the monitor operator may decide to reflect those modifications back to the initial specification or not.

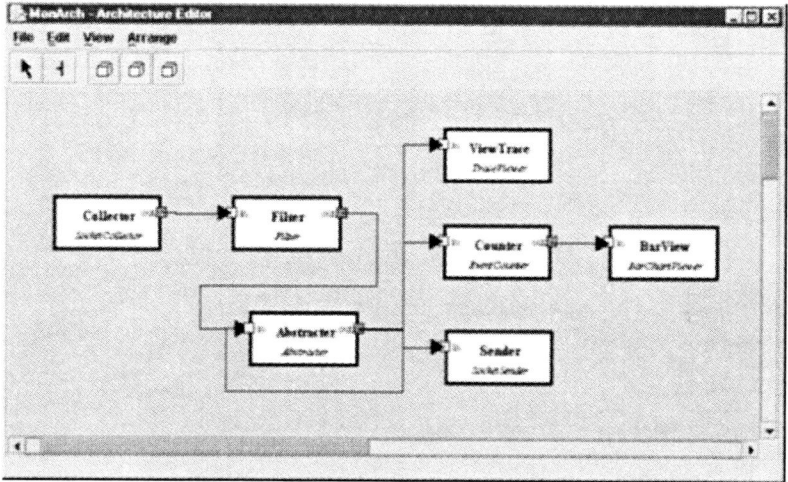

Fig. 10. MonArch Architecture Editor

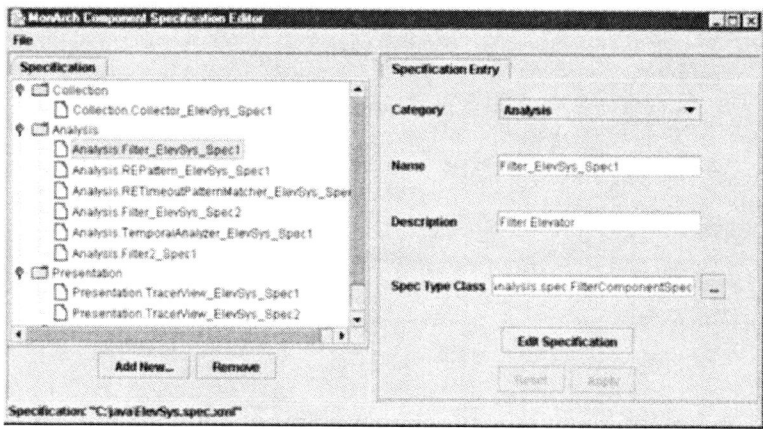

Fig. 11. MonArch Service Specification Editor

3.4 Supporting Tools

While the monitor architecture description is supported by the MonArch Architecture Editor (see Fig. 10), the description of the services for an application is supported by MonArch Specification Editor (see Fig. 11). This prototype tool allows the specification of all services associated to an application. Figure 11 shows the tool being used for the description of services used to monitor the elevator system. After defining what is the type of the service (in Spec Type Class), we can describe the service (edit the specification) either though a GUI Form or directly in XML (see Fig. 12). All services for an application are stored in a single database. The MonArch Architecture Editor is also responsible for supporting the description of projects, associating components in the architecture with service description.

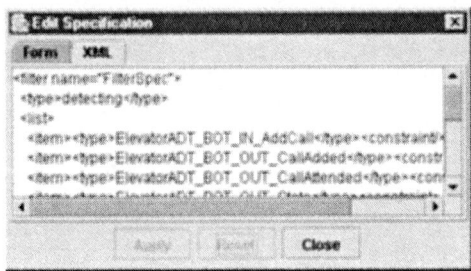

Fig. 12. Editing Filter Service – XML

4 Experiments

We have performed three case studies to verify the adaptability, extensibility and applicability of our approach.

4.1 Elevator System

This system is a simulator for the elevator system of a commercial building. On the contrary of a physical building, it is simple to perform structural modifications to this system. The elevator system was built using the C2 architecture framework (original framework version) [14], which easily allows structural modifications of the system (even on-the-fly modifications).

4.1.1 Experiment Overview
Some details of the elevator system, including its components and variabilities of the system, were discussed before. In this experiment, we have a monitor system connected to the elevator system, performing some analyses over the elevator system execution (we discuss what analyses are performed and how the monitor is connected to the elevator system ahead).

We start the experiment with one configuration of the elevator system, and during its execution, the configuration of the elevator system is (dynamically) modified. As mentioned before, these modifications bring some challenges for analysis and, in order to continue to properly analyze the elevator system, modifications in the monitor system are required and performed. We discuss how modifications happen in the monitor system, in order to show how our approach deals with those challenges. In this experiment, the purpose for monitoring the elevator system is to perform behavioral analysis.

4.1.2 Initial Configuration

In the initial configuration for this experiment, the elevator system has a simple structure (ev1), with just one elevator and no scheduler. The initial monitor configuration (mv1) has the following services: an event collector component (C1); a simple filter component (F1) that filters out irrelevant events for the analysis; a regular-expression pattern matching identifier component (Behavior1) that identifies when event (behavioral) patterns happen during the system execution; and a textual viewer (View) that presents the information about behavioral patterns identified by the analysis.

In the beginning of the experiment, we start to monitor for the following properties:

- **Property 1**: Elevator should not be idle while there still is an unattended call in the building.
- **Property 2**: An elevator should not miss a call (when moving in the same direction and passing by the same floor of the call).

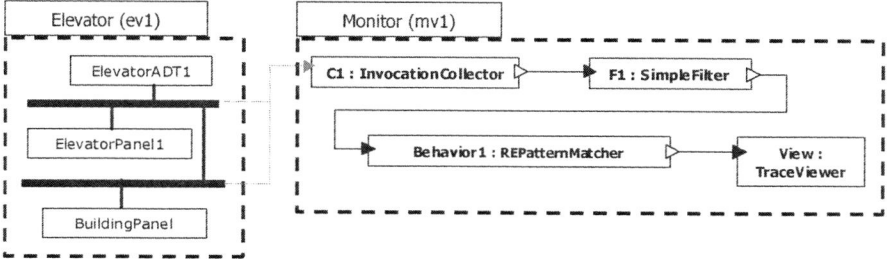

Fig. 13. Elevator Case Study – Initial Configuration (Configuration 1)

In order to analyze these two properties, the services present in the monitoring system (mv1) should be properly specified. While the services provided by InvocationCollector (C1) and TraceView (View) components require no special service specification (in relation to the analysis), we discuss below the specification for the other two services: SimpleFilter (F1) and REPatternMatcher (Behavior1).

4.1.2.1. Service Specification for SimpleFilter (F1)
This is a simple filter service, which requires in its specification basically a list of events collected from the elevator system that should <u>not</u> be filtered out (a "detecting" filter, as opposed to a "blocking" filter) in order to verify properties #1 and #2.

4.1.2.2. Service Specification for RegularExpressionPatternMatcher (Behavior1)
In this service, the specification should describe the properties to be analyzed. In the monitoring system, the identification of a property would be defined as a new event. Therefore, whenever one property is identified by the RegularExpressionPatternMatcher component, a new event is generated and passed to other services.

Below, we present how properties #1 and #2 were described in our experiment:

- **Property 1:** Elevator should not be idle while there still is an unattended call in the building. (Regular Expression for this property, where • represents a sequence operand and variables represent constraints over event attributes)

    ```
    ElevatorADT_BOT_OUT_CallAdded (F:floor;D:direction) •
    NOT ElevatorADT_BOT_OUT_CallAttended(F:floor;D:direction) •
    ElevatorADT_BOT_OUT_State (IDLE:status)
    ```

- **Property 2:** An elevator should not miss a call (when moving in the same direction and passing by the same floor of the call). (Regular Expression for this property)

    ```
    ElevatorADT_BOT_OUT_CallAdded (F:floor;D:direction) •
    ElevatorADT_BOT_OUT_State (MOVING:status;F:floor;D:direction) •
    NOT ElevatorADT_BOT_OUT_CallAttended(F:floor;D:direction) •
    ElevatorADT_BOT_OUT_State(MOVING:status;F2:floor;D:direction)
    ```

4.1.3 Modification of the Analysis Purpose

In this experiment, the first type of modifications we consider is related with the purpose of analysis. Previously, we were analyzing behavioral properties as expressed in regular expressions. At this moment, we also want to perform analysis over temporal properties. For example, we want to include the analysis of a temporal property such as:

- **Property 3:** Every call should be attended in less than one minute.

The service provided by component Behavior1 (RegularExpressionPatternMatcher service) couldn't verify such property. In order to analyze property 3, we need to modify the services provided by the monitor. We discuss two options for modifying the monitor, although other options may be possible as well.

Option 1. Extending RegularExpressionPatternMatcher Service

This option consists in extending the RegularExpressionPatternMatcher into a new service that can handle timing properties. In this case, our extended service (RETimeoutPatternMatcher) can handle properties as described for service REPatternMatcher with an additional (and optional) timeout setting so that, if a property cannot be identified in a specific time interval, a timeout event is fired. Basically, the new service performs a similar analysis of the previous service, but if a partial pattern matching is not completed in the allocated time, a timeout event is fired. Otherwise, it simply identifies the occurrence of a pattern.

Option 2. Adding Extra Service - TemporalAnalyzer

In this option, the analysis of property 3 is not performed completely by one service, but the combination of different services. While the *Behavior1* component perform the identification of event patterns, the additional service (TemporalAnalyzer) performs temporal assessments over the events it receives. The analysis of property 3 would be decomposed into these 2 services: *Behavior1* identifies when a call is attended, and *Temporal* component verifies if the call was attended in less than 1 minute (see). Filter F2 is added to block events of type "Property3_Identified_Event" to bypass the temporal analysis.

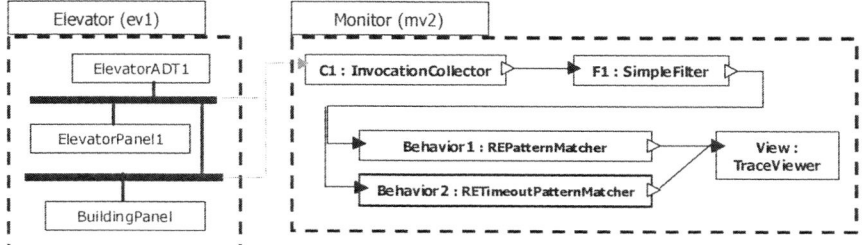

Fig. 14. Modifying analysis purpose by extending service (option 1)

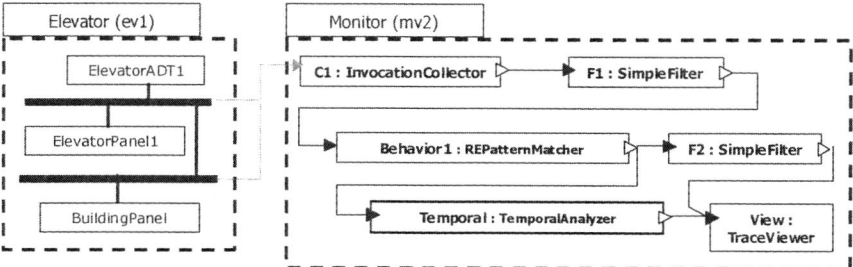

Fig. 15. Modifying analysis purpose by adding new service (option 2)

4.1.4 Modifications in the Elevator System

The second type of modification in the experiment happens in the elevator system. With the reconfiguration of the elevator system, modifications in the analysis are required as well. We considered the following modifications in the elevator system and their implications to the analysis: (1) addition of an extra elevator car, and (2) addition of a scheduler component, which will decide which elevator car should attend a call placed through the building panel component (see Fig. 16).

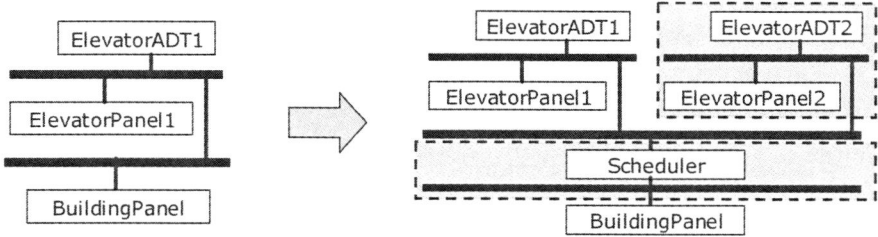

Fig. 16. Reconfiguration of the Elevator System

Revisiting Property #1
Before the reconfiguration, property #1 was "elevator should not be idle while there still is an unattended call in the building". After the reconfiguration, with two elevator

cars, this property would be better expressed as "an elevator should not be idle while there still is an unattended call that was scheduled to it."

The modification performed in the service specification of Behavior1 component (to reflect the change in the description of property #1) was to verify if a previously scheduled call has been attended by (or rescheduled to) another elevator car before the initial scheduled car attend it.

The new property was described as (with the modifications in bold, where the symbol '||' represents an OR operand):

```
ElevatorADT_BOT_OUT_CallAdded(F:floor;D:direction) •
NOT (
   ElevatorADT_BOT_OUT_CallRemoved(F:floor;D:direction) ||
   ElevatorADT_BOT_OUT_CallAttended(F:floor;D:direction)
) •
ElevatorADT_BOT_OUT_State(IDLE:status)
```

Revisiting Property #2
Before the reconfiguration, the property was "An elevator should not miss a call (when moving in the same direction and passing by the same floor of the call)." Similarly to the previous property, this property needs to be adapted to the new situation. Now, one elevator car may miss a call if it was scheduled to another elevator. The modifications in the service description for this new property are similar to property #1. The modification to the previous regular expression for this property are presented below in highlight:

```
ElevatorADT_BOT_OUT_CallAdded (F:floor;D:direction) •
NOT ElevatorADT_BOT_OUT_CallRemoved (F:floor;D:direction) •
ElevatorADT_BOT_OUT_State (MOVING:status; F:floor; D:direction ) •
NOT ElevatorADT_BOT_OUT_CallAttended (F:floor;D:direction) •
ElevatorADT_BOT_OUT_State (MOVING:status; F2:floor; D: direction )
```

4.1.5 Experiment Description

The instrumentation of the elevator system happened in the C2 connectors of the system architecture. Therefore, all C2 messages flowing in the architecture are collected and sent to the monitor. In this experiment, it is in the monitor where events not relevant for the analyses performed are filtered out (by the Filter service). If we have modification on the set of properties being analyzed, or we need additional services, we can adjust the filter service configuration without the need of modifying the instrumentation of the elevator system.

4.2 Air Traffic Control System

Air Traffic Control systems involve high level of complexity, have high availability requirements, and their reliability is crucial for safety and security purposes. Despite all the current technology and advances employed in such systems, we decided to explore such domain for our experiment in face of the events after the September 11th terrorist attacks in the year of 2001. Although simply monitoring the air traffic cannot avoid incidents such as those, it can alert of suspicious maneuvers before the final outcome. In addition, the ability to dynamically adapt the services performed by the monitor would facilitate the modifications to the air traffic control system and possibly reduce the number of days (from 3) the commercial air traffic had to be shut down in the United States.

We used an Air Traffic Control [1] simulator (ATCJ) in this experiment. The simulator allows the user to assume the duties of an air traffic controller without endangering the lives of millions of travelers each year. The user is responsible for directing the flight of jets and prop planes into and out of the flight arena and airports. The speed (update time) and frequency of the planes depend on the difficulty of the arena. This simulator was written in java, with the source code available (an open source project).

The controller needs to transmit commands to airplanes in order to: (1) launch planes at airports; (2) land planes at airports (by instructing them to go to altitude zero when exactly over the airport); and (3) maneuver planes out of exit points. There are many different types of commands the controller can transmit to an airplane, such as change altitude, change direction, turn it towards a beacon, and delay with circle trajectory, among others. However, in this simulator, the controller cannot modify the speed of the planes. Each plane has a destination, either an airport or an exit point. Planes can run out of fuel, miss their target destination, and collide. Collision is defined as adjacency in any of the three dimensions. The simulator displays the current airplanes in the flight arena, their direction and positioning (in the radar), their destination, and their current maneuvers in action (commands). Besides the indication of low fuel in airplanes, no other alert or indication of dangerous situations are displayed to the controller.

We decided to use the ATC in this experiment because it presents a very special domain, where specific analyses are required. Since the simulator performs no analysis over the traffic itself, there are many different types of analyses that are relevant to the controller. Some examples of the types of analysis are: collision detection and avoidance analysis; route-destination analysis; statistics on performance and throughput analysis; identification of all planes that may transit through the route of one specific plane (useful to modify the route of planes in a hijack situation, for example); among others.

The simulator was instrumented in order to have the following types of event collected by the monitoring system:

- **AirplaneStatus Event**: contains the current status information about one airplane, including its ID, positioning, direction, and destination. In every update of the radar, one of such event is collected for each plane in the arena and sent to the monitor.
- **ArenaElementStatus Event**: contains the status information about one arena element, basically including its type (airport, beacon, entry/exit point), ID, positioning, and some extra information depending on the element type. Periodically, but not necessarily at every radar update, one of such event is collected for each arena element and sent to the monitor. In this ATC simulator, the arena cannot be modified dynamically. However, it is useful to have the arena status being updated periodically because, in a real case scenario, the arena may really change (for instance, by having an airport closed

due to difficult weather condition), and current monitor services would be able to handle modifications in the arena.

In order to collect these events in the ATC system, two classes were instrumented – the Plane class (for "AirplaneStatus" event) and the component ATCData (for "ArenaElementStatus" events). No further instrumentation was required in the other components of the ATCJ system.

We started this experiment by monitoring the ATC system and performing collision detection and avoidance analysis.

4.2.1 Collision Detection Analysis

The initial purpose for our monitor is to perform collision detection and avoidance analysis. For this analysis, a CollisionDetection service was developed, where only the positioning of the airplanes is relevant to determine a collision situation. This service keeps a record of airplanes positions, which is updated by incoming AirplaneStatus events. If during a certain period an AirplaneStatus event for one recorded airplane is not collected (for example, after two or three radar updates), the detection service simply removes the airplane record, since the airplane may have exited the flight arena or landed in an airport. It is important to mention that an airplane position may disappear in the radar due to another reason besides exiting or landing and, in such cases, the disappearance should be alerted to the controller, however this kind of analysis is out of the scope of the Collision Detection service – this analysis would be better performed by another monitoring service.

In order to assist in collision avoidance, this service allows different levels of collision safety: from level 5 (green), with no alert of collision, down to level 1 (red), where the collision happens (an actual collision is imminent and possibly unavoidable), with different levels of near-misses in between. Standards for defining these levels may change along the time or be different among various flight arenas.

There were different possible ways to provide the Collision Detection service for this experiment. One option is to use (reusing or developing) a generic analysis service that is based on a formal specification language, and describe the collision detection and avoidance property in such specification language. With exactly the purpose of formally specifying the requirements for TCAS II (Traffic Collision Avoidance System), Leveson et al. [8] have proposed RSML (Requirement State Machine Language) a requirement specification language based on finite state machines and statecharts, simple and readable but with a solid formal and mathematical semantics.

A second option is to use (developing) a domain specific analysis service, with its initial configuration described in a specification language restricted to the domain. The disadvantage of this option in relation with the first option is that this analysis service will only be useful to monitor systems related to Air Traffic Control domain, and perhaps other domains that involve elements in motion in the 3D space. In addition, the domain brings restrictions to the service and the description language, what can reduce the flexibility in modifying the properties analyzed in the service. The advantage of this second option is that description languages specific to a domain, although more restricted, can be simpler and easier to read, write and understand than generic specification languages. Besides, the domain specific analysis services can be optimized for better performance in a more straightforward way.

Instead of taking the approach of the first option, we decided to take the second option in this experiment. Taking the first option would be similar to the approach taken in our first case study. In the first case study, we used a generic analysis service which configuration for analysis was provided by a generic specification language. There, the specification language was based on regular expression semantics; in this case study, the specification language would be based on the semantics of state machines (similarly to the statechart monitoring capability performed in Argus-I [15]). Besides, by deciding on the second option, we want to demonstrate the versatility of the MonArch approach in developing and providing domain specific analyses services as well, in addition to generic analysis services. Since this service is domain specific, the semantics of its specification language is based the concepts of distance between airplanes, difference of altitude, alert sign levels, velocity, direction, among others. The configuration of the monitor system is presented in Fig. 17.

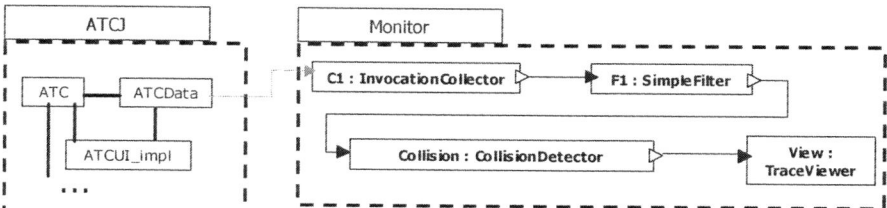

Fig. 17. ATC System and Monitor Configuration

4.2.3 Other Analyses

After configuring the CollisionDetection service, we added some other analysis services to the monitor: Route-Destination analysis and Departure notification.

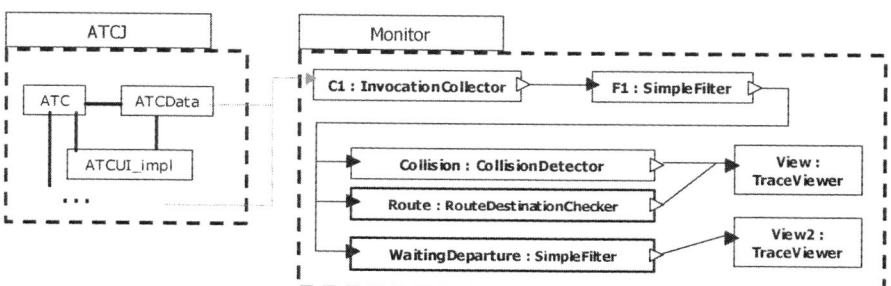

Fig. 18. Other Analysis Services Added to the Monitor

The purpose of the Route-Destination analysis service is to identify those airplanes that are not in the correct route to their destination. This service should consider the flight navigation plan, the commands the airplane received from the controller and all reroutes and delays that may naturally occur. For this experiment, we have a simplified and domain specific service, where navigation plans, reroutes and delays were not considered. The service verifies if the airplane is going towards (or reducing the distance to) its destination.

The Departure notification service basically identifies those planes that are ready for departure but waiting for the controller authorization. Whenever a new plane is waiting for departure, the ATC simulator simply shows the plane in the radar, but no further explicit notification for the controller, and keeping track of all airplanes waiting for departure without an auxiliary mechanism is not reliable and is an unnecessary overhead to the controller. For this service, in this experiment, we used the SimpleFilter service for departure notification, identifying those airplanes that have altitude zero and do not have permission to take off. This filter detects AirplaneStatus events that characterize the mentioned situation, and passes these events to a new visualization service, in order to provide a more organized display to the controller.

4.3 MonArch Version of GEM

GEM [9] is a powerful and generic monitoring system that can be used to process and disseminate events for many different applications, and it allows some level of dynamic configuration of the monitor. The dynamic configuration it supports is dynamic upload of rules (described in GEM specification language) and dynamic distribution and dissemination of processes in a network environment.

We decided GEM would make a good example to mainly evaluate if the MonArch approach supports the development of existent monitors, and how difficult this task would be. In this case study, we studied some of the key features present in GEM, and show how these features are supported in a MonArch version of GEM.

Following the common approach for development of monitoring systems (see Fig. 7), GEM is based on a specification language that describes the processing or analysis to be performed by the monitor. In order to identify the main key features of GEM, we briefly describe some of GEM main features below (details and further discussion of this experiment are presented in [6]).

4.3.1 GEM Main Features
The main set of features provided by GEM (in its services) are the following:

- *Event Attributes*. Every event has some event independent attributes (id, source id, timestamp) and dependent attributes (attributes specific to the event type).
- *Event Correlation and Expressions*. GEM performs event correlation based on extended regular expression notation, with guards and timing features.
- *Guards*. Boolean expressions involving event attributes that work as constraints in the event correlation process.
- *Timed Events (at, every)*. It allows events being triggered based on timing constraints. For example, an event may be generated at a specific time or based on a frequency rate.
- *Detection Window*. Basically, detection window defines the time how long an event should be used for correlation.

- *Notify, Forward and Trigger.* When an event is triggered, GEM tries to fire as many correlation rules as possible with that definition (i.e., a triggered event can be used to trigger other events in the correlation). On the other hand, notify and forward commands sends events to external applications, and these events are not used for further processing in the correlation mechanism.

4.3.2 MonArch Version of GEM

Since GEM basically collects events, processes them, and disseminates the results to other applications or other GEM monitors, no presentation service is provided. Therefore, our MonArch version of GEM has no visualization services in its composition. It has a *Collector* service, which receive events from the external environment, and also a *Sender* service, which disseminates the externally visible events to the external environment (external applications). Most services present in our MonArch version of GEM were reused from our common set of services, including SimpleFilter (a Filter component) and RETimedPatternMatcher (an Abstractor monitor component, which allows configurable detection window). A generic Timed Event Generator component was used in this experiment to provide the same features present in GEM (with commands *at* and *every*). In addition, a new service (the GEM Event Generator) was built in order to reproduce the commands notify, forward and trigger (while notify and forward commands send events to an external application – through the sender service, triggered events are sent back for processing.

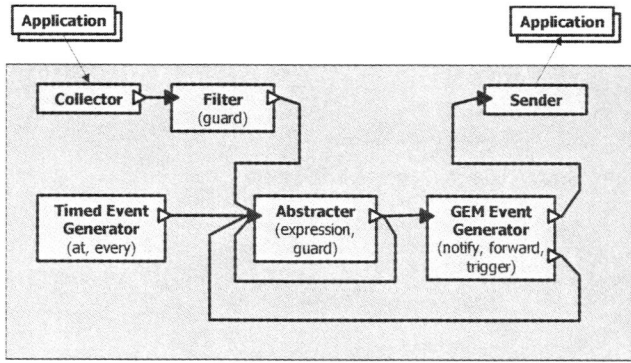

Fig. 19. MonArch Version of GEM

5 Related Work

Monitoring has been around since the early 1960s with the advent of debuggers, and today they monitor distributed applications and are often themselves distributed. There are many monitor systems currently available for different purposes [4]. Monitoring has matured in its ability to give users freedom in defining what is to be monitored. Monitor systems are usually classified [6][11] into traditional monitoring (with focus on post-mortem analysis and presentation - e.g. Historical DB[13]) and online monitoring (focus on analysis and actions at execution time - e.g. EBBA[3], EDEM[7], Argus [15], STAT [16]). The MonArch framework allows the construction of monitor systems that can be in either one of those categories, and also on both at the same time - that is, the MonArch framework and approach allow monitors to perform both online and post-mortem analyses.

Although most existent monitors are target specific and do not allow users to describe what should be monitored, many monitors were developed to allow the user to describe and configure it through a specification language with a well defined semantics, as detailed in [6]. The monitors that allow the user to describe what should be monitored usually permit the description in only one of the following semantics: extended regular expressions (EBBA[3], EDEM[7], GEM[9]), boolean expression trees (HiFi [2]), relational algebra (Historical DB[13]), state machine model (Argus [15], STAT [16]), among others. A more detailed comparison and discussion about those and other monitoring systems is available at [4]. Although most monitors that allow user description require the description to be defined before the monitoring is in execution, some allow dynamic loading or configuration of such descriptions, such as STAT [16]. Similarly, in the MonArch approach, services can be configured not only before execution but also at runtime (although the current implementation only allows this dynamic modification through direct user interaction). In addition, MonArch also allows the configuration of the set of analysis (or other monitoring) services being performed by the monitor, and is not limited to only one specification language.

Although analysis is not the main goal of event-based middleware and publish-subscribe infrastructures, they involve event correlation and its specification, which plays an important role in monitoring service specification as well. Current research on these areas include dynamic configuration (loading) of specification for event correlation during subscription requests (e.g., Yancces [12]). However, to the best of our knowledge, current event-based middleware technology is also limited to specific languages and semantics to describe how event correlation will be performed.

6 Conclusions

Our society becomes every day more dependent on complex software systems with high availability requirements, and many businesses and operations depend on reliable and uninterruptible performance of their systems. Attending to the demands of a fast paced society, maintenance and evolution of such complex and dependable systems are required, but a difficult task to perform, even harder when considering that the services provided by those systems cannot be interrupted.

Software engineers face a critical challenge during maintenance and evolution of dependable systems that is to verify, measure, and ensure their quality. The high availability requirement of such systems demands that maintenance and evolution be performed at runtime. The dynamic evolution of such systems imposes some problems for system verification, and the kinds of analysis may need to be redefined to properly verify the modification in the system.

In addition, even when dependable systems are simply in operation (that is, not passing through maintenance or evolution), their inherent complexity associated with new or unforeseen life situations may require modification in the kinds of analysis necessary to properly verify them.

Given the fundamental role complex and dependable systems play in our society, research concerning verification of such system is very important. This importance becomes even stronger when dealing with maintenance and evolution of such systems, when analysis should be performed: (1) before the changes are put in place in the system (to avoid incorrect system behavior); and also (2) after these modifications happen, to check their actual effect over the system behavior. The focus of this work is in the second point.

6.1 Future Work

In this work, we focused on the analysis (or processing) services supported by monitors. Further exploration in the other types of monitoring services is envisioned, such as services for collection, persistence, distribution, visualization, and actions. Research on services for visualization and actions are very important and interesting, given the importance of properly displaying the results of analysis, and that services (or agents) responsible for taking actions can play a major role in the monitoring system.

One limitation of the current implementation framework is that, although the MonArch approach allows adaptation to the set of analyses and services performed, there is no service (MonArch component) currently available that is able to perform these adaptations automatically, and the human intervention is still required for such dynamic adaptations. And agents are exactly the services that can give more control and power to any monitoring system, allowing it to take actions over itself, over the system under analysis, and also over the environment around it. One of the points to be considered when providing these agent services is the specification of how automatic changes should be applied dynamically to the monitor, and again different agents can provide different mechanisms for this self-adaptation of the monitor system.

The MonArch approach involves the distribution not only of the services, but also the distribution of the overall analysis description. Different services are described separately with the goal to allow dynamic changes in the set of services, and also in the hope to simplify the analysis description within different aspects present in monitoring systems. However, more study is required to assess how more manageable the analysis specification become for the software engineer to describe the analyses. Further research is also necessary on dynamic and automatic mechanisms for instrumentation of the target application.

Future work also involves making better support tools available, using different technologies for the framework, and other supporting mechanisms for service-oriented architectures. Comparing reliability and performance of our approach with different mechanisms and heterogeneous platforms are important to understand and estimate the interference caused by the monitor, and use this information to make the services more aware of their intrusion and allowing them to perform the needed adjustments.

Although we focused on analysis services, these analyses are performed once the changes occur in the target system or in the purpose for analysis. For system evolution, it is also important to explore different types of analysis that need to be performed before the changes take place in the system. The combination of analyses performed before the changes and after the changes is promising and very important for software maintenance and evolution, and to explore this combination is another goal of our future work.

6.2 Contributions

The contributions of this work are:

- **A conceptual framework for classification of the basic services in dynamic analysis.** We developed a conceptual framework presented in [4] providing an organized basis for: (1) comparing and distinguishing types of services present in a monitoring system; (2) separating different concerns of monitor services; and (3) orienting the development of other services.
- **An approach that allows the composition of the analysis based on service-oriented components and the reconfiguration of the monitor system services during system operation.** Different types of analysis may be necessary on highly available and complex systems, and by composing monitors from service-oriented components allows the reconfiguration of the overall analysis, even during the system execution.
- **An approach that allows different specification languages being used to describe the properties of interest for analysis.** The architectural style and the service oriented components allow different analysis services to rely on descriptions written in the same or in different specification languages.
- **An approach that allows and encourages the reuse of services (and specification languages) between different monitoring systems.** The separation of concerns present in the conceptual framework allows generic and not-so-generic analysis services to be reused in different monitors. The approach encourages the existence of a library of analysis services that one can use whenever needed, and use only those services really required, in order to reduce analysis processing and interference on the system execution.
- **A prototype implementation of the approach.** The prototype includes framework and supporting tools for flexibly building and evolving dynamic monitor architectures.

Another important contribution of this work was to highlight that configuration or preparation of a monitor system may happen not only before it is in operation (see Fig. 20). Indeed, when dealing with high available and dependent systems, constant preparation of the monitor system may be required, and reconfiguration mechanisms should be provided, to modify not only the description of the properties being analyzed, but also the set of analyses performed.

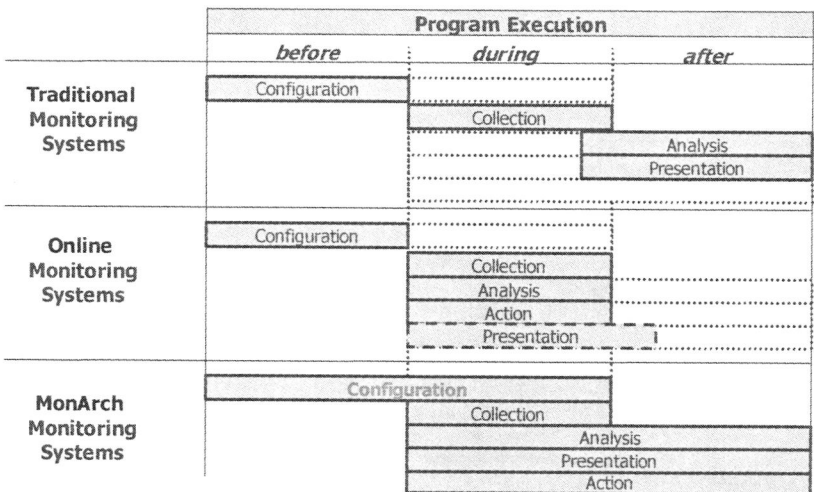

Fig. 20. Monitor configuration performed during system execution

Acknowledgments

The authors gratefully acknowledge the National Science Foundation, which partially supported this work. We are indebted to the ROSATEA research group for their valuable insights.

References

1. Air Traffic Control Simulator – Source Forge Project [http://sourceforge.net/projects/atcj/]
2. E. Al-Shaer, "A Hierarchical Filtering-based Monitoring Architecture for Large-scale Distributed Systems", Ph.D. Dissertation, Computer Science Department, Old Dominion University, December 1998.
3. P. Bates, "Debugging heterogeneous distributed systems using event-based models of behavior", ACM Trans Computer System, vol. 13, n. 1, Feb. 1995, pp. 1 – 31.
4. M. Dias & D. Richardson, "Issues on Software Monitoring", ICS Technical Report, Department of Information and Computer Science, University of California, Irvine, CA, July 2002.
5. M. Dias & D. Richardson, "Issues in Analyzing Dynamic System Evolution", In: Proceedings of the IASTED International Conference on Software Engineering and Applications, Marina del Rey, USA, November 03-05, 2003.
6. M. Dias, "A Flexible and Dynamic Approach for Reconfigurable Software Monitoring", Ph.D. Dissertation, Department of Informatics, School of Information and Computer Science, University of California, Irvine, December 2004.
7. D. Hilbert, "Large-Scale Collection of Application Usage Data and User Feedback to Inform Interactive Software Development", Ph.D. Dissertation, Information and Computer Science Department, University of California at Irvine, 1999.

8. N.L. Leveson, M.P.E. Heimdahl, H. Hildreth, and J.D. Reese, "Requirements specification for process-control systems", IEEE Trans. Software Engineering, vol. 20, n. 9, 1994, pp. 684-707.
9. M. Mansouri-Samani, "Monitoring of Distributed Systems", Ph.D. Dissertation, Department of Computing, University of London, December 1995.
10. N. Medvidovic, D. Rosenblum, R. Taylor, "A Language and Environment for Architecture-Based Software Development and Evolution", In: Proceedings of 21 st International Conference on Software Engineering, Los Angeles, CA, May 1999.
11. B. Schroeder, "On-Line Monitoring: A Tutorial", IEEE Computer, vol. 28, n. 6, June 1995, pp.72-77.
12. R.S. Silva Filho, C.R.B. de Souza, D.F. Redmiles, "The Design of a Configurable, Extensible and Dynamic Notification Service". in Proc. Second International Workshop on Distributed Event-Based Systems (DEBS'03), In conjunction with The ACM SIGMOD/PODS Conference, San Diego, CA, USA, pp.1-8, June 8th, 2003.
13. R. Snodgrass, "A Relational Approach to Monitoring Complex Systems", ACM Trans. on Computer Systems, vol. 6, n. 2, May 1988, pp.156-196.
14. R. Taylor, N. Medvidovic, K. Anderson, E. Whitehead, J. Robbins, K. Nies, P. Oreizy, and D. Dubrow. "A Component- and Message-Based Architectural Style for GUI Software." IEEE Transactions on Software Engineering, vol. 22, no. 6, June 1996, pages 390-406.
15. M. Vieira, M. Dias, D. Richardson, "Analyzing Software Architecture with Argus-I", Proc Int'l Conf on Software Engineering, June 2000, pp. 758 –761.
16. G. Vigna, S.T. Eckmann, and R.A. Kemmerer, "The STAT Tool Suite," in Proceedings of DISCEX 2000, Hilton Head, South Carolina, January 2000, IEEE Press.

Runtime Verification of Statechart Implementations*

Gergely Pintér and István Majzik

Budapest University of Technology and Economics,
Department of Measurement and Information Systems,
Magyar Tudósok krt. 2., H-1117 Budapest, Hungary
{pinter, majzik}@mit.bme.hu

Abstract. Our paper introduces a *runtime verification framework* for concurrent monitoring of applications specified by UML statecharts. The approach offers a considerable degree of granularity by (i) enabling the modeler to focus on specific key dependability criteria by defining *temporal logic formulae* over a *behavioral model* that is available even in early phases of the development and (ii) by supporting the verification of the final implementation against the *fully elaborated UML statechart model*. The paper presents an extension of the propositional linear temporal logic that fits to the advanced constructs of UML statecharts and an advanced watchdog scheme for concurrent supervision of program execution based on the statechart specification.

Keywords: Runtime verification, temporal logic, UML statecharts.

1 Introduction

As the dependence of the society on computer-based systems is increasing the correctness of software artifacts is a primary concern. It is widely recognized that software *model checking* is a complicated task and in case of large systems often infeasible. Traditional *testing* scales well to systems of any complexity and is a commonly used technique, however the fault coverage of testing is hard to measure and it is difficult to reason about the number of remaining faults after the testing phase.

Runtime verification is a combination of formal methods and testing: executable assertions are derived from formal software models and are evaluated in appropriate phases of the execution. This approach avoids several drawbacks of ad-hoc testing and the state space explosion phenomenon of model checking.

Our paper presents a *runtime verification framework* (Fig. 1) for UML statechart realizations and outlines the design and implementation of the key components. The approach offers a *considerable degree of granularity* by simultaneously enabling (i) the definition of dependability criteria even in *early phases of the development* based on temporal logic formulae and (ii) using the fully elaborated behavioral model as reference information for monitoring the implementation:

---

* This research was supported by the Hungarian Scientific Research Fund (OTKA T-046527) and the Bolyai Fellowship of the Hungarian Academy of Sciences.

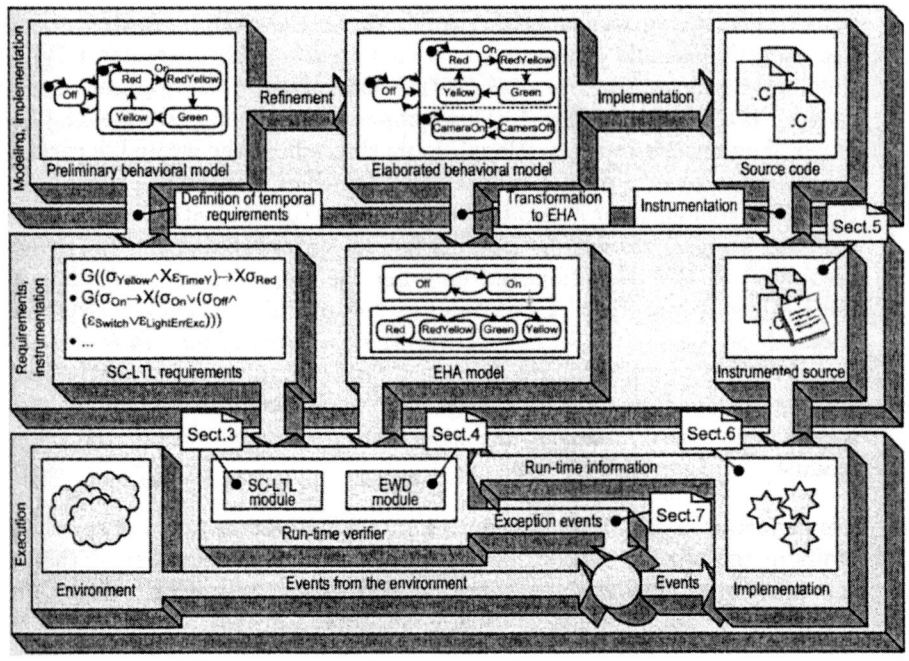

Fig. 1. Runtime verification framework

- The key dependability criteria against software systems are defined during the *requirement analysis* or in the *early modeling* phases (temporal requirements, fail-safe operation etc.) while only *preliminary behavioral models* are available. Since these models specify the most important states and transitions only, they *can not be used* directly for checking the implementation however it would be beneficial to formally define some correctness requirements at the very beginning of the development. Our approach supports the definition of temporal requirements even in the early development phases by providing a *temporal logic language for UML statecharts* (SC-LTL) and a corresponding *runtime verifier component (SC-LTL module* in Fig. 1). Sect. 2 discusses how to *map the key statechart features to Kripke-structures* (the underlying mathematical model of temporal logic languages), Sect. 3 defines the SC-LTL language and outlines an efficient method for *implementing the verifier module*.
- During the subsequent *model refinement steps* the developers prepare the *fully elaborated behavioral model* of the system that is *implemented* following a pattern (template) based systematic approach by manual programming or automatic source code generation. The final behavioral model can be *directly used* for runtime detection of deviations from the behavior specified by the statechart. Our approach is capable of using the elaborated behavioral specification for runtime verification: UML statecharts are transformed to Extended Hierarchical Automata (EHA) that is used as a reference

model for a statechart-level (EHA-level) runtime verifier component. Since the operation of this component is similar to a watchdog processor (WD) that detects deviations from the control flow graph of the application it is called *EWD module* in Fig. 1. This component is capable of detecting behavioral anomalies and operational errors throughout the entire life cycle of the observed object: proper *initialization* (entering the states belonging to the initial configuration), *event processing* (selecting transitions to be fired) and the *firing of transitions* (leaving source states, performing the action associated to the transition and entering the target states) according to the UML semantics. Sect. 2 outlines the *syntax and semantics* of Extended Hierarchical Automata, Sect. 4 specifies the *operation of the runtime behavior monitor* by protocol state machines, Sect. 5 outlines a straightforward way for *implementing the necessary instrumentation* and Sect. 6 presents a discussion about *assessing the error detection capabilities* of the EWD module.

It is important to highlight that during runtime verification we are searching for errors in the *implementation* (programming and refinement errors) that is considered to be a *black box realization of the abstract behavioral model*. This way a *runtime verifier* is significantly different from a *model checker*:

- The runtime verifier is a *passive observer*: while a model checker can simulate *all possible execution paths* for revealing all behavioral errors that *may be exposed* by the system, a runtime verifier can only observe the *behavior actually exposed* by the system. Note that in the user's point of view behavioral anomalies that *potentially* reside within the system but are *never triggered* are of no importance, like buggy code fragments that are never executed.
- The runtime verifier can not conclude about the *overall correctness* of the system since it does not see all possible execution paths (even if it happens to investigate all paths during a sufficiently long execution can not realize this fact because of the black box nature of the approach). Obviously having detected an error by the runtime verifier indicates that the system is incorrect.
- Because of being a passive observer the runtime verifier can not directly evaluate atomic propositions in specific states: it has to *obtain the runtime information* from the implementation. This can be an interface for *polling* the necessary information or a *communication protocol* through which the implementation *pushes* the runtime information to the observer.
- Model checkers are usually applied for proving the correctness of *protocols* or *state machines* that theoretically run for *infinitely long time* by performing cycles in the state space. During runtime verification we are investigating *real software* that is started once and after a time it is shut down – this is the reason for having defined SC-LTL above *finite traces*.
- The runtime verifier is practically an *embedded component* in the system, its CPU requirements and memory consumption should be as low as possible.

Since the temporal logic requirements can be formalized even in a very early stage of the development while the fully elaborated behavioral model is only available before the implementation phase, the errors (besides the operational ones) targeted by the methods can be classified this way (Tab. 1.):

- Requirements formalized by temporal logic in the *early stages* of the development express the correctness criteria in a relatively *non-technical form*, not influenced by the further model refinement decisions enabling this way the *detection of errors introduced in the model refinement process* (e.g., violation of the original behavioral specification by introducing illegal transitions).
- The fully elaborated behavioral model that is available only at *late stages of the development* can be used for *detecting errors introduced during the implementation step* (misunderstood specification, coding bugs etc.).

Table 1. Key characteristics of runtime verification modules

	SC-LTL module	EWD module
Development phase	Requirement analysis (early)	Before implementation (late)
Reference information	Temporal logic (SC-LTL)	Elaborated statechart (EHA)
Targeted faults	Invalid model refinement, misunderstood specification	Implementation faults, operational faults

Detecting temporal and behavioral errors is a key facility in dependable systems but from the point of view of the fault-tolerant behavior it is only the *first step* for initiating the *recovery process* (error confinement, damage assessment, fail-over mechanisms etc.). Our approach enables the developers to apply the advanced modeling constructs and high expressive power of UML statecharts not only for modeling the behavior during *normal operation* but *even in exceptional situations* by introducing the concept of *exception events* for indicating the anomalies detected by the runtime verification facilities. Exception events are ordinary UML statechart events that represent the detection of an exceptional situation that requires some special handling.

Exception events can be used for representing programming language level exceptions and specifying the corresponding exception handling enabling this way the initiation of a *system-level recovery mechanisms* in case of component errors that would be hard to implement when relying only on the facilities provided by the programming language. By introducing the error detection signals as UML statechart events the behavioral model becomes closed *even with respect to the reaction to abnormal situations*: the entire behavior can be specified by the statecharts of the application enabling this way the modeling, model checking and code generation based on the abstract visual language. Sect. 7 outlines our research related to handling exceptional situations by exception events.

The final section of the paper (Sect. 8) concludes the discussion and outlines the directions of our future research.

2 Formal Models

The runtime verification framework proposed in this paper uses multiple behavior specification formalisms. This section discusses the key features of *UML statecharts* (visual behavior specification formalism of the Unified Modeling Language), *Extended Hierarchical Automata* (alternative syntax of UML statecharts) and introduces a direct *Kripke-structure* representation of statecharts.

2.1 UML Statecharts

Abstract Syntax. The State Machine package of UML specifies a set of concepts to be used for modeling discrete behavior through finite state-transition systems. The *syntax* is precisely defined by the metamodel (i.e., a class diagram describing the model elements) in the standard. Besides the fundamental building elements UML statecharts provide several sophisticated constructs.

States model situations during which some invariant condition holds. Optional *entry* and *exit actions* can be associated to them to be performed whenever the state is entered or exited.

Transitions are directed relationships between a source and a target state. An optional action can be associated to them to be performed when the transition fires. Transitions can be *guarded* by Boolean expressions that are evaluated when an event instance is dispatched by the state machine. If the guard is true at that time, the transition is enabled, otherwise it is disabled.

States can be refined into *substates* resulting in a state hierarchy. The decomposition can be simple *refinement* (only one of the substates is active at the same time) or *orthogonal division* where all the substates (called regions) are active at the same time. Join and fork vertices can be used to represent transitions originating from or ending in states in different orthogonal regions. Transitions are allowed to cross hierarchy levels.

Operational Semantics. The *operational semantics* is expressed *informally* in the standard using the terms of a *hypothetical machine*. The key components of this machine are: (i) an *event queue* that holds incoming events until they are dispatched, (ii) a *dispatcher mechanism* that selects and de-queues event instances from the event queue for processing and (iii) an *event processor* that processes dispatched events according to the semantics of statecharts. In the following a short overview is given about the operation.

The semantics of event processing is based on the *run-to-completion* (RTC) assumption i.e., an event can only be dequeued and dispatched if the processing of the previous one is fully completed. After receiving an event a maximal set of enabled transitions is selected that are not in conflict with each other and there is no enabled transition outside the set with higher priority than a transition in the set. The transitions selected this way fire in an unspecified order.

A transition is *enabled* if all of its source states are active, the event satisfies its trigger and its guard is enabled. Two transitions are in *conflict* if the intersection of the states they exit is non-empty. *Priority* of transition t_1 is higher than the priority of t_2 if the source state of t_1 is a directly or transitively nested substate of the source state of t_2. The exact *sequence of actions* to be performed when taking a transition is specified by the standard with respect to the *state refinement hierarchy*: first the exit actions of all states left by the transition are executed starting with the deepest one in the hierarchy, next the action associated to the transition is performed finally the entry actions of states entered by the transition are executed starting with the highest one in the hierarchy.

Events. The UML event concept (Event metaclass) is defined as a "type of an observable occurrence". The base *Event* metaclass is refined to four metaclasses (Fig. 2) indicating that a Boolean expression became true (*ChangeEvent*), expiration of a deadline (*TimeEvent*), request for invoking an operation synchronously (*CallEvent*) and reception of an asynchronous signal (*SignalEvent*) respectively. The *SignalEvent* metaclass is associated to the *Signal* metaclass that represents an asynchronous stimulus received by an object. The *Signal* metaclass is a *generalizable element*. Using this feature UML events can be considered as generalizable classes that can be organized into a *refinement hierarchy*.

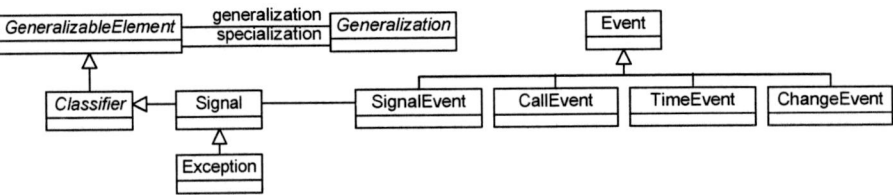

Fig. 2. The UML event concept

For example the left part of Fig. 3 presents the statechart of a traffic light controller as drawn in an early phase of the development, while the class diagram on the right side depicts the event refinement hierarchy. (Since transitions in UML have no names, unique numeric identifiers were assigned and indicated in parentheses before the trigger event in the figure for easier discussion.) The traffic light can be in the normal operational state *(On)* or switched off *(Off)*. Transitions 1 and 6 between the two top states are triggered by the *Switch* event. While being switched on the light can be red, red and yellow, green and yellow (states *Red*, *RedYellow*, *Green* and *Yellow* respectively). Transitions between these states (2, 3, 4, 5) are triggered by the corresponding time events (e.g., the time for switching from green to yellow is signalled by the *TimeG* event). The traffic light implements a basic fail-silent behavior: an internal electronic component detects the failures of the light bulbs and indicates this situation by sending the *LightErr* event. This event triggers transition 7 between *Off* and *On* (the associated action may switch off all the lights in the crossing, etc.).

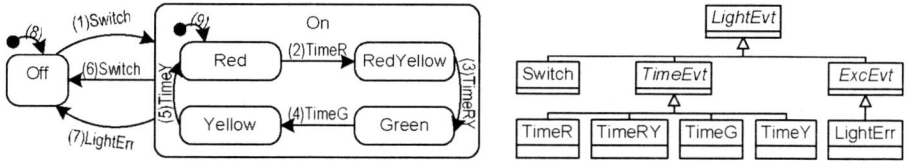

Fig. 3. Preliminary statechart of a traffic light

The root of the event hierarchy is the abstract *LightEvt* class. Two further abstract event classes are derived from it: *TimeEvt* (ancestor of timing-related events) and *ExcEvt* (abstraction of events signalling exceptional situations). The *Switch* event is directly derived from the *LightEvt* base class, the *LightErr* event is derived from *ExcEvt*. *TimeR*, *TimeRY* etc. are derived from *TimeEvt*.

2.2 Extended Hierarchical Automata

Abstract Syntax. Since the operational semantics of UML statecharts is expressed mainly *informally* in the standard, it is not ideal for model-checking purposes [1], [2]. Model-checking approaches published in the literature are based on behavioral description formalisms that have *formally specified operational semantics*. Probably the one that is closest to the advanced features of statecharts is the *Extended Hierarchical Automaton* (EHA) notation [1], [2].

An EHA consists of *sequential automata*. A sequential automaton contains simple (non-composite) *states* and *transitions*. EHA states represent simple and composite states of the UML model. States can be *refined* to any number of sequential automata. All automata refining a state are running concurrently (i.e. a concurrent composite state of a UML statechart is modeled by an EHA state refined to several automata representing one region each).

Source and target states of an EHA transition are always in the same automaton. UML transitions connecting states at different hierarchy levels are represented by transitions with special guards and labels containing the original source and target states called *source restriction* and *target determination* respectively. At most one state in an automaton can be labeled as the *initial state* of the automaton building up the initial *state configuration* of the EHA.

Operational Semantics. The *operational semantics* (transition selection) is expressed by a Kripke-structure in [2]. The EHA semantics is proven to resemble the informal semantics of UML statecharts, which allows using EHA as the representation of statecharts in formal analysis and code generation frameworks.

For example the EHA equivalent of the traffic light's statechart (Fig. 3) is shown in Fig. 4. The top sequential automaton contains two states: *On* and *Off*. The *On* state is refined to a sequential automaton with the states representing the substates of the *On* composite state in the original statechart.

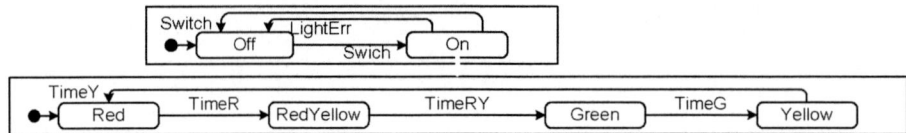

Fig. 4. EHA equivalent of the traffic light

2.3 Kripke-Structure

Kripke-structures can be considered as very simple state machines. States can not be refined, the transitions are expressed by a transition relation and labels are assigned to the states. Kripke-structures are used at two places in our verification framework for formally specifying behavioral models: both the underlying operational semantics of Extended Hierarchical Automata and the SC-LTL temporal logic language are also defined with the terms of a Kripke-structure.

This subsection introduces a *formal notation* for referring to UML statechart features to be used in atomic propositions of the SC-LTL language (states, events, transitions and actions), discusses how to collect information describing all possible RTC steps of the statechart and defines how to represent the operation of the UML statechart with the states and labeling of a Kripke-structure.

Note that for the purpose of runtime checking SC-LTL formulae the Kripke-structure, as defined by the formal operational semantics of the EHA is not sufficient. Checking the temporal ordering of *events*, and *actions* requires to include *run-to-completion steps* (labeled by the corresponding events and actions) in the formal model. Accordingly, the formal model of SC-LTL is obtained by re-structuring and enhancing the formal model of the EHA. In the following, for the sake of easy understanding, the formal model of the SC-LTL is presented directly in terms of the UML statechart instead of using the terms of the EHA.

Formal Notation. Let M be a UML statechart. The *states* of M (simple and composite ones) are in the σ set: $\sigma = \{\sigma_1, \sigma_2, \ldots \sigma_m\}$. The *transitions* of the statechart are in the τ set: $\tau = \{\tau_1, \tau_2, \ldots \tau_n\}$. The classes of *events* possibly received by the statechart are in the ϵ set: $\epsilon = \{\epsilon_1, \epsilon_2, \ldots \epsilon_o\}$.

The event refinement facility of UML is supported by by the *event refinement relation*: $\rho_\epsilon \subseteq \epsilon \times \epsilon$ and $(\epsilon_i, \epsilon_j) \in \rho_\epsilon$ if and only if the event class ϵ_j is directly derived from the event class ϵ_i. Let us use the symbol $\epsilon_\emptyset \in \epsilon$ as an empty trigger event to be used in case of transitions without explicit trigger. Furthermore we introduce the multi-step event refinement relation (ρ_ϵ^N) and the closure of the refinement (ρ_ϵ^*). Informally: ρ_ϵ^N collects those (ϵ_i, ϵ_j) pairs where ϵ_j is derived from ϵ_i in N steps, ρ_ϵ^* collects those (ϵ_i, ϵ_j) pairs where ϵ_j is derived from ϵ_i in any steps. (Obviously the refinement graph is acyclic.)

$$\rho_\epsilon^N = \begin{cases} \{(\epsilon_i, \epsilon_i) | \epsilon_i \in \epsilon\} & \text{if } N = 0 \\ \{(\epsilon_i, \epsilon_j) | \epsilon_i, \epsilon_j \in \epsilon \wedge \exists \epsilon_k \in \epsilon : (\epsilon_i, \epsilon_k) \in \rho_\epsilon \wedge (\epsilon_k, \epsilon_j) \in \rho_\epsilon^{N-1}\} & \text{if } N > 0 \end{cases}$$

$$\rho_\epsilon^* = \{(\epsilon_k, \epsilon_j) | \exists N : (\epsilon_k, \epsilon_j) \in \rho_\epsilon^N\}$$

The entry and exit actions of states and the actions associated to the transitions are represented by the α^E, α^X and α^A sets respectively:

- The α^E set contains an element for each $\sigma_i \in \sigma$ states representing the *entry action* of the corresponding state: $\alpha^E = \{\alpha^E_{\sigma_1}, \alpha^E_{\sigma_2}, \ldots \alpha^E_{\sigma_m}\}$.
- The α^X set contains an element for each $\sigma_i \in \sigma$ states representing the *exit action* of the corresponding state: $\alpha^X = \{\alpha^X_{\sigma_1}, \alpha^X_{\sigma_2}, \ldots \alpha^X_{\sigma_m}\}$.
- The α^A set contains an element for each $\tau_i \in \tau$ transitions representing the *action associated* to the corresponding transition: $\alpha^A = \{\alpha^A_{\tau_1}, \alpha^A_{\tau_2}, \ldots \alpha^A_{\tau_n}\}$.

For example in case of the traffic light (Fig. 3) the sets of states (σ), transitions (τ) and events (ϵ), the state entry actions (α^E referenced using the name of the state in subscript), the event refinement relation (ρ_ϵ) and the closure of the refinement (ρ_ϵ^*) are as follows:

$$\sigma = \{\sigma_{Off}, \sigma_{On}, \sigma_{Red}, \sigma_{RedYellow}, \sigma_{Green}, \sigma_{Yellow}\}$$

$$\tau = \{\tau_1, \tau_2, \tau_3, \tau_4, \tau_5, \tau_6, \tau_7, \tau_8, \tau_9\}$$

$$\epsilon = \{\epsilon_{LightEvt}, \epsilon_{Switch}, \epsilon_{TimeEvt}, \epsilon_{ExcEvt},$$
$$\epsilon_{TimeR}, \epsilon_{TimeRY}, \epsilon_{TimeG}, \epsilon_{TimeY}, \epsilon_{LightErr}\}$$

$$\alpha^E = \{\alpha^E_{\sigma_{Off}}, \alpha^E_{\sigma_{On}}, \alpha^E_{\sigma_{Red}}, \alpha^E_{\sigma_{RedYellow}}, \alpha^E_{\sigma_{Green}}, \alpha^E_{\sigma_{Yellow}}\}$$

$$\rho_\epsilon = \{(\epsilon_{LightEvt}, \epsilon_{Switch}), (\epsilon_{LightEvt}, \epsilon_{TimeEvt}), (\epsilon_{LightEvt}, \epsilon_{ExcEvt}),$$
$$(\epsilon_{TimeEvt}, \epsilon_{TimeR}), (\epsilon_{TimeEvt}, \epsilon_{TimeRY}), (\epsilon_{TimeEvt}, \epsilon_{TimeG}),$$
$$(\epsilon_{TimeEvt}, \epsilon_{TimeY}), (\epsilon_{ExcEvt}, \epsilon_{LightErr})\}$$

$$\rho_\epsilon^* = \{(\epsilon_{LightEvt}, \epsilon_{LightEvt}), (\epsilon_{Switch}, \epsilon_{Switch}), (\epsilon_{TimeEvt}, \epsilon_{TimeEvt}),$$
$$(\epsilon_{ExcEvt}, \epsilon_{ExcEvt}), (\epsilon_{TimeR}, \epsilon_{TimeR}), (\epsilon_{TimeRY}, \epsilon_{TimeRY}), (\epsilon_{TimeG}, \epsilon_{TimeG}),$$
$$(\epsilon_{TimeY}, \epsilon_{TimeY}), (\epsilon_{LightErr}, \epsilon_{LightErr}), (\epsilon_{LightEvt}, \epsilon_{Switch}),$$
$$(\epsilon_{LightEvt}, \epsilon_{TimeEvt}), (\epsilon_{LightEvt}, \epsilon_{ExcEvt}), (\epsilon_{TimeEvt}, \epsilon_{TimeR}),$$
$$(\epsilon_{TimeEvt}, \epsilon_{TimeRY}), (\epsilon_{TimeEvt}, \epsilon_{TimeG}), (\epsilon_{TimeEvt}, \epsilon_{TimeY}),$$
$$(\epsilon_{ExcEvt}, \epsilon_{LightErr}), (\epsilon_{LightEvt}, \epsilon_{TimeR}), (\epsilon_{LightEvt}, \epsilon_{TimeRY}),$$
$$(\epsilon_{LightEvt}, \epsilon_{TimeG}), (\epsilon_{LightEvt}, \epsilon_{TimeY}), (\epsilon_{LightEvt}, \epsilon_{LightErr})\}$$

Configurations and RTC Steps. Let the set C contain all possible configurations of the statechart M ($C \subseteq 2^\sigma$). The special $c_\emptyset$ symbol will be used to represent the uninitialized state of the statechart (before entering the initial configuration). Let us collect information about all possible run-to-completion steps of the statechart into data structures of the format:

$$r_i = (c^{src}, c^{trg}, \epsilon_j, \{\alpha^X_{\sigma_{k_1}}, \alpha^X_{\sigma_{k_2}}, \ldots\}, \{\alpha^A_{\tau_{l_1}}, \alpha^A_{\tau_{l_2}}, \ldots\}, \{\alpha^E_{\sigma_{m_1}}, \alpha^E_{\sigma_{m_2}}, \ldots\})$$

where: (i) $c^{src} \in C$ is the source configuration, (ii) $c^{trg} \in C$ is the target configuration, (iii) $\epsilon_j \in \epsilon$ the class of the event that triggered the RTC step, (iv) the set $\{\alpha^X_{\sigma_{k_1}}, \alpha^X_{\sigma_{k_2}}, \ldots\}$ contains the state exit actions that were performed during the RTC step, (v) the set $\{\alpha^A_{\tau_{l_1}}, \alpha^A_{\tau_{l_2}}, \ldots\}$ contains the actions associated to transitions that were performed in the RTC step and (vi) the set $\{\alpha^E_{\sigma_{m_1}}, \alpha^E_{\sigma_{m_2}}, \ldots\}$ contains the state entry actions that were performed during the RTC step.

It is important to highlight that according to the structure and operational semantics of UML statecharts a specific source and target configuration can be connected by *multiple RTC steps*, e.g., in case of the example in Fig. 3 *Off* can be reached from any substates of *On* through the transitions τ_6 and τ_7 this way the RTC step that takes the statechart from the $\{\sigma_{On}, \sigma_{Red}\}$ configuration to the $\{\sigma_{Off}\}$ configuration can be triggered by an event of the class ϵ_{Switch} (transition τ_6) and by an event of the class $\epsilon_{LightErr}$ (transition τ_7).

Let the set R contain all the structures as collected above and a special element that represents the initialization step during which the statechart reaches its initial configuration: $r_\emptyset = (c_\emptyset, c_{init}, \epsilon_\emptyset, \emptyset, \{\alpha^A_{Tl_1}, \alpha^A_{Tl_2}, \dots, \}\{\alpha^E_{\sigma_{k_1}}, \alpha^E_{\sigma_{k_2}}, \dots\})$ where $c_\emptyset$ is the special configuration representing the uninitialized state of the statechart, c_{init} is the initial configuration, the $\epsilon_\emptyset$ empty event indicates that the initial transition is not triggered by any event class, obviously during the RTC step no exit actions are performed ($\emptyset$) and the last two sets indicate the actions associated to the initial transitions and the entry actions of the states in the initial configuration respectively.

For example the configurations of the traffic light (Fig. 3) are as follows: $C = \{\{\sigma_{Off}\}, \{\sigma_{On}, \sigma_{Red}\}, \{\sigma_{On}, \sigma_{RedYellow}\}, \{\sigma_{On}, \sigma_{Green}\}, \{\sigma_{On}, \sigma_{Yellow}\}\}$. Some examples for the RTC steps to be collected into the R set are: $(c_\emptyset, \{\sigma_{Off}\}, \epsilon_\emptyset, \emptyset, \{\alpha^A_{T_8}\}, \{\alpha^E_{\sigma_{Off}}\})$ (initialization), $(\{\sigma_{Off}\}, \{\sigma_{On}, \sigma_{Red}\}, \epsilon_{Switch}, \{\alpha^X_{\sigma_{Off}}\}, \{\alpha^A_{T_1}, \alpha^A_{T_9}\}, \{\alpha^E_{\sigma_{On}}, \alpha^E_{\sigma_{Red}}\})$ (receiving the *Switch* event in the *Off* state), $(\{\sigma_{On}, \sigma_{Red}\}, \{\sigma_{On}, \sigma_{RedYellow}\}, \epsilon_{TimeR}, \{\alpha^X_{\sigma_{Red}}\}, \{\alpha^A_{T_2}\}, \{\alpha^E_{\sigma_{RedYellow}}\})$ (switching to *RedYellow* from *Red*), etc.

Definition of the Kripke-structure. Having collected data about RTC steps the Kripke-structure can be defined by assigning *states to RTC steps*, specifying the transition relation according to the *possible subsequence of RTC steps* and providing the information related to events, actions etc. by labeling of the states.

Definition 1 (Kripke-structure for representing statecharts). *The UML statechart M can be represented by the Kripke-structure K. K is a tuple $K = (S, T, L)$ and L is decomposed as $L = (L_S, L_{Evt}, L_X, L_A, L_E)$ where:*

S is the state set of K. S contains exactly one $s_r \in S$ state for each $r \in R$ run-to-completion step of M.

T ($T \subseteq S \times S$) is the state transition relation. Since states represent RTC steps of the statechart, the state transition relation represents the possible subsequence amongst RTC steps. It is easy to see that an RTC step r_i may be followed by another RTC step r_j if the configuration reached by r_i is the source configuration of r_j. Let s_{r_i} and s_{r_j} ($s_{r_i}, s_{r_j} \in S$) represent the r_i and r_j structures ($r_i, r_j \in R$ where $r_i = (c_i^{src}, c_i^{trg}, e_i, \alpha_i^X, \alpha_i^A, \alpha_i^E)$ and $r_j = (c_j^{src}, c_j^{trg}, e_j, \alpha_j^X, \alpha_j^A, \alpha_j^E)$:

$$T = \{(s_{r_i}, s_{r_j}) | c_i^{trg} = c_j^{src}\}$$

L_S, L_{Evt}, L_X, L_A and L_E ($L_S : S \to 2^\sigma$, $L_{Evt} : S \to \epsilon$, $L_X : S \to 2^{\alpha^X}$, $L_A : S \to 2^{\alpha^A}$, $L_E : S \to 2^{\alpha^E}$) are the labeling functions. L_S indicates the set of statechart states that are active in the target configuration of the RTC step.

L_{Evt} specifies the class of the event that triggers the RTC step. L_X, L_A and L_E specify the state exit actions, actions associated to transitions and state entry actions that were performed in the RTC step respectively. Let $s_{r_i} \in S$ represent the $r_i = (c_i^{src}, c_i^{trg}, e_i, \alpha_i^X, \alpha_i^A, \alpha_i^E)$ structure ($r_i \in R$). The formal definitions of the labeling functions are as follows:

$$L_S(s_{r_i}) = \{s \in \sigma | s \text{ is active in } c_i^{trg}\}$$
$$L_{Evt}(s_{r_i}) = e_i \quad L_X(s_{r_i}) = \alpha_i^X$$
$$L_A(s_{r_i}) = \alpha_i^A \quad L_E(s_{r_i}) = \alpha_i^E$$

2.4 Application of Formal Models

This subsection has introduced the behavioral description formalisms used in our approach. The efficient visual notation of UML statecharts can be considered as the "user interface" of the runtime verification: statecharts are used for describing the behavior in a UML modeler tool and are automatically transformed [3] to EHA for runtime verification of the implementation. Various artifacts of statecharts will be used as atomic propositions in the SC-LTL language. The main contribution of this section, the Kripke-structure defined in the third subsection establishes the mathematical background of the temporal logic language.

3 Verification of Temporal Requirements

Temporal logic languages have been successfully applied for proving the correctness of *communication protocols* and *finite state-transition systems* with respect to various dependability criteria based on the *model-checking* of the abstract behavioral specifications. Several approaches have been published in the literature [4], [5] [6], [7] or released as commercial software [8] for *runtime verification* of temporal requirements based on the instrumentation of the source code etc. According to our knowledge only a single commercial tool (State Rover from the Time-Rover company) aims at addressing the *runtime verification of UML statechart implementations* and unfortunately very few public information is available about the mathematical background and the operation of this software. The goal of this section is to introduce a linear temporal logic language for UML statecharts (SC-LTL) for bridging the gap between the powerful features of the visual language and the precise mathematical formalism. Defining and checking dependability criteria on UML statecharts offers the following benefits:

– Dependability criteria are typically defined in an *early phase of the development* when only preliminary behavioral models are available. Our approach enables the *direct definition of requirements above the preliminary model* even if it is further refined during the development: there is no need to map the requirements to the final implementation reducing this way the possibility of distorting requirements during the transformation process. This application also enables the *discovery of errors introduced during the refinement process.*

– Our approach *bridges the gap* between the precise mathematical formalism and the visual notation of statecharts enabling this way the more *straightforward application of precise formalism* in engineering practice.

The *temporal operators* used in SC-LTL (*next-time* and *until*) are the same as the ones used in many other temporal logic languages. The expressive power is extended by the introduction of various *atomic proposition classes* that refer to advanced UML statechart constructs like the activity of a *state* in a configuration, the *event* triggering a transition and *actions* performed during a run-to-completion step. These atomic proposition classes were introduced by investigating several informally expressed dependability criteria from the field and mapping their concepts to UML statechart features.

The *notion of time* in SC-LTL corresponds to the *run-to-completion* (RTC) concept of UML statecharts. The finite state-transition model behind the SC-LTL language is the Kripke-structure defined in Sect. 2. SC-LTL formulae are evaluated over a *finite trace* of the Kripke-structure.

Definition 2 (Finite trace). *A Π finite trace of a Kripke-structure is a finite sequence of states: $\Pi = (s_0, s_1, \ldots, s_{n-1})$ connected by the state transition relation: $\forall_{0<i<n}(s_{i-1}, s_i) \in T$. The Π^i suffix of the trace is obtained from Π by dropping the first i steps: $\Pi^i = (s_i, s_{i+1}, \ldots, s_{n-1})(i < n)$.*

3.1 Syntax and Semantics of SC-LTL

Definition 3 (Syntax of SC-LTL). *Below we present an inductive definition of the syntax of SC-LTL formulae and introduce the notion of a formula ϕ being true at the trace suffix Π^i denoted by $\Pi^i \models \phi$.*

$\Pi \models \sigma_i$ iff $\sigma_i \in L_S(s_0)$ (*State proposition*)
$\Pi \models \epsilon_i$ iff $(L_{Evt}(s_0), \epsilon_i) \in \rho_\epsilon^*$ (*Event proposition*)
$\Pi \models \alpha_i^X$ iff $\alpha_i^X \in L_X(s_0)$ (*Exit-action proposition*)
$\Pi \models \alpha_i^A$ iff $\alpha_i^A \in L_A(s_0)$ (*Associated-action proposition*)
$\Pi \models \alpha_i^E$ iff $\alpha_i^E \in L_E(s_0)$ (*Entry-action proposition*)
$\Pi \models \neg e$ iff $\Pi \models e$ in not true   (*Boolean not*)
$\Pi \models e_1 \wedge e_2$ iff $\Pi \models e_1$ and $\Pi \models e_2$ (*Boolean and*)
$\Pi \models \mathcal{X} e$ iff $n > 1 \wedge \Pi^1 \models e$ (*Temporal next*)
$\Pi \models e_1 \mathcal{U} e_2$ iff $\exists_{0<i<n}\Pi^i \models e_2$ and   (*Temporal until*)
                   $\forall_{0<j<i} : \Pi^j \models e_1$

Informally: an atomic proposition about a *statechart state* σ_i is true if σ_i is active in the actual configuration. The name of an *event class* ϵ_i as atomic proposition is true if the RTC step was triggered by an event of that class or of a refining class. Propositions about *actions* indicate that the corresponding entry, associated or exit action was performed in the RTC step. This information is provided by the labeling functions. The semantics of the *Boolean operators* is the same as usually. The single argument of the *next-time* operator ($\mathcal{X}$) is evaluated in the next state of the trace, while the *until* operator ($\mathcal{U}$) indicates that the condition expressed by its second argument should be true some time in the future or even in the actual state and until this the condition expressed by the first argument should hold. Based on the basic operators several *shorthand operators* are introduced:

$$\Pi \models e_1 \vee e_2 \quad \text{iff} \quad \Pi \models \neg(\neg e_1 \wedge \neg e_2) \quad \text{(Boolean or)}$$
$$\Pi \models e_1 \rightarrow e_2 \quad \text{iff} \quad \Pi \models \neg e_1 \vee e_2 \quad \text{(Boolean implication)}$$
$$\Pi \models \top \quad \text{(Boolean true)}$$
$$\Pi \models \mathcal{F} e \quad \text{iff} \quad \Pi \models \top \mathcal{U} e \quad \text{(Temporal finally)}$$
$$\Pi \models \mathcal{G} e \quad \text{iff} \quad \Pi \models \neg \mathcal{F} \neg e \quad \text{(Temporal globally)}$$

For example the requirement "however should the basic statechart in Fig. 3 be refined during the development process, the traffic light can only be switched off by the *Switch* or the *LightErr* events" can be formalized as:

$$\mathcal{G}(\sigma_{On} \rightarrow \mathcal{X}(\sigma_{On} \vee (\sigma_{Off} \wedge (\epsilon_{Switch} \vee \epsilon_{LightErr}))))$$

to be read as "it is always true that if the *On* state is active in the statechart's current configuration (the traffic light is switched on) then after the next RTC step it will be still switched on or it will be switched off but only if the event that triggered the RTC step was *Switch* or *LightErr*".

3.2 Runtime Evaluation of SC-LTL Formulae

In the previous discussion the semantics of SC-LTL was introduced on the basis of Kripke-structures by a straightforward extension of the label set assigned to states of the Kripke-structure. Although the language can be used for defining dependability criteria for model-checking, our primary goal is its application for *runtime verification*. The *runtime checking of temporal-logic formulae* aims at detecting situations when a requirement specified by an SC-LTL formula is violated by the implementation – this can happen even if the model of the application is perfect e.g., because of a misunderstood specification, an invalid refinement of the original model during the development process or simply a programming error. Obviously when the abstract model is faulty the problem can be revealed by a conventional model checker.

In the framework of our research we have designed and implemented a *code generator* that automatically creates the source code of the runtime verifier component (SC-LTL module) on the basis of a set of SC-LTL formulae. Since due to size limitations the exact implementation can not be discussed here: this subsection introduces the main idea behind the implementation and outlines the data structures and algorithms applied in the runtime verifier.

Mathematical Background. The key idea in our approach is to re-structure formulae into a format where the atomic propositions to be evaluated in the actual state and the ones to be evaluated sometime in the future are clearly separated. Iteratively applying this re-formalization enables us to build a virtual "logical chain" consisting of "logical blocks" representing the portion of the verifier logic corresponding to specific states of the system under verification:

- The *outputs* of the logical blocks are the values of arbitrary SC-LTL *expressions to be evaluated* at the corresponding state.
- The *inputs* of a logical block are (i) *atomic propositions* to be evaluated in the actual state and (ii) *sub-expressions* to be evaluated in the *next step*.
- The blocks are connected after each other resulting in a chain of logical blocks. The outputs of a block are the inputs of the previous one in the chain (i.e., the sub-expressions to be evaluated in the future – see (ii) above).
- The system should handle the notion of "unknown value" since during the execution some sub-expressions can only be evaluated at a future step.

The idea of logical blocks is depicted in Fig. 5: In the upper part of the figure the state traversal of a Kripke-structure is shown while the bottom part indicates the building of the logical chain by adding a new logical block in each subsequent step. The original expression requested by the user to be evaluated was $(a \vee b)\mathcal{U}f$. This expression is re-formalized as $f \vee ((a \vee b) \wedge \mathcal{X}((a \vee b)\mathcal{U}f))$ (see the explanation below). This way the output of the first logical block is $(a \vee b)\mathcal{U}f$ (left interface in Fig. 5) and its inputs are (i) the a, b and f atomic propositions obtained from the labeling of the actual state of the Kripke-structure (upper interface) and (ii) the value of the $(a \vee b)\mathcal{U}f$ expression propagated from the output of the next logical block (right interface). Because the original expression simply re-generates itself during the re-formalization, all the logical blocks are the same in this case and have only one outputs (this is obviously not the general case, the example was chosen for simplicity reasons). The internal logic (gates, inverters etc.) represent the Boolean logic operators in the expression. Note that the figure is for illustration purposes: the inputs on the right interface are in *three-state logic* (for enabling the indication that a sub-expression could not have been yet evaluated) this way the implementation of the internal logic is more involved.

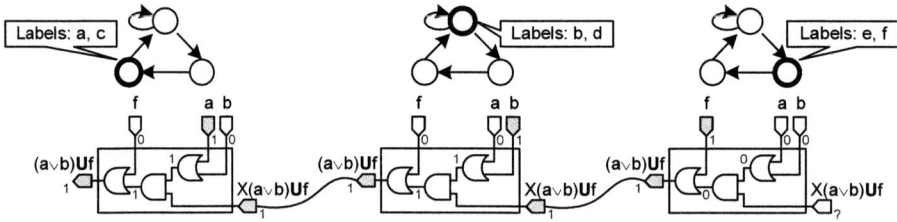

Fig. 5. Building a chain of logical blocks for runtime evaluation of LTL formulae

As introduced above for "designing" the logical blocks we have to *re-formalize* the expressions that are in the outputs of the logical blocks to a format where the atomic expressions to be evaluated at the actual state (Boolean inputs in the upper interface) and the ones to be read from the three-state output of the next logical block (right interface) are *clearly separated*. Since this format is used for "connecting the present and the future" we call this format as *connection normal form* (CNF). It is easy to see that the only operator that needs special attention is the *until* operator ($\mathcal{U}$) since its arguments can not be characterized as sub-expressions referencing *only to the present* state or *only to the future* (e.g., $p\mathcal{U}q$ evaluates to true if q is true in the present state or q is true in some future state but until that point p is true for all intermediate steps). As the definition below introduces, CNF restricts the usage of the $\mathcal{U}$ operator in such way that it can only stand in the scope of a *next-time* subexpression (Def. 4) The restriction does not weaken the language, since *until* expressions can be re-organized to a format that honors this scheme (Thm. 1).

Definition 4 (Connection normal form (CNF)). *An SC-LTL expressions is in* connection normal form *(CNF) is the $\mathcal{U}$ operator appears only in the argument of an $\mathcal{X}$ operator.*

Theorem 1 (Converting SC-LTL expressions to CNF). *For any SC-LTL expression e there exists an SC-LTL expression e' in CNF for which: $\Pi \models e$ iff $\Pi \models e'$ for any Π trace.*

Proof. Let us introduce the $\mathbf{To^{CNF}}$ notation as the "operator for converting an SC-LTL expression to CNF" (this way the CNF equivalent of e can be written as $\mathbf{To^{CNF}}(e)$). The CNF equivalent of e can be achieved by applying the following recursive transformation:

$$\mathbf{To^{CNF}}(\sigma_i|_{\sigma_i \in \sigma}) = \sigma_i \quad \mathbf{To^{CNF}}(\top) = \top$$
$$\mathbf{To^{CNF}}(\epsilon_i|_{\epsilon_i \in \epsilon}) = \epsilon_i \quad \mathbf{To^{CNF}}(e_1 \wedge e_2) = \mathbf{To^{CNF}}(e_1) \wedge \mathbf{To^{CNF}}(e_2)$$
$$\mathbf{To^{CNF}}(\alpha_i^X|_{\alpha_i^X \in \alpha^X}) = \alpha_i^X \quad \mathbf{To^{CNF}}(\neg e) = \neg \mathbf{To^{CNF}}(e)$$
$$\mathbf{To^{CNF}}(\alpha_i^A|_{\alpha_i^A \in \alpha^A}) = \alpha_i^A \quad \mathbf{To^{CNF}}(\mathcal{X} e) = \mathcal{X} e$$
$$\mathbf{To^{CNF}}(\alpha_i^E|_{\alpha_i^E \in \alpha^E}) = \alpha_i^E \quad \mathbf{To^{CNF}}(e_1 \mathcal{U} e_2) = \mathbf{To^{CNF}}(\neg(\neg e_2 \wedge \neg(e_1 \wedge \mathcal{X}(e_1 \mathcal{U} e_2))))$$

The equivalence of the original expression e and $\mathbf{To^{CNF}}(e)$ is obvious from the construction, the only non-trivial transformation is the conversion of $e_1 \mathcal{U} e_2$:

$$\pi \models e_1 \mathcal{U} e_2 \leftrightarrow \exists_{0 \leq i < n} \pi^i \models e_2 \wedge \forall_{0 \leq j < i} \pi^j \models e_1 \leftrightarrow$$
$$\leftrightarrow (\pi^0 \models e_2) \vee (\exists_{1 \leq i < n} \pi^i \models e_2 \wedge \forall_{0 \leq j < i} \pi^j \models e_1) \leftrightarrow$$
$$\leftrightarrow (\pi^0 \models e_2) \vee (\exists_{1 \leq i < n} \pi^i \models e_2 \wedge \forall_{1 \leq j < i} \pi^j \models e_1 \wedge \pi^0 \models e_1) \leftrightarrow$$
$$\leftrightarrow (\pi^0 \models e_2) \vee (\pi^0 \models e_1 \wedge \exists_{1 \leq i < n} \pi^i \models e_2 \wedge \forall_{1 \leq j < i} \pi^j \models e_1) \leftrightarrow$$
$$\leftrightarrow (\pi^0 \models e_2) \vee (\pi^0 \models e_1 \wedge \pi^0 \models \mathcal{X}(e_1 \mathcal{U} e_2)) \leftrightarrow$$
$$\leftrightarrow \pi \models (e_2 \vee (e_1 \wedge \mathcal{X}(e_1 \mathcal{U} e_2))) \leftrightarrow \pi \models \neg(\neg e_2 \wedge \neg(e_1 \wedge \mathcal{X}(e_1 \mathcal{U} e_2)))$$

Implementation of the Runtime Verifier. Based on this idea the algorithm of building the "logical chain", the proof of correctness and the implementation is quite straightforward. The following enumeration outlines the key steps:

1. The "type" (internal structure) of a logical block is defined by the expressions on its outputs (expressions on the left interface in the examples): the internal logic and the inputs are derived from this information. The set of output expressions can be seen this way as the "specification of the logical block".

2. The *next-time* inputs of a logical block (right interface) specify the type of the logical block to be connected after it in the next step: the expressions on the left interface of the next block are the arguments of the outermost $\mathcal{X}$ operators in the right interface of the actual block, e.g., if the inputs on the right interface of the actual block are $\mathcal{X} a$, $\mathcal{X} \mathcal{X}(b \vee c)$ and $\mathcal{X}((a \vee b)\mathcal{U}(c \wedge d))$ then the outputs of the next block should be: a, $\mathcal{X}(b \vee c)$ and $(a \vee b)\mathcal{U}(c \wedge d)$.
3. Converting the expressions on the left interface to CNF and collecting the *next-time* expressions on the right interface (i) defines the interfaces and the internal structure of the actual logical block and (ii) specifies the left interface of the next block. Subsequently applying this algorithm the blocks of the entire chain can be defined. It can be proven that when taking an initial set of SC-LTL expressions to be evaluated (left interface of the first block in the chain), there are always a finite number of "logical block specifications" to be implemented. The proof is based on the idea that the only operator that recursively generates itself is the $\mathcal{U}$ operator and it is easy to see that after a sufficient number of reduction steps the algorithm will generate logical blocks with the same specification (e.g., as $(a \vee b)\mathcal{U} f$ in the example) or empty expression sets (for very simple formulae not containing the $\mathcal{U}$ operator).
4. The "logical blocks" can be straightforwardly implemented in software by generating programming language classes with methods and member variables representing the interfaces and the internals of the blocks. The propagation of logical signals can be simulated by back-propagating the information obtained in the actual step to the previous blocks in the chain (i.e., iteratively copying values occurring on the left interface to the right interface of the previous block and re-evaluating its outputs.
5. It can be proven that the information propagation algorithm outlined above evaluates all the expressions on the left interface of the first chain element (i.e., ones that were requested by the user) at the latest at the final step of the trace. (Obviously expressions that can be evaluated by investigating a prefix of the trace are evaluated at that time but e.g., the violation of a $\mathcal{F} a$ expression can only be proven at the last step of the trace.)

Runtime checking of SC-LTL expressions requires information about the RTC steps taken by the application under verification (states, transitions, currently processed event, actions performed etc.). Almost the same runtime information is required by the EWD module to check the full behavior. Accordingly, the way of obtaining the runtime information (implementation of the necessary instrumentation) is discussed in Sect. 5, after the presentation of the EWD module.

4 Verification of the Behavior

The runtime verification of the behavior is carried out by a statechart-level watchdog component (EWD module) of our framework. The EWD module uses the Extended Hierarchical Automaton equivalent of the statechart as reference information and observes the behavior by receiving signatures from the application. This section outlines the internal operation of the EWD module.

There were several *watchdog solutions* proposed in the literature [9], [10], [11], [12] for concurrent monitoring of hardware-software systems. The simplest *watchdog circuits* are hardware timers that observe the life signals of the application and are capable of restarting it after a long period of inactivity (application crash, infinite loop etc.). The more advanced *watchdog processors* (WDP) are relatively simple co-processors that detect the deviation of the application from the correct control flow. The correct behavior is called the *reference information*, the behavior actually exposed by the observed application is called the *runtime information*.

The WDP obtains the *runtime information* by observing the CPU fetch cycles (*derived signatures*) or by processing signatures of execution explicitly sent by the observed application (*assigned signatures*). Nowadays derived signatures are applicable only in case of low-end CPUs or microcontrollers because the caching and predictive prefetch techniques used in modern CPUs prevent the observation of the internally executed instruction sequence based on bus cycles.

The runtime signatures are checked against the reference information which is typically the *control-flow graph* (CFG) of the application stored in the watchdog [9], [10] or embedded in the signatures sent by the application [11], [12]. Although the CFGs were successfully applied for supervising the execution of relatively low-level programming constructs (functions, interrupt routines etc.) the formalisms lacks the capability of expressing event-driven *hierarchical* state-transition models and *concurrent execution*. While classical WDPs are successful in detecting effects of transient HW impairments, handling SW faults (programming bugs, misunderstood specification, etc.) has remained on open issue.

The *high-level, EHA-based watchdog* (EWD) proposed in this section overcomes the weaknesses identified above by explicitly storing the EHA representation of the application statechart as *reference information* and maintaining a local observer of the state configuration of the supervised one. Note that the EWD module can be implemented on the basis of the EHA, without the need of a Kripke-structure as the reference model. The *runtime information* sent by the application holds identifiers of states and transitions (i.e. assigned signatures). The task of concurrent control-flow verification can be decomposed into two abstraction levels (contexts):

- The *EHA context* is responsible for monitoring the *initialization process* (i.e. exactly those states are entered that are members of the initial configuration and the sequence of entry actions corresponds to the state hierarchy) and the *transition selection method* (i.e. the trigger event is compatible with the event received by the object, the source state and the states in the source restriction set are active and transition priority relations are not violated).
- The *transition context* is responsible for monitoring the firing of a *single transition* i.e. the states exited (entered) by the application are really left (entered) by the transition, the sequence of exit, associated and entry actions correspond to the UML semantics etc.

The implementation of the EWD is based on the hierarchy and behavior of *contexts* identified above. The contexts are defined using protocol state machines

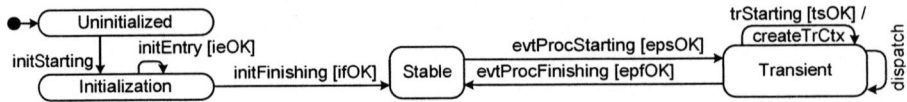

Fig. 6. Operation of the EHA context

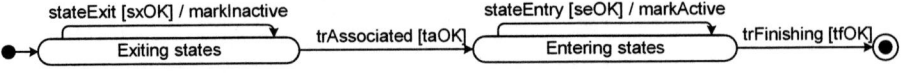

Fig. 7. Operation of the transition context

(PSM) driven by messages (signatures) sent by the application and the reference behavior is obtained from the UML statechart of the application. The PSM of the EHA context (Fig. 6) consists of four states corresponding to the life-cycle of the observed object: during construction (*Initialization* state) the object enters the states (*initEntry* message) belonging to the initial configuration. The start and finish of the initialization phase is indicated by messages (*initStarting* and *initFinishing*). The consistent stable configurations of the observed object are represented by the *Stable* state. While processing an event the configuration is considered to be transient: transitions may be fired (*trStarting* message) and states are left and entered accordingly. Since several transitions may fire simultaneously according to our decomposition scheme a transition context is created for each running transition (*createTrCtx action*) and the messages related to them (e.g. state entry) are forwarded to the appropriate transition context (*dispatch* message). The start and finish of event processing is indicated by messages (*evtProcStarting* and *evtProcFinishing*).

The actual behavior supervision is implemented by *guard predicates* assigned to the transitions of the PSM. Entering a state during the initialization (*ieOK*) is valid if and only if (iff) (i) the state belongs to the initial configuration and (ii) is currently inactive and (iii) all the parent states were already entered. The initialization may be finished (*ifOK*) iff all states of the initial configuration were entered. A transition may be selected for firing (*tsOK*) iff (i) it is triggered by the currently processed event and (ii) its source and source restriction states are active and (iii) it is not disabled by an already started transition and (iv) it does not disable an already started transition. The event processing may be finished (*epfOK*) iff all started transitions were successfully finished. Any messages not triggering a transition of the PSM are considered to be *protocol violations* (e.g. the reception of *initStarting* in *Stable* state). The guards discussed here are automatically derived from the EHA equivalent of the reference statechart.

The PSM of the transition context (Fig. 7) is driven by messages forwarded by the EHA context. Firing a transition involves three steps: (i) exiting the source state and all active states refining it (*Exiting states*), (ii) performing the action associated to the transition and (3) entering the target state and the ones in the target determination set (*Entering states*). While leaving (entering) the source (target) states the application sends the *stateExit* (*stateEntry*) messages and the monitor updates its internal configuration observer accordingly (*markInactive*, *markActive*). Before performing the action associated to the transition or finishing the transition the application sends *trAssociated* and *trFinishing* messages respectively.

A state may be exited (*sxOK*) iff (i) it is the source of the transition or one of its refinements and (ii) it is active and (iii) none of its refinements are active. The action associated to the transition may be performed (*taOK*) iff the source state and all of its active refinements have been left. A state may be entered (*seOK*) iff (i) it is the target of the transition or member of the target determination set and (ii) it is inactive and (iii) all of its parent states have already been entered. The transition may be finished (*tfOK*) iff the target and all states in the target determination set have been entered.

The watchdog discussed above was implemented as a stand-alone utility in ANSI C++. The prototype implementation is capable of supervising the execution of arbitrary number of objects by introducing a new topmost hierarchy level, the *application context* that is responsible for observing object construction and destruction (i.e. capable of detecting some types of memory leaks and corruptions) and dispatching the messages discussed above to EHA contexts.

5 Instrumentation

The concurrent verification scheme proposed in this paper requires the instrumentation of the observed applications: the *SC-LTL module* needs an interface for querying specific atomic propositions about the actual configuration of the statechart implementation and the *EWD module* requires explicit transmission of assigned signatures. The implementation of the interface needed by the SC-LTL module is quite straightforward, this section focuses on the instrumentation needed by the EWD module by proposing a *pattern-based instrumentation scheme* using the emerging paradigm of Aspect-Oriented Programming (AOP).

The observed application has to be instrumented for being observed by the EWD-module in two aspects: (i) the message processing interface of the EWD must be made accessible for the application and (ii) message transfer routines have to be included at key control flow points identified above. The first aspect necessitates the extension of the *static data model* of the application i.e. the association should be implemented, the second task requires the instrumentation of *the behavior*. The approach followed by the application programmer for implementing state-based behavior has an important impact on the instrumentation method to be chosen. Instead of searching for a probably non-existing ultimate solution for instrumenting all possible statechart implementation techniques, we propose a *pattern-based approach* consisting of four steps:

– Identification of *extension points* in the *data model* where the static features for accessing the monitor (e.g. pointers etc.) are to be included.

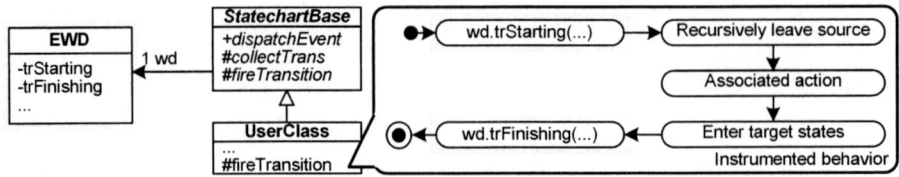

Fig. 8. Instrumentation example

- Identification of *key control points* in the *behavioral model* (e.g. methods recursively leaving the source state of a transition) where message transmission routines are to be included.
- Developing *instrumentation rules* that consist of (i) source code patterns matching one of the *instrumentation points* identified above and (ii) source code *fragments to be applied* (included, substituted etc.) to matching points.
- Algorithmically *applying* the *instrumentation rules* on the source code.

Since the implementation of statechart-based behavior is usually addressed by applying a design pattern, the process outlined above can be seen as developing *instrumentation patterns* for *implementation patterns*.

Fig. 8 illustrates the *identification of extension points* according to our approach in case of a simplified implementation pattern similar to [13] consisting of an abstract base class (*StatechartBase*) providing some fundamental facilities and a descendant class derived from it (*UserClass*) actually implementing the behavior. In this example the EWD module is associated to the application class by adding an association targeting the EWD with role "wd". One of the key methods of the pattern is the *fireTransition* function declared in the base class and implemented in the descendant. This function takes the necessary steps during the firing of a transition i.e. recursively leaves the source state, performs the action associated to the transition and enters the target states. Since the EWD requires the application to send a *trStarting* message before and a *trFinishing* message after firing a transition, the instrumentation inserts these actions in the behavioral model. The instrumentation-related elements (classes, actions etc.) are highlighted by grey surrounding.

For implementing the pattern matching and introduction of static and dynamic instrumentation we propose the application of Aspect-Oriented Programming [14]. AOP aims at separation of concepts and enabling efficient maintenance of application code by distinguishing core and crosscutting concerns:

- *Core concerns* belong to the primary purpose of the application. The design and implementation of core concerns is according to popular methodologies.
- *Crosscutting concerns* are features that should be implemented and integrated into the application but are difficult to design consistently together with the application since their purpose and related artifacts are independent of the primary purpose (e.g. logging, access control).

Adding crosscutting concerns typically introduces several minor code fragments sporadically distributed throughout the entire source resulting in a non-maintainable, unreliable implementation. In order to overcome these drawbacks, AOP provides facilities for defining *programming language-level* (i.e. not primitive textual) patterns, so called *pointcuts* that can be automatically matched against application source. The matching regions are called *join points* while the modifications to be applied at join points are called *advices*. The class-like encapsulation of a set of pointcuts and advices is an *aspect*. Examples for possible patterns are method calls, object creation, accessing specific member variables (reading or writing), exception handling etc. The pattern matching can be recursive: pointcuts can be defined containing other pointcuts. AOP compilers are used to seamlessly *weave aspects* into the the primary application.

In our approach AOP is used for instrumentation of statechart implementations enabling the concurrent supervision by the monitor. In case of the example in Fig. 8 the *association relation* between *UserClass* and *EWD* can be implemented e.g. in Java as adding a member variable of type *EWD* named *wd* to *UserClass*. The instrumentation of the *transition firing method* can be implemented as enclosing the original function body within calls informing the monitor about the start and finishing of the transition respectively. The aspect-oriented (AspectJ) implementation of the instrumentation is shown below. The first entry adds a new member variable to the abstract base class, the second one defines a pointcut as calls for the function *fireTransition* in classes derived from the *StatechartBase* class and finally the latest entry defines the instrumentation (advice) as discussed above (sending the appropriate message to the EWD module before and after performing the original function body).

```
public aspect BehavioralMonitoring {
    // Add a member variable to the base class
    protected EWD StatechartBase.wd;

    // Define a pattern (pointcut) called firingTransitionPattern
    // matching calls for fireTransition in derived classes
    pointcut firingTransitionPattern():
       call(StatechartBase+.fireTransition(Transition tr));

    // Define the advice (instrumentation) to be applied when
    // matching the previous pointcut
    around(): firingTransitionPattern() {
       wd.trStarting(tr);    // Send trStarting to the EWD
       proceed();            // Perform original function body
       wd.trFinishing(tr);   // Send trFinishing to the EWD
    }
}
```

6 Assessment of Error Detection Capabilities

The error detection capabilities of the stand-alone implementation of EWD module was assessed by low-level fault injection experiments [15]. Two inherently different statechart implementation patterns (QHsm [13] and EHA2C [16]) were selected for source-code level instantiation of a benchmark statechart.

The implementation patterns have an important impact on the *binary image* (Fig. 9) of the resulting executables (size and content of code and data sections etc.):

- The QHsm pattern [13] is based on a relatively complex base class and the descendant classes containing one function for each state resulting in a *relatively large code segment* (i.e. larger than the single interpreter function of the EHA2C pattern). These state functions consist of a *switch* statement that performs an *indirect jump* with respect to the actually processed event to the code fragment representing the appropriate *case* edge. Jump target addresses are typically stored in an initialized array in the code section by the C compilers. The *data part is very compact* in case of the QHsm pattern (the QHsm class maintains some pointers for representing the actual state and managing transitions). Pointers are directly used for accessing functions.
- Data structures play a key role in the EHA2C pattern while the interpreter is much simpler than the methods of the *QHsm* class in the QHsm pattern. The *code section is short* containing the single compact interpreter function only (not taking into consideration the test driver, instrumentation etc.). Routines implementing the actions are left empty in both implementations in the investigations presented here. Since the dynamic behavior specification is stored in a constant data structure, the *data segment is relatively large* (*Statechart data* in Fig. 9) containing dominantly *identifiers* (i.e. integers that are used as array indices that can be checked for validity).

Exhaustive fault injection experiments were performed by inverting single bits of the resulting binary executables. The modified programs were executed on a UNIX platform and the observations reported by the SW and HW error detection mechanisms were registered. Although the bit-inversion faults do not exactly model SW faults primarily addressed by the watchdog, the error detection ratio was remarkable in case of the EHA2C pattern when injecting fault in the data section: 21.5% of the detected errors was detected by the EWD only, 40% of injected faults resulted in HW exceptions, the remaining 18.5% were SW assertion failures. In case of the QHsm pattern the error detection effectiveness of HW mechanisms was proven to be higher: 83.39% of detected errors was indicated by HW mechanisms, the EWD detected 7.44%.

Our experiments highlighted that the impairments of the *code sections* are mainly detected by *hardware mechanisms* (illegal instruction or segmentation violation signals) independently of the implementation method. Detection of faults in the *data sections* require different mechanisms in cases of the two patterns: faults of data used directly for addressing in case of the QHsm pattern can be

Fig. 9. Binary layout of the executables

detected by the memory management unit (hardware) while the bit inversions in the complex interpreted data structures used by the EHA2C pattern can be targeted by *software mechanisms* (watchdog, assertions) [15].

Since the primary goal of our error detection mechanisms is the detection of *software errors*, carrying out an experiment series by injecting software faults in the applications and assessing the capabilities of the error detection mechanisms discussed in this paper is subject of our near future research.

7 Indicating Errors by Exception Events

The previous sections introduced our approach for detecting the violations of temporal and behavioral specifications. Obviously the next question after having detected an error by the runtime verifier modules is *how to inform the system about the error for initiating the recovery process*.

looseness 2 Since the behavior of the system under normal circumstances is specified by high-level behavioral models (UML statecharts, activity diagrams, etc.) it would be beneficial to *describe the recovery actions within the same model*. This approach necessitates the introduction of a new event concept that represent the detection of an exceptional situation. As discussed in Sect. 3 one of the refinements of the UML event concept (*Event* metaclass, Fig. 2) is the *SignalEvent* metaclass indicating the reception of an asynchronous signal. The *SignalEvent* metaclass is associated to the *Signal* metaclass representing an asynchronous stimulus received by the system. The UML exception concept (*Exception* metaclass) is derived from the *Signal* metaclass. This way the *SignalEvents* concept is the natural candidate for being used for indicating exceptional situations. Signal events used this way will be referenced as *exception events* in this discussion. Note that we do not need to introduce a new concept and a corresponding metaclass since the *SignalEvent* concept is ideally fitted for being used as error indicator. The introduction of exception events for being used in indicating error detection is quite straightforward (for more detailed discussion see [17]):

- The application processes the events received from the environment by storing them in an event set and consuming them one-by-one. UML does not specify the order in which the events are taken from the queue to enable the implementation of various priority schemes fitted for the application area.
- The operation of the error detection mechanisms is related to the *run-to-completion* steps of the statechart: the EWD module observes the behavior *during* the RTC steps, the SC-LTL module checks the status of the application *after finishing* the RTC steps. When one of the mechanisms detects an error it inserts a corresponding exception event in the waiting set of the application. Exception events should be assigned a high priority (e.g., if the waiting set is implemented as an event queue that is processed in FIFO order, inserting the exception event directly in the head of the queue ensures that the exception event will be processed in the next RTC step).

– Since the UML semantics does not specify the event processing order and
  the run-to-completion operation is not modified, introducing this way the
  error indications into the behavioral model honors the UML semantics.

8 Conclusions and Future Work

This paper has presented our proposal for a *runtime verification framework* for concurrent supervision of UML statechart implementations. The key contributions are a *temporal logic variant* fitted for the artifacts of statecharts, an advanced *statechart-level watchdog*, a proposal for the automatic implementation of the required *instrumentation* and the introduction of the *exception event* concept that enables the developers to specify the behavior even in exceptional situations detected by the verification mechanisms using the visual toolkit of statecharts.

The most important benefits of using our temporal logic language (SC-LTL) is that it enables the straightforward definition of dependability criteria in early phases of the development when only preliminary behavioral models are available, it does not require the developers to "transform" the high-level and typically less-technical terms of the requirement analysis to the technology and implementation-oriented terms of fully elaborated behavioral models.

The EWD module of the framework aims at detecting the errors introduced in the implementation phase by observing the application using the abstract, fully elaborated behavioral model as reference information.

Our framework seamlessly integrates the two aspects of verification (SC-LTL and EWD modules) with the corresponding error-handling by introducing the concept of exception events as error indication signals. Using this facilities the visual toolkit of UML is used not only for modeling the application under normal circumstances but also for specifying the *behavior in exceptional situations* and serves as a *reference information* for error detection.

The components of the framework are in various stages of the development. The prototype of the EWD module was designed and implemented as a stand-alone application. Preliminary fault injection experiments were carried out for assessing its error-detection capabilities and the promising results were published in [15], [18]. Since the fault injection experiments that have been carried out until now (bit inversion faults) do not exactly model the errors EWD module aims at detecting (errors introduced in the implementation phase due to programming errors and misunderstood specification) in the near future we plan to carry out experiments by injecting *software faults* and assessing the error detection capabilities this way. The implementation of the SC-LTL consist of two layers: a general-purpose runtime LTL verifier (checking LTL formulae above execution traces without caring about the semantics of the atomic propositions) and the SC-LTL layer above it that obtains the necessary information from the statechart implementation and translates this data to the labeling abstraction of the general-purpose layer. The general-purpose runtime verifier module has been designed and implemented. Assessing the error detection capabilities is a subjects of our near future research and development.

References

1. Latella, D., Majzik, I., Massink, M.: Automatic Verification of a Behavioural Subset of UML Statechart Diagrams Using the SPIN Model-checker. In: Formal Aspects of Computing. Volume 11., Springer Verlag (1999) 637–664
2. Latella, D., Majzik, I., Massink, M.: Towards a Formal Operational Semantics of UML Statechart Diagrams. In: Proc. FMOODS'99, the Third IFIP International Conference on Formal Methods for Open Object-based Distributed Systems, Florence, Italy (1999) 331–347
3. Varró, D., Varró, G., Pataricza, A.: Designing the Automatic Transformation of Visual Languages. Science of Computer Programming **44** (2002) 205–227
4. Havelund, K., Roşu, G.: Testing Linear Temporal Logic Formulae on Finite Execution Traces. Technical report, RIACS (2000)
5. Finkbeiner, B., Sipma, H.: Checking Finite Traces using Alternating Automata. In Havelund, K., Rosu, G., eds.: Electronic Notes in Theoretical Computer Science. Volume 55., Elsevier (2001)
6. Jayaputera, J., Poernomo, I., Schmidt, H.: Runtime Verification of Timing and Probabilistic Properties using WMI and .NET. In: Proc. EUROMICRO'04 Workshop on Component Based Software Engineering. (2004)
7. Rodríguez, M., Fabre, J.C., Arlat, J.: Wrapping Real-time Systems from Temporal Logic Specifications. In Grandoni, F., Thévenod-Fosse, P., eds.: Proc. EDCC-4. Volume 2485 of Lecture Notes in Computer Science., Springer (2002) 253–270
8. Drusinsky, D.: The Temporal Rover and the ATG Rover. In: Proc. SPIN workshop. Volume 1885 of Lecture Notes in Computer Science., Springer (2000) 323–330
9. Namjoo, M.: Techniques for Concurrent Testing of VLSI Processor Operation. In: Proc. International Test Conference. (1982) 461–468
10. Lu, D.J.: Watchdog Processors and Structural Integrity Checking. In: IEEE Transactions on Computers. Volume "C-31". (1982) 681–685
11. Pataricza, A., Majzik, I., Hohl, W., Honig, J.: Watchdog Processors in Parallel Systems. In: Proc. Euromicro'93, 19th Symposium on Microprocessing and Microprogramming, Barcelona. (1993)
12. Majzik, I., Hohl, W., Pataricza, A., Sieh, V.: Multiprocessor Checking Using Watchdog Processors. In: International Journal of Computer Systems – Science & Engineering. Volume 11 (5). (1996) 125–132
13. Samek, M.: Practical Statecharts in C/C++. CMP Books, Kansas, USA (2002)
14. Kiczales, G., Lamping, J., Mendhekar, A., Maeda, C., Lopes, C.V., Loingtier, J.M., Irwin, J.: Aspect-Oriented Programming. In: Proc. ECOOP, Springer Verlag (1997)
15. Pintér, G., Majzik, I.: Impact of Statechart Implementation Techniques on the Effectiveness of Fault Detection Mechanisms. In: Proc. EUROMICRO'04 Workshop on Component Based Software Engineering. (2004)
16. Pintér, G., Majzik, I.: Automatic Code Generation Based on Formally Analyzed UML Statecharts. In G. Tarnai and E. Schnieder, ed.: Formal Methods for Railway Operation and Control Systems (Proceedings of Symposium FORMS-2003, Budapest, Hungary, May 15-16), L' Harmattan, Budapest (2003) 45–52
17. Pintér, G., Majzik, I.: Modeling and Analysis of Exception Handling Techniques by Using UML Statecharts. In: Proc. FIDJI 2004 International Workshop on Scientific Engineering of Distributed Java Applications. (2004) 69–78
18. Pintér, G., Majzik, I.: High-level Supervision of Program Execution Based on Formal Specification. In: Proc. DSN-2004 Workshop on Architecting Dependable Systems, Florence, Italy. (2004) 292–296

A Framework for Ensuring and Improving Dependability in Highly Distributed Systems

Sam Malek, Nels Beckman, Marija Mikic-Rakic, and Nenad Medvidovic

Computer Science Department, University of Southern California,
Los Angeles, CA 90089-0781
{malek, nbeckman, marija, neno}@usc.edu

Abstract. A distributed software system's deployment architecture can have a significant impact on the system's dependability. Dependability is a function of various system parameters, such as network bandwidth, frequencies of software component interactions, power usage, and so on. Recent studies have shown that the quality of deployment architectures can be improved significantly via active system monitoring, efficient estimation of the improved deployment architecture, and system redeployment. However, the lack of the appropriate tools for monitoring, analyzing, and effecting redeployment at the architectural level makes improving a system's deployment architecture a very challenging problem. To cope with these challenges, developers typically resort to ad hoc solutions that decrease the potential for reuse and understandability. In this paper, we first present an extensible framework that guides the design and development of solutions for this type of problem, enables the extension and reuse of the solutions, and facilitates autonomic analysis and redeployment of a system's deployment architecture. We then discuss a suite of extensible and integrated tools that help developers in realizing the framework.

1 Introduction

Consider the following scenario, representative of a large number of modern distributed software applications. The scenario addresses distributed deployment of personnel in cases of natural disasters, search-and-rescue efforts, and military crises. A computer at "Headquarters" gathers information from the field and displays the current status: the locations and status of the personnel, vehicles, and obstacles. The headquarters computer is networked to a set of PDAs used by "Commanders" in the field. The commander PDAs are connected directly to each other and to a large number of "troop" PDAs. These devices communicate and help to coordinate the actions of their distributed users. Such an application is frequently challenged by network disconnections during system execution. Even when the hosts are connected, the bandwidth fluctuations and the unreliability of network links affect the system's properties such as availability and latency.

For any such large, distributed system many deployment architectures (i.e., distributions of the system's software components onto its hardware hosts) will be typically possible. Some of those deployment architectures will be more dependable than others.

For example, a distributed system's availability can be improved if the system is deployed such that the most critical, frequent, and voluminous interactions occur either locally or over reliable and capacious network links.

Finding a deployment architecture that exhibits desirable system characteristics (e.g., low latency, high availability) or satisfies a given set of constraints (e.g., the processing requirements of components deployed onto a host do not exceed that host's CPU capacity) is a challenging problem: (1) many system parameters (e.g. network bandwidth, reliability, frequencies of component interactions, etc.) influence the selection of an appropriate deployment architecture; (2) these parameters are typically not known at system design time and/or may fluctuate at run time; (3) the space of possible deployment architectures is extremely large, thus finding the optimal deployment is rarely feasible [12]; and (4) different desired system characteristics may be conflicting (e.g., a deployment architecture that satisfies a given set of constraints and results in specific availability may at the same time exhibit high latency).

The above problem is further complicated in the context of the emerging class of decentralized systems, which are characterized by limited system-wide knowledge and the absence of a single point of control. In decentralized systems, selection of a globally appropriate deployment architecture has to be made using incomplete, locally-maintained information.

The work described in this paper builds on our previous work [10,12,13,14], where we have identified and addressed a subset of the above challenges in the context of disconnected operation. We discuss a framework that provides high-level guidelines for devising solutions addressing the challenges identified above. The framework's objective is to provide a library of reusable, pluggable, and customizable components that can be leveraged in addressing a variety of distributed system deployment scenarios. We then describe a suite of integrated tools that help us realize the framework. The tools are extensible along several dimensions and allow for: (1) inclusion of arbitrary system parameters (hardware host properties, network link properties, software component properties, software interaction properties); (2) inclusion of appropriate monitors to extract these parameters from a running system; (3) specification of desirable system characteristics (e.g., high availability, low latency, desired level of security); (4) pluggability of different algorithms targeted at improving the desired characteristics; (5) multiple visualizations of the running system and its properties; and (6) flexible support for both centralized and decentralized systems. Finally, we demonstrate our approach on both a centralized and a decentralized example scenario.

The remainder of the paper is organized as follows. Section 2 briefly outlines the related work. Section 3 presents the deployment improvement framework. Section 4 briefly describes our supporting tools and discusses the specific characteristics of the tools that make them suitable for realizing the framework. Finally, Section 5 demonstrates our approach on two example scenarios. The paper concludes with an outline of our future work.

2 Related Work

One of the techniques for improving a system's dependability is (re)deployment, which is a process of installing, updating, and/or relocating a distributed software system. Carzaniga et. al. [2] provide an extensive comparison of existing software deployment approaches. They identify several issues lacking in the existing deployment tools, including integrated support for the entire deployment life cycle. An exception is Software Dock [5], which is a system of loosely coupled, cooperating, distributed components. Software Dock provides software deployment agents that travel among hosts to perform software deployment tasks. Unlike our approach, however, Software Dock does not focus on extracting system parameters, visualizing, or evaluating a system's deployment architecture, but rather on the practical concerns of effecting a deployment.

The problem of improving a system's deployment architecture has been studied by several researchers:

- I5 [1], proposes the use of the binary integer programming model (BIP) for generating an optimal deployment of a software application over a given network, such that the overall remote communication is minimized. Solving the BIP model is exponentially complex in the number of software components, rendering I5 applicable only to systems with very small numbers of software components and target hosts. Furthermore, the approach is only applicable to the minimization of remote communication.
- Coign [7] provides a framework for distributed partitioning of COM applications across the network. Coign monitors inter-component communication and then selects a distribution of the application that will minimize communication time, using the lift-to-front minimum-cut graph cutting algorithm. However, Coign can only handle situations with two machine, client-server applications. Its authors recognize that the problem of distributing an application across three or more machines is NP hard and do not provide approximative solutions for such cases.
- Kichkaylo et al. [9], provide a model, called component placement problem (CPP), for describing a distributed system in terms of network and application properties and constraints, and an AI planning algorithm, called Sekitei, for solving the CPP model. The focus of CPP is to capture a number of different constraints that restrict the solution space of valid deployment architectures. At the same time, CPP does not provide facilities for specifying the goal, i.e., a criterion function that should be maximized or minimized. Therefore, Sekitei only searches for a valid deployment that satisfies the specified constraints, without considering the quality of the found deployment.
- In our own prior work [10,12,14], we devised a set of algorithms for improving a software system's availability by finding an improved deployment architecture. The novelty of our approach was a set of approximative algorithms that scaled well to large distributed software systems with many components and hosts. However, our approach was limited to a predetermined set of system parameters, and a predetermined definition of availability, and was not extensible to problems with different concerns. Furthermore, it did not consider decentralized systems.

While all of the above projects propose novel solutions for improving a system's properties through the redeployment of software components, the implementation and evaluation of these solutions is done in an ad-hoc way, making it hard to adopt and reuse their results. Furthermore, most of these approaches are aimed at improving specific system properties, which may restrict their applicability.

Also related to our work is the research on architecture based adaptation frameworks, examples of which are [4,16]. As opposed to general purpose architecture-based adaptation frameworks, we are only considering a specific kind of adaptation (i.e., redeployment of components). Therefore, we are able to create a more detailed, and hopefully more practical framework that guides the developers in the design of their solutions.

Finally, Haas et. al. [6] provide a scalable framework for autonomic service deployment in networks. This approach does not address the exponential complexity in the selection of the most appropriate deployment, or that properties of services and hosts may change during the execution.

3 Approach

We have developed a methodology for improving a distributed system's availability via (1) active system monitoring, (2) estimation of the improved deployment architecture, and (3) redeployment of (parts of) the system to effect the improved deployment architecture. Based on this three-step methodology we developed a high-level deployment improvement framework. In this section we describe the framework's components, the associated functionality of each component, and the dependency relationships that guide their interaction. We also describe the framework's instantiation for two classes of solutions.

3.1 Framework Model

Figure 1 shows the framework's overall structure and the relationships among its six high-level components. Note that each of the framework's components can have an internal architecture that is composed of one or more lower-level components. Furthermore, the internal architecture of each component can be distributed (i.e., different internal low-level components may communicate across address spaces). The arrows represent the flow of data among the framework components.

Model. This component maintains the representation of the system's deployment architecture. The model is

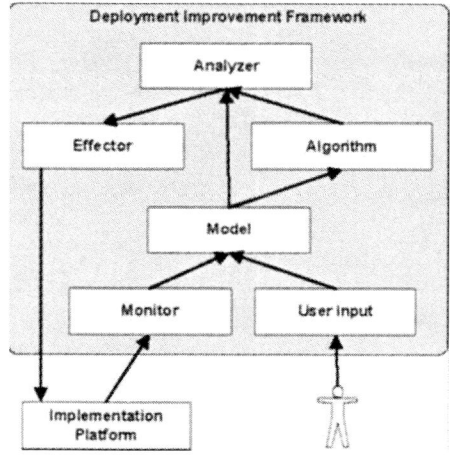

Fig. 1. Deployment improvement framework

composed of four types of parts: hosts, components, physical links between hosts, and logical links between components. Each of these types could be associated with an arbitrary set of parameters. For example, each host can be characterized by the amount of available memory, processing speed, battery power (in case a mobile device is used), installed software, and so on. The selection of a set of parameters to be modelled depends on the set of criteria (i.e., objectives) that a system's deployment architecture should satisfy. For example, if minimizing latency is one of the objectives, the model should include parameters such as physical network link delays and bandwidth. However, if the objective is to improve a distributed system's security, other parameters, such as security of each network link, need to be modelled.

Algorithm. Each objective is formally specified and can either be an optimization problem (e.g., maximize availability, minimize latency) or constraint satisfaction problem (e.g., total memory of components deployed onto a host cannot exceed that host's available memory). Given an objective and the relevant subset of the system's model, an algorithm searches for a deployment architecture that satisfies the objective. An algorithm may also search for a deployment architecture that simultaneously satisfies multiple objectives (e.g., maximize availability while satisfying the memory constraints).

In terms of precision and computational complexity, there are two categories of algorithms for an optimization problem like this: exact and approximative. Exact algorithms produce optimal results (e.g., deployments with minimal overall latency), but are exponentially complex, which limits their applicability to systems with very small numbers of components and hosts. On the other hand, approximative algorithms in general produce sub-optimal solutions, but have polynomial time complexity, which makes them more usable.

In terms of centralization, there are also two classes of algorithms: centralized, which are executed in a single physical location, or decentralized, which are executed on multiple, synchronized hosts. In Section 5, we describe examples of both centralized and decentralized algorithms in more detail.

Analyzer. Analyzers are meta-level algorithms that leverage the results obtained from the algorithm(s) and the model to determine a course of action for satisfying the system's overall objective. In situations where several objective functions need to be satisfied, an analyzer resolves the results from the corresponding algorithms to determine the best deployment architecture. However, note that an analyzer cannot always guarantee satisfaction of all the objectives. Analyzers are also capable of modifying the framework's behavior by adding or removing low-level components from the framework's high-level components. For example, once an analyzer determines that the system's parameters have changed significantly, it may choose to add a new low-level algorithm component that computes better results for the new operational scenario. Analyzers may also hold the history of the system's execution by logging fluctuations of the desired objectives and the parameters of interest. System's execution profile allows the analyzer to fine-tune the framework's behavior by providing information such as system's stability, work load patterns, and the results of previous redeployments.

Monitor. To determine the run time values of the parameters in the model, a monitor is associated with each parameter. The monitor is implemented in two parts: a platform-dependent part that "hooks" into the implementation platform and performs the actual monitoring of the system, and a platform-independent part that interprets and may look for patterns in the monitored data. For example, it determines if the data is stable enough [14] to be passed on to the model. We will discuss an example of this in Section 5.

Effector. Just like monitors, effectors are also composed of two parts: (1) a platform-dependent part that "hooks" into the platform to perform the redeployment of software components; and (2) a platform-independent part that receives the redeployment instructions from the analyzer and coordinates the redeployment process. Depending on the implementation platform's support for redeployment, effectors may also need to perform tasks such as buffering, hoarding, or relaying of the exchanged events during component redeployment.

User Input. Some system parameters may not be easily monitored (e.g., security of a network link). Also, some parameters may be stable throughout the system's execution (e.g., CPU speed on a given host). The values for such parameters are provided by the system's architect at design time. We are assuming that the architect is able to provide a reasonable bound on the values of system parameters that cannot easily be monitored. Furthermore, the architect also must be capable of providing constraints on the allowable deployment architectures. Examples of these types of constraints are location and collocation constraints. Location constraints specify a subset of hosts on which a given component may be legally deployed. Collocation constraints specify a subset of com-ponents that either must be or may not be deployed on the same host.

3.2 Framework Instantiation

Figure 2 shows our framework's instantiation for a centralized system. Centralized systems have a *Master Host* (i.e., central host) that has complete knowledge of the distributed system parameters. *Master Host* contains a *Centralized Model*, which maintains the global model of the distributed system. The *Centralized Model* is populated by the data it receives from *Master Monitor* and *Centralized User Input*. The *Master Monitor* receives all of the monitoring data from the *Slave Monitors* on other hosts. Once all monitoring data from all *Slave Hosts* is received, the *Master Monitor* forwards the monitoring data to the *Centralized Model*. Each Slave Host contains a *Slave Effector*, which receives redeployment instructions from the *Master Effector*, and a *Slave Monitor*, which monitors the *Slave Host's Implementation Platform* and sends the monitoring data back to the *Master Monitor*. Finally, the *Master Effector* receives a sequence of command instructions from the *Centralized Analyzer* and distributes the redeployment commands to all the *Slave Effectors*.

Figure 3 shows our framework's instantiation for a decentralized system. Unlike a centralized software system, a decentralized system does not have a single host with the global knowledge of system parameters. Each host has a *Local Monitor* and a *Local Effector* that are only responsible for the monitoring and redeployment of the host on which they are located. Each host has a *Decentralized Model* that contains some subset of the system's overall model, populated by the data received from the *Local Monitor* and the *Decentralized Model* of the hosts to which this host is connected. Therefore, if there are two hosts in the system that are not aware of (i.e., connected to) each other, then the respective models maintained by the two hosts do not contain each other's system parameters. Each host also has a *Decentralized Algorithm* that synchronizes with its remote counterparts to find a common solution. Finally, in a similar way, the *Decentralized Analyzer* on each host synchronizes with its remote counterparts to determine an improved deployment architecture and effect it.

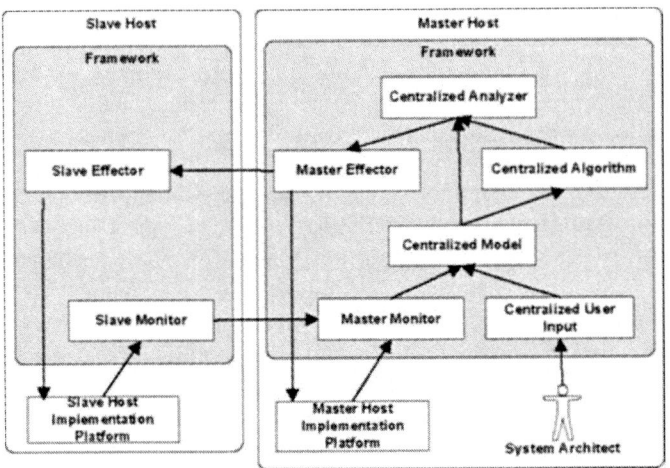

Fig. 2. Framework's centralized instantiation

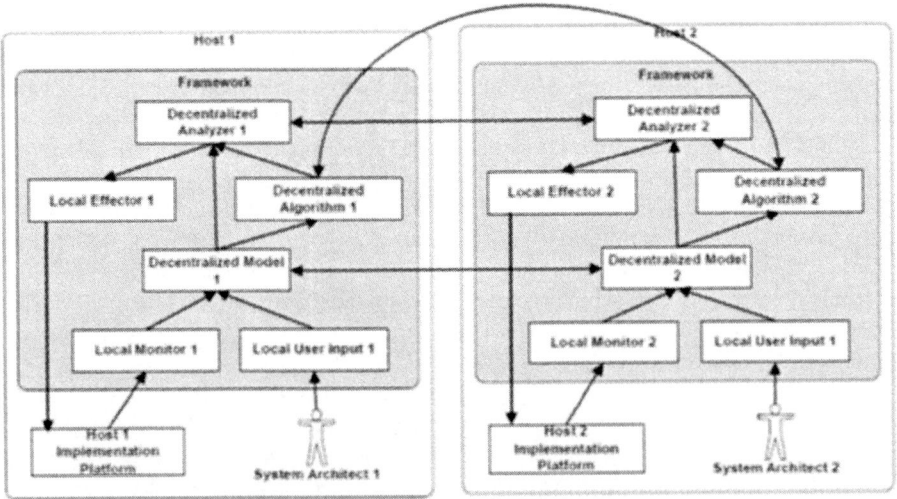

Fig. 3. Framework's decentralized instantiation

4 Tool Suite

While the framework's design is independent of any specific tool or environment, appropriate tool support facilitates the implementation, and automation, of specific deployment improvement solutions using the framework. In this section we describe two tools and their integration, which assist engineers in developing solutions that conform to the framework.

4.1 DeSi

DeSi [13] is a visual deployment exploration environment that supports specification, manipulation, and visualization of deployment architectures for large-scale, highly distributed systems. By leveraging DeSi, an architect is able to enter desired system parameters into the model, and also to manipulate those parameters and study their effects (shown in Figure 9). For example, the architect is able to use a graphical environment to specify new architectural constructs (e.g., components, hosts), parameters (e.g., network bandwidth, host memory), and values for the parameters (e.g., available memory on a host is 1MB). The architect may also specify constraints. For example, the maximum and minimum available resources, the location constraint that denotes the hosts that a component can not be deployed on, and the collocation constraint that denotes a subset of components that should not be deployed on the same host. DeSi also provides a visualization environment for graphically displaying the system's monitored data, deployment architecture, and the results of analysis (shown in Figure 10).

Figure 4 shows the high-level architecture of DeSi. The centerpiece of the architecture is a rich and extensible *Model*, which in turn allows extensions to the *View* (used for model visualization) and *Controller* (used for model manipulation) subsystems.

Model. DeSi's *Model* subsystem is reactive and accessible to the *Controller* via a simple API. The *Model* currently captures three different system aspects in its three components: *SystemData*, *GraphViewData*, and *AlgoResultData*. *SystemData* is the key part of the *Model* and represents the software system itself in terms of the architectural constructs and parameters: numbers of components and hosts, distribution of components across hosts, software and hardware topologies, and so on. *GraphViewData* captures the information needed for visualizing a system's deployment architecture: graphical (e.g., color, shape, border thickness) and layout (e.g., juxtaposition, movability, containment) properties of the depicted components, hosts, and their links. Finally, *AlgoResultData* provides a set of facilities for capturing the outcomes of the different deployment estimation algorithms: estimated deployment architectures (in terms of component-host pairs), achieved availability, algorithm's running time, estimated time to effect a redeployment, and so on.

View. DeSi's *View* subsystem exports an API for visualizing the *Model*. The current architecture of the *View* subsystem contains two components—*GraphView* and *TableView*. *GraphView* is used to depict the information provided by the *Model's GraphViewData* component. *TableView* is intended to support a detailed layout of system parameters and deployment estimation algorithms captured in the *Model's*

SystemData and *AlgoResultData* components. The decoupling of the *Model's* and corresponding *View's* components allows one to be modified independently of the other. For example, it allows us to add new visualizations of the same models, or to use the same visualizations on new, unrelated models, as long as the component interfaces remain stable.

Controller. DeSi's *Controller* subsystem comprises four components. The *Generator*, *Modifier*, and *AlgorithmContainer* manage different aspects of DeSi's *Model* and *View* subsystems, while the *MiddlewareAdapter* component provides an interface to a, possibly third-party, system implementation, deployment, and execution platform (depicted as a "black box" in Fig-ure 4). The *Generator* component takes as its input the desired number of hardware hosts, software components, and a set of ranges for system parameters (e.g., minimum and maximum network reliability, component interaction

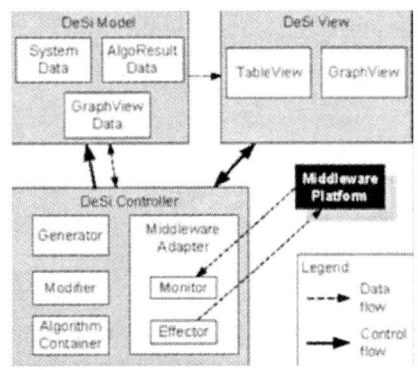

Fig. 4. DeSi's archtecture

frequency, available memory, and so on). Based on this information, *Generator* creates a specific deployment architecture that satisfies the given input and stores it in *Model* subsystem's *SystemData* component. The *Modifier* component allows fine-grain tuning of the generated deployment architecture (e.g., by altering a single network link's reliability, a single component's required memory, and so on). Finally, the *AlgorithmContainer* component invokes the selected redeployment algorithms (examples of algorithms will be presented in Section 5) and updates the *Model's* *AlgoResultData*. In each case, the three components also inform the *View* subsystem that the Model has been modified; in turn, the *View* pulls the modified data from the *Model* and updates the display.

The above components allow DeSi to be used to automatically generate and manipulate large numbers of hypothetical deployment architectures. The *MiddlewareAdapter* component, on the other hand, provides DeSi with the same information from a running, real system. *MiddlewareAdapter's* Monitor subcomponent captures the run-time data from the external *MiddlewarePlatform* and stores it inside the *Model's SystemData* component. *MiddlewareAdapter's Effector* subcomponent is informed by the *Controller's AlgorithmContainer* component of the calculated (improved) deployment architecture; in turn, the *Effector* issues a set of commands to the *MiddlewarePlatform* to modify the running system's deployment architecture. The details of this process are further illuminated below.

4.2 Prism-MW

Prism-MW [11] is an extensible middleware platform that enables efficient implementation, deployment, and execution of distributed software systems in terms of their architectural elements: components, connectors, configurations, and events

[17]. For brevity, Figure 5 shows the elided class design view of Prism-MW. *Brick* is an abstract class that encapsulates common features of its subclasses (*Architecture, Component,* and *Connector*). The *Architecture* class records the configuration of its components and connectors, and provides facilities for their addition, removal, and reconnection, possibly at system run-time. A distributed application is implemented as a set of interacting *Architecture* objects, communicating via *Distribution Connectors* across process or machine boundaries. *Components* in an architecture communicate by exchanging *Events*, which are routed by *Connectors*. Finally, Prism-MW associates the *IScaffold* interface with every *Brick*. Scaffolds are used to schedule and dispatch events using a pool of threads in a decoupled manner. *IScaffold* also directly aids architectural self-awareness by allowing the run-time probing of a *Brick's* behavior, via different implementations of the *IMonitor* interface.

To support various aspects of architectural self-awareness, we have provided the *ExtensibleComponent* class, which contains a reference to *Architecture*. This allows an instance of *ExtensibleComponent* to access all architectural elements in its local configuration, acting as a meta-level component that can automatically effect run-time changes to the system's architecture.

In support of monitoring and redeployment, the *ExtensibleComponent* is augmented with the *IAdmin* interface. We provide two implementations of the *IAdmin* interface: *Admin*, which supports system monitoring and redeployment effecting, and *Admin's* subclass *Deployer*, which also provides facilities for interfacing with DeSi. We refer to the *ExtensibleComponent* with the *Admin* implementation of the *IAdmin* interface as *AdminComponent*; analogously, we refer to the *ExtensibleComponent* with the *Deployer* implementation of the *IAdmin* interface as *Deployer Component*.

As indicated in Figure 5, both *AdminComponent* and *Deployerb Component* contain a ref-erence to *Architecture* and are thus able to effect run-time changes to their local subsystem's architecture: instantiation, addition, removal, connection, and disconnection of components and connectors. With the help of *DistributionConnectors*, *AdminComponent* and *Deployer Component* are able to send and receive from any device to which they are connected the events that contain application-level components (sent between address spaces using the *Serializale* interface).

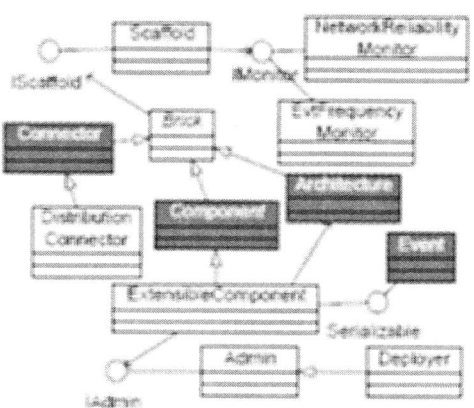

Fig. 5. Elided UML class design view of Prism-MW. The four dark gray classes are used by application developer. Only the relevant middleware classes are shown

4.3 Tool Support for the Framework

To integrate DeSi with Prism-MW, we have wrapped *Monitor* and *Effector* components of DeSi (shown in the *Middleware Adapter* of Figure 4) as Prism-MW components that are capable of receiving *Events* containing the monitoring data from Prism-MW's *Deployer Component*, and issuing events to the *DeployerComponent* to enact a new deployment architecture. Once the monitoring data is received, DeSi updates its own system model. This results in the visualization of an actual system, which can now be analyzed and its deployment improved by employing different algorithms. Once the outcome of an algorithm is selected by the *Analyzer*, DeSi issues a series of events to Prism-MW's *DeployerComponent* to update the system's deployment architecture.

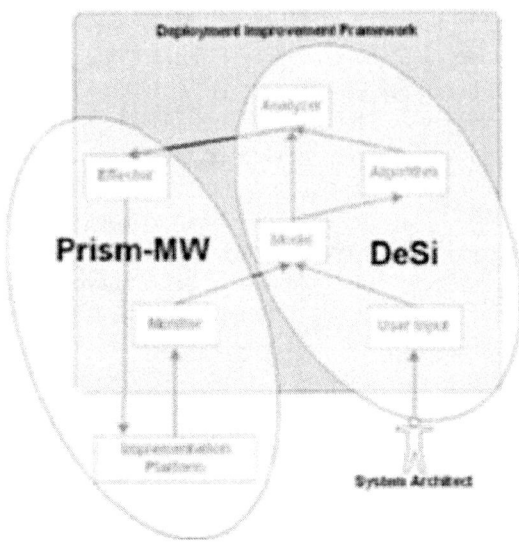

Fig. 6. Realization of the framework via integration of Prism-MW and DeSi

DeSi and Prism-MW are directly leveraged to in realizing our framework, as illustrated in Figure 6. DeSi provides the facilities for implementing *User Input, Model, Algorithm*, and *Analyzer* components, while Prism-MW supports implementation of *Monitor* and *Effector* components. In this section we discuss our realization of each one of the framework components, and their support for pluggability, extensibility, explorability, and adaptability. These characteristics allow the tool suite to be easily tailored to the variation points that arise across different problems.

Model. We leverage DeSi's extensible model to implement the *Model Component* of the framework. DeSi's extensible representation of the system's deployment architecture makes it possible to add or remove new system properties at run-time. The model and the accompanying graphical support make it easy to configure the tool to application scenarios with different concerns and objectives. Once the appropriate model is defined and specified, it is populated with the actual data from a system. The data is provided either at run-time or at design time. Some properties are known at design time (e.g., initial deployment of the system, available memory on each host, etc.), and can be captured in architectural description of the system. To this end, DeSi has been integrated with xADL 2.0 [3], an extensible architecture description language (xADL). Properties that are not available at design time (e.g., reliability of network links, available network bandwidth) are provided by the Monitor component, discussed below.

Algorithm. DeSi provides a pluggable environment for addition and removal of algorithms that run on the model. In order to effectively support reusability and extensibility within different redeployment algorithms, we have identified the following three variation points:

- The objective function (e.g., maximizing availability, increasing security, etc.) that is specified based on the system parameters defined in the model.
- The constraints on the parameters, reflecting the limited resources in the system (e.g., available bandwidth, available memory, etc.), which need to be satisfied by the algorithms when searching for a valid solution.
- The coordination that occurs in decentralized algorithms. There are many decentralized cooperative protocols (e.g., distributed voting [8], auction-based [18]).

We have used these variation points in developing extensible and reusable algorithms in DeSi (as shown in Figure 7). Each algorithm provides an implementation of an abstract API, which is used by DeSi for interfacing with the algorithm. The algorithms are composed of a main body that denotes the algorithm's approach (e.g., greedy algorithm, genetic algorithm, etc.), an objective function, and the relevant constraint functions. Decentralized algorithms are also associated with an implementation of a coordination approach. The above methodology for developing algorithms simplifies the adoption of existing solutions to new problems. The developer first creates the model of the system (as discussed earlier) using the graphical interface, specifies the objective function based on the system parameters, and finally associates the appropriate implementations of the constraint and coordination functions with the algorithm.

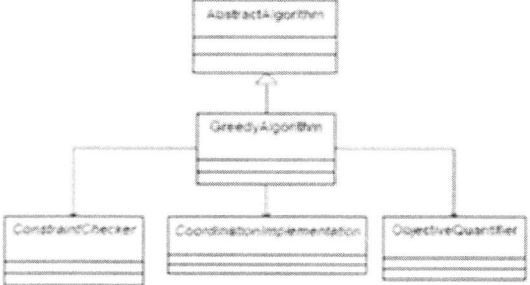

Fig. 7. Class diagram of algorithm development methodology in DeSi for a greedy algorithm

Analyzer. DeSi's visualisation of the deployment architecture and the exploratory utilities allow an engineer to rapidly investigate the space of possible deployments for a given system (real or postulated), and determine the deployments that will result in greatest improvements (while, perhaps, requiring the smallest changes to the current deployment architecture). A user can easily assess a system's sensitivity to changes in specific parameters (e.g., the reliability of a network link) and create deployment constraints (e.g., two components must be located on different hosts). However, while the analysis by a human user may be possible in small centralized systems with few objectives, it is certainly infeasible for large and/or decentralized systems with multiple (and potentially conflicting) objectives. Furthermore, given a deployment improvement problem, there are many decisions and trade-offs associated with improving the deployment architecture: scheduling the time to (re)examine the deployment architecture, selecting the algorithm(s) to run, comparing the results, resolving conflicts, determining the best result, and scheduling the time to effect the solution. Therefore, autonomous solutions for the analysis and conflict resolution are needed. DeSi supports these kind of meta-level algorithms via an API for the modification of DeSi's internal architecture. The API allows for addition and removal of algorithms, modification of the model, and access to DeSi's internal data structure that holds the results of executing algorithms. Via this API, a meta-level algorithm is capable of keeping a profile of the system's history (by monitoring the system's performance), determining the best configuration for the tool, and selecting the result of the best algorithm. Furthermore, in complicated decentralized scenarios, the meta-level algorithms may leverage a decentralized negotiation technique to coordinate their actions with other remote analyzers. Some examples of different analyzers are discussed in Section 5.

Monitor. Prism-MW provides the *IMonitor* interface associated through the *Scaffold* class with every *Brick*. This allows for autonomous, active monitoring of a Brick's run-time behavior. For example, the *EvtFrequencyMonitor* records the frequencies of different events the associated *Brick* sends, while *NetworkReliabilityMonitor* records the reliability of connectivity between its associated *DistributionConnector* and other, remote *DistributionConnectors* using a common "pinging" technique. A meta-level *AdminComponent* (recall Section 4.2) on any device is capable of accessing the monitoring data of its local components via its reference to *Architecture*. In order to minimize the time required to monitor the system, monitoring is performed in short intervals of adjustable duration. Once the monitored data is stable (i.e., the difference in the data across a desired number consecutive intervals is less than an adjustable value ε), the *AdminComponent* sends the description of its local deployment architecture and the monitored data (e.g., event frequency, network reliability, etc.) in the form of serialized Prism-MW Events to the *DeployerComponent*. Figure 8 depicts an application running on top of Prism-MW with the monitoring and deployment facilities instantiated and associated with the appropriate architectural constructs. Our assessment of Prism-MW's monitoring support suggests that monitoring on each host may induce as little as 0.1% and no greater than 10% in memory and efficiency overheads. Note that Prism-MW's extensible design allows for addition of new monitoring capabilities via new implementations of *IMonitor* interface.

Effector. Once a new deployment architecture is selected by one of DeSi's algorithms based on the monitoring data supplied by Prism-MW, DeSi informs the *DeployerComponent* (recall Section 4.2) of the desired deployment architecture, which now needs to be effected. The effecting process requires coordination among different hosts (e.g., ensuring architectural consistency, synchronization, etc.), which is an implementation platform-independent task. Prism-MW's support for coordination is implemented in its Admin and *Deployer Components*:

- The *DeployerComponent* sends events to inform *AdminComponents* of their new local configurations, and of the remote locations of software components required for performing changes to each local configuration.
- Each *AdminComponent* determines the difference between its current and new configurations, and issues a series of events to remote *AdminComponents* requesting the components that are to be deployed locally. If devices that need to

exchange components are not directly connected, the relevant request events are sent to the *DeployerComponent*, which then mediates their interaction.
- Each *AdminComponent* that receives an event requesting its local component(s) to be deployed remotely, detaches the required component(s) from its local configuration, serializes them, and sends them as a series of events via its local *DistributionConnector* to the requesting device.
- The recipient *AdminComponents* reconstitute the migrant components from the received events and invoke the appropriate methods on its *Architecture* object to attach the received components to the local configuration.

Other coordination techniques can also be incorporated into Prism-MW in a similar manner via different implementations of the *DeployerComponent* and *AdminComponent*.

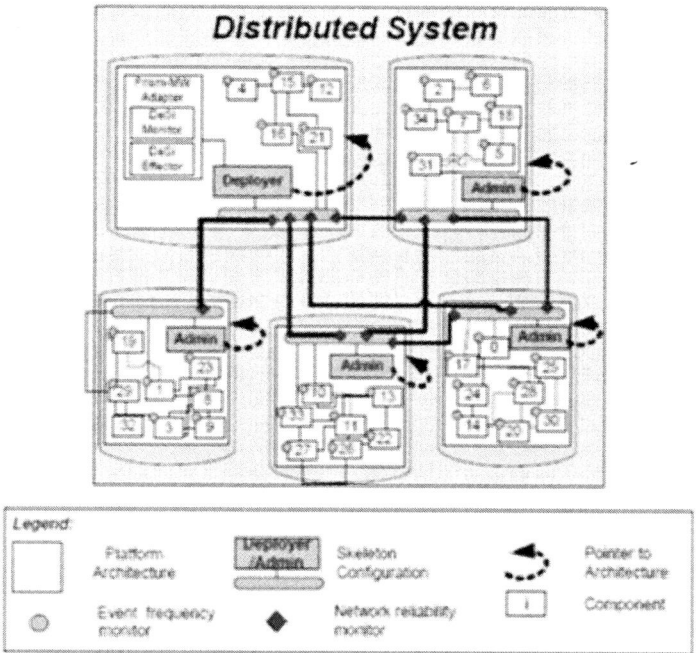

Fig. 8. An example of a distributed system running on top of Prism-MW that is monitored

User Input and Visualization. Once the monitoring data is gathered from all the hosts, the user may invoke one of DeSi's visualization windows to explore the system's deployment architecture and its relevant *parameters*. Figure 9 shows the table-oriented page of the DeSi editor. This page is divided into five sections. In the Parameters table, the properties of every host, component, or link within a software system can be viewed and modified, e.g., to assess the sensitivity of a deployment architecture to specific parameter changes. In the *Constraints* panel, the user can specify different constraints on component locations (e.g., fixing a component to a selected host). Using the set of buttons in the *Algorithms* panel, different algorithms can be invoked and the results displayed in the *Results* panel. Figures 10a and b show the graph-oriented page of the DeSi editor. The thumbnail view in the upper left displays the entire architecture at once and allows users to quickly navigate to any of its portions. Since our framework can support large distributed systems with many hosts and components, DeSi supports the ability to zoom in and out on a visualized system. Hosts are depicted as white boxes while software components are depicted as shaded boxes. The solid black lines between hosts represent physical (network) links and the thin black lines between components represent logical (software) links. At the bottom of the screen, the property sheet allows users to view or modify the properties of the link, host, or component that is currently selected. Components can also be "dragged-and-dropped" from one host to another. In this way, a user can manually create a new system deployment and analyze its effect on system properties (e.g., availability, latency, etc.).

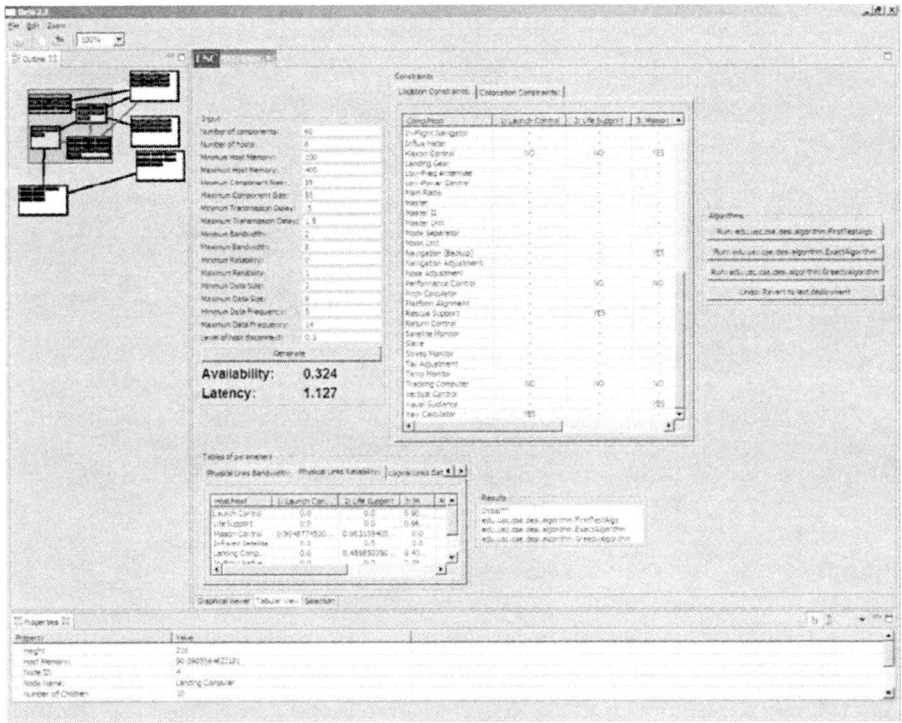

Fig. 9. DeSi's editable tabular view of the system's deployment architecture

5 Example Scenarios

In this section, we describe our experience with the implementation of both the centralized and the decentralized instantiation of the framework targeted at (1) maximizing a distributed system's overall availability, and (2) minimizing the system's overall latency.

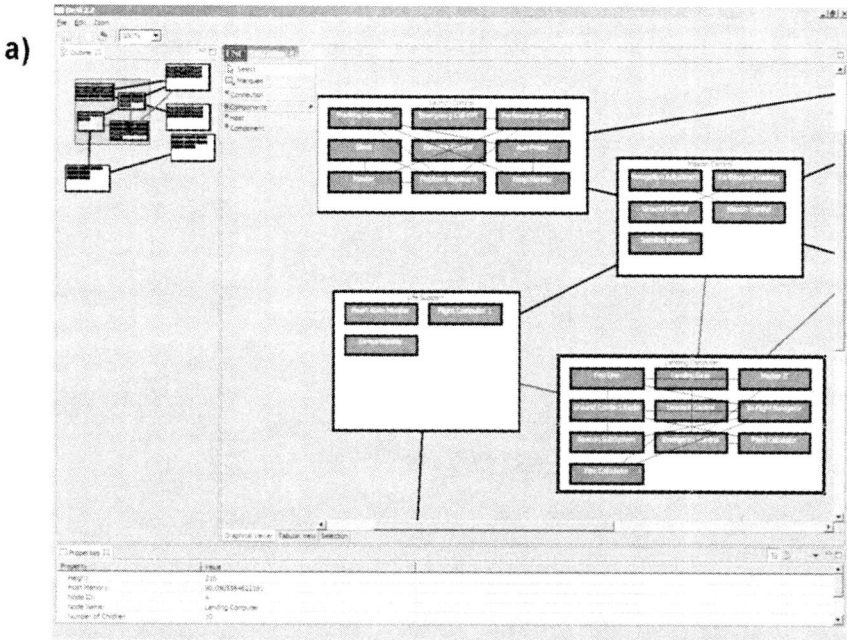
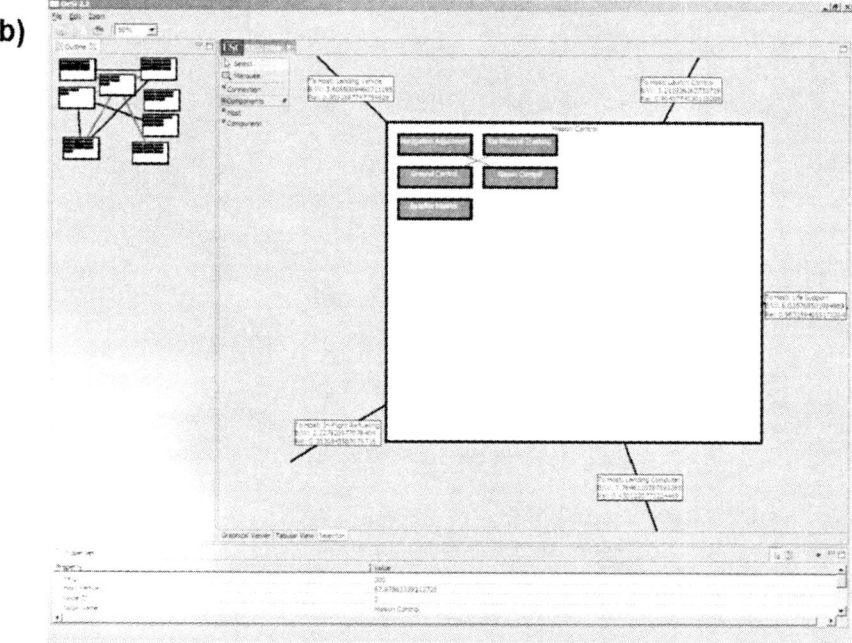

Fig. 10. DeSi's graphical view of a system's deployment architecture: (a) zoomed out view showing multiple hosts; (b) zoomed in view of the same architecture

5.1 Centralized Configuration

In order to achieve the objective of maximizing a system's availability and minimizing the latency we first created an appropriate model. The model is composed of a hierarchical structure of components and hosts that includes the following properties:

- Each component has a required memory size.
- Each host has an available memory.
- Each logical link between components is modelled with a frequency of interaction and an average event size.
- Each physical link among hosts is modelled with a particular network reliability, bandwidth, and transmission delay.
- The system's model contains the location and collocation constraints, discussed in Section 3.1, that restrict the space of valid deployments.

The values for the host's available memory, component's required size, location and collocation constraints are all entered into the model by the user via the DeSi tool. All the modelled properties that are not entered by the user are monitored at run time and added to the model automatically.

We have used three centralized algorithms, called Exact, Stochastic, and Avala [12]. The objective of all these algorithms is to maximize the system's availability by finding a deployment architecture such that the most critical, frequent, and voluminous interactions occur either locally or over reliable and capacious network links. Below we provide a high-level overview of these algorithms.

The Exact algorithm tries every possible deployment, and selects the one that results in maximum availability and satisfies the constraints posed by the memory, bandwidth, and restrictions on software component locations. The Exact algorithm guarantees at least one optimal deployment (assuming that at least one deployment is possible). The complexity of this algorithm in the general case (i.e., with no restrictions on component locations) is $O(k^n)$, where k is the number of hardware hosts, and n the number of software components. By fixing a subset of m components to selected hosts, the complexity reduces to $O(k^{n-m})$.

The Stochastic algorithm randomly orders all the hosts and all the components. Then, going in order, it assigns as many components to a given host as can fit on that host, ensuring that all of the constraints are satisfied. Once the host is full, the algorithm proceeds with the same process for the next host in the ordered list of hosts, and the remaining unassigned components in the ordered list of components, until all components have been deployed. This process is repeated a desired number of times, and the best obtained deployment is selected. Since it needs to calculate the availability and latency for every deployment, the complexity of this algorithm is $O(n^2)$.

Avala is a greedy algorithm that incrementally assigns software components to the hardware hosts. At each step of the algorithm, the goal is to select the assignment that will maximally contribute to the objective function, by selecting the "best" host and "best" software component. Selecting the best hardware host is performed by choosing a host with the highest sum of network reliabilities and bandwidths with other hosts in the system, and the highest memory capacity. Similarly, selecting the best software component is performed by choosing the component with the highest frequency of interaction with other components in the system, and the lowest required memory. Once found, the best component is assigned to the best host, making certain that the location and collocation constraints are satisfied. The algorithm proceeds with searching for the next best component among the remaining components, until the best host is full. Next, the algorithm selects the best host among the remaining hosts. This process repeats until every component is assigned to a host. The complexity of this algorithm is $O(n^3)$.

Our framework's analyzer component automatically decides which one of the algorithms to run based on the following factors:

- The size of the architecture — For example, the Exact algorithm finds the optimal solution, but due to its complexity it can only be used for architectures with very small numbers of hosts (on the order of 5) and components (on the order of 15). Therefore, for large architectures either of the other two algorithms is used.
- The system's availability profile — Analyzer holds a record of the fluctuations in the system's availability (caused by changes in system parameters) that is used to determine when the system should be redeployed and what algorithm should be invoked. For example, the analyzer selects a more expensive algorithm to run if the system is stable (i.e., the system's availability does not fluctuate significantly). On the other hand, if the system is unstable, the analyzer runs a less expensive algorithm that could produce faster results for the immediate improvement of the system's availability.
- The system's overall latency — The algorithms used in this scenario also typically decrease the system's overall latency [12]. However, in rare situations where this is not the case, the analyzer either disallows the results of the algorithms to take effect or modifies the solution such that it does not significantly increase the system's overall latency.

Once the analyzer selects the most appropriate deployment architecture, it creates the appropriate set of redeployment instructions and sends it to the *Master Effector*. The *Master Effector* then forwards the instructions to the appropriate *Slave Effectors*, which leverage Prism-MW's support for the redeployment of software components in the manner described earlier.

5.2 Decentralized Configuration

In the development of the decentralized solution, we were able to reuse the centralized model by extending it to include the notion of "awareness". Awareness denotes the extent of each host's knowledge about the global system parameters. The *Decentralized Model* on each hosts synchronizes its local model with the remote hosts of which it is aware of (i.e., to which it is directly connected), by sending streams of data whenever the model is modified.

Unlike the centralized solution, getting the user input and monitoring is done separately and independently on each host. Similarly to the centralized solution, we leverage DeSi and Prism-MW in gathering data about the system parameters.

We have used a decentralized algorithm, called DecAp [10], that is based on an auction-based protocol to find a solution that significantly improves the system's overall availability. In DecAp, each Decentralized Algorithm component acts as an agent and may conduct or participate in auctions. Each host's agent initiates an auction for the redeployment of its local components, assuming none of its neighboring (i.e., connected) hosts is already conducting an auction. The auction initiation is done by sending to all the neighboring hosts a message that carries information about a component to be redeployed (e.g., name, size, and so on). The agents receiving this message have a limited time to enter a bid on the component before the auction closes. The bidding agent on a given host calculates an initial bid for the auctioned component, by considering the frequency and volume of interaction between components on its host and the auctioned component. Once the auctioneer has received all the bids, it calculates the final bid based on the received information. The host with the highest bid is selected as the winner and the component is redeployed to it. The complexity of this algorithm is $O(k*n^3)$.

The functionality of the decentralized analyzer remains very similar to the centralized version, except that the analyzer uses either the voting or the polling protocol to decide on the appropriate course of action. Once a redeployment decision is made by the analyzers, the redeployment instructions are sent out to the *Local Effectors*, which collaborate in performing the redeployment by leveraging Prism-MW's support for redeployment.

6 Conclusion

A distributed software system's deployment architecture can have a significant impact on the system's dependability, and will depend on various system parameters (e.g., reliability of connectivity among hosts, security of links between hosts, and so on). Improving the deployment architecture such that it exhibits desirable system characteristics is a challenging problem. The lack of a common design framework for improving the system's deployment architecture exacerbates the complexity of this problem. Existing deployment approaches focus on providing support for installing and updating the software system but lack support for extracting, visualizing, and analyzing different parameters that influence the quality of deployment.

In this paper we have presented a design framework for analyzing and improving distributed deployment architectures. We also discussed the integration of Prism-MW, a lightweight architectural middleware that supports system monitoring and run-time reconfiguration, and DeSi, an environment that supports manipulation, visualization, and (re)estimation of deployment architectures for large-scale, highly distributed systems. In concert, Prism-MW and DeSi provide a rich capability for developing solutions that comply to the framework's rules and structure. Our experience has indicated that by leveraging the tool suite to develop solutions we are able to increase the potential for creating pluggable, extensible, and reusable components that could be used to improve deployment architectures in many different scenarios. In our future work we will focus on improving system characteristics beyond availability and latency, such as security, durability, and throughput. We also plan to devise mitigating techniques for situations where different desired system characteristics may be conflicting. There are also many unresolved issues in the decentralized setting that we plan to focus on in the future. For example, modelling user preferences for multiple desired system characteristics in a decentralized environment, and devising decentralized algorithms for non-collaborative hosts are challenging problems. For this we will leverage utility computing techniques to determine a deployment architecture that maximizes the users' overall satisfaction with a distributed system. Furthermore, in the future we plan to extend our framework and tool suite to enhance redeployment with other strategies (e.g., caching and hoarding of data, queuing of remote calls, etc.). These tasks will provide a basis for further assessment and evaluation of our framework and the tool suite.

Acknowledgements

This material is based upon work supported by the National Science Foundation under Grant Numbers CCR-9985441 and ITR-0312780. Effort also partially supported by the Jet Propulsion Laboratory.

References

[1] M. C. Bastarrica, et al. A Binary Integer Programming Model for Optimal Object Distribution. *2nd Int'l. Conf. on Principles of Distributed Systems*, Amiens, France, Dec. 1998.

[2] A. Carzaniga et. al. A Characterization Framework for Software Deployment Technologies. *Technical Report, Dept. of Computer Science, University of Colorado*, 1998.

[3] E. Dashofy, A. van der Hoek, and R. Taylor. An Infrastructure for the Rapid Development of XML-based Architecture Description Languages. *International Conference on Software Engineering (ICSE'04)*, Orlando, Florida, May 2002.

[4] D. Garlan, S. Cheng, B. Schmerl. Increasing System Dependability through Architecture-based Self-repair. In R. de Lemos, C. Gacek, A. Romanovsky, eds., *Architecting Dependable Systems*, 2003.

[5] R. S. Hall, D. Heimbigner, and A. L. Wolf. A Cooperative Approach to Support Software Deployment Using the Software Dock. *International Conference in Software Engineering (ICSE'99)*, Los Angeles, CA, May 1999.

[6] R. Haas et. al. Autonomic Service Deployment in Networks. *IBM Systems Journal*, Vol. 42, No. 1, 2003.

[7] G. Hunt and M. Scott. The Coign Automatic Distributed Partitioning System. *3rd Symposium on Operating System Design and Implementation*, New Orleans, LA, Feb. 1999.

[8] R. Kieckhafer, C. Walter, A. Finn, P. Thambidurai. The MAFT Architecture for Distributed Fault Tolerance. *IEEE Transactions On Computers*, Vol. 37, No. 4, April 1988, pp. 398-405.

[9] T. Kichkaylo et al. Constrained Component Deployment in Wide-Area Networks Using AI Planning Techniques. *Int'l. Parallel and Distributed Processing Symposium*, April 2003.

[10] S. Malek et. al. A Decentralized Redeployment Algorithm for Improving the Availability of Distributed Systems. *Technical Report USC-CSE-2004-506*, 2004.

[11] M. Mikic-Rakic and N. Medvidovic. Adaptable Architectural Middleware for Programming-in-the-Small-and-Many. *ACM/IFIP/USENIX International Middleware Conference (Middleware 2003)*, Rio de Janeiro, Brazil, June 2003.

[12] M. Mikic-Rakic, et. al. Improving Availability in Large, Distributed, Component-Based Systems via Redeployment. *Technical Report USC-CSE-2003-515*, 2003.

[13] M. Mikic-Rakic et. al. A Tailorable Environment for Assessing the Quality of Deployment Architectures in Highly Distributed Settings. *2nd Int'l Working Conf. on Component Deployment (CD 2004)*, Edinburgh, Scotland, May 2004.

[14] M. Mikic-Rakic and N. Medvidovic. Support for Disconnected Operation via Architectural Self-Reconfiguration. *Int'l Conf. on Autonomic Computing (ICAC'04)*, New York, May 2004.

[15] M. Mikic-Rakic and N. Medvidovic. Increasing the Confidence in Off-the-Shelf Components: A Software Connector-Based Approach. *2001 Symposium on Software Reusability (SSR 2001)*, Toronto, Canada, May 2001.

[16] P. Oreizy, N. Medvidovic, and R. N. Taylor. Architecture Based run time Software Evolution. *International Conference on Software Engineering (ICSE'98)*, Kyoto, Japan, April 1998.

[17] D.E. Perry, and A.L. Wolf. Foundations for the Study of Software Architectures. *Software Engineering Notes*, Oct. 1992.

[18] C. A. Waldpurger, et. al. Spawn. A Distributed Computational Economy. *IEEE Trans. on Software Engineering*, February 1992.

Enabling Safe Dynamic Component-Based Software Adaptation*

Ji Zhang, Betty H.C. Cheng, Zhenxiao Yang, and Philip K. McKinley

Software Engineering and Network Systems Laboratory,
Department of Computer Science and Engineering,
Michigan State University, East Lansing, Michigan 48824
{zhangji9,chengb,yangzhe1,mckinley}@cse.msu.edu

Abstract. Recomposable software enables a system to change its structure and behavior during execution, in response to a dynamic execution environment. This paper proposes an approach to ensure that such adaptations are *safe* with respect to system consistency. The proposed method takes into consideration dependency analysis for target components, specifically determining viable sequences of adaptive actions and those states in which an adaptive action may be applied safely. We demonstrate that the technique ensures safe adaptation (insertion, removal, and replacement of components) in response to changing external conditions in a wireless multicast video application.

1 Introduction

Increasingly, computer software must adapt to changing conditions in both the supporting computing and communication infrastructure, as well as in the surrounding physical environment [1]. The need for adaptability is perhaps most acute at the "wireless edge" of the Internet, where mobile devices balance several conflicting and possibly cross-cutting concerns, including quality of service on wireless connections, changing security policies, and energy consumption. To meet the needs of emerging and future adaptive systems, numerous research efforts in the past several years have addressed ways to construct adaptable software. Examples include support for adaptability in programming languages [2, 3, 4], frameworks to design context-aware applications [5, 6], adaptive middleware platforms that shield applications from external dynamics [7, 8], and adaptable and extensible operating systems [9, 10, 11]. In many cases, adaptations involve not only changes to parameters, but reconfiguration of the software structure itself.

Despite these advances in *mechanisms* used to build recomposable software, the full potential of dynamically recomposable software systems can be realized only if the adaptation is performed in a disciplined manner. We use the term "safe adaptation" to mean the program maintains its integrity during adaptation. An adaptation is *safe* if (1) it does not violate dependency relationships and (2) it does not interrupt communication either within a component or between components that would potentially yield

---

* This work has been supported in part by NSF grants EIA-0000433, EIA-0130724, ITR-0313142, and CCR-9901017, and the Department of the Navy, Office of Naval Research under Grant No. N00014-01-1-0744.

erroneous or unexpected results. For discussion purposes, we use the term *critical communication segment* to refer to the communication scenarios mentioned in the second part of the definition. Unless adaptive software mechanisms are grounded in formalisms that codify invariants and other properties that must hold during recomposition, the resulting systems will be prone to errant behavior.

This paper describes an approach to ensure safe adaptation in dynamically recomposable systems. This work is part of the *RAPIDware* project, sponsored by the U.S. Office of Naval Research. RAPIDware addresses the design of adaptive middleware for dynamic, heterogeneous environments. Such systems require run-time adaptation, including the ability to modify and replace components, in order to survive hardware component failures, network outages, and security attacks.

Dynamically adaptive software development comprises four major tasks: *Enabling adaptation* makes a program adapt-ready, that is, capable of run-time reconfiguration. *Program monitoring* instruments the program and monitors condition changes in the execution environment. *Decision-making* determines when and how the program should be adapted. *Process management* ensures safe adaptation. Our previous work [3, 12, 13, 14, 15] has focused primarily on developing techniques for the first three tasks.

This paper focuses on the fourth task, specifically, ensuring that dynamically adaptive actions are performed safely. Adaptive actions can involve the insertion of a new component, removal of a component, or the replacement of an existing component. Our approach to ensuring safeness during adaptation offers three major features. First, we use invariants to specify dependency relationships among multiple components executing across a single or distributed processes. These dependency relationships enable analysis techniques to determine which components are affected during a given adaptation, and consequently the set of safe states in which dynamic adaptations can take place. Second, our approach provides centralized management of adaptations, thus enabling optimizations to be made when more than one set of adaptive actions can be used to satisfy a given adaptation need. Third, our approach provides a rollback mechanism in case an error or failure is encountered during the adaptation process.

We have applied our safeness techniques to adaptive applications primarily in the mobile computing domain. The remainder of this paper is organized as follows. Background is overviewed in Section 2. In Section 3, we describe the theoretical foundations of our approach. Section 4 describes our proposed approach to safe adaptation in detail, and Section 5 describes its application to a video multicasting system. Section 6 discusses related work, and Section 7 concludes the paper and discusses future directions.

2 Background

Many approaches to compositional adaptation are based on computational reflection [16], which refers to the ability of a program to reason about and alter its own behavior. Typically, reflection is defined to include two parts: introspection (observing internal behavior and state) and intercession (modifying internal behavior and state). Whereas programming languages such as Java provide support only for introspection, Adaptive Java [3] also supports intercession, thereby enabling the dynamic reconfiguration of software components. The key programming concept in Adaptive Java is that each component offers three interfaces: *invocations* for performing normal imperative operations on the object, *refractions* for observing internal behavior, and *transmutations* for changing internal behavior. An existing Java class is converted into an adaptable component in two steps. The first step, *absorption*, takes place at compile time and produces an *adapt-ready* component. The second step, *metafication*, occurs at run time and equips the adapt-ready component with a set refractions and transmutations. The refractive and transmutative interfaces, respectively, can be used to sense internal state and effect changes to internal structure [17, 18].

We have used Adaptive Java to develop several adaptable components, including *MetaSockets* [12], which are used in the illustrative example described in Section 5. MetaSockets are constructed from the regular Java Socket and MulticastSocket classes, however, their internal structure and behavior can be modified at run time in response to external conditions. MetaSocket behavior can be adapted through the insertion and removal of *filters* that manipulate the passing data stream. For example, filters can perform encryption, decryption, forward error correction, compression, and so forth. In order to maintain a separation of concerns between the original program and the code responsible for adaptation, we applied an aspect-oriented approach to dynamic adaptation [13], where we wove in code containing MetaSockets to make programs adapt-ready for adaptations at run time.

Safe adaptation is important even in situations where the recomposition is relatively constrained. Imagine a distributed application built upon a substrate of MetaSockets, with different ones adapting to different sets of concerns. Guaranteeing that the adaptations are conducted in a consistent manner that will not corrupt the application behavior can be a challenging task. In the remainder of this paper, we describe our approach to addressing this issue.

3 Theoretical Foundations for Safe Adaptation

The adaptations we consider here are component insertion, removal, replacement, and combinations thereof. A component-based software system can be modeled as a set of communicating components running on one or more processes. Components are considered to be communicating as long as there is some type of interaction, such as message exchange, function calls, IPC, RPC, network communication, and so on. A *communication channel* is the facility for communication, such as a TCP connection, an interface, etc. Communication channels are directed. A two-way communication between two components is represented with two channels with traffic traversing in opposite directions. A component can communicate with another as long as there exists a path of one or more channels connecting these two components.

In general, communication among components can be decomposed into multiple non-overlapping communication segments of various granularity. A coarse-grained segment can be divided into multiple finer-grained segments. For example, the communication between a video server and a video client can be divided into multiple transmission/receive sessions; each session can be divided into multiple frames, where each frame can be divided into multiple packets.

Communication can be either local or global. A *local communication* involves components of only one process, such as an ordinary local procedure. *Global communication* involves components from more than one process. A UDP datagram transmission over a network is an example of global communication, involving both sender and receiver processes.

Unsafe adaptation typically involves communication among components. For a given system, if the execution flow can be altered in order to isolate a given component, then valid adaptations of this component, regardless the order in which they are performed, should not affect the correctness of the system. On the other hand, adaptive actions involving communicating components may disrupt normal functional communication between the adapted component and the rest of the system, thus introducing system inconsistencies.

In a given system, multiple components may collaborate by communicating with each other. We use *dependency relationships* to model these communication patterns. The correct functionality of a component, c, may require the correct functionality of other component(s). Absence of other components may disrupt normal functionality of c.

Dynamic adaptations may interrupt ongoing communication segments. Communication segments whose interruption may cause errors in the system are termed *critical communication segments*. We use a set of finite sequence of indivisible actions (named *atomic actions*) to model the set of critical communication segments CCS. The communication among components in a system is modeled as a (finite or infinite) sequence of *critical communication identifier*, atomic action pairs, where a critical communication identifier is a natural number. Given a communication sequence, S, and a critical communication identifier, CID, we can extract from S the sequence of atomic actions with the same CID, preserving the relative order, denoted S_{CID}. We say an adaptive system does not interrupt critical communication segments if the communication sequence of the adaptive system is S and for all critical communication CID, we have $S_{CID} \in CCS$. Based on the discussion above, we define a *safe dynamic adaptation process* as follows:

Definition: A dynamic adaptation process is *safe iff*

- It does not violate dependency relationships among components.
- It does not interrupt critical communication segments.

In the following subsections, we present our safe dynamic adaptation process.

3.1 Dependency Relationships

Defining Dependency Relationships. In a given system, if the correct functionality of a component A depends on a condition $Cond$ to be true, then we say A *depends* on the condition, denoted as $A \rightarrow Cond$, where "$\rightarrow$" denotes a dependency relationship. The condition takes the form of a logic expression across the components. For example, $A \rightarrow (B_1 \oplus B_2) \cdot C$ means the correct functionality of component A requires the correct functionality of either component B_1 or B_2, and C, where the operator "$\oplus$" represents the logical "xor" operation, and "$\cdot$" represents the logical "and" operation. We use a special type of dependency relationship, *structural invariant*, to specify correct conditions of the system structure. For example, the structural invariant $A \cdot B$ indicates that the correctness of the entire system depends on the correct functionality of both component A and component B.

In a safe adaptation process, the dependency condition of a component should always be satisfied when the component is in its fully operational state. Since dependency relationships are based on communication, if we block the communication channels of a component, then we may temporarily relax the dependency relationships and perform necessary adaptive actions. Before the communication in these channels is resumed, the dependency relationships should be reinforced.

Safe Configurations and Safe Adaptation Paths. A *system configuration* comprises a set of components that work together to provide services. If a dependency relationship predicate *dr* is evaluated to be true when we associate *true* to all components in a configuration, and associate *false* to all components not in the configuration, then we say the configuration satisfies the dependency relationship. If a configuration satisfies all the dependency relationships, then this configuration is considered to be a *safe configuration*, otherwise, it is an *unsafe configuration*. A system can only operate correctly when it is in one of its safe configurations. All safe configurations can be deduced from the dependency relationships and available components.

A system moves from one configuration to another by performing *adaptive actions*. An adaptive action is defined as a function from one configuration to another: $adapt(config_1) = (config_2)$, where $config_2$ is the resulting system configuration when the adaptive action, *adapt*, is applied to $config_1$.

A distributed adaptive action comprises multiple local adaptive actions of individual processes. Each local adaptive action is divided into three parts: *pre-action*, *in-action*, and *post-action*. The pre-action is the preparation operation, such as initializing new components, etc. The in-action alters the structure of the program. The post-action specifies tasks to be performed after the in-action, such as the destruction of old components. Pre-actions and post-actions do not interfere with the functional behavior of the adapting process.

We assume an adaptive action is *atomic* and *isolated*. *Atomicity* of an adaptive action implies that the adaptive action should either not start or run to completion. *Isolation* of an adaptive action implies that the adaptive action is performed without interleaving with other operations, i.e., no other operations take place during the adaptive in-action.

An *adaptation step* is an ordered configuration pair: $step = (config_1, config_2)$, where $step$ represents a system configuration transition from $config_1$ to $config_2$. A safe adaptation process comprises a set of safe configurations connected by a set of adaptation steps. These adaptation configurations and steps together form a *safe adaptation path* that starts from the source configuration of the first step and ends at the target configuration of the last step.

We can construct a *safe adaptation graph* (SAG), where vertices are all safe configurations and arcs are all possible adaptation steps connecting safe configurations. A SAG can be deduced from available adaptive actions. An adaptation step, $(config_1, config_2)$, is in the SAG *iff*

- Both $config_1$ and $config_2$ are safe configurations.
- There exists an adaptive action $adapt$, $adapt(config_1)=config_2$.

3.2 Critical Communication Segments

Performing adaptive actions may disrupt communication among components. A safe adaptation process should maintain the integrity of critical communication segments, i.e., it cannot interrupt critical communication segments. The system state in which the adaptation does not interrupt any critical communication segments is called a *global safe state*.

If a communication is local, then the integrity of its segments can be maintained by a local process. A local process is said to be in a *local safe state*, if the adaptive action does not interrupt local critical communication segments. The integrity of global critical communication segments is guaranteed by a *global safe condition*, meaning that the adaptive action does not interrupt global critical communication segments. For example, the global safe condition for a UDP-datagram transmission is that the receiver has received all the datagram packets that the sender has sent, where the transmission of each datagram packet is a critical communication segment.

A system is in its global safe state *iff*

- All the processes are in their local safe states.
- The global safe condition is satisfied.

3.3 Enabling Safe Adaptation

Next, we introduce the basis for our safe adaptation process, and prove the process is safe. Consider the following two statements.

(a) An adaptation process is safe.

(b) The adaptation process is a process that executes according to a safe adaptation path, where each adaptive action is performed in its global safe state.

We claim that (a) and (b) are equivalent.

Proof sketch: (1) $(b) \rightarrow (a)$

If an adaptation process is performed along a safe adaptation path and each adaptive action is performed in a global safe state, then during the adaptation process, the system is either at a safe configuration or in a transition from one safe configuration to another.

When the system is at a safe configuration, it does not violate dependency relationships (definition of safe configuration). Because no adaptive action is performed, critical communication segments will not be interrupted due to adaptations.

Adaptive actions are performed in global safe states, which implies that no critical communication segments will be interrupted. Adaptations start and end in safe configurations, so dependency relationships will not be violated before and after the adaptive action. Adaptive actions are atomic, thus we can assume there is no intermediate states during an adaptive action. Therefore, dependency relationships are not violated during adaptive actions.

(2) Use proof by contradiction to establish $(a) \rightarrow (b)$

If (b) does not hold, then there are two possibilities: (1) the process is not performed along a safe adaptation path or (2) there is an adaptive action taking place in a state that is not globally safe. In the first situation, there must be a configuration on the adaptation path violating dependency relationships, and therefore, the adaptation process is unsafe. In the second situation, the adaptive action might interrupt a critical communication segment, and thus, the adaptation process is unsafe. Therefore, if (b) does not hold, (a) cannot hold. □

4 Safe Adaptation Process

The safe adaptation method is executed by an *adaptation manager*, typically a separate process that is responsible for managing adaptations for the entire system. The adaptation manager communicates with *adaptation agents* attached to processes involved in the adaptation. An agent receives adaptive commands from the adaptation manager, performs adaptive actions, and reports the status of the local process to the adaptation manager. Communication channels can be implemented to best match the communication patterns of the particular system. For example, both Arora [19] and Kulkarni [20] have used a spanning tree, which is well suited to components organized hierarchically. In contrast, in a group communication system, multicast may be a better mechanism for coordination between the adaptation manager and the agent processes.

Our approach comprises three phases: analysis phase, detection and setup phase, and realization phase. The analysis phase occurs during development time. In this phase, the programmers should prepare necessary information such as determining dependency invariants, specifying critical communication segments, etc. The detection and setup phase occurs at runtime. When the system detects a condition warranting adaptation, the adaptation manager should generate a safe adaptation path. In the realization phase, the adaptation manager and the agents coordinate at runtime to achieve the adaptation along the safe adaptation path established during the previous phase.

4.1 Analysis Phase

At development time, the adaptive software developers should prepare a data structure P, where $P = (S, I, T, R, A)$. S is the set of all configurations. I ($I{:}S \rightarrow BOOL$) is the conjunction of the set of dependency relationship predicates. T is a set of adaptive actions. R ($R{:} T \rightarrow PROGRAM$) maps each adaptive action to its corresponding implementation code in the program, where $PROGRAM$ represents the implementation. The reconfiguration is achieved by the execution of the implementation code. We associate a fixed cost to each adaptive action. Factors affecting cost values include system blocking time, adaptation duration, delay of packet delivery, resource usage, etc. The cost of each adaptive action is defined as a function A ($A{:} T \rightarrow VALUE$), where $VALUE$ represents the cost value.

4.2 Detection and Setup Phase

Once the system detects a condition warranting adaptation, the adaptation manager obtains the target configuration and prepares for the adaptation. This phase contains three steps.

1. **Construct Safe Configuration Set.** Based on the source/target configurations of an adaptation request and dependency relationships, this step produces a set of safe configurations.
2. **Construct Safe Adaptation Graph.** Next, we construct a *safe adaptation graph* (SAG) that depicts safe configurations as nodes and adaptation steps as edges.
3. **Find Minimum Safe Adaptation Path (MAP).** Finally, we apply Dijkstra's shortest path algorithm on the SAG to find a feasible solution with minimum weight, where the weight of a path is the sum of the costs of all the edges along the path.

4.3 Realization Phase

This phase requires the coordination of the adaptation manager and the agents at run time to carry out the actual adaptation according to the safe adaptation path. The adaptation manager should ensure that each adaptive action is performed in its global safe state. We use state diagrams to describe the behavior of each agent and the adaptation manager, respectively.

The state diagram of an agent at each local process is shown in Figure 1, where the Courier font denotes message names. Before an adaptive action is performed, each

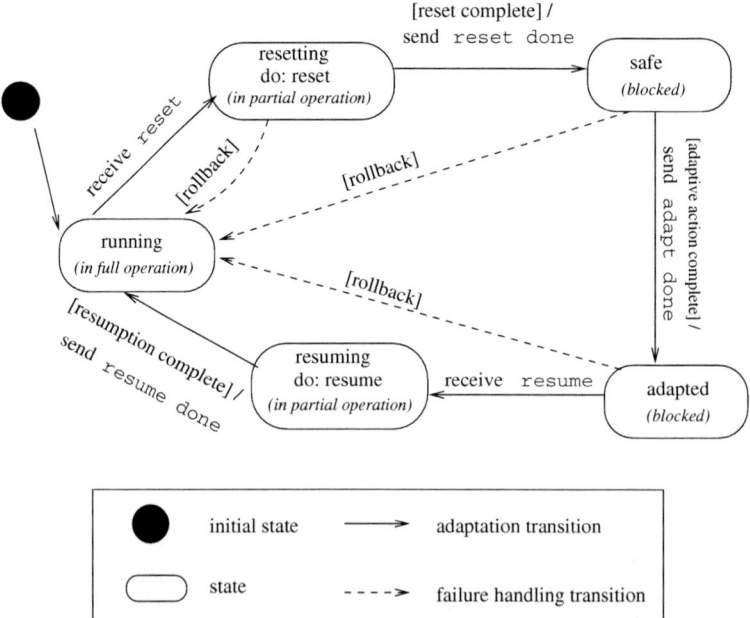

Fig. 1. State Diagram of a Local Process During Adaptation

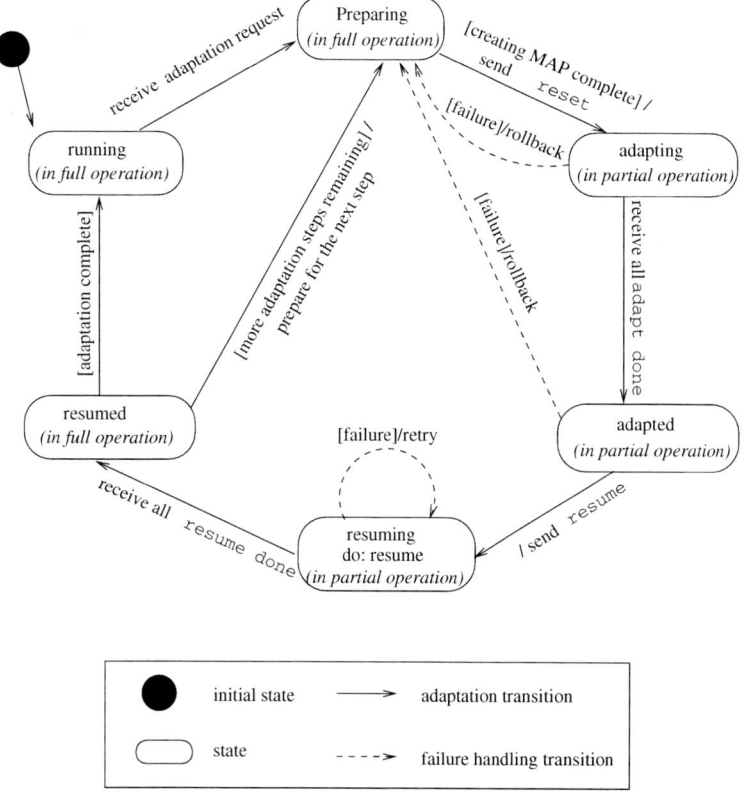

Fig. 2. State diagram of the adaptation manager during adaptation

agent is in a **running** state. In this state, every component in the process is running in its full operation. When the agent receives a `reset` message, then it moves to a **resetting** state. The agent performs the local pre-action, and initiates a reset of the process. In the **resetting** state, the process is only partially operating: Some functionalities related to the adapted component are disabled. When the process achieves its local safe state and the condition required by the global safe condition, the agent performs some actions (such as blocking the process) to hold the process in global safe states, so that the local in-action can be performed safely. Then the agent sends the adaptation manager `reset done` message, after which the process is in a **safe** state. In this state, the agent will perform its local in-action. When the in-action has finished, the agent sends the adaptation manager `adapt done` message and reaches an **adapted** state. If this agent is not the only one involved in this adaptive action, then the process needs to remain blocked in an **adapted** state until it receives a `resume` message. When the agent receives a `resume` message, it knows that all processes have completed their adaptive in-actions, so the process proceeds to a **resuming** state and the agent attempts to resume the process' full operation. If the process is the only one involved in the adaptive action, then it can directly proceed to a **resuming** state from the **adapted** state without blocking. Finally, when the full operation of the process is resumed, the agent sends the manager a `resume done` message and performs the local post-action of the local adaptive action and returns to the original state, running state.

The state diagram of the adaptation manager of the adaptive system is shown in Figure 2. The adaptation manager starts from a running state where the system is fully operational. When an adaptation request is received by the adaptation manager and a MAP is created after the planning phase, it sends `reset` messages to all the agents. Sending the first `reset` message brings the adaptation manager to an adapting state. In this state, the adaptation manager waits for the `adapt done` message from all agents. When all `adapt done` messages are collected, the adaptation manager proceeds to an adapted state. Then the adaptation manager sends `resume` messages to the agents and the manager proceeds to the resuming state. When the adaptation manager collects `resume done` messages from all agents, it transitions to the resumed state. If there are more adaptation steps remaining in the adaptation path, then the adaptation manager will repeat the traversal of preparing, adapting, adapted, resuming, and resumed states until the system configuration matches the target configuration. When the last adaptation step has finished, the adaptation manager returns to the running state.

4.4 Failure During Adaptation Process

We identify two major types of failures based on our experience. First, if the communication between the manager and the agents is not reliable, then the messages between them may be lost, causing loss-of-message failures. Second, when the agent of a local process receives a `reset` message, the local process may not be able to reach a safe state in a reasonably short period of time, thus causing a fail-to-reset failure. Both types of failures can be detected by a time-out mechanism on the manager.

Loss-of-Message Failure. Loss-of-message failures caused by transient network failures can be handled by several attempts to send the messages. However, loss-of-message failures caused by long-term network failure may cause system inconsistencies if the system does not respond to this type of failures correctly. The general rule for handling loss-of-message failures is that if the failures occur before the manager sends out the first `resume` message, then the adaptation should be aborted. That is, the manager should stop sending any new `reset` and `adapt` messages and all the affected processes should roll back to the state prior to the adaptation. If the failure occurs after the manager has sent out a `resume` message, then the adaptation should run to completion. That is, all the related processes should eventually finish adaptation and resume.

Fail-to-Reset Failure. In some cases, when an agent receives a `reset` message, the local process may be engaged in a long critical communication segment, which may prevent it from reaching a safe state in a reasonably short period of time, thus causing a fail-to-reset failure. If a process cannot reach a safe state after it has received a `reset` message, then the adaptation process should be aborted, and all affected processes should roll back to the state prior to the adaptation.

Failure Handling Strategies. In the event that a failure occurs during an adaptation step, there are two possible outcomes: (1) The adaptation step succeeds and the system reaches the target safe configuration. (2) The adaptation step fails and the system reaches a safe configuration prior to the adaptation. If the adaptation step succeeds, then the manager should continue processing the remaining adaptation steps if there are any. If the adaptation step fails, then the manager has four options: (1) Retry the same step. (2) Try other adaptation paths. (3) Attempt to return to the source configuration. (4) Remain at the current safe configuration and wait for user intervention. We use the combination of all options: The adaptation manager first retries the same step once more. If it still fails, then it tries the second minimum adaptation path from the current configuration to the target configuration. If all possible paths to the target configuration have been tried and have failed, then the adaptation manager tries to return to the source configuration. If this attempt also fails, then the adaptation manager notifies the users and waits for user intervention.

The dashed arrows in Figures 1 and 2 show the failure handling transitions on both the manager and the agents. We claim that the adaptation process is still safe with the presence of failures. During an adaptation step, a rollback is invoked only when no process has been resumed, which ensures that no side effect is produced before the rollback. Otherwise, the adaptation will run to completion, which has the same effect as if the adaptation had had no failures. The interaction between the manager and the agents is similar to the two-phase commit protocol [21] if we combine the **safe** state with the **adapted** state in the agents. However, in this work, we consider it clearer to have two separate states. Moreover, our protocol handles multiple adaptation steps where failures may occur at various phases of each step, whereas the two-phase commit protocol only addresses a single adaptation step.

5 Video Streaming Example

We use a video multicasting system to illustrate the safe adaptation process. Figure 3 shows the initial configuration of the application, comprising a video server and one or more video clients. In this example, one client is a hand-held computer (e.g. iPAQ) with a short battery life and limited computing power, and the second client is a laptop (e.g. Toughbook) with reasonable computing power, but limited battery capacity. On the server, a web camera captures video input and a video processor encodes the stream. The encoded video, already packetized, is delivered to the network through a MetaSocket. After traversing a chain of zero or more (encoder) filters, the packets are eventually transmitted on a multicast socket. On each client, the packets are processed by a chain of decoder filters in a receiving MetaSocket. Subsequently, they are passed to the video processor, where they are decomposed into video frames. Finally the frames are displayed in a video player.

In this example, two main encryption schemes are available for processing the data: DES 64-bit encoding/decoding, and DES 128-bit encoding/decoding. The sender has two components: E1, a DES 64-bit encoder and E2, a DES 128-bit encoder. The hand-held client has three components: D1, a DES 64-bit decoder, D2, a DES 128/64-bit compatible decoder, and D3, a DES 128-bit decoder. The laptop client has two components: D4, a DES 64-bit decoder and D5, a DES 128-bit decoder. In general, a DES encoder generates DES encrypted packets from plain packets and a DES decoder decrypts

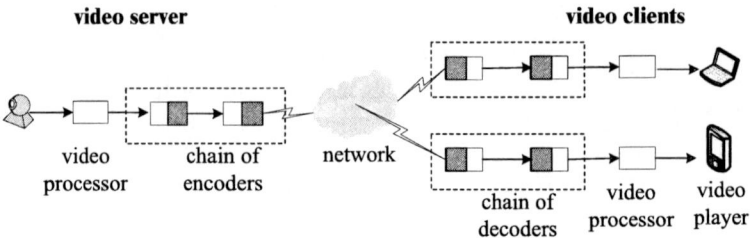

Fig. 3. Configuration of the video streaming application

the DES encrypted packets. Each decoder implements the "bypass" functionality: when it receives a packet not encoded by the corresponding encoder, it simply forwards the packet to the next filter in the chain. The available adaptive actions are: (1) inserting, removing, and replacing a single encoder or decoder; (2) inserting, removing, and replacing an encoder/decoder pair; (3) inserting, removing, and replacing an encoder/decoder triple. The overall adaptation objective is to reconfigure the system from running the DES 64-bit Encoder/Decoders to running the DES 128-bit Encoder/Decoders to "harden" security at run time. We use a separate process to implement the adaptation manager and attach an agent thread to both the server and the clients, respectively. In this particular application and system architecture, the adaptation manager uses a direct TCP connection to communicate with the agents.

5.1 Safe Adaptation Path and MAP

By analyzing the communication patterns between the encoders and the decoders, we find that the correct functionality of a decoder does not require an encoder, but in order to decode a packet generated by an encoder, there must be a corresponding decoder for each encoder. We have the following invariants, where $\otimes$ represents "exclusively select one from a given set of elements".

- System Invariants:
  - **Resource constraint:** $\otimes(D1, D2, D3)$
    One of the receivers, the hand-held device, allows only one DES decoder to be in the system at a given time due to computing power constraints.
  - **Security constraint:** $\otimes(E1, E2)$:
    The sender should have one encoder in the system so that the data is encoded during the adaptation.
- Dependency invariants:
  - $E1 \rightarrow (D1 \vee D2) \wedge D4$
    $E1$ encoder requires the $D1$ or $D2$ decoder to work with the $D4$ decoder.
  - $E2 \rightarrow (D3 \vee D2) \wedge D5$
    $E2$ encoder requires the $D3$ or $D2$ decoder to work with the $D5$ decoder.

We input source and target configurations to the adaptation manager that uses the dependency relationship expressions to generate the safe configuration set. For brevity and automatic processing purposes, we use a 7-bit vector (**D5,D4,D3,D2,D1,E2,E1**) to represent a configuration: If the corresponding bit is "1", then the component is in the configuration, otherwise, it is not. The source configuration is (0100101) and the target configuration is (1010010).

Table 1. Safe configuration set

bit vector	configuration	bit vector	configuration
0100101	D4,D1,E1	1100101	D5,D4,D1,E1
1101001	D5,D4,D2,E1	1101010	D5,D4,D2,E2
1110010	D5,D4,D3,E2	0101001	D4,D2,E1
1001010	D5,D2,E2	1010010	D5,D3,E2

Table 2. Adaptive actions and corresponding cost

Action	Operation	Cost (ms)	Description
A1	$E1 \to E2$	10	replace E1 with E2
A2	$D1 \to D2$	10	replace D1 with D2
A3	$D1 \to D3$	10	replace D1 with D3
A4	$D2 \to D3$	10	replace D2 with D3
A5	$D4 \to D5$	10	replace D4 with D5
A6	$(D1, E1) \to (D2, E2)$	100	A1 and A2
A7	$(D1, E1) \to (D3, E2)$	100	A1 and A3
A8	$(D2, E1) \to (D3, E2)$	100	A1 and A4
A9	$(D4, E1) \to (D5, E2)$	100	A1 and A5
A10	$(D1, D4) \to (D2, D5)$	50	A2 and A5
A11	$(D1, D4) \to (D3, D5)$	50	A3 and A5
A12	$(D2, D4) \to (D3, D5)$	50	A4 and A5
A13	$(D1, D4, E1) \to (D2, D5, E2)$	150	A1 and A10
A14	$(D1, D4, E1) \to (D3, D5, E2)$	150	A1 and A11
A15	$(D2, D4, E1) \to (D3, D5, E2)$	150	A1 and A12
A16	$-D4$	10	remove D4
A17	$+D5$	10	insert D5

The resulting safe configuration set is shown in Table 1. The adaptive actions shown in Table 2 are input to the adaptation manager. Only related actions are listed. The cost column is packet delay in milliseconds. Note, in order to perform some of the actions (e.g., A6-A9), the server has to be blocked until the last packet processed by the encoder has been decoded by the decoder(s) on the client(s). As a result, these actions are much more costly than other actions.

The adaptation manager creates the SAG shown in Figure 4 and uses Dijkstra's shortest path algorithm to obtain the shortest path, which in this example, has cost 50 ms: A2, A17, A1, A16, A4.

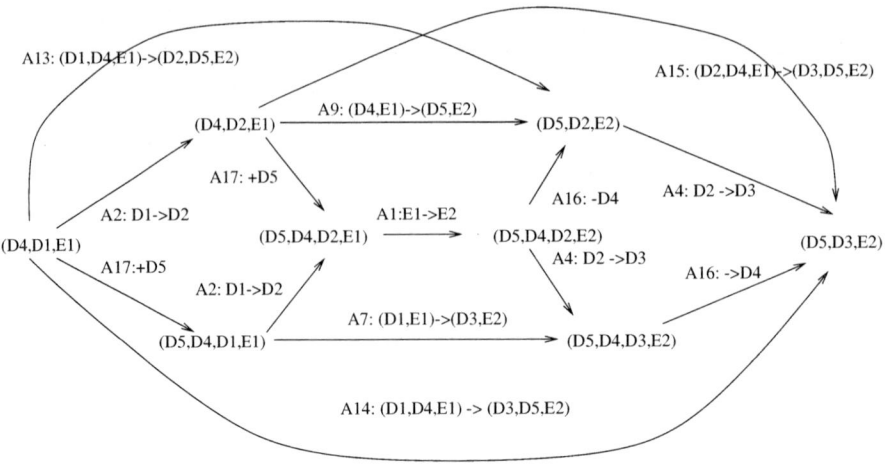

Fig. 4. Safe Adaptation Graph

5.2 Performing Adaptive Actions Safely

The adaptation steps for the safe adaptation path are:

1. **Action A2:** Replace D1 with D2.
2. **Action A17:** Insert D5.
3. **Action A1:** Replace E1 with E2.
4. **Action A16:** Remove D4.
5. **Action A4:** Replace D2 with D3.

Step (1), Action $A2$, only involves the process running the MetaSocket on the handheld. The adaptation manager sends a `reset` message to the agent for the hand-held device. The global safe state of this action is the same as the local safe state of the device: the DES decoder is not decoding a packet. When the agent receives the `reset` message, it sets a "resetting" flag in the MetaSocket. When the decoder finishes decoding a packet, it checks the "resetting" flag. If it is set, then it notifies the agent and blocks itself. At which point, the agent sends a `reset done` message to the adaptation manager and performs the $(A2 : D1 \rightarrow D2)$ action. Then it sends an `adapt done` message to the adaptation manager. When the adaptive action is done, the agent directly resumes the hand-held's full operation and sends a `resume done` message to the hand-held. Other steps (2-5) can be performed in a manner similar to that used in step (1).

6 Related Work

While there have been numerous techniques developed to support dynamic adaptation, we limit our review to work that explicitly addresses the correctness issue of software adaptation. As part of the RAPIDware project, we introduced an aspect-oriented approach to adding dynamic adaptation infrastructure to legacy programs to enable dynamic adaptation [13]. We separated the adaptation concerns from functional concerns of the program, resulting in a clearer and more maintainable design. Also, as part of the RAPIDware project, Kulkarni et al. [20] proposed a distributed approach to safely composing distributed fault-tolerance components at run time. In more recent work [22], they introduced a transitional-invariant lattice technique that uses theorem proving techniques to show that during and after an adaptation, the adaptive system is always in correct states with respect to satisfying the transitional-invariants. Their approach, however, does not guarantee the safeness of adaptation in the presence of failures during adaptation. In contrast, our approach employs a centralized manager, which enables global optimization and ensures safeness.

Other dynamic adaptation techniques have also explicitly addressed correctness issues. Kramer and Magee [23] introduced the notion of a *quiescent state* of a component, in which connections and behaviors of the component can be adapted safely. The concept of quiescent state is close to that of local safe state introduced in this paper. The safe adaptation process in our paper also considers other critical factors such as global conditions and safe configurations. Cactus [24] is a system for constructing highly configurable distributed services and protocols. In Cactus, a host is organized hierarchically into layers, where each layer includes many adaptive components. Chen et al. [24] proposed a *graceful adaptation protocol* that allows adaptations to be coordinated across hosts transparently to the application. Appavoo et al. [25] proposed a *hot-swapping* technique that supports run-time object replacement. In their approach, a *quiescent state* of an object is the state in which no other process is currently using any function of the object. We argue that this conditions is not sufficient in cases where a critical communication segment between two components includes a series of function invocations. Also, they did not address global conditions for safe dynamic adaptation. Amano et al. [26] introduced a model for flexible and safe mobile code adaptation, where adaptations are serialized if there are dependencies among adaptation procedures. Their approach supports the use of assertions for specifying preconditions and postconditions for adaptation, where violations will cancel the adaptation or roll back the system to the state prior to the adaptation. Their work focuses on the dependency relationships among adaptation procedures, whereas our work focuses on dependency relationships among components.

Researchers have also studied architectural description language (ADL)-based approaches to dynamic architectures. Kramer et al. developed Darwin [27], a configuration description language that supports two types of dynamic component instantiations: *lazy instantiation* and *direct dynamic instantiation*. They used π-calculus [28] to define the semantics of the elaboration of Darwin programs. In [29], they used FSP to model adaptive systems, and used a *property automaton* to verify the correctness of adaptations. C2 [30] is an architectural style proposed by Taylor et al. ArchStudio [31] is a management tool for dynamic C2 style software evolution.

7 Conclusions and Future Work

This paper presented an approach to safe dynamic adaptation; the approach can be applied in conjunction with existing dynamic adaptation techniques. We use a centralized adaptation manager to schedule the adaptation process, which results in a globally minimum solution. We block the newly added components until the system has reached a new safe state and thus avoid unsafe adaptation. We also use timeout and rollback mechanisms to deal with possible failures during the adaptation process to ensure atomicity of adaptive actions.

Our approach may greatly benefit from using formal requirements specifications of adaptations [32]. In our approach, the detection and setup phase and the realization phase are largely automated. The algorithms are carried out by the adaptation manager and the agent programs. However, as with other approaches that use dependency relationships, the developers must specify the dependency relationships and the adaptive actions in the analysis phase. We are investigating techniques that enable automatic generation of dependency relationships from formal software requirements specifications. Currently, the developers identify the critical communication segments and safe states based on the requirements and the design. If the requirements are formally specified and there is a strict correspondence between the requirements and the design, then it is also possible to automatically derive the critical communication segments and safe states from the formal requirements specifications. One promising approach is to use a temporal logic formula to specify the set of critical communication segments of a component [32]. The run-time component states can be monitored and the formula can then be dynamically evaluated. If all the obligations of the formula are fulfilled in a state, then the state can be automatically identified as a safe state.

Scalability is a concern for our technique. Because our technique searches the optimal path in a SAG, the computational complexity may be high when there are numerous adaptive components in the system (exponential to the number of components involved in an adaptation). To handle the complexity, we can divide the adaptive components of a system into multiple collaborative sets where component collaborations occur only within each set. The component adaptation of each set can be handled independently, thereby reducing the complexity. Also, Dijkstra's shortest path algorithm requires the entire SAG to be generated. However, in many cases, only a small fraction of the graph is actually related to the given adaptation. We are investigating heuristic-based algorithms that performs partial exploration of the SAG, and would therefore reduce the complexity of this step to $O(n^3)$, where n is the number of components in a collaborative set.

References

1. P. K. McKinley, S. M. Sadjadi, E. P. Kasten, and B. H. C. Cheng, "Composing adaptive software," *IEEE Computer*, vol. 37, no. 7, pp. 56–64, 2004.
2. V. Adve, V. V. Lam, and B. Ensink, "Language and compiler support for adaptive distributed applications," in *Proceedings of the ACM SIGPLAN Workshop on Optimization of Middleware and Distributed Systems (OM 2001)*, 2001.
3. E. Kasten, P. K. McKinley, S. Sadjadi, and R. Stirewalt, "Separating introspection and intercession in metamorphic distributed systems," in *Proceedings of the IEEE Workshop on Aspect-Oriented Programming for Distributed Computing (with ICDCS'02)*, 2002.
4. B. Redmond and V. Cahill, "Supporting unanticipated dynamic adaptation of application behaviour," in *Proceedings of the 16th European Conference on Object-Oriented Programming*, 2002.

5. S. Fickas, G. Kortuem, and Z. Segall, "Software organization for dynamic and adaptable wearable systems," in *Proceedings First International Symposium on Wearable Computers (ISWC'97)*, 1997.
6. J. P. Sousa and D. Garlan, "Aura: An architectural framework for user mobility in ubiquitous computing environments," in *Proceedings of the 3rd Working IEEE/IFIP Conference on Software Architecture*, 2000.
7. G. S. Blair, G. Coulson, P. Robin, and M. Papathomas, "An architecture for next generation middleware," in *Proceedings of the IFIP International Conference on Distributed Systems Platforms and Open Distributed Processing (Middleware'98)*, 1998.
8. F. Kon, M. Roman, P. Liu, J. Mao, T. Yamane, L. C. Magalhaes, and R. H. Campbell, "Monitoring, security, and dynamic configuration with the dynamictao reflective orb," in *Proceedings of the IFIP/ACM International Conference on Distributed Systems Platforms and Open Distributed Processing (Middleware 2000)*, April 2000.
9. B. N. Bershad, S. Savage, P. Pardyak, E. G. Sirer, M. E. Fiuczynski, D. Becker, C. Chambers, and S. Eggers, "Extensibility safety and performance in the SPIN operating system," in *Proceedings of the fifteenth ACM symposium on Operating systems principles*, pp. 267–283, ACM Press, 1995.
10. J. Appavoo, R. W. Wisniewski, C. A. N. Soules, *et al.*, "An infrastructure for multiprocessor run-time adaptation," in *Proceedings of the ACM SIGSOFT Workshop on Self-Healing Systems (WOSS02)*, November 2002.
11. D. R. Engler, M. F. Kaashoek, and J. O'Toole, "Exokernel: An operating system architecture for application-level resource management," in *Symposium on Operating Systems Principles*, pp. 251–266, 1995.
12. S. M. Sadjadi, P. K. McKinley, and E. P. Kasten, "Architecture and operation of an adaptable communication substrate," in *Proceedings of the Ninth International Workshop on Future Trends of Distributed Computing Systems (FTDCS '03)*, May 2003.
13. Z. Yang, B. H. C. Cheng, K. Stirewalt, M. Sadjadis, J. Sowell, and P. McKinley, "An aspect-oriented approach to dynamic adaptation," in *Proceedings of the ACM SIGSOFT Workshop on Self-Healing Systems*, 2002.
14. S. M. Sadjadi and P. K. McKinley, "ACT: An adaptive CORBA template to support unanticipated adaptation," in *Proceedings of the 24th IEEE International Conference on Distributed Computing Systems (ICDCS'04)*, (Tokyo, Japan), March 2004.
15. S. M. Sadjadi, P. K. McKinley, B. H. Cheng, and R. K. Stirewalt, "TRAP/J: Transparent generation of adaptable java programs," in *Proceedings of the International Symposium on Distributed Objects and Applications*, (Agia Napa, Cyprus), October 2004.
16. P. Maes, "Concepts and experiments in computational reflection," in *Proceedings of the ACM Conerfence on Object-Oriented Programming Systems, Languages, and Applications (OOPSLA)*, pp. 147–155, December 1987.
17. P. K. McKinley, E. P. Kasten, S. M. Sadjadi, and Z. Zhou, "Realizing multi-dimensional software adaptation," in *Proceedings of the ACM Workshop on Self-Healing, Adaptive and self-MANaged Systems (SHAMAN), held in conjunction with the 16th Annual ACM International Conference on Supercomputing*, (New York City), June 2002.
18. P. K. McKinley, S. M. Sadjadi, and E. P. Kasten, "An adaptive software approach to intrusion detection and response," in *Proceedings of the 10th International Conference on Telecommunication Systems, Modeling and Analysis*, (Monterey, California), October 2002.
19. A. Arora and M. G. Gouda, "Distributed reset," *IEEE Transactions on Computers*, 1994.
20. S. S. Kulkarni, K. N. Biyani, and U. Arumugam, "Composing distributed fault-tolerance components," in *Proccedings of the International Conference on Dependable Systems and Networks (DSN), Supplemental Volume, Workshop on Principles of Dependable Systems*, pp. W127–W136, June 2003.

21. J. Gray, "Notes on data base operating systems," in *Operating Systems, An Advanced Course*, pp. 393–481, Springer-Verlag, 1978.
22. S. Kulkarni and K. Biyani, "Correctness of component-based adaptation," in *Proceedings of International Symposium on Component-based Software Engineering*, May 2004.
23. J. Kramer and J. Magee, "The evolving philosophers problem: Dynamic change management," *IEEE Trans. Softw. Eng.*, vol. 16, no. 11, pp. 1293–1306, 1990.
24. W.-K. Chen, M. A. Hiltunen, and R. D. Schlichting, "Constructing adaptive software in distributed systems," in *Proc. of the 21st International Conference on Distributed Computing Systems*, (Mesa, AZ), April 16 - 19 2001.
25. J. Appavoo, K. Hui, C. A. N. Soules, *et al.*, "Enabling autonomic behavior in systems software with hot swapping," *IBM System Journal*, vol. 42, no. 1, p. 60, 2003.
26. N. Amano and T. Watanabe, "A software model for flexible and safe adaptation of mobile code programs," in *Proceedings of the international workshop on Principles of software evolution*, pp. 57–61, ACM Press, 2002.
27. J. Kramer, J. Magee, and M. Sloman, "Configuring distributed systems," in *Proceedings of the 5th workshop on ACM SIGOPS European workshop*, pp. 1–5, ACM Press, 1992.
28. R. Milner, J. Parrow, and D. Walker, "A calculus of mobile processes, I," *Information and Computation*, vol. 100, no. 1, pp. 1–40, 1992.
29. J. Kramer and J. Magee, "Analysing dynamic change in software architectures: a case study," in *Proc. of 4th IEEE international conference on configuratble distributed systems*, (Annapolis), May 1998.
30. R. N. Taylor, N. Medvidovic, K. M. Anderson, E. J. Whitehead, Jr., and J. E. Robbins, "A component- and message-based architectural style for GUI software," in *Proceedings of the 17th international conference on Software engineering*, pp. 295–304, ACM Press, 1995.
31. P. Oreizy, N. Medvidovic, and R. N. Taylor, "Architecture-based runtime software evolution," in *Proceedings of the 20th international conference on Software engineering*, pp. 177–186, IEEE Computer Society, 1998.
32. J. Zhang and B. H. Cheng, "Specifying adaptation semantics," in *Proceedings of ICSE 2005 Workshop on Architecting Dependable Systems*, (St. Louis, Missouri), May 2005. accepted for publication.

Architecting and Implementing Versatile Dependability

Tudor Dumitraş, Deepti Srivastava, and Priya Narasimhan[*]

Carnegie Mellon University, Pittsburgh PA 15213, USA
{tdumitra, dsrivast}@ece.cmu.edu, priya@cs.cmu.edu

Abstract. Distributed applications must often consider and select the appropriate trade-offs among three important aspects – fault-tolerance, performance and resources. We introduce a novel concept, called versatile dependability, that provides a framework for analyzing and reasoning about these trade-offs in dependable software architectures. We present the architecture of a middleware framework that implements versatile dependability by providing the appropriate "knobs" to tune and re-calibrate the trade-offs. Our framework can adjust the properties and the behavior of the system at development-time, at deployment-time, and throughout the application's life-cycle. This renders the versatile dependability approach useful both to applications that require static fault-tolerance configurations supporting the loss/addition of resources and changing workloads, as well as to applications that evolve in terms of their dependability requirements. Through a couple of specific examples, one on adapting the replication style at runtime and the other on tuning the system scalability under given constraints, we demonstrate concretely how versatile dependability can provide an extended coverage of the design space of dependable distributed systems.

1 Introduction

Oftentimes, the requirements of dependable systems are conflicting in many ways. For example, optimizations for high performance usually come at the expense of using additional resources and/or weakening the fault-tolerance guarantees. Conversely, distributed fault-tolerance techniques, such as replication, can adversely impact the performance and scalability. It is our belief that these conflicts must be viewed as *trade-offs* in the design space of dependable systems and that only a good understanding of these trade-offs can lead to the development of useful and reliable systems. Unfortunately, many existing approaches offer only point solutions to this problem because they hard-code the trade-offs in their design choices, rendering them difficult to adapt to changing working conditions and to support evolving requirements over the system's lifetime.

---

[*] This work has been partially supported by the NSF CAREER grant CCR-0238381, the DARPA PCES contract F33615-03-C-4110, and also in part by the General Motors Collaborative Research Laboratory at Carnegie Mellon University.

As an alternative, we propose *versatile dependability*[1], a novel design paradigm for dependable distributed systems that focuses on the three-way trade-off between fault-tolerance, quality of service (QoS) – in terms of performance or real-time guarantees – and resource usage. This framework offers a better coverage of the dependability design-space, by focusing on an operating region (rather than an operating point) within this space, and by providing a set of "knobs" for tuning the trade-offs and properties of the system.

Our versatile dependability framework is an enhancement to current middleware systems such as CORBA or Java. While these middleware do have fault-tolerance support (through the Fault-Tolerant CORBA [2] and the Continuous Availability APIs for Java [3] standards), they lack the support for run-time adaptability. Furthermore, tuning these off-the-shelf middleware is an awkward task for their users because, in most cases, the adjustment process requires detailed knowledge of the system's implementation and because the internal tuning mechanisms are hard to control in an effective manner and can produce undesirable side-effects.

For example, the Fault-Tolerant CORBA standard [2] lists a set of "fault-tolerance properties" (*e.g.*, the replication style, the minimum number of replicas, the checkpointing intervals, the fault monitoring intervals and their timeouts), without providing any guidance as to how they ought to be set or how they map into externally-observable properties, such as scalability. We call these internal fault-tolerance properties the *low-level knobs*. The versatile dependability approach advocates the implementation of *high-level knobs*, corresponding to the external properties of the system, that encode the knowledge about the essential trade-offs and that provide the necessary insights on how to configure the system appropriately. Hence, the users of our COTS middleware do not need to quantify or understand the intricate relationships between internal and external properties, while enjoying the full benefits of an increased flexibility.

This paper makes four main contributions in describing:

- A new concept, versatile dependability, directed at achieving tunable, resource and QoS aware fault-tolerance in distributed systems (Section 2);
- A software architecture for versatile dependability with four design goals: tunability, quantifiability, transparency and ease of use (Section 3);
- How to implement the tuning knobs of versatile dependability, including two examples: dynamically adapting the replication style at runtime and adjusting the system scalability under specified constraints (Section 4);
- Why versatile dependability is relevant for several classes of applications, and what are the biggest challenges for extending this research direction (Section 5).

---

[1] An earlier version of this chapter, containing the first mention of versatile dependability, was published as [1].

2 Versatile Dependability

We visualize the development of dependable systems through a three-dimensional *dependability design-space*, as shown in Figure 1, with the following axes: (i) the *fault-tolerance* "levels" that the system can provide, (ii) the *high performance* guarantees it can offer, and (iii) the amount of *resources* it needs for each pairwise {fault-tolerance, performance} choice. In contrast to existing dependable systems, we aim to span larger regions of this space because the behavior of the application can be tuned by adjusting the appropriate settings. In our research, we strive to achieve a high degree of flexibility by evaluating the wide variety of choices for implementing dependable systems, and by quantifying the effect of these choices on the three axes of our {Fault-Tolerance × Performance × Resources} design space. The purpose of this paper is to quantify some of the trade-offs among these three properties and to demonstrate how we can implement the most effective tuning knobs that allow system users and administrators, as well as application designers, to adjust these trade-offs appropriately.

Our general versatile dependability framework consists of:

1. Monitoring various system metrics (*e.g.*, latency, jitter, CPU load) in order to evaluate the conditions in the working environment [4];
2. Defining contracts for the specified behavior of the overall system;
3. Specifying policies to implement the desired behavior under different working conditions;
4. Developing algorithms for automatic adaptation to the changing conditions (*e.g.*, resource exhaustion, introduction of new nodes) in the working environment.

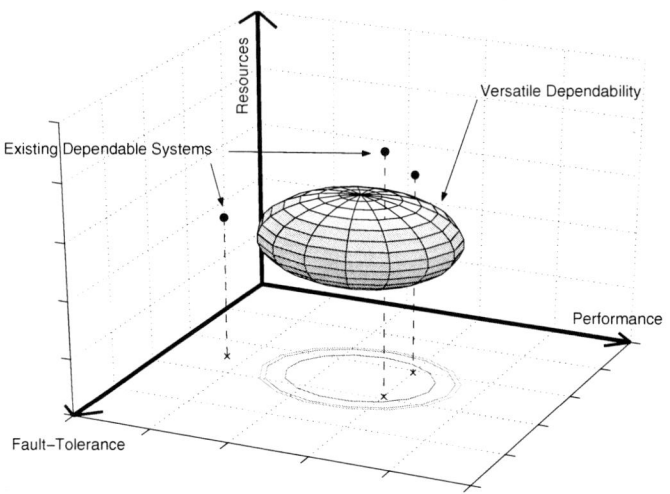

Fig. 1. Design space of dependable systems

Table 1. Mapping from high-level to low-level knobs

High-level Knobs	Scalability	Availability	Real-Time Guarantees
Low-level Knobs	Replication Style, Replication Degree	Replication Style, Checkpointing Frequency[a]	Replication Style, Replication Degree, Checkpointing Frequency
Application Parameters	Request Frequency, Request and Response Size, Resources	State Size, Resources	Request Frequency, Request and Response Size, State Size, Resources

[a] This knob is relevant only for passive replication (see Section 3.1)

Versatile dependability was developed to provide a set of control knobs to tune the multiple trade-offs. There are two types of knobs in our architecture: high-level knobs, which control the abstract properties from the requirements space (e.g., scalability, availability), and low-level knobs, which tune the fault-tolerant mechanisms that our system incorporates (e.g., replication style, number of replicas). The high-level knobs, which are the most useful ones for the system operators, are influenced by both the settings of the low-level knobs that we can adjust directly (e.g., the replication style, the number of replicas, the checkpointing style and frequency), and the parameters of the application that are not under our control (e.g., the frequency of requests, the size of the application state, the sizes of the requests and replies). Through an empirical evaluation of the system, we determine in which ways the low-level knobs can be used to implement high-level knobs under the specified constraints, and we define adaptation policies that effectively map the high-level settings to the actual variables of our tunable mechanisms. This approach complements a formal analysis of the system's correctness and performance and it shows how the system can be tuned and configured in its working environment. Table 1 shows three examples of mapping from high-level knobs to low-level knobs; in a complex system there can be many more such knobs and many other parameters that influence those knobs. In this paper, we consider a representative set of these knobs to illustrate the tuning process.

3 The Architecture of Our Framework

Our framework is based on the Fault-Tolerant CORBA specification [2], which has only primitive support for tunable fault-tolerance. The tuning and adaptation to changing environments are enacted in a distributed manner, by a group of software components that work independently and that cooperate to agree and execute the preferred course of action. In order to add a minimal overhead to the systems that we are continuously monitoring and tuning, we try to keep our system as simple as possible and to limit its functionality to the core

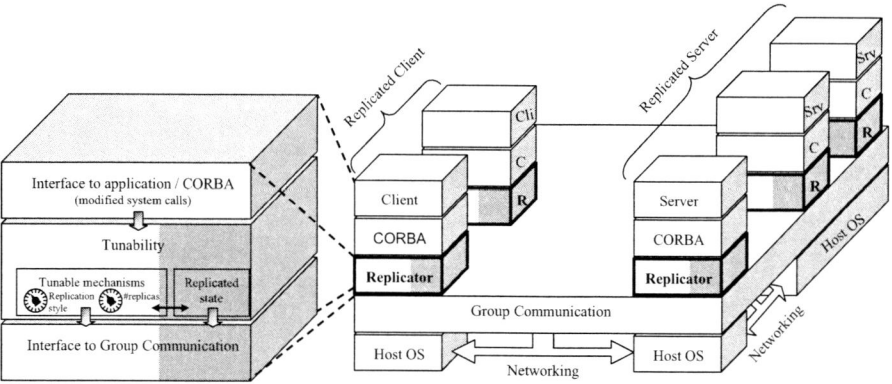

Fig. 2. System Architecture

mechanisms needed to add and adjust fault-tolerance. We believe that this is important, especially since footprint and scalability are major concerns in some critical middleware applications.

This research forms a fundamental part of the MEAD (Middleware for Embedded Adaptive Dependability) project [4] which is currently under development at Carnegie Mellon University. While we currently focus on CORBA systems, which seemed the ideal starting point for this investigation given our previous experiences,[2] our approach is intrinsically independent of the specific middleware platform and can be applied to other systems as well.

3.1 A Tunable, Distributed Infrastructure

To ensure that our overall system architecture enables both the continuous monitoring and the simultaneous tuning of various fault-tolerance parameters, we have four distinct design goals for our system architecture:

- *Tunability and homogeneity:* having one infrastructure that supports multiple knobs and a range of different fault-tolerant techniques;
- *Quantifiability:* using precise metrics to evaluate the trade-offs among various properties of the system and to develop benchmarks for evaluating these metrics;
- *Transparency:* enabling support for replication-unaware and legacy applications;
- *Ease of use:* providing simple knobs that are intuitively easy to adjust.

The taxonomy of low-level and high-level knobs helps us address the flexibility and ease of use requirements of versatile dependability: the knobs preserve

---

[2] MEAD was born out of the lessons that we learned in architecting and implementing the Eternal system [5]; however, Eternal was primarily designed to support fault-tolerant CORBA – real-time, resource-awareness and tunability were not considered in its design.

the tunability of the system's behavior (by not hard coding the trade-off settings in the design choices) and they translate the internal variables of the framework into external properties that make sense for the system operators. The transparency and quantifiability requirements of versatile dependability are achieved through the architecture of our framework, which is discussed below.

We assume a distributed asynchronous system, subject to hardware and software crash faults, transient communication faults, performance and timing faults. The architecture of our system is illustrated in Figure 2. At the core of our approach is the *replicator*, a software module that can be used to provide fault-tolerance transparently to a middleware application. The replicator intercepts the system calls of the CORBA application (on both the client and server sides), redirects the CORBA messages between hosts to a reliable group communication service, and manages groups of client and server replicas. Note that the application and the ORB need not be aware of all these tasks; in fact, we have successfully used the replicator to obtain fault-tolerant versions of legacy, un-replicated applications.

The replicator module is implemented as a stack of sub-modules with three layers. The top layer is the interface to the CORBA application; it intercepts the system calls in order to understand the operations of the application. The middle layer contains all the mechanisms for transparently replicating processes and managing the groups of replicas, as well as the knobs needed to tune the system. The bottom layer is the interface to the group communication package and is an abstraction layer to render the replicator portable to various communication platforms.

The unique feature of the replicator is that its behavior is tunable and that it can adapt dynamically to changing conditions in the environment. Given all the design choices for building dependable systems, the middle layer of the replicator can choose, from among different implementations, those that are best suited to meet the system's requirements. In the following paragraphs, we describe some of the techniques used by the replicator.

Library Interposition. This technique allows the replicator to perform tasks transparently to the application and to CORBA itself [6]. The replicator is a shared library that intercepts and redefines the standard system calls to convey the application's messages over a reliable group communication system. Using linker-related environment variables (*e.g.*, LD_PRELOAD), we can insert the replicator ahead of all the other shared libraries in the CORBA application process' address space. At runtime, symbol definitions of interest to us (primarily socket and network level routines) resolve to the replicator rather than the default operating system libraries. This is accomplished with *no* change to the application, the ORB, or the operating system, thereby achieving transparency. The calls redefined inside the replicator are interposed between the application and the system libraries, such that, at runtime, the application (unknowingly) calls the functions from the replicator, instead of the standard ones. Because the replicator mimics the TCP/IP programming interface, the application continues to believe that it is using regular CORBA GIOP connections. For example, if a client is trying to send a message to a server, we can intercept it and broadcast it (using group communication) to several replicas of that server in order to increase the dependability of the service.

Group Membership and Communication. We are currently using the Spread toolkit [7] for group membership and communication. This package provides an API (based on the extended virtual synchrony model [8]) for joining/leaving groups, detecting failures and reliable multicasting. Spread can provide five types of guarantees for message delivery: best effort (no guarantees), reliable delivery, FIFO ordering (by sender), causal ordering and total ordering. These guarantees enable us to ensure the consistency between the different replicas of the application. The price we have to pay for this consistency is that our system inherits the performance overhead of maintaining virtual synchrony between the nodes and the behavior of the replicator is closely related to the performance of the underlying group communication protocol.

Tunable Fault-Tolerant Mechanisms. We provide fault-tolerant services to both CORBA client and server applications by replicating them in various ways, and by coordinating the client interactions with the server replicas. We implement replication at the process level rather than at the object level because a CORBA process may contain several objects (that share "in-process" state), all of which have to be recovered, as a unit, in the event of a process crash. Maintaining consistent replicas of the entire CORBA application is, therefore, the best way to protect our system against loss of state or processing in the event of software (process-level) and hardware (node-level) crash faults.

Currently, the replicator supports the two canonical replication styles: active replication and passive replication:[3]

- *Active replication*, also called the "state-machine approach" [10], is a technique where all the replicas are running and processing requests simultaneously on different nodes. The client has two choices for determining the correct response:
    - it can accept the first response received, if the server replicas are trusted not to behave maliciously (which is the case in this paper);
    - it can do majority voting on all the responses it receives, if Byzantine failures may occur in the system [11].
- *Passive replication*, also called the "the primary-backup approach" [12], mandates that only one replica, called the *primary*, executes the application, while one or several *backups* are waiting to take over when the primary fails. Depending on how and when the state of the primary is transferred to the backups, this replication style has two flavors:
    - *cold passive* replication, where a backup is launched (by a watchdog) only when the primary crashes, retrieving the state from a log saved on shared permanent storage, and

---

[3] In the future, we plan to include support for other replication styles [9] as well.

- *warm passive* replication, where the backups are in a stand-by mode, periodically receiving state updates from the primary. When the primary crashes, a new primary is chosen from among the running backups, using some deterministic algorithm.

We implement tunability by providing a set of low-level knobs that can adjust the behavior of the replicator, such as the replication style, the number of replicas and the checkpointing style and frequency (see Table 1). Note that versatile dependability does not impose a "one-style-fits-all" strategy; instead, it allows the maximum possible freedom in selecting a different replication style for each CORBA process and in changing it at run-time, should that be necessary.

Replicated State. As the replicator is itself a distributed entity, it maintains (using the group communication layer) within itself an identically replicated object with information about the entire system (*e.g.*, current view of the group membership, resource availability at all the hosts, performance metrics, environmental conditions). This object is needed for certain steps of the replication process (such as failover) and for making consistent decisions when adapting to the conditions in the environment. This is accomplished through MEAD's decentralized resource monitoring infrastructure and through the Fault-Tolerance Advisor [4], whose task is to identify the most appropriate configurations (including the replication style and degree) for the current state of the system.

Adaptation Policies. There are various reasons why a system may need to adapt its fault-tolerance properties. For example, an application may be multi-modal and hence require different fault-tolerance in different modes, or runtime profiling of an application may show different resource availability at different times, and hence fault-tolerance policies would need to be adapted to this. These scenarios require different approaches and hence different adaptation algorithms.

Our system can perform static as well as runtime profiling to adapt the fault-tolerance of the system. It can monitor various system metrics and generates warnings when the operating conditions are about to change. If the contracts for the desired behavior can no longer be honored, the replicator adjusts the fault-tolerant mechanisms to the new working conditions (including modes within the application, if they happen to exist). This adaptation is performed automatically, according to a set of policies that can be either pre-defined or introduced at run time; these policies correspond to the high-level knobs described in Section 2. For example, if the re-enforcement of a previous contract is not feasible, versatile dependability can offer alternative (possibly degraded) behavioral contracts that the application might still wish to have; manual intervention might be warranted in some extreme cases. As soon as all of the instances of the replicator have agreed to follow the new policy, they can start adapting their behavior accordingly.

Application of Adaptation Policies. The decision to act on an adaptation policy must be applied consistently at all the nodes of the distributed system. This can be accomplished in two ways: (i) applying the adaptation without any further communication, based on the replicated state, and (ii) sending a "switch" message through a totally ordered multicast channel to initiate the change. With the first strategy, all the decisions to re-tune the system parameters are made in a distributed manner by a deterministic algorithm that takes the replicated state as input. If each local change is the outcome of events that are consistently delivered[4] at all the nodes by the resource monitoring system, then no further communication is needed; the decisions are based on data that is already available and agreed upon, and virtual synchrony ensures that the adaptation will be applied correctly. This has the advantage that the distributed adaptation process is very swift. With the second strategy, the system sends a "switch" message to all the replicators in a group; reception of this message triggers the adaptation process. This is equivalent to running Consensus to decide when to apply the change, and the "switch" message acts as a checkpoint in the totally ordered stream of messages indicating a time when all the replicas have received the same set of incoming messages and they are in the same state (we give a more detailed example of this strategy in Section 4.1). This approach introduces the delay of a totally ordered multicast between the time when an adaptation decision is made and the time when it is applied.

There are cases when the first strategy cannot be applied. For example, if the Fault-Tolerance Advisor runs as a separate process from the replicator, the decision to change will be communicated through an IPC or a shared memory mechanism. Since our system uses group communication to enforce consistency, using a side-channel (such as IPC or shared memory) may lead to unrecognized causality between the stream of requests and the adaptation decision and, therefore, the change could be applied when the replicas are in inconsistent states.[5] Integrating the replicator, the resource monitoring and the adaptation policy parsing in a single execution thread would remove this shortcoming, but it would increase the overhead of processing the requests. This shows that there is a trade-off between the overhead of the replicator in the average case and the ability to apply the adaptation policies very fast.

High and Low Level Knobs. Using all the mechanisms described above, we can implement the high and low level knobs mandated by versatile dependability. The group communication package allows us to implement a low-level knob that specifies the type of delivery guarantee the messages in the stream of requests have. Depending on the nature of the application, different types of messages may be used to achieve the target performance and dependability (for example, a stateless server requires only reliable message delivery, while a stateful server needs totally ordered messages if the requests contain state updates). Our replication mechanisms let us tune a number of parameters, such as the replication style, the number of replicas and the checkpointing frequency. The aggressiveness

---

[4] In the virtual synchrony model [13, 8], consistent delivery means that the same events are delivered in the same order, but without any timeliness guarantees.

[5] This does not happen when the requests do not update the state or when the replicas are stateless.

of resource monitoring and the strategy for applying adaptation policies define other low-level knobs that can be adjusted to control the overhead and the speed of the adaptation process. Finally, the high-level knobs are implemented on top of all these low-level knobs, using the adaptation policies.

4 Implementation of Tuning Knobs

Our versatile dependability framework includes both knobs that can be used off-line, to configure the system for particular requirements and workloads, and knobs that adapt to conditions in the working environment at runtime. Below, we estimate empirically the performance and the overhead of our framework (Section 4), we show how to implement a low-level knob that allows us to switch between an active and a passive replication style at runtime (Section 4.1), and we show how to construct a high-level knob to tune the system scalability (Section 4.2).

We have deployed a prototype of our system on a test-bed of seven Intel x86 machines. Each machine is a Pentium III running at 900 megahertz with 512MB RAM of memory and running RedHat Linux 9.0. We employ the Spread (v. 3.17.1) group communication system [7] and the TAO real-time ORB [14] (v. 1.4). In our experiments, we use a CORBA client-server test application that processes a cycle of 10,000 requests.

Performance and Overhead of the Replicator. In Figure 3, we examine the raw overhead introduced by the replicator and the replication mechanism. We compare here the latencies of the baseline application (without the replicator), of an operating mode where the system calls are intercepted, but not modified (with just the client, just the server, and both of them intercepted), and of the active and warm passive replication styles (with one client and an unreplicated

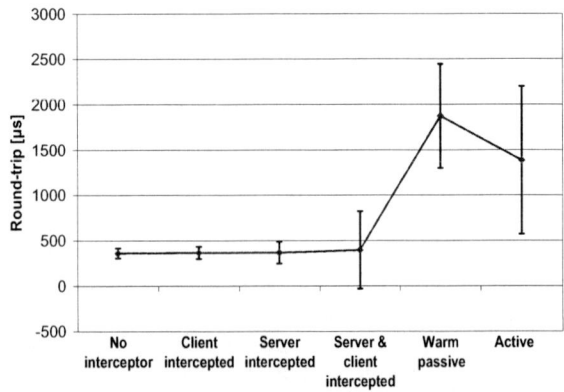

Fig. 3. Overhead of the replicator for a remote client–server application

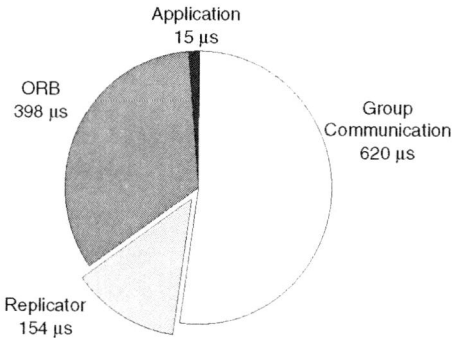

Fig. 4. Break-down of the average round-trip time

server to keep the results comparable). The vertical error bars from the figure indicate the jitter measured in the corresponding experiment. We can see that the replicator itself introduces little overhead, but the replication mechanisms lead to increased latency and jitter.

Figure 4 shows a break-down of the average round-trip time of a request transmitted through MEAD, as measured at the client (in a configuration with one client and an unreplicated server). We notice that the transmission delay through the group communication layer is the dominant contributor to the overall latency (in this paper, by latency we mean round-trip time). The application processing time is very small because we are using a micro-benchmark; for a real application, the time to process the request would be significantly higher. The replicator introduces only 154 μs overhead on average, a fairly small figure compared to the latencies of the group communication system and the ORB.

4.1 Runtime Adaptive Replication

The active and passive replication styles represent different trade-offs between timeliness, recovery and resource usage. In general, active replication is faster in responding to requests and in recovering from faults because checkpointing and rollback are not needed, while passive replication uses more efficiently the resources available, such as bandwidth and CPU cycles. Adaptive systems should be able to modify replication styles on the fly, at run-time, in response to workload changes and application requirements. We implement a low-level knob to switch between replication styles through three steps (see also the pseudocode in Figure 5):

1. One or more replicas initiate the transition process by sending a "switch" message to the entire replica group (duplicate messages are discarded);
2. Each replica, on receiving the "switch" message, starts enqueuing application messages and broadcasts all the information needed by the other replicas to update their local state and to perform the switch;

```
I INITIATE adaptation:
    send switch message

II PREPARE to switch:
    /* Case 1: switch Warm Passive --> Active */
    If (this replica == current Primary)
            prepare to send one more checkpoint before switching
    If (replica == current Backup)
            prepare to wait for one more checkpoint after the switch
    /* Case 2: switch Active --> Warm Passive */
    Choose a new primary
    Prepare to handle outstanding messages, if any, after the switch

III SWITCH to new replication style:
    /* Case 1: switch Warm Passive --> Active */
    New replication style = Active
    If (this replica == previous Primary)
            send one more checkpoint
    If (this replica == previous Backup)
            accept one more checkpoint
            If (no checkpoints received &&
                detect crash of previous Primary)
                    process all outstanding requests
                    in message queue (rollback)
            else
                    continue
    /* Case 2: switch Active --> Warm Passive */
    New replication style = Active
    If (this replica == new backup)
            If (any outstanding requests in message queue)
                    process those requests and then
                    become completely passive
            else
                    continue as backup
```

Fig. 5. Algorithm to switch between replication styles

3. Each replica, on receiving all the information needed to ensure a consistent state, updates its internal state and assumes its role in the new replication style.

The second step is different depending on the direction of the switch: when switching from warm passive to active replication, the backups must synchronize their states with the primary before they can start processing requests. In the case of a crash of the primary, the backups can restore a consistent state by replaying the messages received since the last checkpoint prior to the crash. When switching from active to warm passive replication, a new primary must be selected and the other replicas become backups after finishing to service their current requests.

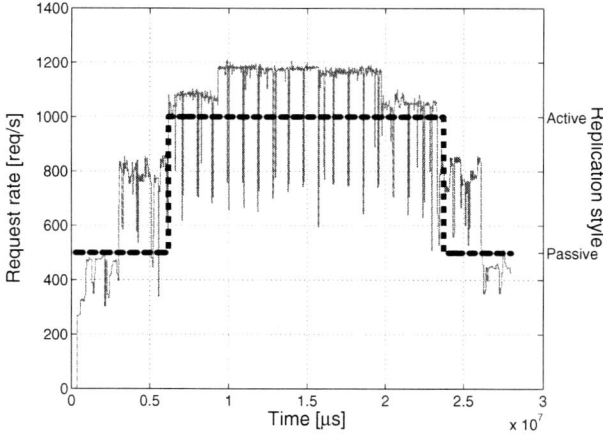

Fig. 6. Low-level knob: adaptive replication

The "switch" messages are sent through a totally ordered, reliable multicast channel using our group communication layer (see Section 3.1), which makes our algorithm tolerant to the crash of any replica. Since fault notifications are ordered consistently with respect to the "switch" and the other messages, the remaining non-faulty instances of the replicator can always determine at which point in the algorithm the crash has occurred and continue the work from that point until the replication style switch is complete. The protocol described in Figure 5 can tolerate the crash failure of either the primary or of any of the backups.

Our adaptive replication style takes the middle ground between the fast, resource-hungry active replication and the slower, resource-efficient passive replication. Figure 6 shows how we can adapt the replication style in response to the load of the system. Since active replication can handle higher request arrival rates than passive replication, in this example we switch whenever the request rate increases above a certain threshold. This simple adaptation policy selects the replication style that is appropriate for the measured request arrival rate at the server.

The observed delays required to complete the switch are comparable to the average response time, and they are negligible at high loads, such as the ones that trigger the adaptation. It is interesting to note that the request arrival rate observed at the server is 4.1% higher in the case of adaptive replication than when using static passive replication with the same workload. This is because active replication can respond faster under such high loads; clients waiting for the replies receive them faster and can send new requests sooner than in the previous case (there is no need for quiescence and checkpointing). This speed-up effect allows the servers to regulate the load imposed by the clients and to increase the throughput of the replicated service.

The adaptive replication knob provides the ability to change the replication style whenever required, either off-line, before the application is launched, or online, during its execution. This flexibility allows us to tune with precision the behavior of dependable systems in the space between active and passive replication, by defining the appropriate adaptation policies. This is essential when the middleware infrastructure needs to support a graceful degradation to operation modes with reduced functionality, (*e.g.*, when taking the system in a safe mode when the loss of redundancy threatens the reliability and safety of the system). However, adaptive replication is most useful for implementing high-level knobs that correspond to external system properties, as described in the next section.

4.2 Tuning System Scalability

In this section, we show we can tune the *scalability* of the system (*i.e.*, the number of clients it can service) under specified resource and performance constraints. The first step in implementing a scalability knob is to gather enough data about the system's behavior in order to construct a policy for implementing a high-level knob (see Section 3.1). We examine the average round-trip latency of requests, under different system loads and redundancy levels (because we were limited to eight computers, we ran experiments with up to five clients and three server replicas). In Figure 7-(a), we can see that the active replication incurs a much lower latency than warm passive replication, which makes the round-trip delays increase almost linearly with the number of clients. With five clients, passive replication is roughly three times slower than active replication.

The roles are reversed in terms of resource usage. In Figure 7-(b), we notice that, although in both styles the bandwidth consumption increases with the number of clients, the growth is steeper for active replication. Indeed, for five clients, active replication requires about twice the bandwidth of passive replication. Thus, when considering the scalability of the system, we must pay attention to the trade-off between latency and bandwidth usage. While this is not intuitively surprising, our quantitative data will let us determine the best settings for a given number of clients.

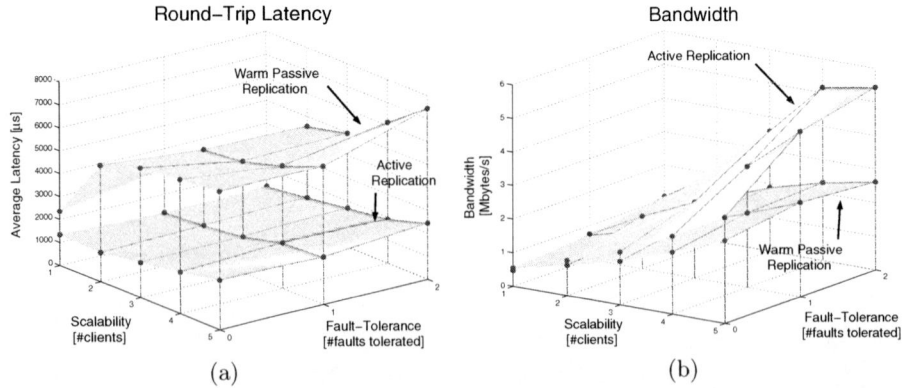

Fig. 7. Trade-off between latency and bandwidth usage

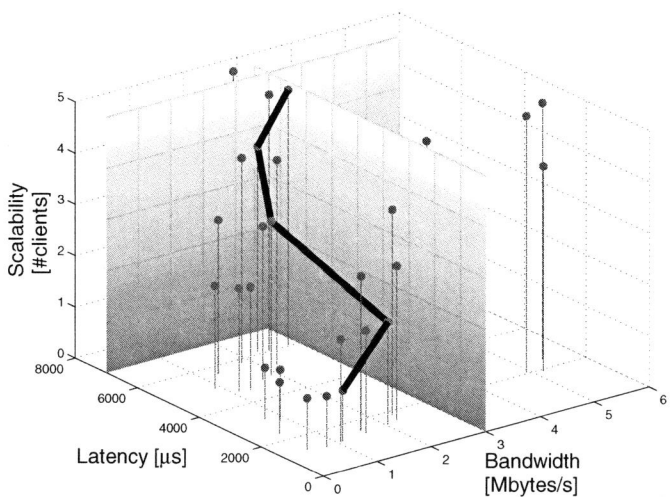

Fig. 8. High level knob: scalability

Implementing a "Scalability" Knob. We would like to implement a knob that tunes the scalability of the system under bandwidth, latency, and fault-tolerance constraints. In other words, given a number of clients N_{cli}, we want to decide the best possible configuration for the servers (*e.g.*, the replication style and the number of replicas). Let us consider a system with the following requirements:

1. The average latency shall not exceed 7000 μs;
2. The bandwidth usage shall not exceed 3 MB/s;
3. The configuration should have the best fault-tolerance possible (given requirements 1–2);
4. Among all the configurations i that satisfy the previous requirements, the one with the lowest:

$$Cost_i = p\frac{Latency_i}{7000\mu s} + (1-p)\frac{Bandwidth_i}{3MB/s}$$

should be chosen, where $Latency_i$ is the measured latency of i, $Bandwidth_i$ is the measured bandwidth and p is the weight assigned to each of these metrics.[6]

This situation is illustrated in Figure 8. The hard limits imposed by requirements 1 and 2 are represented by the vertical planes that set the useful configurations apart from the other ones. For each number of clients N_{cli}, we

---

[6] The cost function is a heuristic rule of thumb (not derived from a rigorous analysis), that we use to break the ties after satisfying the first 3 requirements; we anticipate that other developers could define different cost functions. Here, we use $p = 0.5$ to weight latency and bandwidth equally.

select from this set those configurations that have the highest number of server replicas to satisfy the third requirement. If, at this point, we still have more than one candidate configuration, we compute the cost to choose the replication style (the number of replicas has been decided during the previous steps). The resulting policy is represented by the thick line from Figure 8, and its characteristics are summarized in Table 2.

Note that, while for up to four clients the system is able to tolerate two crash failures, for five clients only one failure is tolerated because no configuration with three replicas could meet the requirements in this case. This emphasizes the trade-off between fault-tolerance and scalability under the requirements 1–4, which impose hard limits for the performance and resource usage of the system. Furthermore, since in both the active and passive replication styles, at least one of the metrics considered (*i.e.*, bandwidth and latency) increases linearly, it is likely that, for a higher load, we cannot satisfy the requirements. In this case, the system notifies the operators that the tuning policy can no longer be honored and that a new policy must be defined in order to accept any more clients.

5 Discussion

Scalability is only one possible high-level knob that versatile dependability can tune; we could similarly implement other high-level knobs such as availability, reliability, sustained throughput, etc. In fact, each one of the requirements specified in Section 4.2 probably corresponds to a high-level knob that can be tuned independently. Achieving a separation of concerns between these knobs, by reducing the influence they have on each other, is therefore an important research challenge for the future of versatile dependability.

However, in its current stage versatile dependability rises to the challenge of enabling adaptive systems with a tunable range of reliability and performance guarantees. Figure 9 displays the trade-off between the active and passive replication styles in the dependability design space (which was introduced in Figure 1). The data set displayed here is the same one from Figure 7, where the fault-tolerance, performance and resource usage of each configuration are normalized to their maximum values. We can see that each of the two replication styles corresponds to a larger region in this space and includes multiple possible

Table 2. Policy for scalability tuning

N_{cli}	1	2	3	4	5
Configuration[a]	A (3)	A (3)	P (3)	P (3)	P (2)
Latency [μs]	1245.8	1457.2	4966	6141.1	6006.2
Bandwidth [MB/s]	1.074	2.032	1.887	2.315	2.799
Faults Tolerated	2	2	2	2	1
Cost	0.268	0.443	0.669	0.825	0.895

[a] Active/Passive (number of replicas); *e.g.*, A(3) = 3 active replicas.

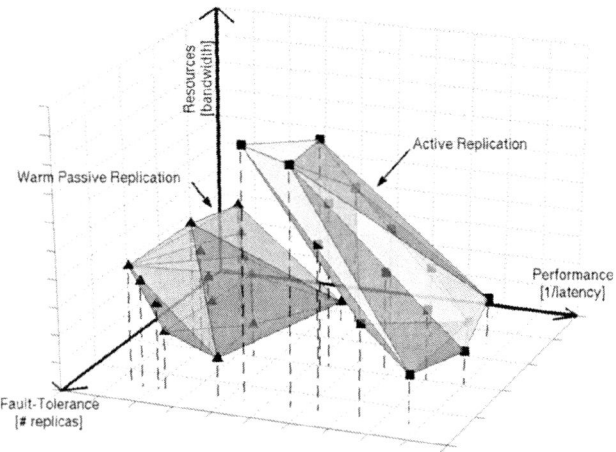

Fig. 9. Active and passive replication in the dependability design space

configurations of the system. The two regions are non-overlapping; however, by using low and high-level knobs such as the ones described above, we can position the system in any configuration desired.

Versatile dependability is essential for long-running applications that cannot be stopped (*e.g.*, during a space flight), but that have several modes of operation with different resource and performance requirements (*e.g.*, simulation/ training and mission modes). The high performance provided by active replication can be used when gathering data and performing actuation must be done within narrow time limits, when there are limited windows of opportunity and data is critical, because of the faster response and recovery times. The more conservative passive replication is needed when the resources are scarce and cannot be wasted by running several active replicas in parallel. When both these conditions are present (*e.g.*, in a network of sensors), the infrastructure must be able to tune the replication style to run in a resource-conservative mode most of the time, and to switch to the high-performance mode only during the limited window of opportunity. The ability to express the tuning problem in terms of external properties (the high-level knobs), rather than internal parameters of the system (the low-level knobs), facilitates the configuration and management of complex distributed systems because it does not require a detailed knowledge of the system's implementation and the internal fault-tolerant mechanisms used.

6 Related Work

Among the first attempts to reconcile soft real-time and fault-tolerance, the Delta-4 XPA project [15] used semi-active replication (*the leader-follower model*) where all the replicas are active but only one designated copy (the leader) transmits output responses. In some conditions, this approach can combine the low synchronization requirements of passive replication with the low error-recovery delays of active replication. The ROAFTS project [16] implements a number of traditional fault-tolerant schemes in their rugged forms and operates them under the control of a centralized network supervision and reconfiguration (NSR) manager.

Traditionally, research on adaptive software systems has focused on either system architectures to support the adaptation process [17, 18], or on domain-specific strategies for adaptation under given constraints encountered in practical situations [19, 20]. The former approach does not make use of any domain knowledge about the application and, thus, only enables hooks for adaptation while leaving the actual implementation details to domain experts; the latter approach usually focuses on one particular (often domain-specific) instance of the problem and does not build a generic framework around the proposed solution.

For instance, the AQuA framework [19] proposes a technique to support graceful QoS adaptation by requiring applications to specify the criticality of their timeliness and consistency requirements in probabilistic terms. This probabilistic QoS model can be implemented through replication and a combination of virtual synchrony and lazy propagation of updates that effectively provides a tunable range of consistency guarantees. Based on the client's request and the measured conditions in the environment (*e.g.*, current network latencies and replica staleness), the framework detects whether the client's QoS specification can be met with the required probability. In this case, AQuA automatically selects the subset of replicas to service the invocation using a greedy algorithm. Note that, in our terminology, AQuA's tunable QoS guarantees are analogous to a high-level knob.

However, in some cases, the QoS requirements and the environmental conditions can change so drastically that a switch to a completely different algorithm is necessary. Cactus [17] proposes a generic software architecture for adaptive systems based on fine-grained software modules that implement abstract QoS properties. The adaptation framework uses fitness functions associated with each module to determine the best one for the current requirements and execution environment. The adaptive action is performed after all the distributed components have agreed to select the corresponding software modules in a consistent way. This adaptation mechanism is similar to a low-level knob from our framework, such as the one described in Section 4.1.

It has also been noted that hybrid replication strategies can be conceived, and these can be combined with caching in order to give more flexibility to the application designer [21]. For example, some of the replicas can be active and some can be passive in order to increase the scalability of the system while keeping low fail-over delays. There are possibly 50–100 such hybrid strategies which give a much finer control of the operational parameters of the system. An analysis of all these combinations, emphasizing the most useful ones of them, would result in a better coverage of the presently very sparsely populated space of replication strategies.

For example, the DARX framework [22] is aimed at providing adaptive fault-tolerance for multi-agent software platforms. This infrastructure associates a replication policy with each agent, and the replication style and degree are adjusted according to the importance of each agent with respect to the rest of the application. This derives from a fundamental assumption that the importance of an agent evolves over time and so do its fault-tolerance requirements.

An offline approach to selecting the appropriate trade-off between fault-tolerance and real-time guarantees was adopted by the MARS project [23] and its successor, the Time-Triggered Architecture (TTA) [24] which are based on time-triggered protocols with strong temporal predictability. Fault-tolerance is achieved in the TTA by using a static schedule (created at design time) that allows enough slack for the system to be able to recover when faults occur. This approach does not provide a generic solution because it delegates the responsibility for reconciling fault-tolerance and real-time requirements to the application designer who establishes the static schedule.

7 Conclusions

Tunable software architectures are becoming important for distributed systems that must continue to run, despite loss/addition of resources, faults and other dynamic conditions. Versatile dependability is designed to facilitate the resource-aware tuning of multiple trade-offs between an application's fault-tolerance and QoS requirements. We propose the concept of "knobs" as a convenient architectural feature that helps designers reason about the system trade-offs and that expresses the tuning process in terms of externally-observable properties of the system. The architecture described in this paper provides abstract high-level knobs for tuning system-level properties such as scalability and low-level knobs for selecting implementation choices, such as the replication style. We detail the implementation of such knobs based on empirical observations, and present the expanded trade-off space covered by our current implementation of versatile dependability.

References

1. Dumitraş, T., Narasimhan, P.: An architecture for versatile dependability. In: Workshop on Architecting Dependable Systems, International Conference on Dependable Systems and Networks, Florence, Italy (2004)
2. Object Management Group: Fault Tolerant CORBA. OMG Technical Committee Document formal/2001-09-29 (2001)
3. Java Community Process: J2EE APIs for Continuous Availability. Java Specification Request, JSR117 (2003)
4. Narasimhan, P., Dumitraş, T., Paulos, A., Pertet, S., Reverte, C., Slember, J., Srivastava, D.: MEAD: Support for real-time, fault-tolerant CORBA. Concurrency and Computation: Practice and Experience **17** (2005)
5. Narasimhan, P.: Transparent Fault-Tolerance for CORBA. PhD thesis, University of California, Santa Barbara (1999)

6. Levine, J.R.: Linkers and Loaders. Morgan Kaufmann Publishers, San Francisco, CA (2000)
7. Amir, Y., Danilov, C., Stanton, J.: A low latency, loss tolerant architecture and protocol for wide area group communication. In: International Conference on Dependable Systems and Networks, New York, NY (2000) 327–336
8. Moser, L.E., Amir, Y., Melliar-Smith, P.M., Agarwal, D.A.: Extended virtual synchrony. In: The 14th IEEE International Conference on Distributed Computing Systems (ICDCS). (1994) 56–65
9. M. Wiesmann et al.: Understanding replication in databases and distributed systems. In: International Conference on Distributed Computing Systems, Taipei, Taiwan, R.O.C. (2000) 264–274
10. Schneider, F.B.: Implementing fault-tolerant services using the state machine approach: a tutorial. ACM Computing Surveys **22** (1990) 299–319
11. Lamport, L., Shostak, R., Pease, M.: The Byzantine Generals problem. ACM Transactions on Programming Languages and Systems **4** (1982) 382–401
12. Budhiraja, N., Schneider, F., Toueg, S., Marzullo, K.: The primary-backup approach. In Mullender, S., ed.: Distributed Systems. ACM Press - Addison Wesley (1993) 199–216
13. Birman, K., Joseph, T.: Exploiting virtual synchrony in distributed systems. In: Symposium on Operating Systems Principles (SOSP). (1987) 123–138
14. Douglas C. Schmidt et al.: The design of the TAO real-time Object Request Broker. Computer Communications **21** (1998)
15. Barrett, P.A., Bond, P.G., Hilborne, A.M.: The Delta-4 extra performance architecture (XPA). In: Fault-Tolerant Computing Symposium, Newcastle upon Tyne, U.K. (1990) 481–488
16. Kim, K.H.: ROAFTS: A middleware architecture for real-time objectoriented adaptive fault tolerance support. In: Proceedings of IEEE High Assurance Systems Engineering (HASE) Symposium, Washington, DC (1998) 50–57
17. Chen, W.K., Hiltunen, M., Schlichting, R.: Constructing adaptive software in distributed systems. In: International Conference on Distributed Computing Systems, Phoenix, AZ (2001) 635–643
18. Nett, E., Gergeleit, M., Mock, M.: Guaranteeing real-time behaviour in adaptive distributed systems. In: Symposium on Large Scale Systems: Theory and Applications, University of Patras, Greece (1998)
19. Cukier, M., Ren, J., Sabnis, C., Sanders, W.H., Bakken, D.E., Berman, M.E., Karr, D.A., Schantz, R.: AQuA: An adaptive architecture that provides dependable distributed objects. In: Proceedings of the IEEE 17th Symposium on Reliable Distributed Systems, West Lafayette, IN (1998) 245–253
20. González, O., Shrikumar, H., Stankovic, J., Ramamritham, K.: Adaptive fault tolerance and graceful degradation under dynamic hard real-time scheduling. In: IEEE Real-Time Systems Symposium, San Francisco, CA (1997) 79–89
21. Bakken, D., Bjune, G., Ahmad, M.: Towards hybrid replication and caching strategies. In: Digest of FastAbstracts presented at the International Conference on Dependable Systems and Networks, New York (2000)
22. Marin, O., Bertier, M., Sens, P.: Darx - a framework for the fault-tolerant support of agent software. In: International Symposium on Software Reliability Engineering, Denver, USA (2003)
23. Kopetz, H., Merker, W.: The architecture of MARS. In: Fault-Tolerant Computing Symposium (FTCS-15), Ann Arbor, MI (1985) 247–259
24. Kopetz, H., Bauer, G.: The time-triggered architecture. Proceedings of the IEEE **91** (2003) 112–126

A Feature-Oriented Alternative to Implementing Reliability Connector Wrappers

J.H. Sowell and R.E.K. Stirewalt

Michigan State University,
East Lansing, Michigan 48824, USA
{sowellje, stire}@cse.msu.edu

Abstract. Connectors and connector wrappers explicitly specify the protocol of interaction among components and afford the reusable application of extra-functional behaviors, such as reliability policies. Ideally, these specifications can be used for more than just modeling and analysis. We are investigating how to use them in the design and implementation of the middleware substrate of a distributed system. This paper reports our experience elaborating connectors and connector wrappers as instantiations of a feature-oriented middleware framework called Theseus, which supports the design of asynchronous distributed applications. The results of this case study indicate that the relationship between specification features and implementation-level features is not one-to-one and that some specification features have complex, often subtle, manifestations in Theseus' design. This work reports the lessons learned designing these strategies and suggests techniques for designing middleware frameworks and composition tools that more explicitly reify and expose the features specified by connectors and connector wrappers.

1 Introduction

Increasingly, distributed computing systems are deployed in volatile environments in which network connectivity is sporadic and unreliable. In response, a variety of *reliability policies* have been devised to shield users from the effects of this volatility. For example, *automatic retry* detects when a service request fails and automatically resends that request rather than propagating the exception to the client program. More sophisticated policies, such as *failover*, exploit redundant servers: When a request to one server fails that request is automatically forwarded to another rather than propagating the exception to the client program. In each case, an unreliable service is promoted to one that is reliable without altering the implementation of the unreliable service. Consequently, such policies tend to be incorporated into the middleware layer by *wrapping* an unreliable middleware implementation with code that intercepts service requests and performs the extra functionality.

To understand how to use wrappers to apply and compose reliability policies, Spitznagel and Garlan [1] developed a technique based on a formal behavioral model of architectural connection [2]. These *connector wrappers* impose policies on an existing connector specification by extending and/or restricting its observable behaviors. Moreover, each connector wrapper has an implementation counterpart that can be applied to incorporate the policy into an existing middleware implementation. These *implementation wrappers* compose with the flexibility of their specification counterparts by treating the underlying middleware as a black box. Unfortunately, the resulting implementations may incur redundancies and inefficiencies that are unacceptable on the resource-constrained devices that are most often exposed to volatile environments.

This paper describes an alternative implementation of connector wrappers as *reusable refinements* rather than black-box wrappers. Reusable refinements appeal to an algebraic model of software composition called AHEAD [3] and are similar to ML functors [4] and mixin layers in C++ [5]. Refinements compose functionally, just like wrappers; however refinement composition is more fine grain and thus affords a tighter integration that enables the reuse and extension of existing abstractions. Designers may thus customize a base middleware with reliability strategies by applying refinements in a manner analogous to the application of connector wrappers, and the resulting configurations will not exhibit the redundancy and inefficiency introduced by implementation wrappers.

Our results exploit the fact that reliability strategies often employ the same design abstractions that are used to implement basic middleware services. For instance, many middleware systems use the *asynchronous completion token* pattern [6] to demultiplex asynchronous operation requests and responses. This pattern is also used to implement a strategy for *warm failover* [7] whereby clients copy outgoing requests to a redundant backup server, which silently serves each request in parallel with the primary. Were such a strategy implemented using a wrapper, the wrapper would require logic for demultiplexing requests and responses with the backup server even though such logic exists in the underlying middleware. Further, some reliability strategies may need to suppress behaviors, such as suppressing the responses sent by a server that is intended to play the role of a silent backup. Wrappers suppress behavior by *masking* the observable effects rather than forestalling the behavior itself. Using refinements, both duplication of functionality and masking of behaviors can be avoided.

We believe that implementing reliability strategies as refinements will enable system architects to easily construct efficient middleware solutions subject to a variety of reliability policies. To validate this claim, we implemented and applied a set of reliability refinements to Theseus, which is an asynchronous middleware implementation that we designed using the AHEAD model. In prior work, we described three reliability refinements and showed that these exhibit the compositional properties as their specification counterparts [8]. We have since implemented other refinements, including one for warm failover that is useful for comparing our approach with black-box wrappers. In the sequel, we describe the design of Theseus and how refinements compose to produce new middleware that incorporates various reliability policies. We then compare our refinement-based implementation of warm failover to the wrapper-based design of [9].

2 Background

By way of background, we first introduce the use of wrappers to enhance reliability in distributed systems and the connector-wrapper formalism, which models the behavior of these wrappers. Wrappers and connector wrappers exhibit a useful structural correspondence between implementation and specification; however wrappers also incur redundancies and inefficiencies that are unacceptable to resource-constrained devices. We contend that reliability enhancements can be implemented so as to exhibit the same correspondence with connector wrappers but without incurring the redundancies and inefficiencies of wrapper-based implementations. The key is to implement the enhancements as reusable refinements under the AHEAD model of composition, which supports the definition of modules whose implementation abstractions are left open for further refinement by other modules under composition. This section concludes with a brief introduction to the AHEAD model.

2.1 Reliability-Enhancing Wrappers

Software architects often wish to augment communication among the components in a distributed system to incorporate extra functionality, such as logging, encryption, and even strategies for enhancing reliability in the face of network failures. Augmentation is accomplished by *intercepting* messages that cross the boundary between client components and the communication or middleware layer. Once intercepted, these messages are then either dropped, transformed and then forwarded to their original destination, or routed to another destination. Interception has proved useful for adding reliability to a variety of system calls (C.f., [10,11]). The technique is now supported directly in modern middleware systems (C.f., CORBA's portable interceptor interface [12,13]).[1]

This paper is concerned with reliability enhancements that are implemented using wrappers, which serve to both mediate client access to a service as well as augment that service with extra-functionality, as with interception. To preserve the original interface, these wrappers are implemented based on the proxy pattern [15][2]. As an example, consider the addition of logging and data encryption to messages sent by client components to a remote server component. Suppose the class `MiddlewareStub` represents the type of the client-side stub object, such as might be generated from an IDL specification of the server component. The additional functionality is implemented by a hierarchy of wrapper objects that conform to the class model in Figure 1. Commensurate with the wrapper pattern, each class implements a common interface, which in this example is called

---

[1] A powerful model of interception is captured by the composition-filters object model, which allows designers to deploy filters that intercept and drop, modify, or reroute messages among arbitrary objects in a system [14].
[2] Readers familiar with GoF design patterns will notice *wrapper* is a synonym for the adapter and not the proxy pattern; we use the term *wrapper* for consistency with Spitznagel's wrappers, which also implement the proxy pattern[9].

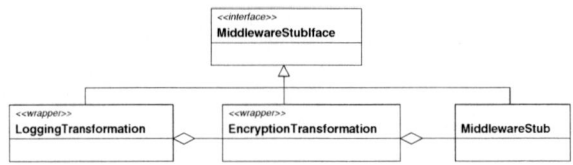

Fig. 1. Adding functionality using wrappers

`MiddlewareStubIface`, and the two wrappers implement their methods by delegation. Software architects typically use wrappers to augment middleware with new functionality, to suppress existing behaviors, or to mask faults.

While easy to implement, wrappers (and interception techniques generally) suffer from two problems. First, components of the original system (that being wrapped) may be "orphaned" when their behaviors are suppressed in favor of behaviors introduced via interception and wrapping. Such orphans, even though no longer actively contributing to the behavior of the system, remain in place and continue to consume resources, both computational and spatial. Second, the extra functionality may incur redundancies and inefficiencies that are unacceptable on the resource-constrained devices that are most often exposed to volatile environments. In the case of wrappers, these redundancies owe to the treatment of the service being wrapped as a black box whose internal resources (i.e., those that might be reasonably reused by the extra functionality) are not accessible to the wrapper. Interception-based techniques suffer a similar problem.

To overcome this obstacle requires the ability to reconfigure a base system when augmenting it with extra functionality. The earliest work in this regard uses static recomposition based on object-oriented frameworks, the most notable of these being Schmidt's ACE framework [16]. More recent work has investigated the development of software modules that, when composed with a base system, are able to reconfigure that system. Such compositions must be able to refine existing components, including those hidden behind an opaque API, to support extra-functional behaviors or replace them with components that do support the desired behaviors. More recent work (C.f., [17,18]) applies dynamic recomposition to introduce reliability enhancements. In these cases, reflection and/or meta-object protocols are used to reconfigure the original application to use the components that best fit the environment at hand. Further still, such techniques have also been combined with class loading technologies, in particular the JBoss extensible middleware platform, to completely add and/or remove components from a running system [19].

2.2 Connector Wrappers

The term *connector* refers to a mechanism for composing architectural components [20]. Connectors abstract communication mechanisms and protocols, such as procedure calls, remote procedure calls, pipes in a pipe-and-filter system, and many of the communication services that are generally referred to as "middleware". More abstractly, a connector represents a pattern of *interaction* among a set of components, called the *roles* of the connector. Allen and Garlan developed a formal model of connectors as stylized CSP specifications, thereby enabling an architect to rigorously specify an architecture as the composition of components and connectors and use formal analysis tools to reason about the resulting behavior [2].

To facilitate reasoning in the presence of wrappers, Spitznagel and Garlan developed a theory of *connector wrappers*, which are stylized CSP specifications designed to compose with a connector specification to yield a new connector, whose behaviors are an extension or restriction of the original [1]. Connector wrappers are useful for specifying different strategies for implementing reliability policies, such as retry and failover, in isolation without regard to the details of a particular connector. The basic idea is to introduce (via parallel composition) additional processes that synchronize with messages at the component–connector interface to precisely model the behavior of the aforementioned wrapper modules. Because connector wrappers faithfully model the structure and behavior of wrappers, an architect may specify a new connector as the composition of one or more connector wrappers with some connector and then semi-automatically generate a conforming implementation. Spitznagel's system provides generation tools that implement this capability.

Unfortunately, connector wrappers cannot yet utilize reconfiguration-based mechanisms, which generally do not adhere to an algebraic model of composition. The next section describes a model of composition that is algebraic in nature and that supports fine-grained recomposition of the base system, allowing for both reuse of abstractions and the avoidance of orphaned components.

2.3 AHEAD

AHEAD is an algebraic model of software composition in which complex, feature-rich programs are synthesized from base programs by applying reusable refinements [21]. Here, a base program is a collection of classes, and a refinement is a collection of classes and/or *class fragments*, which can be applied to extend an existing program with new functionality by using and/or refining the classes defined by that program. AHEAD treats base programs and refinements as *layers*. A base program is a stand-alone layer or *constant* (i.e., the layer contains no class fragments) and a refinement is a parameterized layer (i.e., layer that must "plug in" to another, subordinate layer).

The composition of AHEAD refinements and simple programs is depicted visually using diagrams such as Figure 2(a). This figure illustrates the refinement of a base program (const). Here, the inner-most boxes are classes or class fragments. The solid rectangles demarcate refinements. The dotted lines from one class to another indicate the refinement of a class with the code and data in a class fragment; for example, b_{const} is refined by b_{f1}. Because const is the bottom-most layer, it contains only classes and not class fragments.

Moving up one level, f1 is a refinement whose constituents refine two classes, and that adds a new class e which uses classes from the subordinate layer. Composing this refinement with const effectively synthesizes a new collaboration

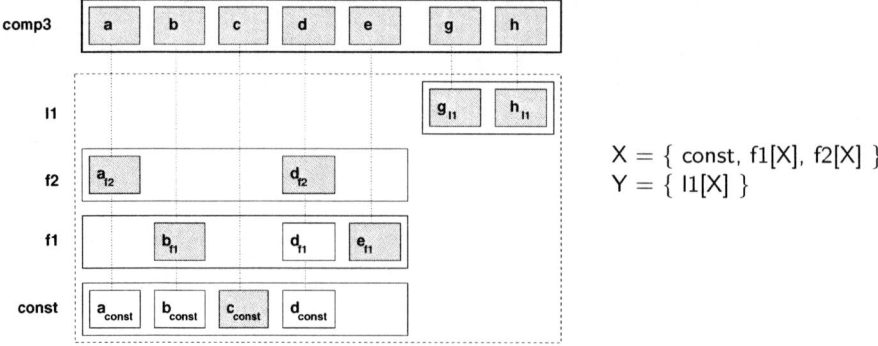

Fig. 2. Layered refinement in AHEAD

that implements that of const augmented by the feature implemented by f1 and results in a new, composite layer we will refer to as comp1. This composition is specified textually via the *type equation* comp1 = f1⟨const⟩. Moving up another level, f2 comprises two class refinements, which collaborate to implement another new feature. In this example, f2 refines comp1, thus creating a new layer that implements the functionality of const augmented with the features of both f1 and f2. The resultant type equation is comp2 = f2⟨f1⟨const⟩⟩.

Figure 2 applies one final refinement, l1, which contains complete classes and no fragments. While l1 may appear to be a constant, it is a refinement in the sense that it adds new abstractions (g_{l1} and h_{l1}) that use classes in the subordinate layer. For this type of refinement, we will will often simply say layer l1 *uses* comp2. The uppermost layer (comp3, in bold) illustrates the final composition that implements this collaboration. Notice that the classes in this uppermost layer are the most refined of each subordinate layer, as indicated by the grey boxes.

AHEAD also employs a type system for reasoning about, classifying, and codifying the relationships between layers. In this type system, layers that share a common interface are elements of a *realm*, and that common interface can be thought of as the *realm type*. For example, the layers of Figure 2(a) and their relationships are expressed in Figure 2(b). In this figure, const is a constant of realm X whose classes implement the interfaces that comprise the type of this realm, namely the class interfaces a, b, c, and d. As we saw earlier, f1 and f2 refine the layers below them; here, this is formalized by the presence of a realm parameter that conveys that these layers augment layers of type X.

Based on this small set of layers, many different compositions may be instantiated, e.g., f1⟨const⟩, f2⟨f1⟨const⟩⟩, and l1⟨f2⟨const⟩⟩. Each of these instantiations synthesizes a set of classes, whose instances collaborate to implement all the features of the base program and each of the refinements. We call such a collection of collaborating objects a *configuration*. Notice that some type equations denote new refinements rather than whole programs. For example, the type equation cf1 = f1⟨f2⟩ denotes a valid composition, but because the class refinements of f2 depend on classes provided by its realm parameter, cf1 is simply a composite refinement; it cannot be instantiated as specified to produce a configuration of collaborating objects. When a composition may not denote a complete program, we may opt to use the more general functional composition operator (∘). For example, we could rewrite the definition of cf1 as cf1 = f1 ∘ f2.

As noted in the Section 1, reliability strategies do not always map to a single layer; rather, they are often implemented by a collection of layer refinements that collaborate to implement a complete reliability strategy. For instance, consider a reliability strategy that is implemented by the collaboration of l1 and f1. In AHEAD, such collaborations may also be represented by {l1, f1}, which is a *collective* (set of layers) that represents the collaboration implemented by this composite refinement. Under AHEAD, a *model* is a set of constants and refinements (each of which may themselves be collectives) whose constituents are the building blocks of a product line[21].

In our example, such a product line would comprise configurations represented by, e.g., const, f1⟨const⟩, l1⟨f2⟨const⟩⟩, and so on. A model of this product line is

$$M = \{\{\text{const}\}, \{\text{f1}\}, \{\text{l1}, \text{f2}\}, \{\text{l1}, \text{f1}\} \ldots\} \quad (1)$$

Here, M comprises a constant ({const}) and a set of refinements (the remaining collectives). A member of this product line is instantiated by

$$\text{rs} = \{\text{l1}, \text{f1}\} \circ \{\text{const}\} \quad (2)$$
$$= \{\text{l1}, \text{f1} \circ \text{const}\} \quad (3)$$
$$= \text{l1} \circ \text{f1} \circ \text{const} \quad (4)$$
$$= \text{l1}\langle \text{f1}\langle \text{const}\rangle\rangle \quad (5)$$

Using collectives, we can represent a reliability strategy as a single unit that can be applied to a base program even when that unit comprises multiple refinements. We use such a model and its constituent collectives to mirror the application of connector wrappers, each of which corresponds to a collective that implements a reliability strategy, to connectors, i.e., base middleware implementations. This model of reliable middleware is presented in Section 4.

3 Theseus

One of the goals of our approach is to augment middleware services with reliability by refining the abstractions used in the implementation of these services rather than by treating the services as a black box and wrapping them with extra functionality. To accomplish this goal requires a middleware framework whose design exposes these major abstractions and makes them available for further refinement. We developed a middleware framework called Theseus that is organized according to an AHEAD model. This section describes this model and shows how it is used to synthesize custom asynchronous middleware services that support a variety of different reliability policies. The Theseus model comprises two realms: MSGSVC, whose layers implement a variety of different message services, and ACTOBJ, whose layers implement variants of the distributed active object pattern. Most of the layers in these realms implement different reliability strategies (or low-level services that support different reliability strategies). Using Theseus, an architect can easily customize middleware services to support specific reliability policies without the duplication and efficiency burdens inherent in the use of wrappers.

3.1 Message Service

In Theseus, the message service provides queue-like communication abstractions that implement a simple, reliable[3] message-oriented middleware. A client of the message service sends data by enqueuing a message in a peer's inbox (which typically resides in a separate address space on a remote machine) and receives data by retrieving messages from its inbox. The sending end of the message service is a peer messenger whose interface is specified by PeerMessengerIface; the receiving end is a message inbox whose interface is specified by MessageInboxIface (Figure 3). An inbox is bound to a universal resource identifier (URI) and listens

```
public interface MessageInboxIface {
  public Serializable retrieveNextMessage ();
  public LinkedList retrieveAllMessages ();
  public boolean hasMessages ();
  public int numQueued ();
}

public interface PeerMessengerIface {
  public void sendMessage ( Serializable msg );
  public void setURI ( String URI );
  public ResourceIdentifierIface getURI ();
  public void connect ();
}
```

Fig. 3. Interfaces in the message service

for, receives, and queues messages sent to that URI. These details are hidden by MessageInboxIface, through which the inbox client treats the network like a queue, receiving messages with calls such as retrieveAllMessages. A peer messenger connects to an inbox, given its URI, and sends messages (in our case, any serializable object) by invoking sendMessage.

Figure 4 depicts the MSGSVC realm, whose layers define and refine these abstractions. The constant in this realm is rmi[4], which comprises classes that

---

[3] In the sense that it is built atop a connection-oriented transport such as TCP.
[4] For convenience, we built our message service atop RMI; the message service abstractions are general and may also be implemented atop object streams, TCP, or any other connection-oriented transport.

MSGSVC = { rmi, idemFail[MSGSVC], bndRetry[MSGSVC],
           indefRetry[MSGSVC], cmr[MSGSVC], dupReq[MSGSVC] }

Fig. 4. Message service realm layers

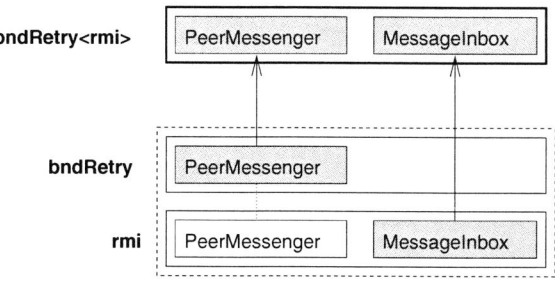

Fig. 5. Visual stratification of bndRetry⟨rmi⟩

implement the most basic form of these abstractions. The remaining layers are reliability-enhancing refinements, which we will describe as the need arises. One such refinement is bndRetry (bounded retry), which augments an existing PeerMessenger[5] to, in the event of a communication failure, suppress the communication exception(s) and retry some number of times ($maxRetries > 0$) before giving up and throwing the exception.

Figure 5 shows the layered representation of an assembly that applies bndRetry to the basic message service rmi. In Figure 5, bndRetry refines classes of the rmi layer, namely, PeerMessenger. In the remainder of our diagrams, the grey classes are the most refined, and the layer in bold represents the client's view of the assembly. Clients always use the most refined implementation of an interface (indicated by the arrows); in the case of the PeerMessengerIface, the most refined implementation is that of bndRetry. Because the bndRetry layer did not refine MessageInbox, the rmi implementation remains the most refined implementation of MessageInboxIface.

3.2 Active Objects

Theseus' second realm is called ACTOBJ because its layers define classes and class refinements that implement different variations of the distributed active object pattern [6]. An *active object* is an object that has its own thread of control (the *execution thread*), listening for operation requests and executing the corresponding operations when the requests arrive. A complete operation execution in this model has three phases: invocation and queueing, dispatching and execution, and returning results. In the first phase, a *proxy* (in the sense of [15]) marshals the invocation into an operation request (referred to simply

---

[5] An implementation of PeerMessengerIface; our classes follow the convention that interfaces are suffixed by "Iface" and the corresponding implementation is not.

as a *request*) and queues it on an *activation list*. The execution phase is initiated by the *scheduler*, which is a loop (running in the execution thread) that dequeues requests from the activation list to be executed. In the simplest case, the scheduler dequeues these in FIFO order. Once dequeued, requests are passed to the *dispatcher* to be invoked on the *servant*, which is an object that actually implements the behavior modeled by the active object [6]. When the servant completes this invocation, the results are returned to the client.

The distributed active object pattern follows the same basic architecture, except that the operations invoked by a client are executed in an object that lives in a separate address space. Middleware stubs and skeletons insulate the client from the details of communication with the remote active object [6]. The stub behaves like the proxy, except rather than queuing the requests on an activation list, they are sent via some form of inter-process communication (IPC) to the skeleton, which resides in the same address space as the servant. This skeleton comprises a scheduler that schedules requests to be executed in the execution thread. Once a request has been dequeued, unmarshaled, and executed, the results are then sent back to the client via IPC.

The ACTOBJ realm type comprises interfaces, such as SchedulerIface and DispatcherIface, whose instances collaborate to implement distributed active objects. The layers that implement and refine these are shown in Figure 6. Notice this realm contains no constants. The core layer is parameterized by

$$\text{ACTOBJ} = \{\ \text{core}[\text{MSGSVC}],\ \text{respCache}[\text{ACTOBJ}],\ \text{eeh}[\text{ACTOBJ}],\ \text{ackResp}[\text{ACTOBJ}]\ \}$$

Fig. 6. Active object realm layers

the MSGSVC realm. Among others, core contains two classes, StaticDispatcher and FIFOScheduler, which implement the DispatcherIface and SchedulerIface interfaces respectively, and which are designed to use subordinate services that are defined in the MSGSVC realm type. Nothing in the implementation of class FIFOScheduler (respectively StaticDispatcher) depends on the particular implementation of the MessageInboxIface (respectively PeerMessengerIface) interface. Thus, core is "parameterized by" the MSGSVC realm.

3.3 Synthesizing Middleware Services

To create a set of middleware services, we instantiate objects from the classes defined in the assembly core⟨rmi⟩, which is our most basic middleware assembly and the one that is refined to create all of the other variants. Here, the message service is refined to include core's abstractions for building active objects, as is depicted in Figure 7. Notice that none of the classes in core refine any of those in the rmi layer. Rather, core uses rmi's concrete classes in the same sense that FIFOScheduler uses MessageInboxIface. Notice also that the rmi classes are still visible in the assembly and are thus available for further refinement, as

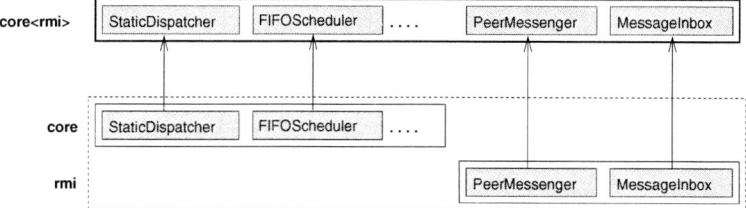

Fig. 7. Layers of a simple middleware

are the classes in core. That the classes defined in a subordinate layer remain visible to superior layers allows the functionality defined in these superior layers to tap into and reuse the basic abstractions used to implement the subordinate functionality.

To illustrate how this visibility accommodates refinement, consider a bounded retry policy that prescribes (1) suppressing errors, (2) performing a bounded number of retries, and (3) throwing an exception if these retries fail. Our basic middleware, specified by core⟨rmi⟩, comprises classes that implement the minimum functionality necessary to implement active objects; accounting for any type of exceptional conditions is not part of that minimal functionality. Now consider how this basic middleware assembly must be modified to implement a bounded retry strategy: The first two requirements are met by the bounded retry augmentation of the message service. To meet the third requirement, we must augment the stub, which does not account for exceptions, to properly transform internal exceptions thrown by the message service into those declared to be thrown by the active-object interface. To this end, we refine the pertinent classes in the active object layer.

The stub is implemented by an instance of the active object's interface that performs the first phase of invocation marshaling. To create such an instance of an arbitrary active object interface, we generate these instances using Java's Dynamic Proxy Framework [22]. Such an instance is referred to as a dynamic proxy and is generated by a static factory method that is parameterized by a metaobject representation of the interface [6] and an instance of the InvocationHandler interface, which will be used by the dynamic proxy to process operations invoked on the proxy. The dynamic proxy itself is an object that marshals invocations of its operations into two objects: an instance of class Method that represents the operation invoked and an array of Objects that are the parameters of this invocation, which it immediately passes to its instance of InvocationHandler for processing.

The core layer defines a class TheseusInvocationHandler that is responsible for completing invocation marshaling. This class implements the InvocationHandler interface; thus its instances can be passed to the static factory method that generates the dynamic proxy. At run-time, these instances use an instance of class PeerMessengerIface to send the resultant request to

---

[6] i.e., an instance of class Class in Java used to generate the dynamic proxy itself.

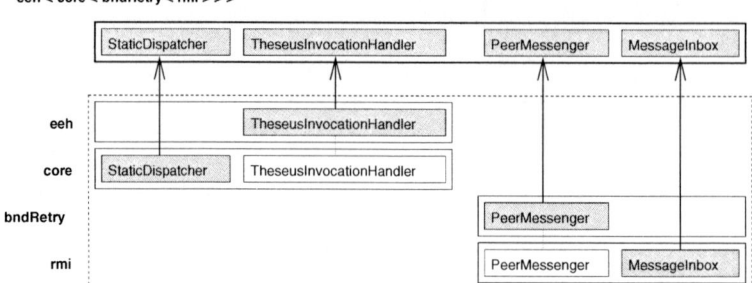

Fig. 8. Layered implementation of the bounded retry strategy

the skeleton of the active object. In the minimal assembly, i.e., core⟨rmi⟩, the invocation handler does not account for exceptions. In the more realistic case, the underlying network may fail or the server on which the active object resides may crash; in either event, the peer messenger that is used by the invocation handler will throw an `IPCException`[7]. To accommodate this possibility, we refine the `TheseusInvocationHandler` to transform these exceptions into the exceptions that the active object's interface declares in its throws clause.

The refinement that performs this transformation is eeh (exposed exception handler) and is depicted in Figure 6. A minimal middleware augmented by eeh is expressed by eeh⟨core⟨rmi⟩⟩. Adding bounded retry to the message service completes the functionality specified by the bounded retry policy; the configuration then becomes eeh⟨core⟨bndRetry⟨rmi⟩⟩⟩. The layers that implement this configuration are shown in Figure 8.

3.4 Efficiency Improvements in Bounded Retry

To see how our design forestalls the duplication that arises when implementing reliability strategies via wrappers, consider a wrapper-based implementation of the bounded retry policy. The wrapper would have to be applied to the server stub, i.e., the object returned by RMI's `Naming.lookup` call. Upon communication failure, a remote exception is propagated from the underlying transport up to the wrapper, where it is caught and responded to by invoking the operation on the base stub again. Notice that in this scenario, each retry subsequent to the initial failure must perform the entire client side invocation process, including the re-marshaling of the same invocation.

In Theseus, by contrast, the class of the object that is used to send the marshaled invocation, i.e., the class that implements the `PeerMessengerIface`

---

[7] The astute reader will notice that `PeerMessengerIface` does not declare any exceptions; `IPCException` is an unchecked runtime exception that need not be declared in a throws clause. To avoid polluting the interfaces of realm types with throws declarations for checked exceptions they may or may not have to handle, we encapsulate all checked exceptions in runtime exceptions, placing the responsibility for managing such exceptions on the developer.

interface, is available for further refinement. And indeed, the bndRetry layer refines this class with the retry logic, thereby placing the retry logic "beneath" the marshaling logic. Consequently, this implementation avoids the cost of re-marshaling for each retry. The composite (bold) layer in Figure 8 depicts the synthetic collaboration whose participants include the eeh-augmented invocation handler and the bndRetry-augmented peer messenger. Instances of these refined classes collaborate to implement our bounded retry strategy. In the next section, we describe a model that facilitates applying such collaborating refinements to a middleware as a single unit.

4 An AHEAD Model of Reliable Middleware

In the previous section we implemented a strategy for bounded retry in two phases. The first phase refined the message service to suppress exceptions and retry some bounded number of times before giving up. The second phase refined the active object layer to transform internal exceptions into those declared by the active object interface, i.e. those a client of the stub would expect based on the active object's interface. Consequently, the functionality associated with the bounded-retry connector wrapper manifests not as a single layer, but rather as a collective that comprises two layers. In fact, most of the connector wrappers specified in Spitznagel's thesis cannot be implemented as a single layer without some degree of duplication. However, all of them can be implemented using collectives that comprise multiple layers.

We now show how to represent this product line as an AHEAD model whose elements are collectives. The resulting model contains one constant, the most-basic assembly core⟨rmi⟩, and one collective for each reliability strategy. As we describe our model and how it is used, we also focus on how we use our AHEAD model to group the structural changes affected by refinements such that they correspond to reliability connector wrappers. As we will see, a base middleware, such as core⟨rmi⟩, corresponds to a middleware connector specification and collectives that implement a reliability strategy correspond to reliability connector wrappers. As we describe our model, we will make these correlations explicit.

4.1 A Reliable Middleware Model

Our model THESEUS, is

$$\mathsf{THESEUS} = \{\mathsf{BM}, \mathsf{RS}_0, \mathsf{RS}_1, \ldots, \mathsf{RS}_n\} \tag{6}$$

where BM is a collective that represents the base middleware and each RS_i ($0 \leq i \leq n$) is a collective that represents some reliability strategy. Our base middleware (BM) is $\{\mathsf{core}_{\mathsf{ao}} \circ \mathsf{rmi}_{\mathsf{ms}}\}$, which is equivalent to $\{\mathsf{core}_{\mathsf{ao}}, \mathsf{rmi}_{\mathsf{ms}}\}$[8] where

---

[8] Recall uses relationship described in Section 2.3; $\mathsf{core}_{\mathsf{ao}}$ uses $\mathsf{rmi}_{\mathsf{ms}}$, as illustrated in Figure 7.

the subscripts ao and ms indicate layers in the active object and message service realms, respectively. Similarly, each strategy RS_i is a collective of the form $\{\text{refinement}\_i_{ao}, \text{refinement}\_i_{ms}\}$, where refinement$\_i_{ao}$ applies to (refines) an active-object layer and refinement$\_i_{ms}$ applies to a messages-service layer.

Elements of this product line are synthesized by choosing a set of reliability strategies and then applying these in sequence to the base-middleware assembly. An example application of the first two strategies, RS_0 and RS_1, is

$$\text{rm} = RS_1 \circ RS_0 \circ BM \tag{7}$$
$$= \{\text{ref}\_1_{ao}, \text{ref}\_1_{ms}\} \circ \{\text{ref}\_0_{ao}, \text{ref}\_0_{ms}\} \circ \{\text{core}_{ao}, \text{rmi}_{ms}\} \tag{8}$$
$$= \{\text{ref}\_1_{ao}, \text{ref}\_1_{ms}\} \circ \{\text{ref}\_0_{ao} \circ \text{core}_{ao}, \text{ref}\_0_{ms} \circ \text{rmi}_{ms}\} \tag{9}$$
$$= \{\text{ref}\_1_{ao} \circ \text{ref}\_0_{ao} \circ \text{core}_{ao}, \;\; \text{ref}\_1_{ms} \circ \text{ref}\_0_{ms} \circ \text{rmi}_{ms}\} \tag{10}$$

There are three important properties of this composition. First, refinements naturally apply to layers in the realm that they refine. In Equation 9, the active-object refinement ref$\_0_{ao}$ composes with core$_{ao}$, and the message-service refinement ref$\_0_{ms}$ composes with rmi$_{ms}$. Second, the order of refinement is preserved. Namely, Equation 7 indicates the refinements should be applied right to left: RS_0, then RS_1. In Equation 10 this ordering has been preserved in the refinement of both the active-object and message-service layers.

The third property is this structural representation's high-level mapping to connectors and connector wrappers. Here, BM implements the base middleware and corresponds to a connector that specifies the behavior of communication among components that use this base middleware. The collectives RS_0 and RS_1 correspond to reliability connector wrappers that augment BM. The collectives that implement reliability strategies decompose further into reusable refinements, much like Spitznagel's connector wrappers decompose into connector transforms, but do not exhibit a strict one-to-one correspondence.

4.2 Reliable Middleware Examples

We now illustrate three applications of synthesis using the THESEUS model.

Bounded Retry As noted earlier, our bounded retry strategy is implemented by the bounded retry (bndRetry$_{ms}$) refinement of the message-service realm and the exposed exception handler (eeh$_{ao}$) refinement of active-object realm. Under our model, this strategy is implemented as the collective

$$BR = \{\text{eeh}_{ao}, \text{bndRetry}_{ms}\} \tag{11}$$

A model of a bounded retry augmented middleware bri is thus

$$\text{bri} = BR \circ BM \tag{12}$$
$$= \{\text{eeh}_{ao}, \text{bndRetry}_{ms}\} \circ \{\text{core}_{ao}, \text{rmi}_{ms}\} \tag{13}$$
$$= \{\text{eeh}_{ao} \circ \text{core}_{ao}, \text{bndRetry}_{ms} \circ \text{rmi}_{ms}\} \tag{14}$$

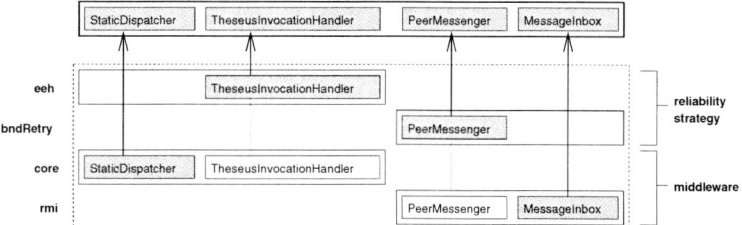

Fig. 9. Grouping bounded-retry layers into a collective

The visual stratification of the layers, as specified by Equations 12 and 13 is shown in Figure 9. In this figure, the bottom two layers implement the middleware and the top two are the refinements that implement the bounded retry strategy. This visual stratification is expressed by Equation 14, whose layers are the same as in Figure 8. Because each refinement in this model is local to a specific realm (either message service or active object) the refinements may be applied in arbitrary order; however refinements are not, in general, commutative.

Figures 8 and 9 visually depict the tighter binding of AHEAD refinements that is shown equationally in Equations 12-14. Figure 9, and the corresponding Equation 12, appear much as we would expect under connector wrapper composition, applying BR, which implements the bounded retry reliability connector wrapper, to BM, which implements an existing connector.

Idempotent Failover. The idempotent failover policy specifies that, in the event of a communication failure, the client should connect to a known backup. In the simple version of failover, operations are assumed to be idempotent and therefore the original (primary) server and backup need not be synchronized with one another. Upon failure of the primary, a failover refinement will suppress the exception and silently switch over to the backup. Further, this policy assumes a perfect backup that never fails; thus, once failover occurs, no additional communication exceptions will arise.

Our implementation of this strategy is very similar to that of the bounded retry refinement of the message service. In this case, instead of initiating a retry loop on a communication exception, the class refinement simply resets the URI of the peer messenger (via `setURI`, Figure 3) to that of the backup, connects (via `connect`, Figure 3) to the corresponding inbox, and proceeds as normal. Under our model, the strategy is

$$\mathsf{FO} = \{\mathsf{idemFail}_{\mathsf{ms}}\} \tag{15}$$

and an application is

$$\mathsf{foi} = \mathsf{FO} \circ \mathsf{BM} \tag{16}$$
$$= \{\mathsf{idemFail}_{\mathsf{ms}}\} \circ \{\mathsf{core}_{\mathsf{ao}}, \mathsf{rmi}_{\mathsf{ms}}\} \tag{17}$$
$$= \{\mathsf{core}_{\mathsf{ao}}, \mathsf{idemFail}_{\mathsf{ms}} \circ \mathsf{rmi}_{\mathsf{ms}}\} \tag{18}$$

In this example, FO comprises only a refinement of the message service. Because failover is "perfect", no exceptions propagate up to the client. As such, there is no need to refine the active object with exception transformation logic such as exposed exception handler.

Bounded Retry and Idempotent Failover. As a final illustration of the model, consider the application of both the bounded retry and idempotent failover strategies. The idea behind this composite reliability strategy is to retry the primary some finite number of times before failing over to the backup. As such, we apply bounded retry first, then failover; the application of this composite strategy is

$$\text{fobri} = \text{FO} \circ \text{BR} \circ \text{BM} \tag{19}$$
$$= \{\text{idemFail}_{\text{ms}}\} \circ \{\text{eeh}_{\text{ao}}, \text{bndRetry}_{\text{ms}}\} \circ \{\text{core}_{\text{ao}}, \text{rmi}_{\text{ms}}\} \tag{20}$$
$$= \{\text{idemFail}_{\text{ms}}\} \circ \{\text{eeh}_{\text{ao}} \circ \text{core}_{\text{ao}}, \text{bndRetry}_{\text{ms}} \circ \text{rmi}_{\text{ms}}\} \tag{21}$$
$$= \{\text{eeh}_{\text{ao}} \circ \text{core}_{\text{ao}}, \text{idemFail}_{\text{ms}} \circ \text{bndRetry}_{\text{ms}} \circ \text{rmi}_{\text{ms}}\} \tag{22}$$

Attending to the refinements of the message service, bounded retry is applied first, then failover, as intended. Under these refinements,

1. A communication exception thrown by rmi_{ms} will be suppressed by $\text{bndRetry}_{\text{ms}}$, which will attempt to reconnect and resend the marshaled request some bounded number of times.
2. If the bndRetry does not successfully reconnect, it will throw the communication exception.
3. idemFail will suppress this exception, connect to the backup, and resend the marshaled request.

In Spitznagel's connector-wrapper specification of each strategy, exceptions are modeled by the action error [1]. In these specifications, the error action is intercepted and triggers recovery; in this case, first a bounded retry, then failover. Here, we see AHEAD collectives also compose, both structurally and behaviorally, in the same manner as connector wrappers.

Now consider if the order were changed to

$$\text{fobri} = \text{BR} \circ \text{FO} \circ \text{BM} \tag{23}$$

idemFail would immediately switch over to the backup on failure, occluding any communication exception from reaching bndRetry and would be functionally equivalent to Equation 16. This is also the case in the corresponding connector specification; the juxtaposition finds the error action immediately triggering failover behavior, just as the exception does in our implementation.

This also illustrates how a semantic conflict, namely the overlapping of the recovery strategies used, may cause one refinement to occlude another. Because a failover augmented middleware will never throw a communication exception, the eeh_{ao} is not needed and adds unnecessary processing. Under AHEAD, this is a problem of composition optimization. While it is possible to inspect such an equation and remove exposed exception handler, this optimization is not "automatic" and requires some form of higher reasoning about the semantics of composite refinements.

5 Contrasting Implementation Strategies

We believe that our AHEAD-style implementation of reliability strategies offers a useful alternative to wrappers without sacrificing the flexibility of composition and reasoning provided by the connector-wrapper formalism. In previous sections we briefly illustrated a simple efficiency improvement in a message service implementation of bounded retry (Section 3.4). We now describe the implementation of a more complex reliability policy, warm failover, and identify where our approach eliminates both redundancy and the need for additional logic for suppressing behavior.

5.1 Warm Failover

Warm failover is a reliability policy that uses a backup server providing reliability via redundancy in a client-server architecture. This policy is a variation of process pairs and takeover in transaction systems[23]. The original server is referred to as the primary. The backup is "warm" in the sense that it is kept in sync with the primary via some strategy dependent mechanism. Under this policy, if the primary fails, the client uses the backup to recover lost responses. The client then promotes the backup to the role of primary, which means the client sends requests to and expects responses from the backup and the backup, correspondingly, accepts requests from and sends responses to the client. This policy assumes a "perfect" backup that will not fail, and, as such, does not account for the failure of the backup.

The strategy we employ to implement warm failover is referred to as silent backup. Under this strategy, the client sends each request to both the primary and the backup. The primary processes these requests and sends the responses to the client. The backup also processes requests (and is thus in sync with the primary) but, rather than send the responses to the client, the backup caches these in an outstanding response cache, which is keyed on the response's unique id (an asynchronous completion token). This cache is intended to store only the responses that the client has yet to receive from the primary. To maintain the cache as such, the client is obligated to send acknowledgements (that comprise a response id) to the backup when it receives a response from the primary, indicating that response may be removed from the cache. Upon failure of the primary, the client sends a control message to the backup indicating this failure and promotes the backup to the role of primary. When the backup receives such a message, it sends any outstanding responses to the client and, henceforth, upon processing a request, sends the response to the client rather than caching it.

5.2 Theseus Refinements

To implement silent backup, we must augment the client and create a backup that fulfills the responsibilities outlined above. The primary remains unchanged.

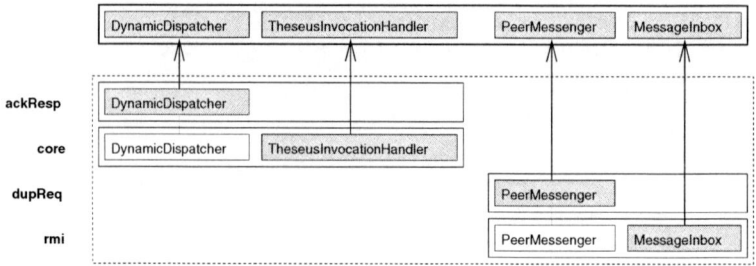

Fig. 10. Silent backup client configuration

Client Refinements. To implement the client's responsibilities, we send each request to both the primary and the backup, activate the backup in case the primary fails, and send acknowledgements to the backup as the primary's responses arrive such that the backup may purge these from the response cache. The following describes the refinements that fulfill these responsibilities.

*Duplicate Request (*dupReq*)* refines `PeerMessenger` to connect to and send requests to both the primary and the backup. In the event that the primary fails, the peer messenger sends a special activate message to the backup, which indicates the backup should assume the role of the primary. Once the activate message has been sent, the peer messenger sends requests only to the backup.

*Acknowledge Response (*ackResp*)* refines the active object layer to send acknowledgements indicating a response has been received. In Theseus, a variant of the dispatcher (`DynamicDispatcher`) is used to dispatch responses to threads dedicated to processing responses and making them available to the client. Here, this type of dispatcher is refined to send acknowledgements to the backup as it dispatches these responses.

The client side of silent backup is implemented by the collective SBC.

$$\mathsf{SBC} = \{\mathsf{ackResp_{ao}}, \mathsf{dupReq_{ms}}\} \tag{24}$$

The warm failover client wfc is instantiated by

$$\mathsf{wfc} = \mathsf{SBC} \circ \mathsf{BM} \tag{25}$$
$$= \{\mathsf{ackResp_{ao}}, \mathsf{dupReq_{ms}}\} \circ \{\mathsf{core_{ao}}, \mathsf{rmi_{ms}}\} \tag{26}$$
$$= \{\mathsf{ackResp_{ao}} \circ \mathsf{core_{ao}}, \mathsf{dupReq_{ms}} \circ \mathsf{rmi_{ms}}\} \tag{27}$$
$$\tag{28}$$

The visual depiction of these layers is shown in Figure 10.

Backup Server Refinements. The backup server should have all the functionality of the original server, modulo features for handling control messages, caching responses, and switching from the role of silent backup to that of primary. To this end, we refine our minimal middleware (core⟨rmi⟩) with the following refinements:

*Control Message Router (*cmr$_{ms}$*)* is a refinement of the message service that accommodates specially formed control messages (acknowledgement and activate messages) that have the same expedited properties as TCP's out-of-band data [24] using existing operations of the `PeerMessengerIface` and `MessageInboxIface`. Control messages are serializable objects that implement `ControlMessageIface`, which provides getters for retrieving both the command type (such as "ACK" and "ACTIVATE") and the data payload of the message (such as the id of the response being acknowledged). When such an object is passed to `PeerMessenger`'s `sendMessage` operation, it delivers that object to the corresponding inbox as normal. The control message router layer refines the inbox to filter control messages so they are handled immediately (expedited) and not mistakenly passed along as service requests. On the inbox side of communication, listeners implement a `ControlMessageListenerIface` and register themselves as listeners, indicating which command type they are interested in being notified of. When a command of that type arrives, the inbox invokes the `postControlMessage` operation of the interested listeners.

*Response Cache (*respCache$_{ao}$*)* augments the active object layer to cache responses. In a Theseus skeleton, the stub logic that marshals requests (Section 3.3) is used to marshal responses. We refine the invocation handler that participates in marshaling responses to store these in the cache rather than send them to the client. Further, the refined invocation handler implements `ControlMessageListenerIface` and is registered with the control message router to listen for both acknowledgement and activate messages. Upon acknowledgement of a response, the invocation handler removes that response from the cache. Upon activate, the backup starts delegating requests to a live invocation handler (one that sends responses to the client rather than storing them), effectively switching to a configuration that is equivalent to that of the primary.

Our implementation of the server half of the silent backup strategy, SBS, is

$$\mathsf{SBS} = \{\mathsf{respCache}_{ao}, \mathsf{cmr}_{ms}\} \tag{29}$$

When instantiated, the corresponding configuration, sb, is

$$\mathsf{sb} = \mathsf{SBS} \circ \mathsf{BM} \tag{30}$$
$$\mathsf{sb} = \{\mathsf{respCache}_{ao}, \mathsf{cmr}_{ms}\} \circ \{\mathsf{core}_{ao}, \mathsf{rmi}_{ms}\} \tag{31}$$
$$\mathsf{sb} = \{\mathsf{respCache}_{ao} \circ \mathsf{core}_{ao}, \mathsf{cmr}_{ms}, \mathsf{rmi}_{ms}\} \tag{32}$$

The visual depiction of these layers is shown in Figure 11.

5.3 Implementing Silent Failover with Middleware Wrappers

We now contrast our implementation of silent failover with a wrapper implementation constructed using Spitznagel's wrapper transformations.

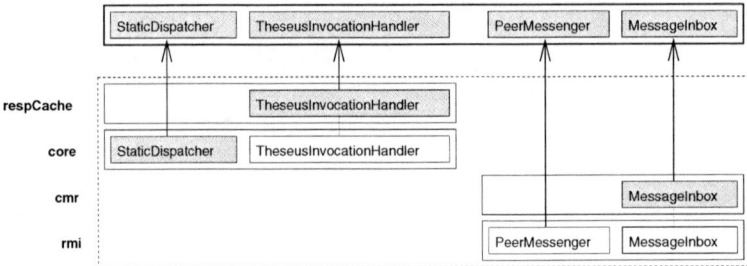

Fig. 11. Backup server configuration

Duplicating Requests. To duplicate requests sent by the client, the add observer wrapper is applied. This wrapper creates a duplicate middleware stub for communicating with the backup server. Each time an operation is invoked, the corresponding request is sent to both the primary and the backup. As such, the marshaling due to the second invocation is both functionally and structurally equivalent to the first, introducing redundant processing in redundant components. Because our approach refines the peer messenger to send the marshaled request to both the primary and the backup in the message service, we avoid the processing redundancy inherent in marshaling the same invocation twice.

Managing the Response Cache. Acknowledging responses and maintaining a response cache requires the introduction of unique identifiers (asynchronous completion tokens) to both the request and the response and the introduction of an out-of-band message service comparable to our control message service. The easier of the two is the application of a data translation wrapper that introduces unique identifiers such that they are available for use by middleware wrappers. Upon client invocation, a data-translation wrapper cannot modify the marshaled request, but it can add a unique identifier to the invocation parameters. On the backup, a dual data translation wrapper wraps the servant and removes this identifier. Also on the backup, this wrapper must apply the unique identifier to the return data (the response) and store that response in a response cache. While these wrappers work, the introduction of unique identifiers is redundant with the corresponding middleware identifiers used to coordinate requests and responses (such as CORBA's object id[25] and RMI's UID[26]). In Theseus, refinements such as ackResp and respCache have access to the existing identifier marshaled into a request. As such, they non-destructively re-use these identifiers to maintain the response cache.

An auxiliary concern that arises when treating the middleware as a black box is how to "silence" the backup server. Silencing the backup requires somehow, non-invasively orphaning the components that send responses. Under black box wrapping, on the server side, wrappers are applied to the servant that is registered with the middleware. When a request is received by that middleware, it invokes the corresponding invocation on the servant and expects that servant to return some data that is to be sent back to the client. As such, one must affect suppression of the reply, caching it instead, when the servant returns. In some middleware systems, interceptor techniques (such as CORBA's interceptors[12,13]) can be used to suppress replies by intercepting, caching, and then discarding each without sending them. However, not all systems support such facilities and would have to send some form of response to the client. As such, the client must suppress this behavior by discarding responses sent by the backup. In the latter case, the backup can not be made silent and will create additional traffic that silent backup was intended to avoid. In contrast, we silence the backup by applying a refinement (respCache) that replaces the invocation wrapper that sends the responses with one that caches them, effectively removing this component rather than orphaning it.

The more difficult part of managing the response cache is sending the expedited control messages needed to acknowledge responses and activate the backup server. Because conventional middleware, by its nature, hides the underlying communication primitives, expedited control messages and the corresponding out-of-band data channel must be implemented completely independently of the stub and skeleton infrastructure. To this end, client wrappers must contain hooks for communication with objects that instantiate and maintain an additional communication channel between the client and the backup for such expedited messages. Correspondingly, the wrapper on the backup must maintain similar hooks to objects that implement a server that listens for such messages and handles the connections between itself and its clients. This solution introduces both complexity and a duplicate communication channel, further increasing system resource usage. Using refinements, the developer of silent backup may refine the existing message service to filter out control messages and post them to their listeners immediately, preserving the expedited nature of the out-of-band messages. Moreover, this refinement re-uses the existing channel and avoids the need for an auxiliary message service to manage out-of-band channels.

Recovery from Failure. As per silent backup, in the event of an error, the client activates the backup, the backup sends outstanding responses to the client, and then the backup assumes the role of the primary. Implementing these with wrappers requires adding fairly extensive recovery logic that uses the out-of-band data channel to resend responses. This logic is added to both the client and backup server. On the backup, when the activate message is received, the responses are sent over the out-of-band data channel (because the middleware occludes access to the underlying communication channel), to the client. After sending the activate message, the client waits to receive these responses and delivers the corresponding results to the client via hooks into the stub wrappers. Depending on the type of middleware being wrapped, the delivery mechanisms will differ. For instance, if the wrapper augments a message-oriented middleware, the wrapper simply needs to add the response to a queue and invoke a notification method that indicates a new message has arrived. In the case of a synchronous middleware stub, the client is blocked on a synchronous call to the stub wrapper and is awaiting its return; delivery logic must use a setter method that allows it to set the return value of that wrapper and then notify it such that it will return that value to the client.

In our refinement-based implementation, by virtue of our ability to re-use existing abstractions, recovery is drastically simplified. Because the refined invocation handler caches the responses as it receives them, the recovery initiated by the activate message may simply iterate through these responses, replaying them to a live invocation handler (one whose configuration is identical to that of the primary's invocation handler) that will send them to the client via a peer messenger. From the perspective of the client, because these are sent by an invocation handler identical (in configuration) to that of the primary, these responses are sent directly to the client's inbox, where they will be retrieved and delivered exactly as if they had been sent by the primary.

Promoting the Backup to Primary. To complete the transition from backup to primary requires transitioning the backup from silent to active. This returns us to the concern of how to silence the backup. If this was possible via a mechanism such as portable interceptors, the logic for processing activate message ought to reverse this augmentation such that the backup sends responses to the client. If the backup is already sending responses, the client's promotion of the backup to the primary should cause the client to begin accepting responses from the client rather than discarding them as before.

Using refinements, the implementation of this transition is also drastically simplified. Recall that the backup was made silent by replacing the live invocation handler with one that caches responses. Reversing the process is just as simple: the caching invocation handler is replaced with a live invocation handler, cached responses are replayed, and subsequent responses are sent to the client by the now live invocation handler.

5.4 Discussion

Both wrappers and AHEAD collectives an be used to augment middleware with reliability. Wrappers are more reusable in that they do not require the underlying middleware to have been designed according to an AHEAD model. Consequently, legacy systems may benefit from wrapper based reliability, transparent to both the original communication system and the applications that use these. However, with this reusability comes the potential for redundancy and inefficiency. Moreover, additional complexity may be introduced if existing components must be orphaned by an augmentation.

By contrast, we sacrifice reusability across multiple middleware implementations for a mechanism that accommodates fine-grain composition and refinement. As such, we avoid the complexity of suppressing, bypassing, or accommodating behaviors of a former middleware incarnation in favor of those behaviors expressed by newer strategies. Further, our type expressions make the structural composition of these systems clear.

The skeptical reader may question the redundancy and efficiency gains afforded by the seemingly minor improvements, such as removing duplicate stubs.

These "minor" inefficiencies may snowball in a system in which thousands, or even millions, of stubs and skeletons are managing the sessions of an equal number of client-server interactions. At this scale, the cumulative gain is substantial. These improvements are especially important in systems with tight resource constraints, such as small devices, real-time systems, and high-availability systems. In such cases, computational and storage resources are at a premium.

6 Conclusions and Future Work

In her work implementing connector wrappers, Spitznagel identified a covering set of transforms that can be used to implement a variety of reliability strategies and may be applied to many different middleware implementations. Because these wrappers treat middleware as a black box, this portability comes at the cost of redundancy and increased resource consumption, neither of which are acceptable for small, mobile devices that are most in want of reliability.

This paper descibes an alternative implementation that capitalizes on the compositional properties of systems built under the AHEAD-model. Under this model, a system is enhanced by augmenting the base middleware with refinements that are relevant to the reliability policy at hand and recomposing the system. These refinements may then reuse resources that implement common middleware abstractions, allowing the refinement itself to implement only the essence of the policy at hand.

To validate our alternative, we illustrate how a minimal middleware may be augmented by refinements to implement various reliability policies. Moreover, we provide a model that groups the refinements that collaborate to implement reliability strategies into collectives that may be applied as a single, composite refinement, analogous to how connector wrappers are applied to connectors. Finally, our evaluation of silent backup illustrates that our refinements do indeed avoid redundancy when compared with a wrapper-based approach.

Our future work intends to extend Theseus with the ability to incorporate reliability enhancements at run-time, using dynamic-reconfiguration techniques, such as [27,28]. We expect this work to leverage dynamic recomposition representations, such as Dynamic WRIGHT[29], to support a design tool that allows developers to design multiple configurations and then evaluate the possible transitions between them.

Acknowledgements. Support for this work was provided by the Office of Naval Research grant N00014-01-1-0744 and by NSF grants EIA-0000433 and CCR-9984726.

References

1. Spitznagel, B., Garlan, D.: A Compositional Formalization of Connector Wrappers. In: Proceedings of the 2003 International Conference on Software Engineering, Portland, Oregon, USA (2003)
2. Allen, R., Garlan, D.: A Formal Basis for Architectural Connection. ACM Transactions on Software Engineering Methodology **6** (1997) 213–249

3. Batory, D., Sarvela, J.N., Rauschmayer, A.: Scaling step-wise refinement. In: Proceedings of the 25th International Conference on Software Engineering, IEEE Computer Society (2003) 187–197
4. Milner, R., et al.: The Definition of Standard ML - Revised. The MIT Press (1997)
5. Smaragdakis, Y., Batory, D.: Implementing layered designs with mixin layers. In: Proceedings of the European Conference on Object-Oriented Programming (ECOOP), Springer-Verlag LNCS 1445 (1998) 550–570
6. Schmidt, D., Stal, M., Rohnert, H., Buschmann, F.: Pattern-Oriented Software Architecture: Patterns for Concurrent and Networked Objects. Volume 2. John-Wiley & Sons (2000)
7. Avizienis, A., Laprie, J.C., Randell, B.: Fundamental concepts of dependability. Technical Report 010028, UCLA (1984)
8. Sowell, J.H., Stirewalt, R.E.K.: Middleware Reliability Implementations and Connector Wrappers. In: Proceedings of ICSE 2004 Workshop on Architecting Dependable Systems, Edinburgh, Scotland, UK (2004)
9. Spitznagel, B.: Compositional Transformation of Software Connectors. PhD dissertation, School of Computer Science, Carnegie Mellon University, Pittsburgh, PA, USA (2004)
10. Becker, T.: Application Transparent Fault Tolerance in Distributed Systems. In: Proceedings of 2nd International Workshop on Configurable Distributed Systems, Pittsburgh, Pennsylvania, USA (2004)
11. Zandy, V.C., Miller, B.P.: Reliable network connections. In: MobiCom '02: Proceedings of the 8th annual international conference on Mobile computing and networking, ACM Press (2002) 95–106
12. : Portable Interceptors. In: Common Object Request Broker Architecture: Core Specification . Object Management Group (2002) 21-1–21-64. http://www.omg.org/technology/documents/formal/corba_2.htm.
13. C.Marchetti, L.Verde, R.Baldoni: CORBA Request Portable Interceptors: A Performance Analysis. In: Proceedings of the 3nd International Symposium on Distributed Objects and Applications (DOA 2001). (2001) 208–217
14. Bergmans, L., Aksits, M.: Composing crosscutting concerns using composition filters. Commun. ACM **44** (2001) 51–57
15. Gamma, E., Helm, R., Johnson, R., Vlissides, J.: Design Patterns: Elements of Reusable Object-Oriented Software. Addison-Wesley (1995)
16. Schmidt, D.: The ADAPTIVE Communication Environment: Object-Oriented Network Programming Components for Developing Client/Server Applications. In: Proceedings of the 12th Sun Users Group Conference. (1994)
17. Fabre, J.C., Perennou, T.: A Metaobject Architecture for Fault Tolerant Distributed Systems: The FRIENDS Approach. IEEE Transactions on Computers, Special Issue on Dependability of Computing Systems **41** (1998) 78–95
18. Parlavantzas, N., Coulson, G., Blair, G.: An Extensible Binding Framework for Component-Based Middleware. In: Proceedings of EDOC 2003, Brisbane, Australia (2003)
19. Fleury, M., Reverbel, F.: The jboss extensible server. In: Middleware. (2003) 344–373
20. Shaw, M., DeLine, R., Klein, D.V., Ross, T.L., Young, D.M., Zelesnik, G.: Abstractions for software architecture and tools to support them. IEEE Trans. Softw. Eng. **21** (1995) 314–335
21. Batory, D., Sarvela, J.N., Rauschmayer, A.: Scaling step-wise refinement. IEEE Trans. Softw. Eng. **30** (2004) 355–371

22. : Package java.lang.reflect. (http://java.sun.com/j2se/1.4.2/docs/api/java/lang/reflect/package-summary.html)
23. Gray, J., Reuter, A.: Transaction Processing: Concepts and Techniques. Morgan Kaufmann Publishers (1993)
24. Stevens, W.R.: UNIX Network Programming, Volume 1, Second Edition: Networking APIs: Sockets and XTI. Prentice Hall (1998)
25. : Common Object Request Broker Architecture: Core Specification. Object Management Group (2002)
26. : Class java.rmi.server.uid. (http://java.sun.com/j2se/1.4.2/docs/api/java/rmi/server/UID.html)
27. Kramer, J., Magee, J.: The evolving philosophers problem: Dynamic change management. IEEE Trans. Softw. Eng. **16** (1990) 1293–1306
28. Hillman, J., Warren, I.: An open framework for dynamic reconfiguration. In: ICSE '04: Proceedings of the 26th International Conference on Software Engineering, IEEE Computer Society (2004) 594–603
29. Allen, R., Douence, R., Garlan, D.: Specifying and analyzing dynamic software architectures. In: Proceedings of the 1998 Conference on Fundamental Approaches to Software Engineering (FASE'98), Lisbon, Portugal (1998)

Concerning Predictability in Dependable Component-Based Systems: Classification of Quality Attributes

Ivica Crnkovic[1], Magnus Larsson[2], and Otto Preiss[3]

[1] Mälardalen University, Department of Computer Science and Engineering
Box 883, 721 23 Västerås, Sweden
`ivica.crnkovic@mdh.se`
`http://www.idt.mdh.se/~icc`
[2] ABB Corporate Research, 721 59 Västerås, Sweden
`magnus.larsson@se.abb.com`
[3] ABB Corporate Research, CH-5405 Baden-Daettwil, Switzerland
`otto.preiss@ch.abb.com`

Abstract. One of the main objectives of developing component-based software systems is to enable efficient building of systems through the integration of components. All component models define some form of component interface standard that facilitates the programmatic integration of components, but they do not facilitate or provide theories for the prediction of the quality attributes of the component compositions. This decreases significantly the value of the component-based approach to building dependable systems. If it is not possible to predict the value of a particular attribute of a system prior to integration and deployment to the target environment the system must be subjected to other procedures, often costly, to determine this value empirically. For this reason one of the challenges of the component-based approach is to obtain means for the "composition" of quality attributes. This challenge poses a very difficult task because the diverse types of quality attributes do not have the same underlying conceptual characteristics, since many factors, in addition to component properties, influence the system properties. This paper analyses the relation between the quality attributes of components and those of their compositions. The types of relations are classified according to the possibility of predicting properties of compositions from the properties of the components and according to the influences of other factors such as software architecture or system environment. The classification is exemplified with particular cases of compositions of quality attributes, and its relation to dependability is discussed. Such a classification can indicate the efforts that would be required to predict the system attributes which are essential for system dependability and in this way, the feasibility of the component-based approach in developing dependable systems.

1 Introduction

Component-based development (CBD) is of great interest to the software engineering community and has achieved considerable success in many engineering domains. CBD has been extensively used for several years in desktop environments, office applications, e-business and in general in Internet- and Web-based distributed applications. The component technologies (for example COM/DCOM, CORBA, EJB and .NET) used in these domains originate from object-oriented (OO) technologies. The basic principles of the OO approach, such as encapsulation and class specification have been further extended. The importance of component interfaces has increased; a component interface is treated as a component specification and the component implementation is treated as a black box [26]. A component interface is also the programmatic means of integrating the component in an assembly. Component technologies include the support of component deployment into a system through the component interface. On the other hand, the management of the component quality attributes has not been supported by these technologies. This topic has instead been treated separately from the applied component-based technologies.

In many other domains, for example dependable systems, CBD is utilized to a lesser degree for a number of different reasons [3]. One is the difficulty of implementing the same component technologies because of various system constraints such as limited resources which is one typical characteristic of small embedded systems. Another reason is the unclear distinction between system components which include both hardware and software parts and software components which may be encapsulated in system components or distributed through several system components. In this article, whenever we use the term "components" we assume "software components". Finally an important reason is the inability of component-based technologies to deal with quality attributes as required in these domains. For dependable systems, a number of quality attributes are as important as the functions these systems provide, and the development effort related to realizing quality attribute requirements is most often greater than the effort related to the implementation of particular functions. In general, the problem of CBD for dependable systems is that, if components are considered black boxes, it is difficult to obtain evidence that they behave according to their specifications. Moreover, depending on the deployment and usage context a component's behavior might change. Dependability arguments can be obtained only if the complete behavioral specification of a component is known beforehand. If the advantages of component-based technologies are limited to the functional domain only and cannot be utilized in the domain of quality attributes, or, even worse, introduce difficulties in the management of quality attributes, these technologies cannot be fully utilized.

The component-based approach is closely related to software architecture. The use of a component-based technology decreases chances to get an architectural mismatch by standardizing certain architectural decisions. A software component model specifies rules for component composition and interoperation and in this way simplifies the development process and similar to software architecture makes it possible to reason about quality properties largely independent of a particular application. The main difference between a software component-based approach and the software architecture-oriented approach is that the former focuses on reusability of already existing components, whereas the latter focuses on a conceptual approach in identifying components, their interconnections and evaluation of overall configuration.

Some of the main advantages of CBD are reusability, higher abstraction level and separation of the system development process from the component development process [3,4]. These advantages have however implications on other aspects of software and system development. The final success of the utilization of CBD depends not only on its advantages but also on these implications – the degree to which they are positive and negative. Since for dependable systems, particular quality attributes are of the greatest importance, a question which arises is to what extent does CBD influence the achievement of these properties: CBD can introduce new difficulties, it can be irrelevant for those properties, or can have a positive effect. For this reason it is of interest to analyze the ability of CBD to cope with requirements related to quality attributes.

Component-based software engineering (CBSE) faces two types of problems in dealing with quality attributes. The first, common to all software development, is the fact that the quality attributes are often imprecisely defined or difficult to estimate and measure. Further, values of certain properties may be different in different contexts. The second, specific to component-based systems, is the difficulty of relating system properties to component properties. In CBD one desired feature is that components can be selected and integrated in an automatic and efficient way. This goal is achieved for the functional part; components are selected and integrated through their interfaces. It is questionable if a similar approach can be applied to quality attributes.

For component-based systems crucial questions in relation to quality attributes are the following:

- Given the system quality attributes required, which attributes are required of the components concerned and which attributes are required from the component design- and runtime infrastructure?
- Given a set of component attributes, which system attributes are determined?
- How can the quality attributes of a system be accurately predicted, from the quality attributes of components which are determined with a certain accuracy.
- To which extent, and under which constraints are the emerging system attributes determined by the component attributes?

These and similar questions have been addressed at a series of CBSE symposia [4], and particular models of certain properties have been analyzed [14], but so far very little work has been done in the systematization and classification of quality attributes in accordance with the questions above. Although there are other classifications of quality attributes such as [6,7,17,23], these have not considered the predictability and composability aspects of the quality attributes.

Some system quality attributes can be derived directly from the component attributes; others might require a complex calculation model, related to the component model and the system architecture. Some system attributes, such as safety, do not exist on the component level and are the result of a complex combination of the system interaction with its environment, system architecture and different attributes of components involved.

In this paper, our intention is to demonstrate the diversity of quality attributes and the different methods which can be used for predicting system properties from the properties of the components involved. The quality attributes can be classified according to our ability to accurately calculate their compositions, i.e. the ability to predict the properties of component compositions. Such a classification indicates the feasibility of the component-based approach for building dependable systems.

The paper is organized as follows: Section 2 provides basic definitions needed for a classification and a classification framework which is used in our CBD-specific classification. Section 3 identifies the types of properties according to the principles for predicting the properties of component assemblies. Section 4 discusses the proposed classification with respect to a possibility of combining the types identified in the previous section, and with respect to recursive composition. Section 5 analyzes composability of properties of dependable systems and discusses possible benefits for dependable models of utilizing CBD and Section 6 concludes the paper.

2 Composability of Quality Attributes

In this section we will take a more fundamental look at what quality attributes or properties are and what they are good for. We then investigate the various notions of property decompositions, so that we can properly position our empirical and composition-oriented classification of properties.

2.1 What Are Properties?

The discussion in this paper is not primarily concerned with the theories behind individual types of properties (such as what is *green*, or what is *having a latency of,* or *what is security*). It is rather concerned with how we can generalize our understanding of the notion of property or its synonyms to a level where we can suggest a principled manner to conceptualize them in the context of software systems and software components where we can suggest a principled manner to reason about them in a decompositional way.

2.2 The Philosophical View on Properties – What Are Properties Good for?

Coming to grips with properties is pervasive in philosophy. Plato's theory of Forms ([19], p. 93) (where Form is said to be Plato's term for property,) seems to be one of the earliest accounts on what is today called properties. The term property includes attributes, qualities, features, or characteristics of things. It even encompasses relations such as *being faster than*.

The need for properties is motivated by their explanatory roles they have to fill. They came into being to describe phenomena of *interest* (like when we say: the system response is *very fast*). Because a stakeholder is a role that represents groups of people who have similar interests in the same phenomenon, the choice of properties and their importance is clearly related to certain stakeholders or stakeholder classes.

From an ontological viewpoint, the existence of properties is determined empirically. As a first important rule this means that properties and their definitions are conceived by humans and there is no a priori, logical or conceptual method to determine which properties exist [24]! This also means that the notion of a property and every type of property is an abstract concept only. As with any concept, humans define its name as well as its definition and its related theories. We therefore do not have to argue about the universal truth behind or correctness of a property as long as its definition and purposeful theory fulfills our goals.

From a natural language viewpoint, there is no single idiom to talk about and use properties. In other words, properties are distinct from their representations and *the same property may have different representations*. In the English language for example, properties can appear as single terms with any of the many suffixes such as '-ity', '-ness', '-hood', '-kind', '-ship', etc. (e.g. as in '*safety*'), or as predicative expressions in multiple ways (e.g., '*executes safely*', '*is safe*'). Hence, since properties are conceived by humans, not only their meaning need to be defined but also their possibly numerous, not only natural language-based, representations.

As with any concept (i.e. purely knowledge-related construct), humans tend to categorize also properties, i.e. we describe properties by means of inherent characteristics of certain categories. Two such inherent characteristics that are very important in the discourse of "quality attribute compositions": complexity, and specificity.

Complexity refers to the fact that properties can be simple or compound/complex. A complex property is some form of a logical structure or combination of properties. This combination must of course be defined to understand a complex property. As an example for a complex property consider 'being my grandfather'. It implies that the person this property is ascribed to is 'male and older than I am'. Or 'being CMM Level 3 certified' implies that the software development unit this property is ascribed to 'has a software process that is documented and standardized, and that all software projects use an approved, tailored version of this standard software process for developing and maintaining software'[22].

Specificity refers to the fact that a property can be a determinable or a determinate. The distinction, however, is relative in that a determinate property is a more specific version of a determinable. For example, "up-time" is a determinate property (i.e. a more specific one) of the determinable "availability". The measure "time passed between failures" is in turn one possible determinate of "up-time". The hierarchy of determinables and determinates is generally expected to bottom out in completely specific, absolute determinates. In software engineering, such leave determinates would be called quality-carrying properties, or direct properties, or tangible/measurable properties, to name a few.

In software engineering, hierarchies or taxonomies of properties, which are fundamentally based on the notions of complexity and specificity, are at the heart of the decompositional approaches of quality models (e.g. [8] and its predecessors).

2.3 Realization-Oriented Decomposition Versus Other Forms of Property Decompositions

Before we proceed to the patterns of realization-oriented decomposition/traceability in the next main chapter, we want to clarify by means of Fig 1 how two other types of property decompositions are related to the realization-oriented decomposition: (1) classification oriented quality attribute decompositions, and (2) the analysis-oriented decomposition for non-functional requirements.

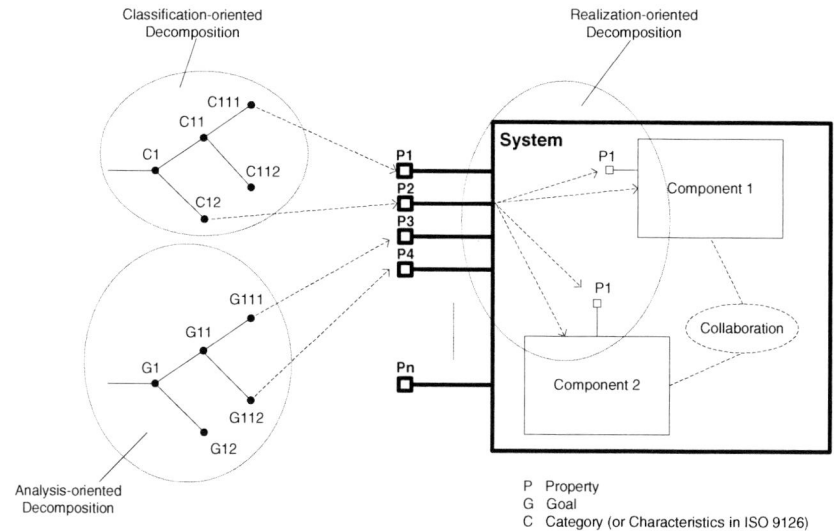

Fig. 1. Different Types of Property Decompositions

Fig 1 shows a *System* and its ascribed properties *P1...Pn*. The System is composed of two components (*Component 1* and *Component 2*) that engage in a *Collaboration*. In this simple example, every component has just one property *P1*. If we envision a designer who needs to design a *System* with the required properties *P1...Pn*, the constituents of the *System* would be called the realization elements.

In a **realization-oriented decomposition** we want to relate a system-level property to the elements that realize the system and that cause the property to manifest in the requested way. Fig 1 illustrates a simple case in which the *Component 1* and *2* and their respective property *P1* realize the system-level property *P2*. Let us take the simple case where *P2* of the *System* expresses its power consumption in Watts. *P1* of *Component 1* and *2* would simply be the respective consumption per component. Hence, *P2* of the *System* is no more than the sum of the two properties *P1* of the two components. This is of course the simplest case and it is, in fact, the subject of the rest of this paper to elaborate on other types of realization-oriented decompositions.

A **classification-oriented decomposition** on the contrary refers to a hierarchy represented as a tree of determinables and determinates, where the leaf determinates could be selected as the relevant, required properties of a system. Hence, it is a classification that serves the purpose of knowledge structuring. It represents a decomposition of high-level properties into more tangible ones so as to end with a set of quantifiable properties on some scale. The ISO/IEC 9126-1 [8] is a representative for such a classification because it defines a set of characteristics, which are decomposed into subcharacteristics, which in turn shall be decomposed into potentially measurable properties. Such a classification can therefore serve as starting point for defining the system-level properties to be realized. In Fig 1, such a classification is used to derive the required properties *P1* and *P2* of the *System*. For instance, *P1* could be the required physical property power consumption, whose value must be below a certain threshold. *P1* could have resulted from the ISO/IEC 9126-1 derived classification Efficiency (*C1*) -> Resource Utilization (*C11*) -> Power Consumption (*C111*).

The third kind of decomposition - **analysis-oriented decomposition** – is shown in the figure for completeness reasons only. It relates to the decomposition of requirements. For more details of this category and in general on these classes of decomposition refer to [18].

2.4 Definitions of Certain Terms

We feel that terms such as non-functional property, extra-functional property, quality attribute, etc. are very often not used carefully enough. Based on our research, we would suggest the following distinction which we used in this paper.

- *Attribute/property* are treated as synonymous and are used in the most general sense as defined by standard dictionaries, e.g.: "a construct whereby objects and individuals can be distinguished" [15] "a quality or trait belonging and especially peculiar to an individual or thing" or "an effect that an object has on another object or on the senses" [16]
- A *required attribute/property* is expressed as a need or desire on an entity by some stakeholder. We may call such a property a *requirement*.
- An *exhibited attribute/property* is an attribute/property ascribed to an entity as a result of evaluating the entity. The evaluation may be direct, in the sense that one does some measurement with the entity in question, or it may be indirect. The latter may be the case when we ascribe a property to an entity because we evaluate related artifacts or because someone made us believe that the entity has this (typically conceptual) property, although we can hardly measure it on the entity itself.
- *Quality*: The totality of exhibited attributes/properties of an entity that bear on its ability to satisfy stated or implied needs, i.e. to satisfy its requirements. Quality thus represents the set of all exhibited attributes/properties that have a relationship to required properties.
- *Quality attribute/property*: Refers to an exhibited attribute/property that is part of the Quality of an entity.

Having discussed the basic classes of property decompositions that are being used today, we can now focus on the conceptualization of the realization-oriented decompositions that go along with building software-intensive systems based on software components.

3 Classification of Properties

A great number of quality attributes are encountered in software engineering. They are classified in many different ways, frequently in a non-orthogonal manner. One example of classification is related to the system lifecycle: run-time properties (visible and measurable during the program execution) and lifecycle properties (those that characterize different phases in a development and maintenance process). Another example is the quality model defined in ISO/EIC 9126-1 "Software engineering -

product quality" standard [8], which classifies quality attributes as external and internal. Quality attributes are the measurable, quantifiable properties of a software product. The latter also includes all its intermediate development artifacts. Quality attributes that refer to the internal quality – internal quality attributes - are typically applied to intermediate deliverables at certain development stages (e.g. attributes of a design specification, source code, etc.). Internal therefore has the connotation of "development internal view". The relation between internal and external quality attributes is not unambiguous though; an internal quality attribute may have impact on different external quality attributes and of course an external quality attribute is a result of combination of internal attributes.

The classification we consider here is related to *composability*. We classify properties according to the principles applied in deriving the system properties from the properties of the components involved. Instead of the term "system", we shall use a generic term *Assembly (A)* which simply denotes a set of interacting components. Such an assembly can be a part of a software system (for example a functional unit, or a subsystem), or the entire system. The only characteristic we want to relate to an assembly is a set of integrated components – an assembly can be assumed as a component (however composed of other components). Some properties, however, cannot be related only to an assembly, but are explicitly related to the entire system and its interaction with the environment. In such cases we refer to a *System (S)*.

We distinguish the following types of properties:

a. *Directly composable properties.* A property of an assembly which is a function of, and only of, the same type of property of the components involved.
b. *Architecture-related properties.* A property of an assembly which is a function of the same type of property of the components and of the software architecture.
c. *Derived properties.* A property of an assembly which depends on several different properties of the components.
d. *Usage-depended properties.* A property of an assembly which is determined by its usage profile.
e. *System environment context properties.* A property which is determined by other properties and by the state of the system environment.

Let us discuss these cases and give examples in the following subsections.

3.1 Directly Composable Properties

Definition: *A directly composable property of an assembly is a function of, and only of the same property of the components.*

$$P = \text{attribute}, \quad A = \text{assembly}, \quad c = \text{component}$$
$$A = \{c_i : 1 \leq i \leq n\} \tag{1}$$
$$P(A) = f(P(c_1), P(c_2), \ldots, P(c_n))$$

Note that the property of the assembly is the same as the component property. Further, the component technology is not explicitly specified in the relation (1). However it is obvious that the function f itself is dependent on the technology since the mechanisms to assemble components is provided by the component technology.

An example of a property of this type is the static memory size of a component or an assembly, this is also known as the memory footprint. The simplest composition model is the calculation of the static memory of an assembly as the sum of the memories used by each component:

$$M(A) = \sum_{i=1}^{n} M(c_i) \qquad (2)$$

M = memory size, A = assembly, c_i = components

The function M(ci) is different for different technologies. For example in the case of the separation of composition time from run-time which is usually used in embedded systems, M(ci) will be a constant, possibly parameterized by configuration factors. In such cases the static memory size of an assembly will be a constant. A more complicated model can be found in the Koala component model [25], in which additional parameters, such as size of glue code, interface parameterization and diversity are taken into account (i.e. the parameters determined by the component technology used).

The equation (2) is also valid for a dynamic memory, with the difference that M(ci) is not a constant, but a function which may depend on the usage profile. When using a particular technology, design patterns or parameterized resources this function may be limited on a particular value or budgeted. In such a case the total amount of memory can be calculated.

$$M(A) \leq \sum_{i=1}^{n} M_{\max}(c_i) \qquad (3)$$

The properties of this type can be calculated directly from the component properties if the components comply with particular restrictions for memory allocation. These restrictions can be built in component technologies.

For this type of composition there are no other assumptions and therefore these properties are the easiest to specify and predict. This does not mean that the composition functions are easy or even possible to express formally. However the fact that the property is visible on component and assembly level, and that the assembly property is dependent only on the component properties simplifies the prediction procedure and makes the prediction valid in any application using these components.

3.2 Architecture-Related Properties

Definition: *An architecture-related property of an assembly is a function of the same property of the components and of the software architecture.*

$$A = \{c_i : 1 \leq i \leq n\}$$
$$P(A) = f(P(c_1), P(c_2), \ldots, P(c_n), SA) \qquad (4)$$
$$SA = \text{software architecture}$$

In this case the assembly properties depend not only on the component properties but on the architectural structure. The software architecture is often used as a means for improving particular properties without changing the component properties. These types of properties can be tuned by different architectural solutions or variations. An example of such a property is a performance predictability model for J2EE (Java 2 Platform, Enterprise Edition) application presented in [9,29]. A typical application implemented in this technology would be a distributed web-based application in which the variability in scalability is achieved by it being possible to add new clients and new computational (business) components to the server as illustrated in Fig 2. To achieve concurrency the components are executed in different threads. A possible extension variation of this architecture is the possibility to include several nodes with web servers and business applications.

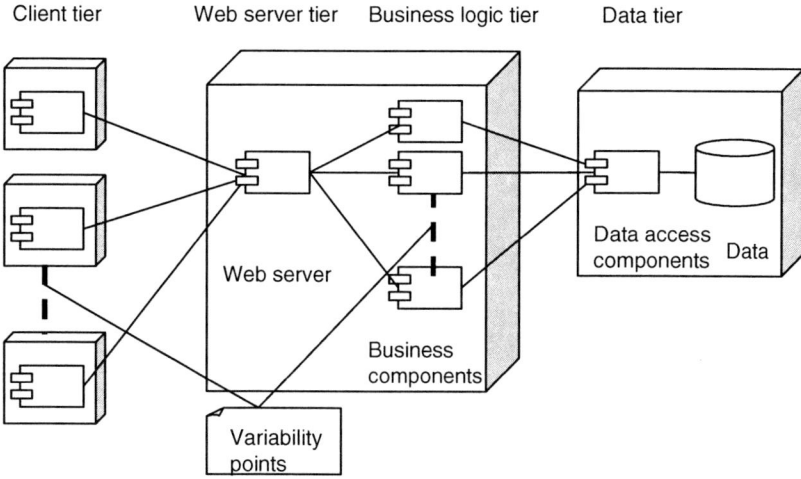

Fig. 2. A typical multi-tier architecture with client and servers variability points affecting the performance quality property

The performance of the system shown in the Fig 2 is related to the number of clients and the number of server components. A typical requirement for such applications is the performance and scalability, i.e. the dependencies between the performance and number of clients and active business components.

According to [9,29] the time per transaction T/N expressed in equation (5) depends on several factors related to the system architecture: The first factor comes from the concurrent requests that compete for service from the server component. This includes the network bandwidth and underlying transport mechanisms. The second factor describes a case in which accepted requests compete for a thread to execute the business components. The third factor results from concurrent access to the database by the concurrent server threads.

The first factor is proportional to the number of clients, the second to the number of clients and inversely proportional to the number of threads (i.e. number of components on the server) and the third factor is proportional to the number of threads.

$$T/N = ax + b\frac{x}{y} + cy \qquad (5)$$

T/N = execution time per transaction

x = number of clients; y = number of components

a, b, c = proportional factors for a particular implementation

The form of the equation shows that it is possible to calculate the optimal number of threads in relation to the number of clients to achieve a minimum respond time per transaction.

3.3 Derived Properties

Definition: *A derived property of an assembly is a property that depends on several different properties of the components.*

$$A = \{c_i : 1 \leq i \leq n\}$$

$$P(A) = f \begin{pmatrix} P_1(c_1), P_1(c_2), \cdots, P_1(c_n), \\ P_2(c_1), P_2(c_2), \cdots, P_2(c_n), \\ \vdots \\ P_k(c_1), P_k(c_2), \cdots, P_k(c_n) \end{pmatrix} \qquad (6)$$

P = assembly attribute

$P_1 ... P_k$ = component attributes

In the same way that a function of an assembly is more than the sum of the component functions, there are properties that are the result of the composition of different component properties.

An example of such a property in a real-time system is the end-to-end deadline (a maximal response time) that is a function of different component properties, such as worst case execution time (WCET) and execution period as shown in the following example. Let us consider real-time port-based component models with provided and required interfaces and interfaces to an underlying operating system or I/O devices, as discussed in [5,10,28]. In these models, components are implemented as tasks, parts of a task or a set of tasks. An assembly consisting of two components, where every component is realized as a task is shown on Fig 3. Each basic component includes properties such as WCET and execution period. A composition of this simple model is achieved by connecting ports and identifying provided and required interfaces.

The question is whether we can calculate WCET for an assembly of components executing with different periods. In a case in which the execution periods are the same, this would be possible. In a case in which these periods are different, we cannot specify WCET of the assembly, but we can specify end-to-end deadline and a period.

An end-to-end deadline is the maximum time interval between the start of the first component in an assembly and the finish of the last component in the assembly. The assembly period will be a number to which the components periods are divisors.

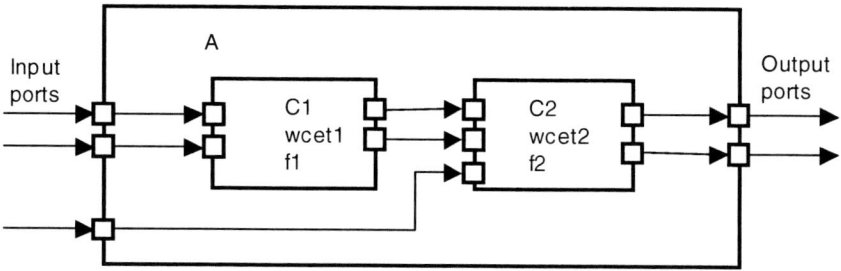

Fig. 3. Composition of port-based components

In a similar way we can calculate latency, or response time, from the real-time properties of components if particular assumptions about real-time system characteristics, such as scheduling policy, and mapping between component and real-time entities are taken. In a case in which components are mapped to tasks and the fixed priority scheduling is used, a worst case latency of component c_i, L(c_i), can be calculated as [11]:

$$L^{n+1}(c_i) = c_i.wcet + B(c_i) + \sum_{\forall c_j \in hp(c_i)} \left\lceil \frac{L^n(c_i)}{c_j.T} \right\rceil c_j.wcet \quad (7)$$

B is the blocking time, $hp(c_i)$, is the set of components having tasks with higher priority than component i, $c_j.T$ is the period and $c_j.wcet$ is the worst-case execution time of component c_i.

Emerging properties, i.e. properties that are pertinent on a system (or an assembly) level but are not visible on the component level are of special interest in this category. For such properties the major challenge is to identify the properties of the components that have impact on them.

3.4 Usage-Dependent Properties

Definition: *A Usage-dependent property of an assembly is a property which is determined by its usage profile.*

$$P(A, U_k) = f(P(c_i, U'_{i,k})) : i, k \in N$$
P = attribute for a particular usage profile
U_k = assembly usage profile $\quad (8)$
$U'_{i,k}$ = component usage profile

The behavior of an assembly and consequently of a system depends not only on the internal properties of the components and their composition but also on the particular use of the system. A usage profile U_k which determines a particular attribute P_k must be transformed to the usage profile $U'_{i,k}$ to determine the properties of the components.

Properties of this type introduce particular problems as they depend on the use of the system. This means that the component developers must predict as far as possible the use of the component in different systems – which may not yet exist. A second problem is the transfer of the usage profile from the assembly (or from the system) to the component. Even if the usage profile on the assembly level (U_k) is specified, the usage profile for the components ($U'_{i,k}$) is not easily determined especially when the assembly (and the system) configuration is not known.

A particular problem with this type of property is the limited possibility of reusing measured and derived properties. If the usage profile is changed, the properties must be re-calculated or re-measured. An example of such property is reliability which in software is calculated or measured for particular usage profiles. The question arising here is the possibility of reusing previous specifications of the property [5]. The first thought would be that this is possible if the domain of the new usage profile is a sub-domain of an old usage profile. In this case the value of a property will be within the range of possible values of the property for the old usage profile; the local maximum and minimum value being in the range of values for the old usage profile (see Fig 4).

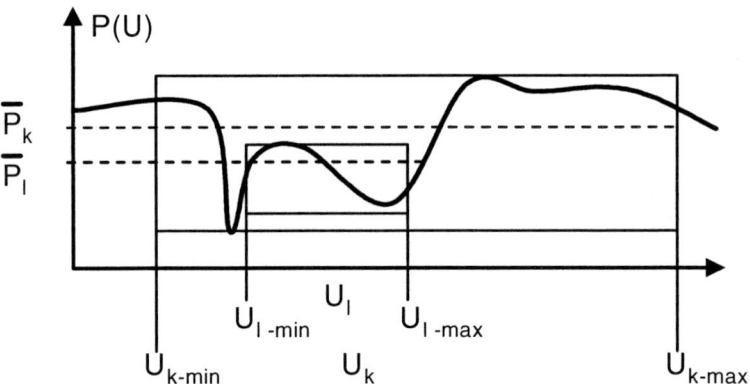

Fig. 4. Property for different usage profiles

If the new requirements of a property in a new usage profile are equal of or less stringent than the old requirements, we can use the property value from the old usage profile. This means, for example, that we do not need to measure the component properties.

$$U_l \subseteq U_k \Rightarrow P_{k-\min}(A, U_k) \leq P_l(A, U_l) \leq P_{k-\max}(A, U_k) \tag{9}$$

In a case in which a property is expressed as a statistical value (such as a mean value), the property value in an interval can be changed in an unwanted direction; Fig 4 illustrates such example in which the mean value of the property P(U) in the interval [U_{l-min}, U_{l-max}] is lower than in the entire interval [U_{k-min}, U_{k-max}], although the minimum and maximum values are higher. For certain properties (such as availability, or different quality of services) in certain domains (for example multimedia) the average plays a more important role than min or max values.

3.5 System Environment Context Properties

Definition: *A System Environment Context property is a property which is determined by other properties and by the state of the system environment.*

$$P(A, U_k) = f(P(c_i, U'_{i,k}), C_k) : i, k \in N$$

P = attribute for a particular usage profile
U_k = system usage profile (10)
C_k = system context
$U'_{i,k}$ = component usage profile

The property depends not only on the system property determined by the usage profile, but also on the environment in which the system is used (denoted by C_k in (10)). This case of composition is very much related to the "Usage dependent properties" type of composition, because the set of system profiles include a subset of all usage profiles. However, the property itself can be different in different contexts (i.e. surrounding environment) in which the system is placed. By this we emphasize that it is not possible to determine the value of the property even the if the usage profiles are known. An example of such a property is safety. As the safety property is related to the potential catastrophe, it is obvious that in different circumstances, the same property may have different degrees of safety even for the same usage profile. We can argue that these properties are out of the scope of the predictable assembly, as they depend on the surrounding environment. In contrast to "compositionally" deriving assembly properties from component properties, the approach for such kinds of properties is more like "given the system environment and the system properties, what are the requirements on the assembly and component properties. Nonetheless, system environment context properties are also dependent on component properties. Further, for most of the cases an environment can be assumed or even be required for a usage profile.

A system can exhibit numerous properties and certainly not all of them have the same characteristics; some are easy to perceive and measure while others are very difficult to analyze, or measure (for instance administrability). Analyzable properties, which can be measured, are potential candidates for automatic reasoning about the behavior of a system. Properties that depend on the environment in which a system is deployed are generally hard to derive from the component properties.

4 Composition of Properties

For a classification it is important that it is complete and orthogonal. The completeness assumes that all cases fit into the classification. The orthogonally means that a particular case belongs to and only to a particular type in the classification. The presented classification is an idealization and an abstraction; in systems, in particular in complex systems, we could have many properties that are important for the stakeholders but are by their nature not precisely and formally specified, and which have different manifestations at component and system levels. While the question whether there are other types of properties, i.e. that there are types which do not fit into the classification cannot be formally justified or falsified, we can certainly find properties whose composition is the result of a combination of the principled types described in the previous section. For this reason it is of interest to see which combinations of these basic types are feasible and which combinations are of fundamental character. Further, there is a question related to recursive composability. Similarly to the question "can we provide component models that support recursion, in which we treat assemblies as components?" we can state a question: which properties and under which constraints are recursively composable?

In this section we discuss these two aspects of composability: composition of different types of properties and recursive compositions.

4.1 Composition Combination of Different Types of Properties

We are analyzing here a possibility of combining basic types of properties; can a system property be a result of a combination of different composition types? Theoretically we can have 26 combinations (single, double, triple, fourfold and fivefold combinations) of basic property types. Some of the combinations do not make sense. For example, a derived (emerging) property by definition cannot be at the same time a directly composable property. Similarly, combinations between directly composable and usage-dependent, or system environment-related properties are not feasible. This reduces the number of combinations. Further we shall see that some of the combinations cannot be found in practice.

In [11] we have analyzed and classified many properties grouped with respect to different concerns and validated the classification by inquiring a dozen researchers through a questionnaire to classify almost 100 properties. Since in general the properties and their definitions are the result of concerns, limitations and requirements it is possible to find an arbitrary number of different properties. To make the questionnaire manageable we have collect properties in groups, which correspond to different concerns (such as performance, dependability, usability, business, etc.). The results of the questionnaire indicated that there are many properties, in particular emerging properties, which are a combination of two, three or more basic classification types.

Here follows all possible combinations of the basic types of properties and identify those which we have never seen in practice (indicated by N/A), and give examples of possible combinations. From Table 1 we can see that a rather small number of combinations seem to be feasible.

Table 1. Examples of properties that are related to combinations of basic types of properties (a. Directly composable properties (DIR), b. Architecture-related properties (ART), c. Derived properties (emerging properties) (EMG), d. Usage-depended properties (USG), and e. System environment context properties (SYS))

No	a) DIR	b) ART	c) EMG	d) USG	e) SYS	Concerns/Properties Examples
1	x	x				Performance/Scalability
2	x		x			N/A
3	x			x		N/A
4	x				x	N/A
5		x	x			Performance/Timeliness
6		x		x		Dependability/Reliability
7		x			x	N/A
8			x	x		N/A
9			x		x	N/A
10				x	x	Dependability/Security
11	x	x	x			N/A
12	x	x		x		Performance/Responsiveness
13	x	x			x	N/A
14	x		x	x		N/A
15	x		x		x	N/A
16	x			x	x	N/A
17		x	x	x		Dependability/Security
18		x	x		x	N/A
19		x		x	x	N/A
20			x	x	x	Dependability/Safety
21	x	x	x	x		N/A
22	x	x	x		x	Business/Cost
23	x	x		x	x	N/A
24	x		x	x	x	N/A
25		x	x	x	x	N/A
26	x	x	x	x	x	N/A

4.2 Recursive Composition of Quality Properties

We have used the generic term "assembly" for a set of integrated components. In section 2 it is shown that specification of some properties should distinguish between an assembly and a system; the difference is whether only internal parameters are assumed, or a combination of internal and external factors, not part of the system, are included. A software system may consist of a set of assemblies, which turns out to be a set of components. Several questions arise when composing assemblies: Can the assemblies composed be treated as components in the new assembly, or are they treated in the new assembly as a set of the original components loosing the assembly identity? A similar question we can state for a properties; can a property be expressed in a recursive form of (the same) properties of hierarchical components? An ideal situation would be to have a means of using a hierarchical and recursive model which permits the same reasoning on all levels of the hierarchy.

We can distinguish two types of assemblies supported by existing component technologies. The first is the 1st order assembly which is not treated as a component in the component model. This type of assembly is merely a set of components integrated together, creating an application or a part of an application. In this case an assembly is seen as a virtual boundary of the component set and not as a separate entity. An assembly of the 1st order does not follow the semantics of a component. The second type of assembly is hierarchical which means that the assembly, created from components, is treated as a new component inside the component model.

There are different criteria which must be satisfied if an assembly is to be treated as a component. The basic criteria are the ability to provide recursive principles on (i) operational (construction) interface, (ii) component deployment and (iii) component quality properties.

The way to obtain the property value of an assembly is different from obtaining assemblies from components, and a recursive composition of properties is not related to the (recursive) constructions of assemblies. Rather it depends of the type of the property. For example the directly composed properties are by definition recursive; for recursive assemblies these properties will be recursive. In this way a property of an assembly of assemblies will be a composition of assembly and component property functions. For example, the properties of type (a) from the section 3 will be derived in the following way:

$$
\begin{aligned}
&P(A_a) = f(P(A_k)) = f(f(P(c_i))); i,k \in N \\
&A_a = \{A_k\}; A_k = \{c_i\} \\
&P = property, A_a = assembly\ of\ assemblies \\
&A_k = assemblies,\quad c_i = components
\end{aligned}
\quad (11)
$$

For the memory consumption case in equation (2), we have:

$$M(A_a) = \sum_{i=1}^{k} M(A_i) = \sum_{i=1}^{k}\sum_{j=1}^{n} M(c_{ij}) \quad (12)$$

For derived properties, it is in general not possible to achieve recursion. The same is valid for component properties which are not relevant on the assembly level.

5 Composability of Dependability Properties

To illustrate the property classification, we take dependability as an example. Dependability is defined as the ability of a system to deliver service that can be trusted and the ability of a system to avoid failures that are more severe and frequent than are acceptable to the users. According to [1] dependability is a complex property including six basic attributes, namely, availability, reliability, safety, confidentiality, integrity and maintainability.

The questions of interest to component-based software engineering or development are:

- To which category belong the dependability properties? In particular, which of the dependability properties are emerging or derived system properties, and which are both system and component properties?
- How are these properties in a component-based system related to other component properties?
- To which extent (and how) can these properties can be determined from component properties?
- To which extent can the unpredictability of these properties be minimized and how much is it related to the uncertainty of the component properties?

Reliability

The definition of reliability originates from the probability that a system will fail within a given period of time. The probability of failure is directly dependent on the usage profile and context of the module under consideration. One possible approach to the calculation of the reliability of an assembly is to use the following elements [20,21]:

- Reliability of the components – Information that has been obtained by testing and analysis of the component given a context and usage profile;
- Usage paths – Information that includes usage profile and the assembly structure. Combined, it can give a probability of execution of each component, for example by using Markov chains.

A model based on this approach needs the means for calculating or measuring component reliability and an architecture which permits analysis of the execution path. Component models that specify provided and required interface make it possible to develop a model for specifying the usage paths. This is an example in which the definition of the component model facilitates the procedure of dealing with the quality attribute. The system reliability can be analyzed by (re)using the reliability information of the assemblies and components (which can be derived or measured).

Availability

Availability is defined as the probability of a module being available when needed. The difference between reliability and availability is that availability is not only dependent of the system properties but also on a repair process, which implies that the availability of an assembly cannot be derived from the availability of the components in the way that its reliability can be derived from the reliability of its components. If the repair rate of the components are known, it also must be known the repair time of the system integration. In a larger context, non run-time attributes must be taken into a consideration; availability is related to the maintenance and support of the components constituting the assembly.

Safety

Safety is an attribute involving the interaction of a system with the environment and the possible consequences of the system failure [12]. It is a system attribute, neither a component nor an assembly attribute. Its safety depends on where and how the system is deployed. Since safety is a system attribute that is dependent on the system's environment, a means for analyzing safety is a top-down architectural approach, a decomposition rather than composition. Examples of such approach can be found in [2,27] In the analysis process, the components' attributes are used as selection criteria or are identified as demands that should be met. For this reason a component-based approach might not have the apparent advantage – on the contrary, if the starting idea is a reuse of existing components, the components' attributes cause new constraints and in this way might decrease the system safety. However, when the constraints are identified and unambiguously related to the constraints on the system level, the system safety can increase. Also, some attributes, such as reliability, might improve the accuracy of the system safety prediction, especially if known or measured when used in other applications.

Confidentiality and Integrity

Security properties, confidentiality and integrity, defined as follows apply to dependable systems [1].

- Confidentiality is defined as a measure of the absence of unauthorized disclosure of information;
- Integrity is defined as the absence of improper system state alterations.

From the definitions it is apparent that these attributes are not directly measurable and composable, and this is the main obstacle to the development of a theory for their prediction. Confidentiality and integrity are emerging system attributes that can be tested and analyzed on the system and architectural level but not on the component level. Usage profiles can be used for testing and analysis, but it is impossible to automatically derive these attributes from the component attributes.

Maintainability

Maintainability is related to the activities of people and not of the system itself, although there exists self-repairable systems which in some cases can reconfigure themselves in order to continue to provide services. Component technologies might provide support for dynamic upgrading/deployment of components which can improve the maintainability of a system. In this case the maintainability is much a matter of component technology, and not of the component itself. The system architecture thus has an impact on maintenance.

There are many parameters that can be measured and then used to estimate the maintainability of a code (for example McCabe Metrics for complexity [13]). These parameters can be identified for each component. It is however not clear how these parameters can be defined on the assembly level. One possibility is to define a mean value of all components normalized per lines of code.

6 Conclusion

The full advantage of the component-based approach to developing software will only be achieved when, in addition to a compositional reasoning of a system's functionality, we are able to more easily and accurately predict the system behavior with its quality attributes. When systems are designed and build from components, many system properties can be derived from the component properties. Hence, a generic support for the definition and measurement of the properties, which is built into the component models and technologies, would be greatly welcomed. However, the predictability of properties does not depend only on such a support in the component models but more on the types of properties themselves. Consequently, there is no silver bullet to deal with all types of properties. For each type of property, a theory of the property, its relation to the component model, composition rules and their contextual dependence and relation to requirements must be known.

Dependability properties belong to a class of properties which compositions are the most difficult; they are system properties and are result of different properties on component level, and system usage context. The feasibility of a bottom-up approach is questionable, but a more feasible challenge is to achieve an incremental composability when adding a new or modifying a component in a system, and being able to reason about the system properties from the properties of the old system and the properties of new component.

Because no generic approach will do, the paper suggests a classification of properties according to their principled way of compositional reasoning. Each type of the classification is characterized by the required parameters for obtaining predictability on the system level. Some types show clear composable characteristics, while others are not directly related to compositions.

The existing component models differ considerably and how the assemblies' and components' properties are treated will be highly dependent on these models, especially for those properties that are directly composable or are related to the architecture. For example, if the component model has independently deployable components with a 1st order assembly model, it is likely that the properties of the components cannot be propagated further than the assembly level without considering the environment.

In spite of diversity of properties, technologies, and theories, it should be possible to create reference frameworks that by identifying type of composability of properties can help in estimation of accuracy and efforts required for building component-based systems in a predictable way. These frameworks can be built for particular component-models in combination with architectural solutions and particular domains. Our future work will continue in these directions in which different component technologies and architectural solutions in the domain of embedded systems, such as automotive or automation systems will be considered.

Acknowledgements

We would like to express our gratitude to the reviewers for their excellent analysis of the paper and their valuable suggestions to improve it.

References

1. Avizienis, A.; Laprie, J.-C.; Randell, B.; Landwehr, C., *"Basic concepts and taxonomy of dependable and secure computing"*, IEEE Trans. Dependable Sec. Comput., Vol. 1, Issue 1, 2004
2. Bondavalli, A., Chiaradonna, S., Cotroneo, D., Romano, L.: Effective Fault Treatment for Improving the Dependability of COTS and Legacy-Based Applications, *IEEE Trans. Dependable Sec. Comput.* Vol. 1, Issue 4, 2004
3. Bouyssounouse, B., J. Sifakis (Eds), *"Embedded Systems Design - The ARTIST Roadmap for Research and Development"*, Springer-Verlag, LNCS Vol. 3436, 2004
4. Crnkovic I., Schmidt H., Stafford J., and Wallnau K. C., "5th Workshop on Component-Based Software Engineering: Benchmarks for Predictable Assembly", In *Software Engineering Notes*, Vol. 27, Issue 5, 2002.
5. Crnkovic I., and Larsson M., *Building Reliable Component-Based Software Systems*, Artech House, 2002.
6. Dromey G.R., "A Model for Software Product Quality", In *IEEE Transaction on Software Engineering*, Vol. 21, Issue 2, 1995.
7. ISO/IEC, *Information technology - Software product quality - Part 1: Quality model*, report ISO/IEC FDIS 9126-1:2000 (E), ISO, 2000.
8. ISO/IEC, *"Software engineering - Product quality - Part1: Quality model"*, ISO/IEC, International Standard 9126-1:2001(E).
9. Jogalekar P., and Woodside M., "Evaluating the Scalability of Distributed Systems", *IEEE Transactions on Parallel & Distributed Systems*, Vol 11, Issue 6, 2000.
10. Hissam S. A., Hudak J., Ivers J., Klein M., Larsson M., Moreno G. A., Northrop L., Plakosh D., Stafford J., Wallnau K. C., and Wood W., *Predictable Assembly of Substation Automation Systems: An Experience Report*, report CMU/SEI-2002-TR-031, Software Engineering Institute, Carnegie Mellon University, 2002.
11. Larsson M., *Predicting Quality Attributes in Component-based Software Systems*, PhD Thesis, Mälardalen University Press, Västerås, Sweden, March 2004
12. Leveson, N., *"Software: System Safety and Computers"*, Addison-Wesley, 1995
13. McCabe T.J., *"A Complexity Measure"*, *IEEE Transaction on Software Engineering*, Vol. 2, 1976.
14. Moreno G. A., Hissam S. A., and Wallnau K. C., "Statistical Models for Empirical Component Properties and Assembly-Level Property Predictions: Toward Standard Labeling", *Proceedings of 5th ICSE workshop on CBSE*, 2002.
15. Miller, G. A. (2002). WordNet®. Cognitive Science Laboratory, Princeton University [Online]. Available: http://www.cogsci.princeton.edu/~wn/
16. Merriam-Webster (2004, May), *"Collegiate Dictionary: Merriam-Webster Online"*, [Online]. Available : http://www.m-w.com/dictionary.htm
17. Preiss O., Wegmann A., and Wong J., "On Quality Attribute Based Software Engineering", *Proceedings of EUROMICRO 2001, Component Based Software Engineering workshop*, IEEE, 2001.
18. Preiss O., *Foundations of Systems and Properties: Methodological Support for Modeling Properties of Software-Intensive Systems*, PhD Thesis Nr. 3013, Swiss Federal Institute of Technology, Lausanne, May 2004.
19. Russell B., (2002, July 20). The Problems of Philosophy. Home University Library [Online]. Available: http://www.ditext.com/russell/russell.
20. Schmidt H. and Reussner R. H., "Parametrized Contracts and Adapter Synthesis", *Proceedings of 5th ICSE workshop on CBSE*, 2001.

21. Schmidt H., "Trustworthy components: compositionality and prediction", In *Journal of Systems & Software*, Vol. 65, Issue 3, 2003.
22. SEI. (2003, November). Capability Maturity Model® for Software (SW-CMM®). Carnegie Mellon Software Engineering Institute [Online]. Available: http://www.sei.cmu.edu/
23. Svahnberg M., *Supporting Software Architecture Evolution*, Ph.D. Thesis, Blekinge Institute of Technology, Sweden, 2003.
24. Swoyer, C.. (2002, July). Properties. The Metaphysics Research Lab, Stanford University [Online], http://www.science.uva.nl/~seop/entries/
25. van Ommering R., "The Koala Component Model", in Crnkovic I. and Larsson M. (editors): *Building Reliable Component-Based Software Systems*, Artech House, 2002.
26. Szyperski C., *"Component Software - Beyond Object-Oriented Programming"*, Second Edition, Addison-Wesley/ACM Press, 2002
27. Valérie Issarny, Apostolos Zarras: Software Architecture and Dependability, *LNSFM 2003*, LNCS Vol. 2804
28. Wall A., Larsson M., and Norström C., "Towards an Impact Analysis for Component Based Real-Time Product Line Architectures", *Proceedings of Euromicro Conference on Component Based Software Engineering*, IEEE, 2002.
29. Yan L., Gorton I., Liu A., and Chen S., "Evaluating the scalability of enterprise javabeans technology", *Proceedings of 9th Asia-Pacific Software Engineering Conference*, IEEE, 2002.

Architecture-Based Reliability Prediction for Service-Oriented Computing

Vincenzo Grassi

Università di Roma "Tor Vergata", Italy
vgrassi@info.uniroma2.it

Abstract. In service-oriented computing, services are dynamically built as an assembly of pre-existing, independently developed, network accessible services. Hence, predicting as much as possible automatically their dependability is important to appropriately drive the selection and assembly of services, in order to get some required dependability level. We present an approach to the reliability prediction of such services, based on the partial information published with each service, and that lends itself to automatization. The proposed methodology exploits ideas from the Software Architecture- and Component-based approaches to software design.

1 Introduction

The service-oriented computing (SOC) paradigm has recently emerged as a new approach to the development of complex distributed applications in a timely and cost-effective way [14]. According the SOC paradigm, an application is built as composition of services (including both "basic" services, e.g. computing, storage, communication, and "advanced" services that incorporate some complex business logic) provided by several independent providers. A strong overlapping exists between this paradigm and component-based development (CBD) approaches [18]. As a distinguishing feature, the SOC paradigm requires that services are provided as Internet accessible functionalities that can be discovered, selected and assembled in an automated way. The "Web services" and "Grid computing" frameworks represent standardization efforts in this area [4, 6, 7].

An important issue for applications built in this way is how to assess the degree of trustworthiness one can have about the resulting service quality, for instance their performance or dependability characteristics. In particular, the *prediction* of such characteristics is important to drive the selection of the services to be assembled [3 (chapt. 9)]. In this respect, automatic and efficient predictive analysis methodologies should be devised, to remain compliant with the SOC requirement that most of the activities connected with service discovery and composition should be performed automatically.

In this paper, we focus on dependability aspects, and provide an approach to predict the *reliability* of a service, defined as a measure of its ability to successfully carry out its own task when it is invoked. The main goal of this approach is to define an automatic and compositional way for the reliability prediction, that reflects the underlying structure of a service realized as an assembly of other services, exploiting information published by each assembled service. To achieve this goal, we exploit ideas taken from Software Architecture- and Component-based approaches to software design.

Approaches to the reliability analysis of service- and component-based systems have been already presented (e.g. [5, 15, 17, 19]). We briefly discuss them in a "related work" section (section 5). What distinguishes our approach is the exploitation of a "unified" service model that helps in modeling and analyzing different architectural alternatives, where the characteristics of both "high level" services (typically offered by software components) and "low level" services (typically offered by physical devices) are explicitly taken into consideration. This model allows us to explicitly deal also with the reliability impact of the infrastructure used to assemble the services and make them interact. Moreover, we point out in this work the importance of considering the impact on reliability of service sharing, that could typically happen in a SOC framework, when we assemble originally independent services in such a way that they exploit some common service, so being no longer independent. Finally, to better support compositional analysis, we also point out the need of explicitly dealing with the dependency between the input parameters for some service and the input parameters of cascading service requests that the service itself generates, as also pointed out in [9].

The paper is organized as follows. In section 2 we discuss general issues for an architecture-based approach to quality of service (QoS) prediction in a SOC/CBD framework. In section 3 we focus on reliability, and present an approach to its architecture-based prediction, that lends itself to automatization. In section 4 we present a simple example, while in section 5 we discuss related work. Finally, section 6 concludes the paper.

2 An Architectural Approach to Predictive QoS Analysis

According to the Software Architecture approach [2], an application is seen as consisting of a set of *components* that offer and require services, connected through suitable *connectors*, where the latter model some selected "interaction infrastructure". In particular, special emphasis is given to the connector concept, that is intended to embody all the issues concerning the connection between offered and required services [12]; hence, a connector can also represent a complex architectural element carrying out tasks that are not limited to the mere transmission of some information, but could also include services such as security and fault-tolerance; this means that a connector can be seen as the proper architectural element to model also the middleware aspects of some assembly of software services and components.

We note that, in a broad SOC perspective, who assembles services should be allowed to select not only "high level" services, needed to implement some complex functionality, but also the underlying "low level" services; these include the interconnection architecture (communication services) used to make high level services interact. Different ways of connecting the same set of high level services can have different impact on the overall non functional characteristics (as a simple example, a "local call" connection to some service is generally more dependable and more efficient than a "remote procedure call" (RPC) connection). Hence, besides being an important architectural concept, connectors are valuable also from the viewpoint of QoS prediction for a service assembly. Indeed, by providing an easily identifiable architectural elements, connectors support and encourage the explicit modeling of the interconnection infrastructure; moreover, they facilitate the QoS analysis and comparison of different interconnection architectures, that in principle can be modeled by simply connecting the same set of services using different connectors models, each with its own QoS characteristics.

For these reasons we base our analysis methodology on the Software Architecture "component-connector" framework, remarking in particular that the connector concept should be explicitly introduced in any analysis of some non functional characteristic of SOC applications. Within this framework, according to a SOC perspective, we adopt a unifying "service model", looking at both components and connectors as entities offering and requesting services (with the services of connectors often implicitly invoked to support some higher level service). As an example, an RPC connector offers a connection service implicitly invoked during the invocation of some remote service, and requires in its turn processing and communication services to marshal/transmit/unmarshal the service request and response.[1]

In a SOC framework (but, also, more generally, in CBD approaches) a service is expected to publish a description that includes not only of its signature, but also a description of a related set of required services, plus a set of attributes and constraints that further specify conditions for a correct matching between offered and provided services.

To support predictive analysis of some non-functional property of a service composition, for example its reliability, it has been argued that each service (or resource) should also publish some *analytic interface* (see [10]), that is a representation at a suitable abstraction level of the actual service behavior and requirements, that lends itself to the application of some analysis methodology. Based on the above discussion, we assume that an analytic interface is associated with each service offered by both resources and connectors, which should include:

(a) an abstract description of the offered service;

(b) an abstract description of the *flow* of requests that will be possibly addressed to other resources and connectors to carry out that service (abstract usage profile).

We now give some detail about how these two parts of an analytic interface can be structured.

With regard to point (a), the abstraction should concern both the service itself and the domains where its formal parameters, used to specify a particular service request, can take value; for example, the abstract description of a processing service can be

---

[1] In the following, we will use generally the term *resource* rather than *component*, since the latter seems too strictly tied to the idea of software resource. Hence, by *resource* we mean something that offers one or more services (and possibly requires others), thus encompassing both software components and physical resources, like processors, communication links, or other devices (like printers and sensors).

defined in terms of a service that executes a single kind of "average" operation (at some constant speed) and whose formal parameter is the number of such operations that must be executed, rather than their actual list. In general, the abstraction with respect to the real service parameter domains can be achieved by partitioning the real domain into a (possibly finite) set of disjoint subdomains, and then collapsing all the elements in each subdomain into a single "representative" element [9]. The processing service example is an extreme case, where the entire set of operations is collapsed into a single average operation.

With regard to point (b), we assume that the abstraction consists in giving a probabilistic description of the flow of requests. For this purpose, we assume that the "abstract" flow of requests generated by a service is modeled by a discrete time Markov chain. Each node of the Markov chain transition diagram models a set of actual (abstract) service requests, with the underlying assumption that the requests in this set must be fulfilled according to some completion model before a transition to the next node can take place. We discuss in the next section possible completion models.

Finally, we make the consideration that it is reasonable to assume the possible existence of a dependence between the parameters that characterize a particular service and the cascading service requests that it addresses to other resources. For example, the size of a list to be ordered sent as input parameter to some sort service has an impact on the request of processing service addressed by the sort service itself to some processing resource. This has an obvious impact also on the resulting QoS. Indeed, continuing with the sort service example, the probability of a hardware failure occurrence in the processing resource while sorting the list increases with the time taken to sort the list, i.e. with the size of the list sent as parameter to the sort service.

For this reason, we argue that modeling this dependency is necessary to achieve a real QoS compositional analysis. To model it, we assume that both the transition probabilities and the actual parameters of the service requests in a flow may be defined as functions of the formal parameters of the offered service they are associated with. In the next sections we will provide examples to better clarify this point.

3 Architecture-Based Reliability Prediction

As stated before, the reliability of a service is a measure of its ability of completing its task, where, according to the adopted framework, a service is generally realized by a suitable composition, through appropriate connectors, of services offered by several resources. Let us introduce the following notation:

- S (Sj): a service offered by some resource (including a connector);
- fp: the list of formal parameters associated with a service S;
- apj: the list of actual parameters used by a service S to call a service Sj; to model the dependency (as discussed above) between apj and fp, we assume that the actual parameters apj of Sj are a function of the formal parameters fp of S ($apj = apj(fp)$); however, for the sake of conciseness, in the following we will write apj instead of $apj(fp)$;

- *Pfail(S,fp)*: the probability that a service S is unable to complete its task, expressed parametrically in terms of the service formal parameters *fp*;
- *Pfail(Sj,apj)*: the probability that a service Sj is unable to complete its task, when Sj is invoked with actual parameters *apj*;
- *i*: a state of the Markov chain modeling the flow of service requests generated by S;
- Start: a special state of the Markov chain, representing the entry point for the flow it models;
- End: an absorbing state of the Markov chain, representing the successful completion of the service task;
- $Ai1, \ldots Ain$: the set of service requests included in a state i of the flow, $i \neq$Start, $i \neq$End (i.e., $Aij \equiv call(Sj,apj)$); note that by "service request" we mean all the activities involved in the service invocation and execution.

Using this notation, the reliability of S can be expressed as $1 - Pfail(S,fp)$. In the following, we show how to calculate *Pfail(S,fp)*, exploiting information about how S has been architected. To this end, we distinguish two types of services:

- *simple services*, that do not require the services of any other resource to carry out their own task; these include, for example, the services offered by basic processing and communication resources ("cpu" and "network" resources), but also the services offered by "black-box" software components strictly tied to a particular computing platform; the reliability of such services depends only on the service internal characteristics/operations; we assume that this reliability is a known function of the service formal parameters;
- *composite services*, that do require the services of other resources to carry out their own task: these services include, typically, those offered by software components; each of these services is characterized by a flow modeling its usage profile of other service [2] their reliability depends on both the service internal characteristics/operations and on the reliability of the services they require; moreover, it also depends on the reliability of the connectors used to connect required and offered services; we assume that a composite service can only provide information about the "internal part" of its reliability, expressed by some suitable reliability measure (e.g., software failure rate in the typical case of software components).

Moreover, in the following discussion, we assume a "fail-stop" behavior (i.e. each failure causes a service interruption), and that no repair occurs [11].

3.1 Reliability of Simple Services

As stated above, we assume that the reliability of such services is explicitly expressed by some known function of the service parameters. In this section, we limit ourselves to explicitly presenting examples for the cases of processing and communication services. For each of these services, we use the name of the resource offering it as name of the service itself, under the assumption that such resources offer a single service.

---

[2] Note that a service offered by a software component that does not call any other component, but can be deployed to different computing platform is a composite service in our framework, since it can be modeled as a service issuing requests for a processing service.

Let us consider first a cpu-type resource offering a processing service. In an abstract characterization of this service (analytic interface), we model it as a service with an integer valued abstract parameter N, used to specify the number of operations to be executed during a request for that service. Moreover, the processing service analytic interface includes two attributes: a speed s (operation/time-unit) and a failure rate λ (failure/time-unit). Assuming an exponential failure rate, the probability of a failure during the execution of N operations is expressed by the following function of N:

$$Pfail(cpu,N) = 1 - e^{-\lambda N/s} \qquad (1)$$

Then, let us consider a network-type resource offering a communication service. The analytic interface of this service is characterized by an integer valued abstract parameter B representing the number of bytes to be transmitted. Moreover, the interface includes two attributes: a bandwidth b (byte/time-unit) and a failure rate β (failure/time-unit). Assuming again an exponential failure rate, the probability of a failure during the transmission of B bytes is expressed by the following function of B:

$$Pfail(net,B) = 1 - e^{-\beta B/b} \qquad (2)$$

Within this type of services, we also include as a special case the connectors that do not have any flow of service requests associated with them. In our unified "service-connector" framework, this is in particular the case of connectors we use to model a simple association between required and offered services, like a "local processing" connector between a software component and the cpu-like resource of the same node where the component is located.[3] These "connectors" are used only for modeling purposes, but do not actually make use of any resource and do not correspond to any tangible artifact; hence we assume that their failure probability is equal to zero.

3.2 Reliability of Composite Services

In this case, we are considering services carried out by resources that exploit the services offered by other resources, as modeled by the flow of requests specified in their analytic interface. This case also include "interaction" services offered by connectors that exploit other resources (typically communication and, possibly, processing resources) to carry out them; in the following we do not make any basic distinction between such connectors and generic complex resources, from the viewpoint of the reliability evaluation of the service they offer.

Given our flow model, we have:

$$Pfail(S,fp) = 1 - p^*_{S,fp}(\underline{Start},\underline{End}) \qquad (3)$$

where $p^*_{S,fp}(\underline{Start},\underline{End})$ denotes the probability of reaching in any number of steps the $\underline{End}$ absorbing state for the flow associated with S, starting from its $\underline{Start}$ state. For a flow modeling only the functional aspects of a service execution, this probability would be trivially equal to one. To calculate a non trivial value for such a probability, we must specialize the flow model to the dependability domain, taking into consideration the possibility that a failure may occur at any flow stage. In terms of our model this means

---

[3] In a UML modeling framework, this type of connector would correspond to a *deployment relationship* between a software service and a processing resource.

that we must add a "failure structure" to the flow model; under the fail-stop and no repair assumptions, this corresponds to adding a new Fail absorbing state to the Markov chain, and then adding an additional transition from each state i of the Markov chain to the Fail state with probability $p_{S,fp}(i,\text{Fail})$, weighing with a probability $1-p_{S,fp}(i,\text{Fail})$ the already existing transitions to other states (except transitions from the Start state, since we assume that it does not represent any real behavior, and hence no failure can occur in it). Standard Markov methods can be exploited to evaluate $p^*_{S,fp}(\text{Start},\text{End})$ once the failure structure has been added to the original flow model (see, for example, [19]). Hence, the basic problem is how to evaluate $p_{S,fp}(i,\text{Fail})$ for each node i. In this section, we focus on issues related to the evaluation of $p_{S,fp}(i,\text{Fail})$, exploiting architectural information.

Recalling that each state i includes a set of service requests $Ai1, \ldots Ain$, we must take into account the following factors to evaluate $p_{S,fp}(i,\text{Fail})$:

a) the failure probability of each service request Aij included in state i;
b) how the individual failure probabilities of the Aij's combine together to determine $p_{S,fp}(i,\text{Fail})$.

Point b) in turn requires considering the following factors:

b1) a completion model for the requests $Ai1, \ldots Ain$, to determine when a successful transition to the next flow stage is enabled, even if some Aij has failed;
b2) the existence of possible dependencies among the $Ai1, \ldots Ain$, that can affect their overall failure probability.

In the following, we first briefly discuss separately these points, and then, based on this discussion, we go into the details of the evaluation of $p_{S,fp}(i,\text{Fail})$.

Failure probability of each Aij. To evaluate the probability of a failure of Aij, that we denote by $\Pr\{fail(Aij)\}$,[4] we must take into account the following failure probabilities:

- *Pfail_int(Aij)*: probability of "internal" failure, i.e. depending on the internal characteristics of the service issuing the request Aij; we discuss at the end of the section some issues concerning a more precise definition of this probability;
- *Pfail_ext(Aij)*: probability of "external" failure related to the service request Aij (i.e. "call(Sj,apj)"); this probability depends in its turn on the probability of failure of the service Sj itself, and on the probability of a failure in the connector Cj that "transports" the request, that is on $Pfail(Sj,apj)$ and $Pfail(Cj,[Sj,apj])$ (where $[Sj,apj]$ is the actual parameter for the connection service offered by Cj).[5]

Completion model for $Ai1, \ldots Ain$. We take into consideration two possible completion models for the service requests in state i:

---

[4] Note that $Pfail(Sj,apj)$ and $\Pr\{fail(Aij)\}$ denote the probability of two different events, where the former corresponds to a failure during the execution of the service Sj once it has been called, while the latter corresponds to a failure during the overall invocation process of Sj, that includes a failure during the execution of Sj.
[5] For the sake of simplicity, we are identifying the name of the connector with the name of the service it offers.

- *AND* model: all the requests $Ai1, ... Ain$ must be fulfilled to enable a transition to the next state;
- *OR* model: at least one of the requests $Ai1, ... Ain$ must be completed to enable a transition to the next state.[6]

Other completion models could be considered as well (e.g. "k out of n"), but we do not analyze them in this paper.

Dependency model for $Ai1, ... Ain$. With this model we take into account the sharing of some common service, that could typically occur in a SOC framework:
- *no sharing*: the requests $Ai1, ... Ain$ do not share any common service, and hence are assumed independent of each other;
- *sharing*: the requests $Ai1, ... Ain$ do share a common service, and hence their failure probabilities are not independent.

In particular, in the *sharing* model we restrict our attention to the case where all the $Ai1, ... Ain$ are actually requests for the same service Si offered by a single resource, accessed through a single connector Ci. Note that a very simple example for this case is when n software components are allocated to the same processing node, thus requesting the same processing service offered by that node.

Using the above defined probabilities, and completion and dependency models, we can now define expression for the probability $p_{S,fp}(i,\underline{Fail})$ of a failure in state i of the flow. Let us start with the calculation of $p_{S,fp}(i,\underline{Fail})$ under the two completion models:

- *AND* model: the failure of any activity in state i causes a failure in that state; hence we have:

$$p_{S,fp}(i,\underline{Fail}) = 1 - \Pr\{\bigwedge_{j=1}^{n} nofail(Aij)\} \qquad (4)$$

- *OR* model: the failure of all the activities in state i causes a failure in that state; hence we have:

$$p_{S,fp}(i,\underline{Fail}) = \Pr\{\bigwedge_{j=1}^{n} fail(Aij)\} \qquad (5)$$

Now, let us see how we can calculate the two probabilities in the right hand side of (4) and (5) under the two defined dependency models.

- *no sharing* model: for the *AND* case, thanks to the independence assumption among the $Ai1, ... Ain$, we can rewrite (4) as:

$$p_{S,fp}(i,\underline{Fail}) = 1 - \prod_{j=1}^{n} (1 - \Pr\{fail(Aij)\}) \qquad (6)$$

analogously, for the *OR* case, we can rewrite (5) as:

$$p_{S,fp}(i,\underline{Fail}) = \prod_{j=1}^{n} \Pr\{fail(Aij)\} \qquad (7)$$

---

[6] The *OR* model allows us to consider, for example, the presence of fault-tolerance features within a component

According to the discussion about the failure probability of each A_{ij}, the failure probability $\Pr\{fail(A_{ij})\}$ in equations (6) and (7) can be calculated as follows:

$$\begin{aligned}\Pr\{fail(A_{ij})\} &= 1 - (1 - Pfail\_int(A_{ij})) \cdot (1 - Pfail\_ext(A_{ij})) \\ &= 1 - (1 - Pfail\_int(A_{ij})) \cdot (1 - Pfail(C_j, [S_j, ap_j])) \cdot (1 - Pfail(S_j, ap_j)))\end{aligned} \quad (8)$$

since each A_{ij} does not fail only if neither an internal nor an external failure occurs, and, in its turn, the external failure does not occur if neither the used connector nor the requested service fail.

- *sharing* model: in this case the requests $A_{i1}, \dots A_{in}$ are no longer independent, since they request the same service S_i. Let us denote by *extfail* and *noextfail* the events "external failure occurrence" and "no external failure occurrence" in the service requests $A_{i1}, \dots A_{in}$, respectively. In the *AND* case we rewrite (4) as follows:

$$\begin{aligned}p_{S,fp}(i,\text{Fail}) = 1 - \Pr\{ &\bigwedge_{j=1}^{n} nofail(A_{ij}) \mid noextfail\} \Pr\{noextfail\} \\ - \Pr\{ &\bigwedge_{j=1}^{n} nofail(A_{ij}) \mid extfail\} \Pr\{extfail\}\end{aligned} \quad (9)$$

Analogously, in the *OR* case we rewrite (5) as follows:

$$\begin{aligned}p_{S,fp}(i,\text{Fail}) = \Pr\{ &\bigwedge_{j=1}^{n} fail(A_{ij}) \mid noextfail\} \Pr\{noextfail\} \\ + \Pr\{ &\bigwedge_{j=1}^{n} fail(A_{ij}) \mid extfail\} \Pr\{extfail\}\end{aligned} \quad (10)$$

Now, note that when no external failure occurs, each A_{ij} can only fail because of an internal failure; in the opposite case, that is when an external failure occurs for some A_{ij}, it causes the failure of all the $A_{i1}, \dots A_{in}$ with probability one, since they share the same external service S_i and the same connector C_i, and we have assumed that no repair occurs. Hence, reasonably assuming that the internal failures are independent, we can refine equation (9) and (10) as follows. For equation (9) we have:

$$\begin{aligned}p_{S,fp}(i,\text{Fail}) &= 1 - \prod_{j=1}^{n} (1 - Pfail\_int(A_{ij})) \cdot \prod_{j=1}^{n} (1 - Pfail\_ext(A_{ij})) \\ &\quad - 0 \cdot (1 - \prod_{j=1}^{n} (1 - Pfail\_ext(A_{ij}))) \\ &= 1 - \prod_{j=1}^{n} (1 - Pfail\_int(A_{ij})) \cdot \prod_{j=1}^{n} (1 - Pfail\_ext(A_{ij}))\end{aligned} \quad (11)$$

For equation (10) we have:

$$\begin{aligned}p_{S,fp}(i,\text{Fail}) &= \prod_{j=1}^{n} Pfail\_int(A_{ij}) \cdot \prod_{j=1}^{n} (1 - Pfail\_ext(A_{ij})) \\ &\quad + 1 \cdot (1 - \prod_{j=1}^{n} (1 - Pfail\_ext(A_{ij})))\end{aligned}$$

$$= 1 - \prod_{j=1}^{n} (1 - Pfail\_ext(Aij))) \cdot (1 - \prod_{j=1}^{n} Pfail\_int(Aij)) \qquad (12)$$

Note that in equations (11) and (12) the probability *Pfail_ext(Aij)* can be expressed as:

$$Pfail\_ext(Aij) = 1 - (1-Pfail(Si,api)) \cdot (1-Pfail(Ci,[Si,api])) \qquad (13)$$

Let us now compare the expressions for the *AND* completion model under the *no sharing* and *sharing* models (i.e. expressions (6) and (8) with expressions (11) and (13). With some simple manipulation, we see that they are identical. Hence, under the fail-stop and no-repair assumption, the reliability of requests to be completed under the *AND* model is unaffected by the possible sharing of a service.

On the other hand, let us compare the expressions for the *OR* completion model under the *no sharing* and *sharing* models (i.e. expressions (7) and (8) with expressions (12) and (13). In this case, we can see that they provide different results.

These results remark the importance of carefully considering the possible dependencies between completion models and service sharing in the reliability analysis of a composition of services.

Finally, note that in the above analysis we have introduced the term *Pfail_int(Aij)* to denote the "internal" failure probability for a service requets $Aij = call(Sj,apj)$. We conclude this section by giving some suggestion about how the internal failure probability *Pfail_int(Aij)* can be defined. We recall that in a service-oriented approach, information about the internal failure characteristics is the only kind of failure-related information that a service can directly publish. For this purpose, we distinguish two cases:

a) *Aij* is the request for a service offered by some software resource, and hence typically corresponds to an actual method call; in this case, the internal operations related to this request just consist of the "call" of such service, while other operations connected to the request (e.g., parameters marshaling/unmarshaling) in our architectural vision are captured, together with their reliability, under the connector concept; hence, we must give some suitable value to *Pfail_int(Aij)* reflecting the reliability of the call operation only; this value could also be set equal to zero, if we assume that a method call is a reliable operation that does not cause a failure by itself;

b) *Aij* is the request made by a software component to a processing service to execute N operations (i.e. $Aij = call(cpu,N)$); this case actually corresponds to the execution of the "internal" operations of some component; in this case *Pfail_int(Aij)* must depend on N and represents the probability that the software code that implements the N operations contains a software fault that manifests itself as a failure; this probability should be expressed as some function of N, according to some suitable software reliability model. For example, assuming that the software failure rate of the component requesting the processing service is φ (that represents the probability of a software failure in an operation), we could write:

$$Pfail\_int(Aij) = Pfail\_int(call(cpu,N)) = 1 - (1-\varphi)^N \qquad (14)$$

3.3 A Recursive Procedure for the Reliability Evaluation of a Service Assembly

The reliability evaluation methodology presented above lends itself to the definition of a procedure for the evaluation of the reliability of a service assembly, that can be easily automated.

Let S be a (composite) service provided by some services assembly Σ, and let *Pfail_Alg(S, fp)* denote the procedure that calculates the absorbing probability in the Fail state for the service S with formal parameters fp. This procedure can be defined as follows:

1. *Pfail_Alg(S, fp)* :
2.   add a Fail state to the flow of S;
3.   **for each** state i of the flow of S **do**
4.   **case** (completion model / sharing model of state i) :
5.   AND / any: $f := p_{S,fp}(i,\underline{Fail})$ /* (expression (6)) */
6.   OR / no sharing: $f := p_{S,fp}(i,\underline{Fail})$ /* (expression (7)) */
7.   OR / sharing: $f := p_{S,fp}(i,\underline{Fail})$ /* (expression (12)) */
8.   **endcase**;
9.   **for each** outgoing transition from i to k with probability $p(i,k)$ **do**
10.   replace $p(i,k)$ with $(1-f) \cdot p(i,k)$
11.   **endfor**;
12.   add a transition from i to Fail with probability f;
13.   **endfor**
14. **return** $1 - p^*_{S,fp}(\underline{Start},\underline{End})$ /* (expression (3)) */

Note that *Pfail_Alg(S, fp)* is actually a recursive procedure, as the evaluation of $p_{S,fp}(i,\underline{Fail})$ in the statements 5, 6 and 7 implies the recursive call of *Pfail_Alg(Sj, ap)* for all the services Sj that are required in state i. The bottom of this recursion is given by the simple services included in Σ, whose unreliability can be directly calculated as shown, for example, in section 3.1. At the end of the evaluation, we get *Pfail(S, fp)*, that is the unreliability of the composite service realized by the assembly Σ.

Finally, we point out that this recursive evaluation procedure does not work in the case of a service assembly where some services recursively call each other. In this case, the recursive procedure outlined above would incur in an infinite loop, and the assembly reliability should be expressed by a fixed point equation, for which appropriate evaluation methods should be devised. In this work we do not investigate this point.

4 Example

We use a very simple example to illustrate the proposed methodology. For this purpose, we consider a resource that offers a *search* service for an item in a list. To carry out this service, the resource requires in its turn a *sort* service (to possibly sort the list before performing the search) and a *processing* service (for its internal operations). The search service has three formal parameters, with the former two used to receive the item to be searched and the list, respectively, while the third is used to return the search result (true or false). In an abstract characterization of this service (i.e. in its analytic interface), the abstract domain of the former two parameters is the set of integer numbers, used to specify, respectively, the size of the element to be searched and the list size. Moreover, the analytic interface of this service includes an attribute specifying the service software failure rate φ.

We consider two different ways of assembling the search service with the services it requires:

- *local assembly*: the sort service is a local service (*sort1*), that is both the components providing the search and sort services are allocated to the same processing node (*cpu1*) providing the needed processing service;
- *remote assembly*: the sort service is a remote service (*sort2*), that is the components providing the search and sort services are allocated to two different processing nodes (*cpu1* and *cpu2*, respectively), connected by a communication network (*net12*).

We assume that both sort services (*sort1* and *sort2*) are characterized by analogous analytic interfaces, with one formal parameter used to receive from and return to the caller the list to be sorted, and an attribute specifying a software failure rate (φ1 and φ2, respectively).

Figure 1 depicts the flows associated with the search and sort services, where beside each state it is shown the associated service request with its actual parameters. Note how these parameters are defined as functions of the service formal parameters. In this figure, q denotes the probability that the list is not already sorted.

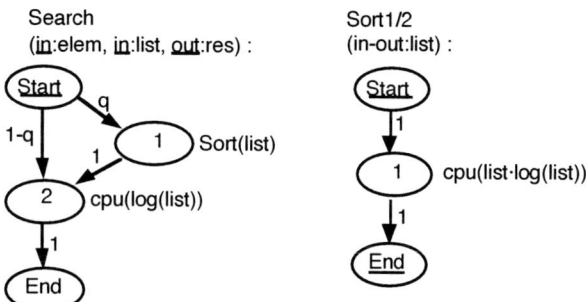

Fig. 1. Flows of the search and sort services

For what concerns the processing nodes (*cpu1* and *cpu2*), and the communication network (*net12*), we assume that they are modeled as resources offering simple processing and communication services, respectively, with each service characterized by one abstract parameter used to provide the number of operations to be processed, and the bytes to be transmitted. The two processing resources (*cpu1* and *cpu2*) are also characterized by speed attributes (*s1* and *s2*) that specify the number of operations per unit time that they are able to process, and by failure rates $\lambda 1$ and $\lambda 2$.

Analogously, the communication resource has a bandwidth attribute (b) that specifies the number of bytes per unit time that the resource is able to transmit, and a failure rate γ.

Let us now consider how these services are connected. In the local assembly case, the *search* and *sort1* services are connected through a "local procedure call" (LPC) connector, while in the remote assembly case the *search* and *sort2* services are connected through an RPC connector. From a reliability viewpoint, these connectors play a role similar to composite services, as they require other services (processing and communication) to carry out their own interaction service.

Figure 2 shows the flows associated with these connectors, where the input and output (abstract) formal parameters *ip* and *op* are intended to represent the size of the data transmitted from the client to the server and vice-versa, respectively. In the local case, we assume a shared memory communication model; hence, the *lpc* connector requires only a processing service (modeling the few operations needed for the control transfer from *search* to *sort1* and vice versa). Given the shared memory assumption, we assume that the number of these operations is independent of the value of *ip* and *op*, and is given by some constant l. We also assume that the software failure rate of this connector is equal to zero (i.e. the software used to code its functionality is perfectly reliable).

On the other hand in the remote case, both the processing requirements of the *rpc* connector for the parameters marshaling and unmarhaling and the communication requirements are defined as linear functions of *ip* and *op* (through the constants c and m, respectively). Also for this connector we assume a software failure rate equal to zero.

Finally, figures 3 and 4 graphically show the two assemblies. Note that in these figures we also depict some "local processing" connectors, modeling the association between the local processing requested by some resource and the processing service offered by the node where that resource is allocated. As discussed in section 3.1, these connectors are pure modeling artifacts, and their reliability is equal to one.

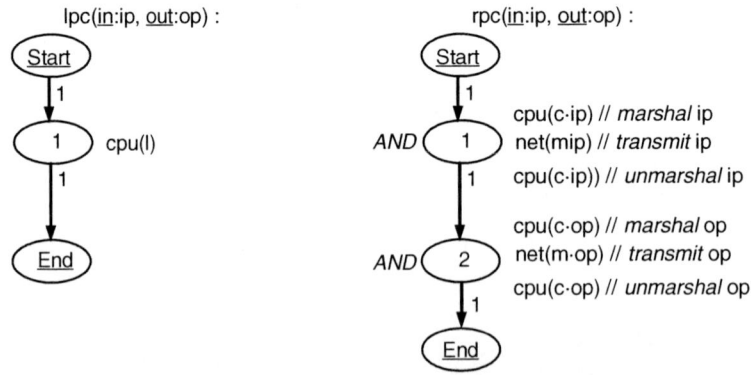

Fig. 2. Flows of the LPC and RPC connectors

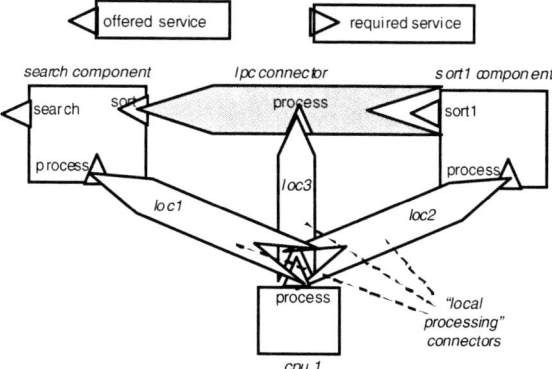

Fig. 3. Graphical representation of the local assembly

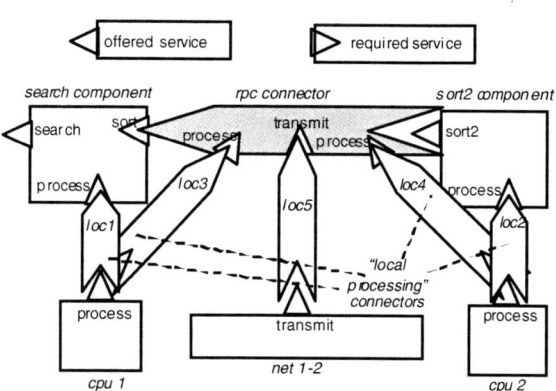

Fig. 4. Graphical representation of the remote assembly

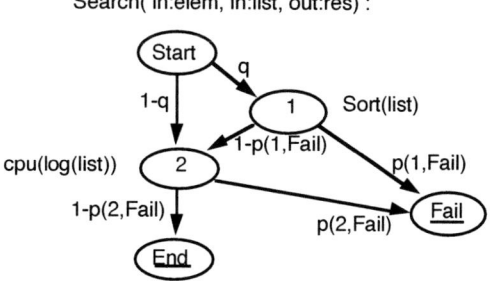

Fig. 5. Flow of the search service augmented with the failure structure

To evaluate the reliability of this assembly of services, we must add failure information to the service flows, as discussed in section 3.2. As an example, figure 5 shows the modified search service flow.

Now, we can evaluate the search service reliability using the methodology of section 3. Given the simplicity of the example, we can directly calculate the service reliability in a symbolic way, without using matrix-based operations to numerically calculate the absorbing probabilities into the <u>Fail</u> state for each service flow. These operations should be implemented for more complex examples.

Thanks to the possibility of a symbolic evaluation, we can directly start from the bottom of the recursion described in section 3.3, going up to upper levels. In particular, looking at figures 3 and 4, we readily see that we can identify three recursion levels, namely:

- *level 0* (simple services): *cpu1, cpu2, net12, loc1, loc2, loc3, loc4, loc5*;
- *level 1* (services requiring only level 0 services): *lpc, rpc, sort1, sort2*;
- *level 2* (services requiring level 0 and level 1 services): *search*.

Note that under the level 0 services we include also those offered by the "local processing" connectors *loc1, loc2, loc3, loc4, loc5*. As remarked above, their reliability is equal to one. On the other hand, for the *cpu1, cpu2, net12* services we assume that their reliability is given by the expressions (1) and (2), respectively. Hence, we have:

$$Pfail(cpu1,N) = 1 - e^{-\lambda 1 \cdot N/s1} \tag{15}$$

$$Pfail(cpu2,N) = 1 - e^{-\lambda 2 \cdot N/s2} \tag{16}$$

$$Pfail(net1\text{-}2,B) = 1 - e^{-\gamma B/b} \tag{17}$$

Now, let us consider the level 1 services. For the *sortx* service ($x = 1, 2$) we get, using its flow model augmented with the failure information, and expressions (6), (8), (14) and (16):

$$\begin{aligned} Pfail(sortx,\text{list}) &= \Pr\{fail(\text{call}(cpux,\text{list}\cdot\log(\text{list})))\} \\ &= 1 - (1\text{-}Pfail\_int(\text{call}(cpux,\text{list}\cdot\log(\text{list})))) \\ &\quad \cdot(1\text{-}Pfail(loc2)) \\ &\quad \cdot(1\text{-}Pfail(cpux, \text{list}\cdot\log(\text{list}))) \\ &= 1 - (1\text{-}\varphi x)^{\text{list}\cdot\log(\text{list})} \cdot 1 \cdot e^{-\lambda x \cdot \text{list}\cdot\log(\text{list})/sx} \end{aligned} \tag{18}$$

Note how in expression (18) the formal parameter N of the *cpux* reliability expressions (15) and (16) has been substituted by an actual parameter list·log(list) defined as function of the *sortx* formal parameter "list".

On the other hand, for the connector services *lpc* and *rpc*, we note that the assumption of zero software failure probability for their code implies that $Pfail\_int(\text{call}(cpu1,l)) = Pfail\_int(\text{call}(cpu1,c\cdot ip)) = Pfail\_int(\text{call}(cpu1,c\cdot op)) = Pfail\_int(\text{call}(cpu2,c\cdot ip)) = Pfail\_int(\text{call}(cpu2,c\cdot op)) = 0$. Using this assumption, the flow models of figure 2, and expressions (6), (8), (15), (16) and (17), we get (we omit some intermediate result):

$Pfail(lpc,\text{ip},\text{op}) = \Pr\{fail(\text{call}(cpu1,l))\}$
$= 1 - (1-Pfail\_int(\text{call}(cpu1,l)))$
$\qquad \cdot (1-Pfail(cpu1, l))$
$= 1 - e^{-\lambda 1 \cdot l/s1}$ (19)

$Pfail(rpc,\text{ip},\text{op}) = 1 - (1 - \Pr\{fail(\text{call}(cpu1,c\cdot\text{ip}))\})$
$\qquad \cdot (1 - \Pr\{fail(\text{call}(net12,m\cdot\text{ip}))\})$
$\qquad \cdot (1 - \Pr\{fail(\text{call}(cpu2, c\cdot\text{ip}))\})$
$\qquad \cdot (1 - \Pr\{fail(\text{call}(cpu2,c\cdot\text{op}))\})$
$\qquad \cdot (1 - \Pr\{fail(\text{call}(net12,m\cdot\text{op}))\})$
$\qquad \cdot (1 - \Pr\{fail(\text{call}(cpu1, c\cdot\text{op}))\})$

$= 1 - e^{-\lambda 1 \cdot c(\text{ip}+\text{op})/s1} \cdot e^{-\gamma \cdot m(\text{ip}+\text{op})/b} \cdot e^{-\lambda 2 \cdot c(\text{ip}+\text{op})/s2}$ (20)

Also in this case we can note how the actual parameters of the requests addressed to the *cpux* and *net12* services are expressed as a function of the *lpc* and *rpc* formal parameters, thus achieving a more effective composition of the reliability of each service with the requests it receives. Finally, let us consider the level 2 *search* service. Using its flow model and expressions (6), (8), (14), (15) and (16), we get (omitting again some intermediate result):

Pfail(search,elem,list,res)

$= (1 - q) \cdot \Pr\{fail(\text{call}(cpu1,\log(\text{list})))\}$
$+ \quad q \cdot (1 \quad - \quad (1-\Pr\{fail(\text{call}(cpu1,\log(\text{list})))\}) \cdot (1-\Pr\{fail(\text{call}(sortx,\text{list}))\})$

$= (1 - q) \cdot (1 - (1-\varphi)^{\log(\text{list})} \cdot e^{-\lambda 1 \cdot \log(\text{list})/s1})$
$+ q \cdot (1 - (1-\varphi)^{\log(\text{list})} \cdot e^{-\lambda 1 \cdot \log(\text{list})/s1}$
$\qquad \cdot (1-Pfail\_int(\text{call}(sortx,\text{list})))$
$\qquad \cdot (1-Pfail(connect,\text{elem}+\text{list},\text{res}))$
$\qquad \cdot (1-Pfail(sortx,\text{list})))$ (21)

where *connect* = *lpc, rpc*;

Assuming that a method call made within the search service is perfectly reliable (i.e. $Pfail\_int(\text{call}(sortx,\text{list})) = 0$) we get from (21):

Pfail(search,elem,list,res)

$= (1 - q) \cdot (1 - (1-\varphi)^{\log(\text{list})} \cdot e^{-\lambda 1 \cdot \log(\text{list})/s1})$
$+ q \cdot (1 - (1-\varphi)^{\log(\text{list})} \cdot e^{-\lambda 1 \cdot \log(\text{list})/s1}$
$\qquad \cdot (1-Pfail(connect,\text{elem}+\text{list},\text{res})) \cdot (1-Pfail(sortx,\text{list})))$
$= (1 - q) \cdot (1 - (1-\varphi)^{\log(\text{list})} \cdot e^{-\lambda 1 \cdot \log(\text{list})/s1})$
$+ q \cdot (1 - (1-\varphi)^{\log(\text{list})} \cdot e^{-\lambda 1 \cdot \log(\text{list})/s1}$
$\qquad \cdot (1-Pfail(connect,\text{elem}+\text{list},\text{res}))$
$\qquad \cdot (1-\varphi x)^{\text{list} \cdot \log(\text{list})} \cdot e^{-\lambda x \cdot \text{list} \cdot \log(\text{list})/sx})$ (22)

In expression (22), the (1-*Pfail*(*connect*,elem+list,res)) term can be substituted by expression (19) or (20) when *connect* = *lpc* (and x=1) or *connect* = *rpc* (and x=2), respectively. Finally, depending on the values assigned to the services parameters and attributes (e.g. list size, failure rates, processor speeds, network bandwidth) we can use expression (22) to determine which of the two service assemblies considered in this example provides a higher reliability.

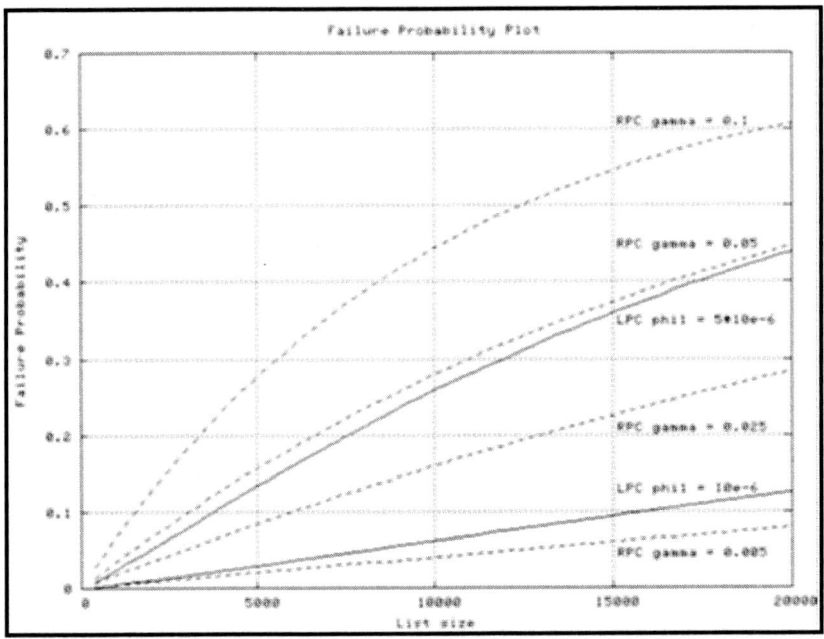

Fig. 6. Reliability comparison of the local (continuous lines) and remote assemblies (dashed lines), for different values of φ1 and γ

Figure 6 shows an example of comparison between the reliabilities of the two assemblies, as a function of the list size, with respect to different values of the reliability of the local sort service and the reliability of the communication infrastructure used to access the remote service. In particular, we have set φ1 = 10^{-6} or φ1 = $5 \cdot 10^{-6}$ for the *sort1* local service software failure rate. On the other hand, we have set φ2 = 10^{-7} for the *sort2* remote service software failure rate (i.e. one order of magnitude smaller than φ1), while the *net12* communication service failure rate is γ = 10^{-1}, γ = $5 \cdot 10^{-2}$, γ = $2.5 \cdot 10^{-2}$ or γ = $5 \cdot 10^{-3}$. Hence, looking only at the reliability of the two services, the local service is considerably less reliable than the remote one, and the remote assembly should be preferred. However, this simple consideration does not take into account the impact of the communication infrastructure reliability. As figure 6 shows, the remote assembly is actually more reliable only when the *net12* failure rate is γ = $5 \cdot 10^{-3}$. For the higher values of γ considered in this example, the local assembly is always more reliable when the *sort1* failure rate is $\varphi 1 = 10^{-6}$. Only if we assume a still higher *sort1* unreliability ($\varphi 1 = 5 \cdot 10^{-6}$) the remote assembly is more reliable for γ values greater than $5 \cdot 10^{-3}$ and less than $5 \cdot 10^{-2}$.

5 Related Work

Approaches to the reliability analysis of service- and component-based systems have been already presented (e.g. [5, 15, 17, 19]). According to the classification proposed in [8], [5] presents a *path-based* model, where the reliability of an assembly of components is calculated starting from the reliability of possible component execution paths. This model only considers sequential executions of services (so excluding, for example, *OR* completion models), and does not take into account the impact of the interconnection architecture; it also does not consider possible dependencies among services in the evaluation of the overall reliability. On the other hand [15] and [19] present *state-based* models [8], where probabilistic control flow graphs are used to model the usage patterns of components. In both models also the impact of the interconnection architecture is considered, through the introduction of the concept of connector reliability. The model presented in [15] considers only a single activity in each flow graph node (so excluding, for example, *OR* completion models), while the model in [19] take into consideration the *AND* and *OR* completion models for multiple activities in a single flow graph node. However, both models do not consider the possible dependency between services caused by service sharing, thus implying that they implicitly assume a *no sharing* dependency model. Also the model discussed in this paper is a state-based model, where we take into account both *AND* and *OR* completion models, and the possibility of service sharing (even if in the limited form of a single service shared by other services).

For what concerns the dependency between the request a particular service has to fulfil and the cascading service requests that it addresses to other resources, this concept has been explicitly introduced and modeled in [15] through the concept of *parameterized contract*. In this perspective, the Markov chain obtained by augmenting the flow graph of an offered service with suitable failure probabilities is presented in [15] as an example of such a contract, as it depends on (is parametric with respect to) the failure probabilities of the services requested within that flow. In our model we refine this concept, by explicitly introducing the possibility that the failure probability of each requested service in a flow may be expressed as a function of the parameters of the service modeled by that flow. As shown in the example of section 4 this provides a better support to the compositional reliability analysis. None of the models discussed above introduce explicitly the service parameters in the reliability evaluation, so that compositional analysis is not completely supported.

In our model (as also in [15] and [19]), we assume that the Markov model specifying the service usage profile is completely known. Issues related to the actual construction of this Markov model are discussed, for example, in [16], where in particular it is shown how a Hidden Markov model can be used to cope with the imperfect knowledge about the service behavior.

Finally, we point out that if we want to truly integrate the reliability prediction of a service assembly with the automatic service discovery, selection and composition procedures, a key point is the embedding of the analytic interface outlined in sections 2 and 3 into the machine-processable languages used to support the service description and composition. We recall that basic elements of this interface are: a model of the service usage profile (probabilistic flow graph), a model of the "internal" failure probability, (abstract) models of service requests whose actual parameters are defined as function of the calling service formal parameters. Examples of languages that support the service description, discovery and composition are OWL-S [13] and BPEL4WS [1], where both are intended to complement and to extend the basic WSDL language, proposed as a standard for the service description in the Web Service protocol suite [4]. Both languages include syntactic constructs to specify the structure and the flow of control of a composite service, and to specify QoS related infomation. Hence, they already provide some syntactic support that can be used as starting point for the specification of a dependability oriented analytic interface. Starting from this base, to fully specify such an interface, the existing syntactic constructs of these languages should be suitably extended (for example adding constructs for the inclusion of transition probabilities in the control flow graph, and constructs for the specification of failure rates among the QoS related information). Moreover, these syntactic constructs should be bound to some underlying "reliability prediction engine" that implements the algorithm outlined in section 3.3.

6 Conclusions

We have presented an approach to the reliability prediction of an assembly of services, that allows to take into account in an explicit and compositional way the reliability characteristics of both the resources and interaction infrastructures used in the assembly. We remark that predicting the reliability of an assembly of services actually represents only one side of the reliability assessment of an assembly of services, with the other side represented by appropriate monitoring activities to check whether the assembly of selected services will actually achieve the predicted reliability. In this paper we have focused on reliability prediction only.

However, several points require further investigation for what concerns the prediction of reliability. They include, for example, the dependency model, that should be extended to deal with more complex dependencies, and the fail-stop assumption, that should be released to deal also with error propagation aspects [11]. Moreover, as discussed at the end of section 5, another point, that is important in a true SOC perspective, is how to make as much as possible automatic the reliability prediction of a service assembly. This point involves the definition of reliability evaluation algorithms, and the inclusion in SOC oriented machine-processable languages of appropriate constructs to express the dependability-related characteristics of resources and connectors.

Finally, we would like to remark that, even if our focus is on reliability issues, the presented ideas can also be extended, with appropriate modifications, to other QoS aspects (e.g. performance).

Acknowledgements

Work partially supported by the Italian FIRB project "PERF: Performance evaluation of complex systems: techniques, methodologies and tools".

The author would like to thank Vittorio Cortellessa and Raffaela Mirandola for the insightful discussions about these topics, and Antonino Sabetta for his help with the application example.

References

1. T. Andrews *et al.* "Business Process Execution Language for Web Services Version 1.1" May 2003, on line at: http://www.ibm.com/developerworks/library/ws-bpel/.
2. L. Bass, P. Clements, R. Kazman, *Software Architectures in Practice*, Addison-Wesley, New York, NY, 1998.
3. I. Crnkovic, M. Larsson (eds.), *Building Reliable Component-Based Software Systems*, Artech House, 2002.
4. F. Curbera et al. "Unraveling the Web services Web: an introduction to SOAP, WSDL and UDDI" *IEEE Internet Computing*, vol. 6, no. 2, March/April 2002.
5. J. Dolbec, T. Shepard "A component based software reliability model" in *Proc. of the 1995 Conference of the Centre for Advanced Studies on Collaborative Research (CASCON)*, Toronto, Ontario, Canada, 1995.
6. I. Foster, C. Kesselman, S. Tuecke "The Anatomy of the Grid: Enabling Scalable Virtual Organizations", *Int. Journal of Supercomputer Applications*, 15(3), 2001.
7. I. Foster, C. Kesselman, J. Nick, S. Tuecke "Grid Services for Distributed System Integration" *IEEE Computer*, vol. 35, no. 6, 2002.
8. K. Goseva-Popstojanova, A.P. Mathur, K.S. Trivedi "Comparison of architecture-based software reliability models" in *Proc. of the 12th IEEE Int. Symposium on Software Reliability Engineering (ISSRE 2001)*, 2001.
9. D. Hamlet, D. Mason, D. Woit "Properties of Software Systems Synthesized from Components", June 2003, on line at: http://www.cs.pdx.edu/~hamlet/lau.pdf (to appear as a book chapter).
10. S. Hissam et al. "Enabling predictable assembly" *Journal of Systems and Software*, vol. 65, 2003, pp. 185-198.
11. J.C. Laprie "Dependable computing: Concepts, limits, challenges" in *FTCS-25, the 25th IEEE International Symposium on Fault-Tolerant Computing - Special Issue*, Pasadena, CA, USA, June 1995, pp. 42-54.
12. N.R. Mehta, N. Medvidovic, S. Phadke "Toward a taxonomy of software connectors" in Proc. *22nd Int. Conference on Software Engineering (ICSE 2000)*, May 2000.
13. "OWL-S: Semantic Markup for Web Services" White Paper, The OWL Services Coalition, Nov. 2003.

14. M.P. Papazoglou, D. Georgakopoulos "Service oriented computing" *ACM Communications*, vol. 46, no. 10, Oct. 2003, pp. 24-28.
15. R.H. Reussner, H.W. Schmidt, I.H. Poernomo "Reliability prediction for component-based software architectures" *Journal of Systems and Software*, no. 66, 2003, pp. 241-252.
16. R. Roshandel, N. Medvidovic "Toward architecture-based reliability prediction" in Proc. *ICSE 2004 Workshop on Architecting Dependable Systems (WADS 2004)*, (R. de Lemos, C. Gacek, A. Romanowsy eds.), Edinburgh, Scotland, UK, May 2004, pp. 2-6.
17. J. Stafford, J.D. McGregor "Issues in predicting the reliability of composed components" *5th ICSE Workshop on Component-based Sw Engineering*, Orlando, Florida, May 2002.
18. C. Szyperski, *Component Software: Beyond Object-Oriented Programming*, Addison Wesley, 2002.
19. W.-L. Wang, Y. Wu, M.-H. Chen "An architecture-based software reliability model" Proc. *IEEE Pacific Rim Int. Symposium on Dependable Computing*, Hong Kong, China, Dec. 1999.

Fault Injection Approach Based on Architectural Dependencies

Regina Lúcia de Oliveira Moraes[1] and Eliane Martins[2]

[1] State University of Campinas (UNICAMP),
Superior Centre of Technological Education (CESET),
regina@ceset.unicamp.br
http://www.ceset.unicamp.br/~regina
[2] State University of Campinas (UNICAMP),
Institute of Computing (IC),
eliane@ic.unicamp.br
http://www.ic.unicamp.br/~eliane

Abstract. In a previous paper we described a fault injection strategy that applies risk-based analysis to select the system's riskiest components for testing. Among other criteria, this analysis considers the number of upstream and downstream dependencies of a component in a system. In order to obtain this number, we propose the use of architectural-level dependency analysis. One advantage of an analysis at architectural level is that systems may often contain COTS components from which no source code is available. The approach is illustrated with a case study, and the preliminary experimental results are also discussed.

1 Introduction

The increased pressures on time and money make component-based software development a current trend in the construction of new systems. In this method, instead of bespoke design and development, a system integrates *off the shelf* (OTS) components developed by third parties.

Despite the potential benefits of component-based development, the validation of components and component-based systems is still a challenge. The difficulty stems from lack of knowledge [5] [34]. On the one hand, component users do not know the acquired component's quality level, and even if it is known, there is no guarantee that the component will present the same quality level when used in a new context. This means that the acquired component must be validated each time it is used in a new context. However, users generally do not have enough information about the OTS component to perform this task.

On the other hand, using high-quality components is no guarantee that the overall system will present high quality. The complexity of the interaction among components can cause unexpected errors to emerge from component interfaces [35]. According to [35], 50% of bugs are detected after component integration, not during component development.

There is an increasing demand nowadays for high quality, critical and non-critical applications. For example, both e-commerce and military systems require availability and security. In order to achieve these quality properties, a focus on solutions at architectural level can be foreseen. Research into describing software architectures with respect to their dependability properties has recently gained considerable attention [31] [28] [33].

A good architectural solution is an important step, but it is not enough to guarantee that the final system will present the required quality level. Systems are increasingly complex, integrating thousands or millions of (hardware and/or software) components. There are numerous interfaces among these components, which increase design complexity. Components' interfaces comprise the assumptions that components make about each other. Architectural mismatch [13] can arise when the expectations of a component do not match those of other components or the environment in which it operates. Furthermore, the coupling between components to achieve the system's goals makes them highly interdependent; consequently, a failure in one component can rapidly affect the state of other components [35].

Validation is thus a necessary step to establish whether an architectural solution achieves the required system qualities. Moreover, it is important to assess the robustness of the interfaces with respect to component failures as well as problems that enter the system from external sources [34].

We propose the use of Software-Implemented Fault Injection (SWIFI) to observe how interfaces behave when data passing through them are intentionally corrupted. SWIFI is a useful complement to other validation techniques, in that it allows us to observe whether the failures of components or interfaces among components affect the services provided by the system.

Our approach is based on the introduction of interface errors, that is, errors are introduced at a component's interface by affecting input or output parameters, as well as returned results. A component's internal faults can generate errors that may propagate to its interfaces. Thus, interface errors may represent a component's failure modes as well as the failure modes of other components that interact with the target component. Errors are introduced using a software-implemented fault injection tool, Jaca [20], in order to validate Java applications. Jaca does not require access to an application's source code, since it is a solution for the validation of a system that may be composed of multiple, generally black-box OTS. All instrumentation needed for fault injection and monitoring purposes are introduced at byte code level.

Given that a component-based system may contain too many components and interfaces, it may not be practical to inject errors in all of them. Although the system may be composed of OTS components, from which no source code is available, the system is not considered a black-box; the system architecture, representing how various components are interconnected is known. We will use this knowledge to help select a subset of components and interfaces in which to inject errors. One approach that has been used in tests is to perform the selection based on risk analysis: more test effort is concentrated on those parts of the system that may present higher risk of causing the system to fail [4] [27]. Various factors can be considered when evaluating a component's risk. Complexity metrics can be one of them [27]; in a previous work we used a set of OO metrics to select a component to inject [22]. One limitation of this approach was the need of source code to better categorize such metrics.

In the current approach we use dependency analysis, at the architectural level, to guide fault injection. In brief, the idea is to select components based on upstream dependencies (components whose failure will cause cascading failures in the rest of the system) as well as downstream dependencies (components particularly affected by failures in the rest of the system) [4].

In the following section we give a fault injection overview. In Section 3 we describe the dependency analysis approach that we use in this work. The proposed strategy is discussed in Section 4; a case study is presented in Section 5 and the tests' results are presented in Section 6. Finally, in Section 7 we present our conclusions and future research.

2 Fault Injection Overview

2.1 Fault Injection

Fault injection techniques have been widely used to evaluate a system's dependability and to validate its error-handling mechanisms. The technique provides a means to dynamically demonstrate the software quality and to observe the system's behaviour [36]. By doing so, it is possible to know how the system will behave in the presence of faults in its components or in its environment. Fault injection enables accelerated system testing under stressful conditions, and can help uncover design and implementation faults in the systems [3]. This technique is useful to validate the solutions designed to handle exceptional situations.

Fault Injection may be used to validate a fault tolerant system, to help with fault removal aimed at reducing the occurrence of faults and their severity, as well as to assist with faults forecasting. Fault removal and fault forecasting could be used to quantify dependability attributes. In this work we are interested in its fault removal aspects.

Fault Injection approaches may vary according to the system life cycle in which they are applied and to the type of faults that are injected. Among the various existent approaches (see [15] for an overview), software-implemented fault injection has been widely used [9] [12] [26]. It has become more popular due to its lower costs (it does not require specially developed circuits, as does hardware fault injection), better versatility (it is easier to adapt codes to make fault injection in another system than to adapt of circuits) and better control, which together facilitate the observation of the system during tests. One approach of software-implemented fault injection consists of injecting anomalous input data that come into the software through its interface [36], instead of altering a system's code or state in order to emulate the software [34]. This study uses this approach, allowing software acquirers to determine its robustness. The software can be stated as robust if it is fed by anomalous input and does not propagate into a failure, demonstrating that the software can produce dependable service even in presence of an aggressive external environment [36].

For software-implemented fault injection the most common faults considered are memory faults (which alter the content of memory positions), processor faults (which affect the content of registers, the result of calculus, control flux or instruction), bus faults (which affect the addressing lines or data that are being transmitted by the bus) and, in the case of distributed systems, communication faults (which affect messages that are transmitted through a communication channel: they can be lost, altered, duplicated or delayed)[15].

Recently more attention has been given to the consequences of software faults. Software faults represent the faults resulting from mistakes committed by developers during system development or in modifications made in the phases of maintenance. Software faults have turned out to be the main causes of field failures.

In this work we are using a software-implemented fault injection tool, called Jaca, to inject errors and test the system's robustness. A similar approach was presented by Ballista Project [17] and Mafalda tool [11], but in those cases the errors were injected in the parameters of operating system calls instead of the component interfaces.

TAMMER [9] is another similar work in which the injection of interface faults is used to observe fault propagation focusing on code coverage. The tool Jaca, used in this work, is presented in section 2.2.

2.2 The Jaca Tool

Software Fault Injection can affect either the code (source or assembler) or the state of a target system. To alter a system's state, a tool is needed to inject faults or errors during runtime. These tools differ according to the mechanism used to trigger faults [15]. Most of these tools are aimed at emulating hardware faults, so faults are injected at low-level, affecting processor registers, I/O device drivers and memory positions. Nowadays, with the increasing importance of software faults, some studies present tools that aim to inject faults at higher level during runtime [9] [12] [26].

Jaca offers mechanisms for the injection of interface errors in object-oriented systems written in Java language. Jaca is an evolution of the FIRE tool [26] and it uses reflective programming. The reflection mechanism introduces a new architectural model by definition of two levels: the meta-level (implements fault injection and monitoring features) and the base level (implements the system's functionalities) [19]. Computational reflection allows the target system's instrumentation to carry out its functions through introspection (useful for the system's monitoring) or by altering the system during runtime (useful for the injection) without changing the system's structure. Jaca does not need the application source code to perform fault injection. This occurs because Jaca was implemented using the Javassist reflection toolkit [6], which allows the instrumentation to be introduced at byte code level during load time. The source code independency is an important feature of the tool, allowing the validation of a system that may be composed of multiple third-party components. Jaca's current version can affect the public interface of an application by altering attributes' values, method's parameters and return values. The tool needs to get a class's interface information in order to inject the errors, and it can do this through introspection when the source code is not available. Jaca is described in more detail in [18], [20].

2.3 Related Work

The use of fault injection to validate component-based systems is an active research area. This work is an evolution of that presented in [21] in which we test an isolated component. In that work we used an application to activate the component under test; it differs from the current work in two respects: (i) the target is no longer a component in isolation but a system integrating various heterogeneous components, some of which may be black-box; (ii) the units considered are no longer classes, but components. Hence, the strategy cannot use source code dependent metrics as in [21] and the architecture becomes essential for planning fault injection. This work also extends that presented in [23], where we introduced the idea of architectural relevance for testing a component-based system without describing our criteria in detail. Our current work tackles the dependencies criterion.

A closely related approach to the one presented here is the Interface Propagation Analysis (IPA) [33, ch.9.2]. IPA takes a black-box view of software components, injecting faults at the interfaces between hardware and software, as well as between operating system, microkernel and so on. The difference is that we are not considering all components as black-box.

TAMER [9] is another study which describes a tool that injects interface faults aimed at observing fault propagation. The main focus of that work is code coverage. Here we are not interested in source code coverage but in the exceptions raised by the component, as well as whether these exceptions cause the whole system to fail.

The work in [12] is quite similar to ours since they use a tool based on computational reflection, called Java Wrapper Generator (JWG). JWG modifies the bytecode at load time, which in turn provokes an exception and allows the observation of the exception-handlers behaviour. In Fetzer's case, the focus is on objects, whereas in our approach the focus is on a component that may be composed by several classes.

MAFALDA (Microkernel Assessment by Fault injection Analysis and Design Aid) [11] is another tool that provides quantitative information on COTS microkernels to support their integration into dependable systems using error confinement wrappers. The proposal of MAFALDA is the injection of errors in the parameters of operating system calls, instead of the parameters between components as in our case.

The dependency analysis at the architectural level used in our work is strongly influenced by the study in [32] where they propose the chaining concept to reduce the portions of an architecture that must be examined in order to test or debug a system. In our work we use this idea to select the components to inject and monitor the fault injection.

From the Ballista approach [17] we derive the definition of error model, which is proposed by the authors as a means to test robustness.

We also borrow ideas from studies that use risk for test costs reduction. Many risk-based testing strategies have been proposed [4] [27] [30]. The approach presented here is particularly related to [4], from which we use the heuristic risk-based testing presented below.

3 Dependency Analysis at the Architectural Level

Abstractly, software architecture is a representation of the system based on the components that integrate the system and their interactions [29]. The set of components integrated in a system can be component interaction elements or connectors, data elements, processing (or behavioural) elements or state elements that contain the current state of the component both in terms of data and processing elements.

Architecture diagram is a high-level model of software system that represents the system's components and how they are interconnected.

A component may be defined as "unit of composition with contractually specified interfaces and explicit dependencies. A software component can be deployed independently and is subject to composition by third parties" [8]. A component's provided interface allows one component to provide information or stimulus to another component, whereas the required interface allows one component to ask for information or receive stimulus from other components.

Dependency analysis has been traditionally based on control and data flow relationships associated with functions and variables of a program [32]. This has worked primarily for compiler optimization. It has been used widely in software engineering activities such as program understanding, testing, debugging, reverse engineering, and maintenance [7]. It has also been useful for code reviewers and architects when assessing the coupling within an application or library. A limitation of the traditional approaches is that they are generally source-code based. This is not useful to us for two main reasons: (i) the source code of some OTS components might not be available; (ii) polymorphism (the ability to bind a reference to more than one object) and dynamic binding (where a specific bond between a reference and an object is determined at runtime) replace explicit compile-time binding with implicit runtime binding. This means that a receiver of a polymorphic message is only known at runtime. In this way, the interaction among components is better determined through the analysis of the system's architecture.

Dependency relationships at the architectural level appear from the connection between components and the constraints on their interaction [32].
There are several architectural-based dependencies' approaches [16] [1] [24]. The approach used in this work is based on Chaining, dependency analysis technique that was primarily aimed at reducing the part of the architecture to be examined for a given purpose, for example testing and debugging [32]. Individual links in a chain associate architecture components that are directly related. A chain of dependencies includes association among components that are indirectly related.

There are three types of chains: (i) affected-by chains, which contain the set of components that could potentially affect the component of interest; (ii) affects chains, which contain the set of components on which the component of interest can potentially have an effect; (iii) related chains, which are a combination of affected-by and affects chains.

The next section presents how the chaining technique can be useful for fault injection.

4 Using Dependency Analysis for Fault Injection

Dependency analysis can be useful for fault injection in many ways: (i) to help select target components, e.g. components whose interfaces are to be injected; (ii) to establish monitoring points to determine error propagation, and (iii) to select a minimal set of components to monitor for debugging purposes in case of system failure.

As discussed above, components with high affects chain and affected by dependencies are possible targets for fault injection.

Figure 1 illustrates the chains of a given component. In this figure, the component designated as "Target Component" has 5 downstream dependencies (number of elements in its affected-by chain) and 4 upstream dependencies (number of elements in its affects chain). Faults that are introduced in the links indicated in the figure can have an effect on other components that do not need to be directly injected. Faults in a link between the target component and an affects chain component represent failure modes in components used by the target one (its successors) and could be impacted by a change in the target component. Conversely, faults in a link with an affected-by component represent failure modes from components that use the target one (in other words, failures on its predecessors) and may affect it.

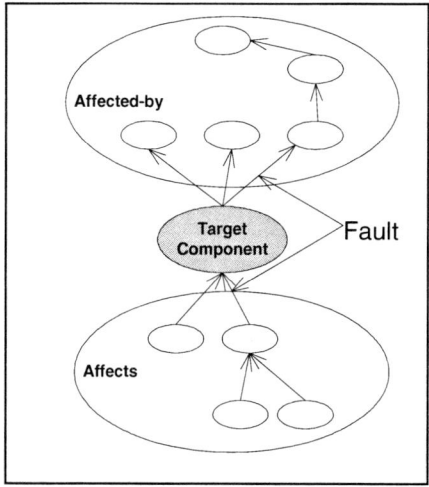

Fig. 1. Chains

We also need to determine where to observe in order to understand the effect of the corruptions. When a selected component does not have the required observability (easiness of monitoring) the observation point should be transferred to another component in the same chain (affected-by or affects).

In this way, we can assess the failure tolerance of the interfaces regarding component failures and corruptions that may enter into the system from external sources.

We must bear in mind that in this context the related chains can comprise any components that integrate the system (protective wrappers, exception handles and so on).

Our approach encompasses the following steps:

1. Modelling the system's architecture
2. Constructing the dependency matrix
3. Determining the chain for each component
4. Determining the component to be injected
5. Determining the failure mode
6. Determining the values to be injected
7. Determining the expected outcomes

The following sections describe these steps in more detail.

4.1 Modelling the System's Architecture

The kinds of dependencies that can be considered among components are influenced by the notation used to represent the system's architecture [32]. In our approach we are interested only in behavioural relationship, particularly in input and output interactions among the components. Figure 2 presents an example of the architectural model considered in this study where the interactions among components through the provided and required interfaces are in relief.

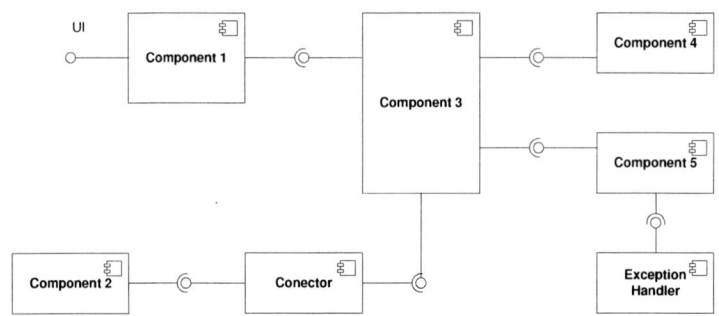

Fig. 2. The System Architecture Model

4.2 Constructing the Dependency Matrix

We use a matrix to represent the components relationships as suggested in [32]. Although the chaining technique considers different types of connections, only the connections between a provided interface and a required interface are being considered in this study. In the dependency matrix, the columns represent the dependent in the relationship. The rows represent the object of dependency in addition to any events generated in the system's environment that can be acquired by an interface (e.g. a user interface - UI). Thus, if component A is dependent on B, the cell at column A and row B hold that relationship (indicated by an "x" in this cell). Table 1 shows the matrix corresponding to the architecture in Figure 2.

Table 1. Dependency Matrix

	Component1	Component2	Connector	Component3	Component5
Connector		X			
Component3	X		X		
Component4				X	
Component5				X	
Exception Handler					X
Component1	X				

4.3 Determining the Chain for Each Component

A component's chain can be determined by creating links when there is a mark (X) in a cell, which indicates that a relationship holds. To determine the affected-by chain for a component, select its corresponding column and locate cells containing an "X" in this column. The component in the corresponding row is in the affected-by chain of this component. To determine the affects chain for a component select its corresponding row and locate cells in this column containing an "X". The component in the corresponding column is in the affects chain of this component. Both affected-by and affects chain are transitive; once you create a link you construct in a similar manner the next link, beginning by the newly identified element in the chain.

For example, to determine the affected-by chain for Component2 in the matrix presented in Table 1, and to identify which component potentially affected it, it is necessary to take the column Component2 and locate all the related rows in the matrix. Only the Connector has been identified. Continuing by the transitivity property, one must take the column Connector and locate all the related rows in the matrix, reaching Component3. Taking the column Component3, Component4 and Component5 are identified and finally the column Component5 identifies the Exception Handler. In this way, the affect-by chain of Component2 is Connector, Component3, Component4, Component5 and Exception Handler.

The affects chain can be obtained in a similar way beginning with the row, for example, taking Component3. To identify which components it may affect, one obtains Component3 affects chain as Component1, Connector, Component2 and information acquired from the boundary of the system through the user interface (UI).

4.4 Determining the Candidate Targets

To select a component in which to inject errors we are considering the number of components in affects chain and affected by chain of each component. Based on Pareto's 80/20 rule [25], the components whose sum of both chains is classified between the top 20%, must be selected to inject the faults.

As mentioned above, these components may affect many others, so we can observe the impact of faults without having to inject all the components' interfaces.

Based on Table 1, where we have six rows, if we apply Pareto's 80/20 rule we should inject errors into one or two components. The highest sum of affected-by and affects chain belongs to Component3, which has this sum equalling seven, followed by Component5 and ExceptionHandler equalling six. If the tester must make a choice and inject error in only one component, Component3 should be selected; otherwise, he should select Component5 and Exception Handler, too.

However, there is a need to cope with constraints on controllability (easiness to inject faults) imposed by fault injection tools. Jaca, namely, can only inject and observe components written in Java. Another limitation is that it can only affect parameters or return values that are not objects. As Jaca, other fault injectors also have their limitations. If the selected component is not considered controllable, the related chain can be used to select another target component.

4.5 Determining Where to Inject

Once the components that should be tested are selected, each component should be considered (CUT) in order to determine in which of their interfaces to inject errors. As we are considering only the connections between a provided interface and a required interface, our focus is on parameters and returned values that flow between components. The locations to inject are:

(i) input parameters provided to the target component by its predecessors (according to links in affected-by chain);
(ii) a returned value (or output parameter) provided by the target component to its predecessors (according to links in affected-by chain);
(iii) input parameters provided by the target component to its successors (according to links in affects chain);
(iv) a returned value (or output parameter) provided to the target component by its successors (according to links in affects chain);
(v) a parameter or returned value that comes into the system through its boundary components.

4.6 Determining the Values to Inject

To determine which values we should inject into input/output parameters or returned values of the operations in a component's interface, one should consider the component's specification when there are valid domains of these values or constraints imposed by the component's contract. In such case, boundary value testing can be used [25]. However, if these domains are not specified, the Ballista approach may be used [17]. In this case, the values to be used for each data type are presented in Table 2.

Table 2. Values to Inject based on Ballista's Approach

Data Type	Values to Inject
Integer	0, 1, -1, MinInt, MaxInt, neighbour value (current value ± 1)
Real Floating Point	0, 1, -1, DBLMin, DBLMax, neighbour value (current value * 0.95 or * 1.05)
Boolean	inversion of estate (true -> false; false ->true)
String	Null

4.7 Determining the Expected Outcomes

An output value space is the set of all possible output values of the program. In this set, as a result of an experiment, the system may fail or tolerate the injected faults. Tolerance to the injected faults means that the system outputs the expected results, i.e. that the architecture offers the required tolerance level. Otherwise, if failure occurs it means that modifications to the system are needed. Failures may be reported, raised exceptions or returned wrong values. Application hangs, application crashes or erroneous values as outputs characterize a non-reported failure.

In order to decide if an output value is a wrong value or not, an oracle mechanism is needed. An oracle is a predicate on input/output pairs that checks whether the desired behaviour has been implemented correctly by some function [34]. Oracles can be obtained from predicates that characterize the system's expected properties. These predicates can be implemented as contract assertions.

To observe the outputs, the tester should collect the assertions at the system's interfaces and the output generated by the system, such as, messages to users, exit codes, generated files, output to hardware devices, exceptions that appear at the system's interface, among others.

Furthermore, error propagation is also observed. Predecessors and successors are useful for the observation of errors propagation, too. Errors can be cancelled (corrupt data is flushed or overwritten) or hidden (corrupt data remains unchanged but unused); these are considered as tolerated by the system. An error is detected when error handlers are activated. Detected errors are considered as recovered when the error handler successfully recovers the system's state, meaning that the system terminates successfully; otherwise a failure of exception handlers may cause the system to fail.

To observe error propagation, the tester should monitor the exception handlers or other error detection mechanism and monitor the injected component output to check if a bad input produces a bad output.

Table 3 presents the observation points related to the injection points presented in the failure mode in section 4.5. They are useful to monitor the system when the injection has been carried out for:

Table 3. Values to Inject based on Ballista's Approach

Failure Mode	Observation Points
(i)	the direct successors and the predecessors of the target component
(ii)	the direct predecessors of the component
(iii)	the target component or its direct predecessors, the first component in the direct successors' affects chain
(iv)	the target component or its direct predecessors
(v)	the direct successors, the direct predecessors of the target components

In all cases, the exception handler and the system boundary components should be observed to detect the outgoing data and raised exceptions that will be seen by the users.

It is possible that the direct CUT' predecessors or successors do not have enough observability (easiness of monitoring). If so, the tester must find in its respective chain the next predecessor or successor directly linked to the CUT. The newly selected component should be as closer as possible to the CUT.

The observation points will guide the tester in developing, monitoring and runtime checking capabilities. One must bear in mind that the monitoring of the system will generate a logfile. Checking should be selected carefully; too little information logged may not be enough for debugging purposes. Too much information, on the other hand, may be too time-consuming to analyze. One can choose to activate observation points only when a failure is detected, and then re-execute the tests. The risk, in this case, is when the situation that has led to a failure is an intermittent failure and perhaps a non-repeatable one.

5 The Case Study

In this section we present a case study that has been utilized in our experiments. The system's specification used in our case study has been retrieved from [2] and implemented by a PhD student whose work we used to better understand the system and the architectural aspects presented in the following sections [14].

Anderson presented a general approach to engineering protective wrappers as a means to detect error and undesired behaviour in a component-based system, composed by some COTS components. The wrappers were also used to launch appropriate recovery actions. Thus, the protective wrappers, allow detection and tolerance of typical errors caused by unavailability of signals, violations of constraints and oscillations. In [2], the author presented experiments' results using a Simulink model of a steam boiler system, together with an Off-the-Shelf (OTS) Proportional Integral and Derivative controller (PID controller).

5.1 The System

The overall system has two main components: the boiler system and the control system. The control system comprises a PID controller (the OTS items), and the ROS, which is simply the remainder of the control system. The control system is represented by three PID controllers dealing with the feed water flow, the coal feeder rate and the airflow. The ROS consists of: (i) the boiler sensors. These are "smart" sensors, which monitor variables providing input to the PID; (ii) controller: Drum Level, Steam Flow, Steam Pressure, Gas Concentrations and Coal Feeder Rate; (iii) actuators. These devices control a heating burner, which can be ON/OFF, and adjust inlet/outlet valves in response to outputs from the PID controller: Feed Water Flow, Coal Feeder Rate and Air Flow; (iv) configuration settings. These are the "set-points" for the system: Oxygen and Bus Pressure, which must be set up in advance by the operators. Smart sensors and actuators interact with the PID controller through a standard protocol.

5.2 The Architectural Solution

The system's architecture presented in [2] was extended in [14] and was implemented as a fault tolerant system. As a system that integrates OTS components, the system should consider these components as a potential source of faults. The overall software system should be able to support OTS components while preventing the propagation of errors. So the system should be able to tolerate faults that may reside or occur inside the OTS components, but should not be able to directly inspect or modify their internal states or behaviour.

An architectural solution to tackle this problem was presented in [14], to encapsulate a COTS component adding fault tolerant capabilities, aiming to improve error detection and error recovery. The main concept used is the idealised C2 component (iC2C), which is an evolution of the C2 architectural style.

The C2 architecture style [33] is a component-based style that supports large grain reuse and flexible system composition. The components in C2 architecture are integrated by connectors that are responsible for message routing, broadcasting and filtering. Wrappers encapsulate each component to cope with interface and architectural mismatches [13]. In C2 style, the system has a layered architecture.

Each side of a connector may be connected to any number of components or connectors. In C2, *requests* are messages that flow up the architecture, and their responses (*notifications*) flow down. Figure 3 shows the Boiler System architecture of the Boiler System that was first presented by [2] and that has now been adapted to the C2 style. By analysing Figure 3 we can infer that the system's boundary is the Conn3 component that represents the interface between the system and the hardware components, and the Boiler Controller that represents the user's interface.

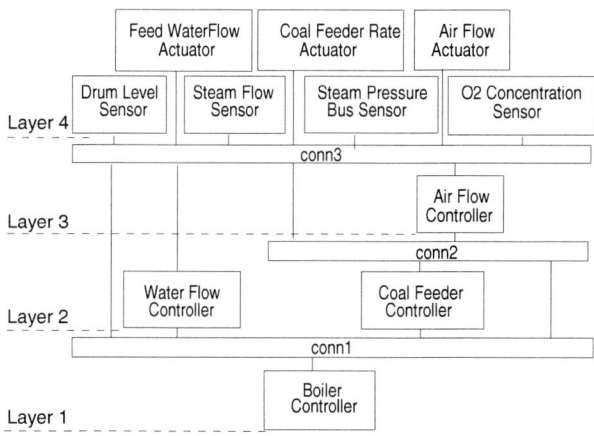

Fig. 3. C2 Configuration of the Boiler System

The iC2C style was proposed to allow the structuring of software architectures compliant with the C2 architectural style [33] [14]. The main idea is the separation of the normal and the abnormal activity parts of the idealised component, in order to minimise the impact of fault tolerance provisions on the system's complexity. The iC2C normal activity component (represented by the Air Flow Controller in Figure 3) implements the normal behaviour. It is responsible for error detection during normal operation as well as for signalling the interface and internal exceptions. The iC2C abnormal activity component (represented by the AFC Error Handler in Figure 3) is responsible for error recovery and for signalling the failure exceptions.

iC2C connectors are specialised reusable C2 connectors and have the following roles: (i) the iC2C_bottom connector (represented by the AFC_bottom in Figure 4), connects the iC2C with the lower components of a C2 configuration and serialises the requests received. When a request is completed, a notification is sent back. This request may be a normal response, an interface exception or a failure exception; (ii) the iC2C_internal (represented by the AFC_internal in Figure 4) controls message flow inside the iC2C selection its destination; (iii) the iC2C_top connector (represented by the AFC_top in Figure 4) connects the iC2C with the upper components of a C2 configuration. The overall structure defined for the iC2C is fully compliant with the component rules of the C2 architecture style, allowing an iC2C to be integrated into any C2 configuration and to interact with components of a larger system.

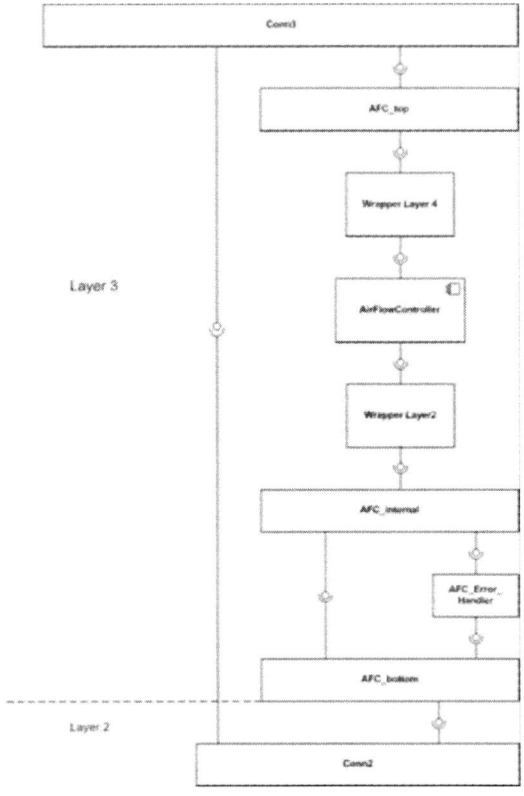

Fig. 4. Configuration for the Layer 3 of the Boiler System (Idealized fault tolerant component)

To improve fault-tolerance capability, a protective wrapper for a COTS software component may be added to the system's architecture, resulting in an idealized COTS component (iCOTS). In this approach, the COTS component (Air Flow controller) is connected to two specialised connectors (Wrapper Layer2 and Wrapper Layer4), which in turn act as error detectors to compose iCOTS normal activity components.

When a constraint violation is detected, the wrappers send an exception notification, which is handled by the abnormal activity component, following the rules defined for the iC2C. The abnormal activity component is responsible for both error diagnosis and error recovery. The abnormal activity component reacts to exceptions raised by the normal activity component and either sends notifications to activate the error handlers or stands as a service provider for requests sent by the error handlers. Figure 4 presents the configuration of the Boiler System, graphically representing all these ideas. The case study consists of a system implementation based on this configuration.

6 Experimental Results and Analysis

6.1 The Case Study Dependency Matrix

We use the architectural model presented in Figures 3 and 4 to construct the dependency matrix for the Boiler System, according to what was explained in Section 4.

For each component with a required interface we create a column in the matrix and for each component that has a provided interface we create a row in the matrix. We also create a row for the user interface (UI) and a row for the interface with the hardware (actuators and sensors).

When a component requires information to a provided interface of another component, we place a mark (X) in the corresponding cell of the matrix. For example, Conn2 has a required interface connected to Conn3. In the matrix presented in Table 4, we put a mark in the cell that crosses these two components. We also place a mark in the respective cell of the component Boiler Controller with the UI and Conn3 with the hardware, since they represent the boundary components of the system. Table 3 presents the resulted matrix.

Table 4. The Case Study Dependency Matrix

	Boiler Controller	conn1	Coal FeederCtl	Water FlowCtl	conn2	Afc_bottom	Afc_cErrorHandler	Afc_internal	Wrapper Layer2	AirFlowCtl	Wrapper Layer4	Afc_top	conn3
UI	X												
Conn1	X												
CoalFeederCtl		X											
WaterFlowCtl		X											
Conn2		X	X										
Afc_bottom					X								
Afc_ErrorHandler						X							
Afc_internal						X	X						
WrapperLayer2								X					
AirFlowCtl									X				
WrapperLayer4										X			
Afc_top											X		
Conn3		X		X	X							X	
Hardware													X

6.2 Determining the Chain for Each Component

After constructing the dependency matrix, we have to obtain the related chains for each component, as presented in section 4.3. These chains are represented in Figure 5.

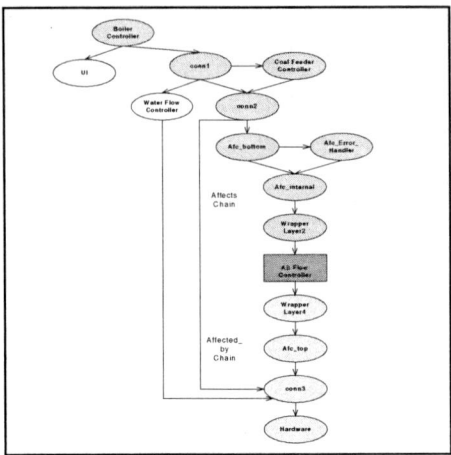

Fig. 5. Chain among components

Based on the graph in Figure 5, Table 5 presents the number of components in affected-by and affects chain for each component.

Table 5. Number of affected-by and affects chain

Component	Affected-by	Affects	Total
Boiler Controller	14	0	14
conn1	12	1	13
Coal Feeder Controller	10	2	12
Water Flow Controller	2	2	4
conn2	9	3	12
Afc_bottom	8	4	12
Afc_Error_Handler	7	5	12
Afc_internal	6	6	12
Wrapper Layer2	5	7	12
Air Flow Controller	4	8	12
Wrapper Layer4	3	9	12
Afc_top	2	10	12
conn3	1	12	13

6.3 Selecting the Target Components

According to Table 5, we should select the top 20% components with the highest number of affected-by and affects chain. As we have 13 components in the matrix row, we should select three components. These three components are emphasized in

Table 5. We should analyse the chain and select parameters and returned values in accordance with the failure mode presented in 4.5 for each component.

6.4 Summary of the Experiments

Table 6 summarizes the experiments executed with the three selected components. Experiments were also carried out with the other components to compare the results obtained. For the sake of space these experiments are not described, but the values injected are similar, according to Table 2.

Table 6. Injection Points based on the Strategy

Component	Interface Method	Injection Location	Values to Inject
Boiler Controller	setConfiguration	1st Parameter	0, 1, 1.1, -0.9 DBLMax, DBLMin
Boiler Controller	setConfiguration	2nd Parameter	0, 0.1, -0.9, 0.2, DBLMax, DBLMin
BoilerController	connectTop	1st Parameter	null
conn1	connectTop	1st Parameter	null
conn1	setConfiguration	1st Parameter	0, 1, 1.1, -0.9, DBLMax, DBLMin
conn1	setConfiguration	2nd Parameter	0, 0.1, -0.9, 0.2, DBLMax, DBLMin
conn3	ReadO2Concentration	Returned Value	0, 1, 1.1, -0.9, DBLMax, DBLMin
conn3	readSteamFlow	Returned Value	0, 125, 126, -0.9, DBLMax, DBLMin
conn3	readBusPressure	Returned Value	0, 20, 21, -0.9, DBLMax, DBLMin
conn3	setFeedWaterFlow	1st Parameter	0, 1, 1.1, -0.9, DBLMax, DBLMin
conn3	SetAirFlow	1st Parameter	0, 0.1, -0.9, 0.2, DBLMax, DBLMin

6.5 Results

Table 7 contains the results obtained. The column "#Errors" indicates the number of errors injected. The "#Detections" column shows the number of times an error detection mechanism is activated. The next column indicates the number of successful executions, which comprises: (i) number of experiments in which the errors injected were non-effective (errors were masked, flushed or remained latent), (ii) number of experiments where the error detection mechanisms were activated, the exception was handled and the system recovered execution. The last columns contain the number of failures, which can be reported or non-reported. A reported failure means that an exception was raised and then the system crashed. A non-reported failure represents the case in which invalid values are not detected and the system terminates normally. This is a dangerous situation because the system violates safety conditions.

The reported failure occurred when errors were injected when the connections between components and connectors were being established. In the C2 architecture, these connections are established during runtime. This result indicates that the C2 framework components also need a protective wrapper.

Table 7. Results Obtained

Component	#Errors	#Detections	#Successes	#Failures	
				Reported	Non-reported
Boiler Controller	13	4	12	1	0
conn1	13	4	12	1	0
CoalFeeder Controller	16	0	16	0	0
WaterFlow Controller	1	0	0	1	0
conn2	13	4	12	1	0
Wrapper Layer2	6	4	6	0	0
AirFlow Controller	6	4	6	0	0
Wrapper Layer4	12	8	12	0	0
conn3	30	4	30	0	16
Total	110	32	106	4	16

As expected, the results obtained when injecting the rest of the components (ROC) were similar to the ones obtained when injecting the selected ones. Nevertheless, when analyzing the execution log that Jaca generates, we observed that the components were effectively executed according to the dependency graph in Figure 5.

The system's behaviour was similar when we injected the Boiler Controller component and the conn1 connector. One may think that only one of them could have been selected, but the Boiler Controller is the only component in which fault injection can emulate operator faults (in this case, erroneous values provided through the system interface). On the other hand, by selecting conn1 connector it is possible to affect the Coal Feeder Controller, given that this component is not on the affected-by chain of neither the Boiler Controller nor the conn3 connector.

6.6 Approach Limitations

When fault injection technique is used to validate a system, the intrusion caused by the tool is unavoidable. However, in previous experiments [21] we had evaluated the performance of a system composed by a benchmark application interacting with an object-oriented database management system (ODBMS). To analyze the impact of the tool's intrusion on the ODBMS's performance, the application was executed threefold: 1)without the use of Jaca, 2) using Jaca without the injection of errors and 3) using Jaca to inject errors. The tests were executed using the operations available on benchmark application (create, query match and query traversal). For each experiment the execution timing presented by the benchmark's interface was noted (each injection was repeated five times with the same parameters and the average was taken as result). Before each execution of the experiment, the object manager as well as the operational system were re-initiated so that no information residue from the cache memory or temporary disk storage were used (the aim was to avoid compromising the results). From the results it was possible to see that the benchmark presented a similar performance in all case. Some small variations were observed when Jaca was used only to monitoring and to inject the errors, since the difference between one case and another is the execution of arithmetic operations between the injected error and the value previously existent.

Currently, we are working to test the ODMBS through error injection, with the aim to evaluate the impact of those errors in the application.

Another limitation is the analysis of the system's architecture as we could fall into two situations: (i) when the system is composed of several components and (ii) when there is no information about the system's architecture. In both case we could use a tool to analyze the dependencies. There are some tools, however, that show the dependencies through the analysis of the bytecode [10] and do not need the source code for this purpose.

7 Conclusion and Future Work

This study represents a first step toward our investigation on the use of a risk-based fault injection approach. The main contribution of this study is the use of architectural analysis to guide fault injection. Specifically, a dependency analysis technique was applied to establish the relationships among components, based on the interactions through their provided and required interfaces.

Fault injection can be a valuable approach to validate whether an architectural solution achieves the required reliability level. An advantage in analysing a system's architecture is that fault injection can be planned early in the development process. Another advantage is that it allows dependencies to be established even when the source code is not available, which can be the case when third-party components are used in a system.

Dependency analysis can be used for many purposes, one of them being change impact determination. It can be helpful in fault injection to determine the components that are worth injecting. In other words, under time or cost pressures, fault injection efforts can be concentrated on those components whose failures may have greater impact on the system. Moreover, when a component of interest has low controllability (or observability), the dependency relationships can be used to determine the target components in which to inject the faults (or to observe): components that can be affected by the one of interest (to determine the impact of a faulty component on the rest of the system) or those that can affect the component of interest (to determine the effect on the latter when the rest of the system fails).

A simple case study and its experiments' results were used to show the benefits of the approach. Clearly, further experiments must be made in order to corroborate these results. The value of this approach will also be tested in a real world application.

Acknowledgment

The authors wish to thank Carlos Eduardo Rodrigues de Almeida , a UNICAMP student, for performing the experiments and also for his invaluable support with the Jaca tool. This research is partly supported by CNPq – Brazil's National Council for Scientific and Technological Development – through the ACERTE project and the State of São Paulo's Research Foundation.

References

1. Allen, R., Garlan, D.: Formalizing Architectural Connection. In: Proc. of the 16th International Conference on Software Engineering, IEEE Computer Society, (1994) 71-80
2. Anderson, T. et. al.: Protective Wrapper Development: A Case Study. Lecture Notes in Computer Science (LNCS), Vol. 2580, Spring Verlag, (2003) 1-14
3. Arlat, J., Aguera, M., Amat, L., Crouzet, Y., Fabre, J. C., Laprie, J. C., Martins, E., Powell, D.: Fault Injection for Dependability Validation–A Methodology and some Applications. IEEE Transactions on Software Engineering, Vol. 16 (2), (1990) 166-182
4. Bach, J.: Heuristic risk-based testing. Software Testing and Quality Engineering Magazine, (1999)
5. Beydeda, S., Volker, G.: State of the art in testing components. In: Proc. Of the International Conference on Quality Software, (2003)
6. Chiba, S.: Javassist – A Reflection-based Programming Wizard for Java. In: Proc of the ACM OOPSLA'98 Workshop on Reflective Programming in C++ and Java, (1998)
7. Chen, Z., Xul, B., Zhao, J.: An Overview of Methods for Dependence Analysis of Concurrent Programs. ACM SIGPLAN Notices, Vol. 37, Issue 8 (2002) 45-52
8. Clemens, S.: Component Software: Beyond Object-Oriented Programming, New York, Addison-Wesley, (1998)
9. De Millo, R. A., Li, T., Mathur, A. P.: Architecture of TAMER: A Tool for dependability analysis of distributed fault-tolerant systems. Purdue University, (1994)
10. Dependency Finder tool project, http://depfind.sourceforge.net/, (2005)
11. Fabre, J-C, Rodriguez, M., Arlat, J., Sizum, J-M.: Building dependable COTS microkernel-based systems using MAFALDA. In: Proc. of 2000 Pacific Rim International Symposium on Dependable Computing - PRDC'00, Los Angeles, USA, (2000)
12. Fetzer, C., Högstedt, K., Felber, P.: Automatic Detection and Masking of Non-Atomic Exception Handling. In: Proc. of DSN 2003, San Francisco, USA, (2003) 445-454
13. Garlan, D., Allen, R., Ockerbloom, J.: Architectural Mismatch: Why Reuse is so Hard. IEEE Software, Vol. 12(6), (1995) 17-26

14. Guerra P. et. al.: A Dependable Architecture for COTS-based Software Systems using Protective Wrappers. Lecture Notes in Computer Science (LNCS), Vol. 3069, Spring Verlag, (2004) 147-170
15. Hsueh, Mei-Chen, Tsai, Timothy, Iyer, Ravishankar.: Fault Injection Techniques and Tools. IEEE Computer, (1997) 75-82
16. Inverardi, P., Wolf, A.L., Yankelevich, D.: Checking Assumptions in Component Dynamics at the Architectural Level. In: Proc. of the 2nd International Conference on Coordination Models and Languages, Springer-Verlag, (1997)
17. Koopman, P., Siewiorek, D, DeVale, K., DeVale, J., Fernsler, K., Guttendorf, D., Kropp, N., Pan, J., Shelton, C., Shi, Y.: Ballista Project : COTS Software Robustness Testing. Carnegie Mellon University, http://www.ece.cmu.edu/~koopman/ballista/, (2003)
18. Leme, N. G. M.: A Software Fault Injection Systems based on Patterns. Master Thesis, UNICAMP, Brasil, (2001) (in Portuguese)
19. Maes, P.: Concepts and Experiments in Computational Reflection. In: Proc. of OOPSLA'87, (1987) 147-155
20. Martins, E., Rubira, C. M. F., Leme N.G.M.: Jaca: A reflective fault injection tool based on patterns. In: Proc of the 2002 International Conference on Dependable Systems & Networks, Washington D.C. USA, (2002) 483-487
21. Martins, E., Moraes, R.: Testing Component-based Applications in the Presence of Faults. In: Proc. of the 7th World Multi-conference on Systemic, Cybernetics and Informatics, (2003) 112-117
22. Moraes, R, Martins, E.: A Strategy for Validating an ODBMS Component Using a High-Level Software Fault Injection Tool. In: Proc. of the First Latin-American Symposium, LADC 2003, São Paulo, Brazil, (2003) 56-68
23. Moraes, R., Martins, E.: An Architecture-based Strategy for Interface Fault Injection. In: Proc. of the International Conference no Dependable Systems and Networks, Firenze, Italy, (2004)
24. Naumovich, G., Avrunin, G.S., Clarke, L. A., Osterweil, L.J.: Applying Static Analysis to Software Architectures. In: Proc. of the 6th European Software Engineering Conference, Springer-Verlag, (1997)
25. Pressman, R. S.: Software Engineering a Practitioner Approach. Mc Graw Hill1, 4th edition, (1997)
26. Rosa, A.: A Reflexive Architecture to Inject Faults in Object-Oriented Applications. Master Thesis, UNICAMP, Campinas, Brasil, (1998) (in Portuguese)
27. Rosenberg, L, Stapko, R, Gallo, A.: Risk-based Object Oriented Testing. In: Proc. of 13th International Software / Internet Quality Week (QW2000), San Francisco, California USA, (2000)
28. Saridakis, T., Issarny, V.: Developing Dependable Systems using Software Architecture. In: Proc. of the 1st Working IFIP Conference on Software Architecture, (1999) 83-104
29. Shaw, M., Clements, P. C.: A Field Guide to Boxology: Preliminary Classification of Architectural Styles for Software Systems. In: Proc. of the 21st International Computer Software and Applications Conference, (1997) 6-13
30. Sherer, S. A.: A Cost-Effective Approach to Testing. IEEE Software, (1991)
31. Sotirovski, D.: Towards Fault-Tolerant Software Architectures. In: R. Kazman, P. Kruchten, C. Verhoef, H. Van Vliet, editors, Working IEEE/IFIP Conference on Software Architecture, Los Alamitos, CA, (2001) 7-13
32. Stafford, J.A., Richardson, D.J., Wolf, A.L.: Chainning: A Software Architecture Dependence Analysis Technique. Technical Report CU-CS845-97, Department of Computer Science, University of Colorado, (1997)

33. Taylor, R. N., Medvidovic, N., Anderson, K.M., Whitehead Jr.E.J., Robbins, J.E., Nies, K.A., Oreizy, P., Dubrow, D.L.: A Component and Message-based Architectural Style for GUI Software. IEEE Transactions on Software Engineering, Vol. 22(6): 390-406, (1996)
34. Voas, J., McGraw, G.: Software Fault Injection: Inoculating Programs against Errors. John Wiley & Sons, New York, EUA, (1998)
35. Voas, J., Charron, F., McGraw, G., Miller, K., Friedman, M.: Predicting how Badly Good Software can Behave. IEEE Software, (1997) 73–83
36. Voas, J.: Marrying Software Fault Injection Technology Results with Software Reliability Growth Models. Fast Abstract ISSRE 2003, Chillarege Press, (2003)

Problem Structure and Dependable Architecture

Michael Jackson

Faculty of Mathematics & Computing, The Open University,
Milton Keynes MK7 6AA, England
jacksonma@acm.org
http://mcs.open.ac.uk/mj665

Abstract. An approach to software development is sketched in which problem structuring is separated from software architecture. The problem is decomposed into subproblems of familiar classes that can be considered in isolation; then the interactions among the subproblems are considered. The architectural task is seen as the task of composing the software machines associated with each subproblem and with the more complex interactions among them. It is suggested that such an approach embodies a good separation of concerns that can contribute to achieving system dependability.

1 Introduction

Software architecture, according to Shaw and Garlan [9] is concerned with "... the organization of a system as a composition of components; global control structures; the protocols for communication, synchronization and data access; the assignment of functionality to design elements; the composition of design elements; physical distribution; scaling and performance; dimensions of evolution; and selection among design alternatives." We may ask how these concerns impinge on system dependability, and—if they do—how to address them in a way that will improve dependability.

An obvious analogy is with the dependability of engineered physical structures. Many notorious engineering failures can be traced to structural design faults. A structure that has been incorrectly designed to carry the imposed loads will fail in use. The careful investigation that follows a failure reveals the design error; popularising books on engineering [7, 2, 5] provide lucid explanations for lay readers. But it is far from clear that the analogy is sound. Software is not itself a physical product, and the forces imposed on it are, for the most part, not usefully quantifiable like the forces on a beam or a truss. There are, of course, aspects of some systems where numerical calculations of bandwidth, network traffic, response times, or computational complexity are critical to successful design. But for most aspects of the broad range of systems this is not so.

Another important difference is that software is extremely malleable. Software for a digital computer evokes a computation describable by a state machine: the transitions of this machine can be grouped and configured in many different ways without affecting the evoked computation. Presenting two candidate modularisations of the KWIC problem [6], Parnas wrote:

"The systems are substantially different even if identical in the runnable representation. This is possible because the runnable representation need only be used for running; other representations are used for changing, documenting, understanding, etc. The two systems will not be identical in those other representations."

The 'runnable representation' is only one of several architectures of a system. Other representations—and hence other architectures—are largely concerned with human understanding. They embody attempts to master the complexity of a real-world problem and of the software that must lie at the core of its solution, and to ensure that all important concerns are adequately addressed. The goal for the software architect is to avoid certain classes of system failure. Not all failures can be avoided by software structure aimed at mastering complexity: examples of those that can not include failures arising from poorly designed human interfaces, configuration errors, unreliable hardware, slow response, inadequate throughput, and from many other causes. But one important class that can be so addressed is functional failure, in which the observable behaviour of the system is not what was intended or desired. In this class we include failures to meet requirements of safety and reliability, and also failures to repair or conceal or mitigate a malfunction where such response to the malfunction is, or should be, a functional requirement of the system.

2   A View of Software Development

The principal parts[1] of a software development problem are:

- the *problem world*, where the problem is located: for a lift control system this is the users, floors served, lift car and shaft, doors, request buttons, winding gear, indicator lights, floor sensors, and so on;
- the *requirement*, which is the behaviour to be established and maintained in the problem world: for example, that the doors open only when the lift car is at a floor, and that the lift comes when summoned and goes to the requested floor;
- the *machine*, which is the hardware-plus-software computer to be designed and installed in the problem world and connected to it by the *machine interface*: for the lift system this interface would be the port connections to the motor control, button sensors, indicator lights, floor sensors, and so on.

The goal of the development is to devise, specify and build a machine that will guarantee satisfaction of the requirement by exploiting and respecting the given properties of the problem world. In the lift control problem these are the physical properties that cause the lift car to rise when the motor is set *on* and *up*, the floor sensor to close when the lift car arrives at the floor, and so on.

Because the requirement and the problem world are complex, the development can fail in many ways. The requirement may have been misunderstood; the given properties of the problem world may have been misunderstood; the machine that is built may not satisfy its specification; the specification may be faulty—not guaranteeing satisfaction of the requirement even if the requirement and the problem world properties have been correctly understood and represented. It is a principal goal

---

[1] 'Principal parts' is a term taken from [8].

3 Architecture and Decomposition

The key to mastering complexity is the separation of concerns, but we must clarify what this means for software development. Architecture is concerned with structuring the machine by organising it "as a composition of components" and with "the assignment of functionality to design elements". This demands a structuring of functionality. The problem must be structured into *subproblems*, whose solutions can eventually be assigned to software components. This structuring into subproblems is primarily a decomposition of the problem requirement. Each subproblem has its own requirement and its own problem world, which is a projection of the problem world originally given. The problem world too demands to be structured, both to support the problem decomposition and to separate parts whose interactions will be mediated by the machine. For example, it is convenient to separate the lift car in the shaft from the buttons and lights. We will regard the problem world, then, as an assemblage of *problem domains*, but we must not expect that exactly the same structuring will be appropriate for all subproblems. As Shaw and Garlan point out, there will be a need for "the composition of design elements". In fact we can go further: there will be a need for composition of problem elements more generally, including requirements and problem domains. Composition, as we shall see, is a major development task in its own right, with its own characteristic concerns.

The structuring of requirements or functionality is rarely a concern in the established branches of engineering, where most design work is *normal*, rather than *radical*, design [10]. The engineer engaged in normal design knows the *operational principle* of the device to be designed: that is, how it works, and how its characteristic parts fulfil their special function in combining to an overall operation which achieves the purpose. The designer of a car, for example, does not spend effort in decomposing the functionality that converts fuel combustion into movement of the car. Normal design dictates a decomposition into reciprocating engine, flywheel, gearbox, cardan shaft, differential gear, half-shafts and road wheels, arranged in a standard configuration and connected by well-understood interfaces.[2]

In software, by contrast, the decomposition of functionality is very often a task of radical design [1], in which:

"... how the device should be arranged or even how it works is largely unknown. The designer has never seen such a device before and has no presumption of success. The problem is to design something that will function well enough to warrant further development."

A developer confronted by a genuinely radical design task can do little but resort to general principles and broadly formulated methods or design disciplines. They are, of course, a very inferior substitute for an established normal design practice specialised to the problem in hand.

---

[2] Where there are choices—for example, between front-wheel and rear-wheel drive—the designer must choose from a very small number of such standard configurations.

4 A Problem Decomposition Discipline

One approach to the development task [4] is to regard it initially, and primarily, as a task of problem decomposition rather than of solution design. The approach does not aim at 'seamless development': no assumption is made that the problem structure will suffice for the solution architecture. Taking the view presented earlier of the principal parts of a software problem, the developer seeks to decompose the problem into a collection of subproblems, each with its problem world, requirement, and machine.

At this stage, conceptually, each subproblem is considered in isolation, supposing all the remaining subproblems to have been solved. For example, the *service* requirement of one identified subproblem might be to provide normal lift service on the assumption that the electromechanical equipment is functioning correctly, while the *safety* requirement of another is to monitor the equipment behaviour and, if serious malfunction is detected, to apply the emergency brake and hold the motor switch off. Then in the service subproblem the problem world properties take no account of possible malfunction or of the emergency brake. In the safety subproblem the problem world properties take no account of service requests or of indicator lights; the requirement is to monitor only the lift and door movements in response to the changing motor and door control states, and to take appropriate action in the event of malfunction.

This functional decomposition is guided above all by a need to identify subproblems of known classes. The space, *a priori*, of possible decompositions is very large. By insisting, so far as possible, that the arrangement and characteristics of the principal parts of each subproblem must conform to a known pattern or *problem frame* [4], the developer aims at two related goals, both contributing directly to dependability. First, it becomes easier to grasp and communicate the decomposition itself because an appropriate vocabulary is ready to hand. Just as a developer who uses an object-oriented design pattern [3] such as *Decorator* can easily hold in mind and communicate the pattern elements and the part of the problem to which it relates, so too a developer who identifies a *WorkPieces* or an *Information Display* subproblem can do the same. Second, a known problem frame to which an identified subproblem conforms should already be, or can eventually become, the object of specialised normal design practice and knowledge. The decomposition itself is locally validated by the knowledge that the identified subproblem is soluble and that its solutions have certain properties.

If the whole requirement has been structured as a set of subproblems of known classes then the design task is radical only in the sense that it is a novel composition of normally-designed components. The radical aspect of the development is restricted to the *composition concerns* (which we discuss in a later section), and does not reach down to the individual subproblems. Being able to treat the subproblems as objects of normal design has a large positive effect on dependability. This positive effect goes well beyond the saving of development effort by the adoption of ready-made, tested, solutions. Any software-intensive system that interacts with the natural world is potentially vulnerable to that world's unbounded capacity for varied and novel behaviour. Developing a successful system depends on identifying and selecting those behaviours that are likely to prove significant, and making soundly judged decisions about the system properties needed to deal with them effectively. This selection and judgment can scarcely be achieved by working from first principles: it emerges as the fruit of long experience of the kind that is captured in a normal design.

5 The Impact of Decomposition

The kind of problem decomposition discussed here departs from current common practice. It is basically parallel rather than hierarchical. The service and the safety subproblems for the lift are parallel: neither one is a part of the other; and their solutions must run concurrently. Monitoring for equipment malfunction must continue alongside the provision of lift service in the absence of serious malfunction. Essentially, each subproblem is directly connected to the parts of the problem world that are relevant to satisfying its requirement.

This is not to say that there is no hierarchical structure anywhere in the decomposition. The practice of normal design is itself concerned with a structure of parts fulfilling a requirement, and this structure may be partly hierarchical. Normal design practice for the safety subproblem, for example, may dictate a decomposition into a monitoring subproblem and an action subproblem, and a further decomposition of the monitoring subproblem into a part that builds and maintains a model or simulacrum of the equipment and its behaviour, and another that diagnoses malfunctions from the model. Within the safety subproblem, then, there is a local hierarchical structure fitting into the larger parallel structure of the whole problem.

The basic decomposition technique achieves a simplification of the individual subproblems. The developer of the service subproblem is not concerned with the possibility of malfunction: it has been specifically excluded from consideration. Similarly the developer of the safety subproblem is not concerned with whether or how lift service is provided: the problem world to be monitored is simply one in which motor and door control states are changing spontaneously, and the states of the door and floor sensors may or may not be changing as they should in response. This separation of concerns is quite subtle, but, like many successful separations, it makes a substantial contribution to the reduction of complexity: for the safety problem the rich possibilities of scheduling lift movements in response to service requests are abstracted away, leaving only a much simpler world of spontaneous changes of motor and door control states.

Another impact of this decomposition is that the problem worlds of different subproblems intersect, but analysis and solution of the subproblems may depend on assuming different—and possibly incompatible—properties of their problem worlds. This difference may be no more than a difference in the granularity with which the behaviour of a particular problem domain is viewed; but it may be much more than that. For example, in the service problem the analysis assumes that the lift car always moves upwards when the motor state is *on* and *up*; in the safety subproblem the assumption is that it may fail to do so because of some equipment malfunction.

6 Composition Concerns

A very large part of the complexity of any realistic system lies in the interaction of subproblems. A major motivation for decomposition into distinct subproblems is to avoid the combinatorial explosion of the possible states in each subproblem. Misguided decomposition can lead to gratuitous complexity, forcing the developer to consider combinations of requirements or behaviours that a better decomposition would reveal to be orthogonal. But some of the subproblem interaction complexity is inherent in the problem.

The form of decomposition we are discussing here postpones consideration of problem interactions until the interacting subproblems have been identified and analysed. The interactions then present themselves in the form of composition concerns. If we imagine conjunctions of all the subproblems' machine behaviours, all the problem domain properties on which they depend, and all their requirements, we may ask whether these conjunctions, taken together, constitute an adequate analysis and solution of the original problem? If not, what additions and changes are necessary? To ask and answer these questions is to address the composition concerns.

One example of a composition concern is direct requirement conflict. The requirements of two subproblems may, in some circumstances, contradict each other. If a malfunction has been detected in the lift equipment at a time when a user has just pressed a button to request lift service, then the service requirement demands that the motor be switched on to move the lift car in response to the request, while the safety requirement demands that the motor be switched off. To address this concern it is necessary to give precedence to one of the conflicting requirements, and to describe their composition in a way that embodies this decision. This may, in some cases, demand the recognition of a fresh subproblem, in which the machines of the subproblems to be composed appear as problem domains and the composition rule is regarded as a fresh requirement to be satisfied by the new machine.

Another example of a composition concern is interference. If the safety subproblem has been decomposed into a part that builds and maintains a model of the lift equipment behaviour, and another part that diagnoses malfunctions by inspecting the model, then the composition must deal with the resulting interference. The model is shared data for the two subproblem parts, and a suitable granularity must be chosen for the necessary mutual exclusion.

As a third example, consider a decomposition of a lending library system in which one subproblem deals with membership, regarding book loans as atomic events, and another deals with loans, regarding membership as static. In their composition it is necessary to deal with the interactions that arise from these two simplifications. What, for example, is the required system behaviour when a two-week book loan is requested by a member whose membership is due to lapse in one week?

These composition concerns seem to arise from the simplification (oversimplification, we may honestly say) of the subproblems. But they were always present in the original problem, and the decomposition has merely placed them in a context in which they can be dealt with explicitly. In a more usual approach the composition concerns are dealt with piecemeal as they come to attention in each subproblem. This piecemeal approach has severe disadvantages. One disadvantage is the added complication of the subproblem while its basic substance is not yet well understood: this is an unwelcome distraction from the subproblem concerns in hand. Another is that the composition concern itself is then being approached from one side rather than the other, leading potentially to an asymmetry that distorts what may very well be a symmetric composition concern. Another, deeper, disadvantage is that the composition itself may well merit the status of a subproblem in its own right, but yet be denied the appropriate focused concentration of the developers' attention.

7 Architectures and Subproblem Implementations

Having addressed the decomposition, the resulting subproblems, and their subsequent composition, the development must proceed to an implementation. In the view we are taking here, this obligation focuses on designing a software structure that will accommodate all[3] of the subproblem machines—including any additional machines arising from their composition.

We may identify this design task with a central aspect of what is usually considered to constitute software architecture design. The functionality of the system, including the subproblem interactions, has been fully specified in the machines to be accommodated in the architecture. These specifications, however, are still in some respects abstract. Consider, to take a simple example, a pair of subproblem machines $M1$ and $M2$ that interact by respectively writing and reading a sequential data stream S. The granularity of the interaction has already been determined, but the interleaving of the machines, and the interfaces they present to other software components, have not. The possible implementations, exploiting the malleability of software, include:

- $M1$ and $M2$ are run as separate threads communicating by a bounded buffer S that enforces the necessary write-read exclusion;
- $M1$ and $M2$ are run sequentially in that order, communicating by a buffer S (possibly on disk) that accommodates the whole of S;
- $M2$ is implemented as a procedure invoked by $M1$, each invocation passing a record of S from $M1$ to $M2$;
- $M1$ is implemented as a procedure invoked by $M2$, each invocation passing back a record of S from $M1$ to $M2$.

Choosing an implementation from such a set of possibilities is a local choice of architectural style: there is no reason *a priori* to assume that the choice of architectural style must be global for the system. The primary concern in architectural design of this kind is clearly to accommodate the subproblem machines correctly, ensuring that their inputs are made available, their outputs sent to the appropriate destinations, their persistent data preserved, enough compute cycles provided for their execution, and so on.

Many other architectural concerns must also be addressed. One important such concern is reliability with respect to failures— for example, failures of computer hardware —that can not be addressed conveniently, or at all, except in the context of architectural design. In the problem analysis that conceptually precedes architectural design, it is a useful separation of concerns to assume that the computer executing the

---

[3] For brevity and simplicity, we are ignoring the possibility of an implementation using distributed hardware.

software for each subproblem machine is perfectly reliable: unreliability in the problem world—for example, malfunction of the lift equipment—is dealt with as a problem decomposition concern, but computer malfunction is not. It is a part of architectural design to consider the use of such techniques as triple modular redundancy to avoid system failure in the presence of computer hardware malfunction.

The possibility of failures of the software itself, due to faults in the problem analysis, subproblem machine specification, or programming, must also be addressed. In addressing requirement conflict among the composition concerns it was necessary to establish a precedence among requirements: the safety requirement was more important than the service requirement, so the safety requirement took precedence in the event of conflict. The conceptual relationship between these two requirements is clear: ideally we would like both good service and safety; but if we are ever forced to choose we will choose safety. A similar conceptual relationship holds with respect to functional dependability in the presence of software faults: ideally we would like all system functions to be fully dependable; but if we are forced to choose we would certainly prefer a system in which the safety function is more dependable than the service function. To ensure this ordering of dependability is an architectural concern. Suppose, for example, that the dependability of the requirement satisfied by our subproblem machine *M1* is more important than that of the requirement satisfied by *M2*. Then the architect must choose an implementation structure in which software failure of *M2* can not cause failure of *M1*. This consideration should probably lead the architect to exclude, for example, the tightly-coupled architectural designs in which the two components are connected by procedure call.

8 Summary

The approach roughly sketched here pays explicit attention to the problem architecture before addressing the software architecture. Subproblems of familiar classes can be solved more reliably than unfamiliar problems, because their solutions draw on the communal experience that is embodied in normal design practice. In the problem architecture subproblems of familiar classes are identified, and their composition in the problem space is then considered. The implementation and configuration of the resulting machines then becomes the central theme of the software architecture. The time ordering of development tasks implicit in this sketch can be viewed as a methodological prescription for development. But it can also be viewed more abstractly as a basis for understanding the relationship of problem structure to software architecture, or even for reverse-engineering an existing architecture to expose its structural relationship to the problem it solves.

Both in the analysis of the problem and the design of the software architecture the approach could be characterised as bottom-up rather than top-down. Subproblem composition is deferred until the subproblems have been analysed and, essentially, solved. Software architecture is deferred until the components—the subproblem machines—that are to be accommodated are well understood. Essentially this means that the requirements and problem domain properties have been analysed and a specification has been derived of the external behaviour of the machine that can guarantee satisfaction of the requirement. Much of the complexity of software development, and hence the potential for failure, springs from undesired or unforeseen interactions. By postponing composition until the parts to be composed—whether subproblem requirements or subproblem machines—are well understood, the approach aims to get a better grasp of interaction complexity and so to improve system dependability.

References

1. E W Constant; *The Origins of the Turbojet Revolution*; The Johns Hopkins University Press, Baltimore 1980.
2. Eugene S Ferguson; *Engineering and the Mind's Eye*; MIT Press, 1992.
3. Erich Gamma, Richard Helm, Ralph Johnson, and John Vlissides; *Design Patterns: Elements of Object-Oriented Software*; Addison-Wesley, 1994.
4. Michael Jackson; *Problem Analysis and Structure*; in *Engineering Theories of Software Construction*, Tony Hoare, Manfred Broy and Ralf Steinbruggen eds; Proceedings of NATO Summer School, Marktoberdorf; IOS Press, Amsterdam, Netherlands, August 2000, pp3-20.
5. Matthys Levy and Mario Salvadori; *Why Buildings Fall Down: How Structures Fail*; W W Norton and Co, 1994.
6. D L Parnas; *On the Criteria To Be Used in Decomposing Systems into Modules*; Communications of the ACM Volume 15 Number 12, pages 1053-1058, December 1972.
7. Henry Petroski; *To Engineer is Human: The Role of Failure in Successful Design;* St. Martin's Press, New York, 1985; Macmillan, London, 1986.
8. G Polya; *How To Solve It*; Princeton University Press, 2nd Edition 1957.
9. Mary Shaw and David Garlan; Software Architecture: Perspectives on an Emerging Discipline; Prentice-Hall 1996.
10. Walter G Vincenti; What Engineers Know and How They Know It: Analytical Studies from Aeronautical History; The Johns Hopkins University Press, Baltimore, paperback edition, 1993.

The Lost Art of Abstraction

Matti A. Hiltunen and Richard D. Schlichting

AT&T Labs - Research, 180 Park Avenue,
Florham Park, NJ 07932, USA
{hiltunen, rick}@research.att.com

Abstract. System abstractions such as virtual memory simplify the construction of software by hiding details of the underlying system and by providing higher-level functionality on which to build. While the value of building systems as layers or hierarchies of abstractions has long been known, the application of this principle has been uneven when it comes to using it as the basis for architecting dependable distributed systems. This paper gives an overview of issues that arise when using abstractions in this area and proposes some approaches to addressing these issues. The latter include the use of translucent abstractions that expose some of the internal workings of the abstraction implementation, customizable abstractions that allow attributes to be matched to the application requirements and execution scenario, and an intrusion-stop process abstraction that potentially provides a basis for architecting survivable systems.

1 Introduction

Abstraction in the context of computing systems means constructing a simplified model of a real-life entity (e.g., a software or hardware component) or system function by extracting the essential features while omitting unnecessary details. A good abstraction makes it easier to understand the system structure and facilitates the design and implementation of systems by providing higher-level functionality on which to build. Virtual memory is a good example of such an abstraction. It provides the easy-to-understand concept of an arbitrary size homogeneous memory segment that is made available to a program, while masking the details of implementing such a segment using physical memory and secondary storage.

The value of abstraction and the advantages of structuring systems as layers of abstractions have been known and used in different domains in computer systems for many years. For example, in the area of operating system design, the THE multiprogramming system was designed with six layers of abstraction: hardware, CPU scheduling, memory management, operator console device driver, buffering for I/O, and user programs [1]. Similarly, such a layered approach has been used in the design of communication protocols; for example, the seven layer ISO OSI model consists of physical, data link, network, transport, session, presentation, and application layers [2]. Ideally, each layer provides a useful abstraction that makes the higher layers and applications easier to construct. For example, a memory management layer provides the abstraction of virtual memory, while the network layer of the OSI model provides the abstraction of a logical communication link or connection between a sender and a receiver that may, in reality, be connected by a network path consisting of a number of different types of network links, routers, and bridges.

Using the right abstractions can similarly simplify the problem of architecting dependable systems. Abstractions that have been introduced for this purpose include failure models, which can be viewed both as an assumption about the failure behavior of the underlying platform and as an abstract virtual machine that is implemented by underlying hardware and software layers. For example, the *fail-stop processor* abstraction is a virtual processor that fails only by crashing in a detectable way [3], and that can implemented using solutions to the Byzantine Generals' problem [4]. Such an abstraction makes it easier to build dependability into higher-level applications. For example, a fault-tolerant service can be constructed on fail-stop processors using the primary-backup approach, where the backup simply becomes active when it detects the failure of the primary. Using the abstraction of *virtual synchrony* can further simplify the construction of such fault-tolerant services by allowing applications to be written as if execution of the system was synchronous [5]. Essentially, virtual synchrony guarantees that events such as message arrivals or membership changes are received in a consistent order by all the distributed components of the application.

Here, we argue not only that such abstractions are important for architecting dependable systems, but that the design of good systems abstractions is in danger of becoming a lost art. Rather than focusing exclusively on algorithms and protocols, what is needed in our view is more emphasis on developing abstractions that, like processes and virtual memory, are so natural and elegant that people soon do not even realize they are abstractions. Of course, the need to factor in dependability attributes makes the problem much more challenging and the solutions much less obvious. Therefore, we propose a number of extensions that can help simplify the process of developing good abstractions.

2 Dependability Abstractions

Architecting dependable distributed systems is very difficult and system designers must consider a number of issues. For one thing, programmers have to deal with the typical complications of concurrency, such as coordinating the use of shared data and other shared resources. Furthermore, various types of accidental faults and intentional security attacks ranging from benign ones, such as a message getting lost in the network, to more severe ones, such as a computer being taken over by a malicious intruder, may occur. Since the events may occur at arbitrary times during the execution of the software, designing the software so that it behaves correctly at all times is a significant challenge. Finally, the execution environment can be dynamic, often requiring the software to adapt its behavior; for example, response times or throughput of the underlying network may fluctuate due to congestion or changes in the load.

A number of useful services and abstractions for dependable distributed computing have evolved over the years. For example, *atomic multicast* provides a method for transmitting a message to a set of receivers atomically and in a consistent order [6,7,8]. Similarly, as mentioned above, *virtual synchrony* provides a consistent view of process group membership and consistent ordering of events among group members, thereby simplifying the problems associated with failures. A variety of *consistent time* abstractions make it easier to construct time-driven algorithms in distributed systems. Such time abstractions may be virtual (e.g., logical clocks [9]) or may be based on synchronized physical clocks [10]. Other important service abstractions include *atomic actions*, a collection of operations whose execution is indivisible despite concurrency and failures [11,12]; and *stable storage*, storage whose contents survives failures [11].

Paradigms for structuring fault-tolerant software further simplify developing applications by essentially providing patterns for implementing applications, services, or their underlying abstractions. The *replicated state machine approach* is a paradigm for building fault-tolerant services using replication [13]. A service is constructed using a collection of identical deterministic state machines, with client requests being sent to all replicas for execution using atomic ordered multicast. This approach is an example of *active replication*, where every replica executes the same operations. In the *primary/backup paradigm*, only one of the replicas actively executes client requests [14], with the state of the other backup replicas being updated periodically. This approach is an example of *passive replication*. In the *object/action paradigm*, the system is constructed of passive objects that export actions, i.e., operations, that modify the state of objects [15]. Applications of this approach to reliable computing are discussed in [16]. In all these paradigms, abstractions such as atomic multicast and membership are key components of the supporting infrastructure.

One issue that makes implementing dependability abstractions and services difficult is that they often incorporate multiple different *attributes* that characterize the guarantees, or properties, of the abstraction. For example, the atomic multicast service in [8] has the following attributes:

- *Termination*: Every message broadcast by a correct sender is delivered to all correct receivers after some known time interval.
- *Atomicity*: Every message whose broadcast is initiated by a sender is either delivered to all correct receivers or to none of them.
- *Total order*: All messages delivered from all senders are delivered in the same order at all correct receiving nodes.

Consider a distributed application built on this abstraction. The application consists of software components, here called *nodes*, executing on different computers in a distributed system. Let one node transmit a message to the others using the atomic multicast service. Due to the attributes of the service, a node receiving this message has significant information about the distributed state of the application, even independent of the message contents. For one, because of atomicity, it knows that all other correct nodes have already received or will receive the same message. Thus, if this message causes a state change at the node, it knows that this change will occur at all other nodes as well. Furthermore, because of termination, it knows that this change will occur within a known time bound. Finally, if two or more nodes send a multicast at approximately the same time, these messages will be delivered in the same order on all nodes. Therefore, the corresponding state changes occur in the same order. Note, however, that all applications do not require all of the atomic multicast attributes. For example, for some applications the order of message delivery is not important.

The attributes defined for transactions are another example of abstraction attributes. A transaction is a collection of operations that is executed as a unit despite concurrency and potential failures during the execution. Typically, transactions have the following four, so-called ACID, attributes [17]:

- *Atomicity*: Either the transaction completes or it has no effect, despite failures of some of the components involved in the transaction.
- *Consistency*: A transaction takes the database from one consistent state to another.
- *Isolation*: The intermediate states of the data manipulated by a transaction are not visible outside the transaction.
- *Durability* or *Permanence*: The effect of a transaction that has completed will not be undone by failure.

In essence, the ACID attributes guarantee that each transaction is executed on what appears to be a dedicated system with limited failures, even though in reality a number of other transactions may be executing concurrently and failures may occur. While all of the ACID attributes are useful for many applications, when database systems are used in certain specific application areas such as CAD, engineering, and artificial intelligence, some of the properties have been found to be too restrictive [18]. Similarly, subsets of the ACID properties have been found to be useful for transactions in an operating system context [19].

3 Problems and Limitations

3.1 Abstraction Failures

Abstractions provide a simplified model of an actual entity or service by hiding some details. Abstractions in dependability often hide failures or make the failures easier to deal with by simplifying the failure semantics. For example, the abstraction of stable storage ideally hides any hardware and software failures, while a fail-stop processor ensures that the only possible failure is a crash that can be reliably detected by other components in the system, the latter being a simple issue but one proven impossible in true asynchronous distributed systems [20].

It is impossible to implement an abstraction such as these that guarantees the required properties under all conditions. For example, an implementation of stable storage may use multiple independent disks to store data in a redundant fashion, but it is always possible that all of them will fail at the same time. Similarly, the implementation of fail-stop processors and similar abstractions use multiple physical processors to implement a single virtual processor, and assume that only a certain fraction of these physical processors can fail simultaneously. Therefore most, if not all, dependability abstractions are inherently probabilistic. However, the fact that an abstraction can fail does not need to be a fundamental problem as long as this possibility is factored into the overall system reliability requirement. For example, consider some service S that uses abstraction A. Let the probability of abstraction failure be $p_f(A)$ and the probability of S failing independent from A be $p_f(S)$. Now, if the reliability requirement for service S is less than $(1 - p_f(A)) * (1 - p_f(S))$, the system still satisfies its reliability requirements. The concept of *assumption coverage* [21] formalizes such reasoning about overall system dependability.

The failure of a dependability abstraction becomes especially important when high dependability is needed in applications beyond life-critical systems where it is economically feasible to build in enough redundancy that such failures are rare. Nowadays, with increased reliance on computer systems throughout society, dependability becomes an important issue even for embedded systems at homes and offices. In such domains, it is not economically feasible to use massive redundancy and as a result, the likelihood that the resulting service abstractions may fail becomes an issue. This implies that the higher-level system must now be designed to be aware of, and deal with, the possibility of abstraction failure.

Note that abstraction failure is not only relevant for dependability abstractions, but also for traditional system abstractions such as virtual memory. As applications grow larger and operate on larger data sets, they can exhaust even the secondary storage assigned as the backing store for virtual memory. Also, even if the memory is not exhausted, its response time may become unacceptably slow if a large part of the virtual memory has to be stored on the slower secondary storage. Indeed, it has been argued that "all non-trivial abstractions, to some degree, are leaky", that is, may fail [22].

3.2 Composing Abstractions

Dependable distributed systems are architected using, in essence, a hierarchy of abstractions, including abstractions provided by the operating system (e.g., processes, virtual memory, file system) and abstractions provided by middleware layers (e.g., remote procedure call, atomic multicast, secure sockets). Therefore, it is usually necessary to compose abstractions, i.e., to use them in combination to provide the required application-level functionality. Composition of abstractions has always been problematic, however. For example, the implementations of many database systems choose to bypass the file system abstraction provided by the operating system and directly manage the physical disks instead for performance reasons. In general, the implementation of any abstraction has a performance penalty since the implementation has to do something to enhance the underlying system to implement the abstraction's attributes. This performance penalty is negligible in many cases, but some abstractions are very expensive and in some cases, even a small performance penalty may be too much for a demanding application.

Composing dependability abstractions is an even bigger issue, in part because the different dependability attributes—reliability, availability, timeliness (real time), and security—have fundamental conflicts and tradeoffs. For example, replicating data and processing for reliability and availability increases the vulnerability of the system to security attacks, since if even one of the nodes is compromised, the privacy of the data is lost. Furthermore, the implementation of reliability and security abstractions often requires extra communication (e.g., update backup) and extra processing (e.g., cryptography) that can increase the response time of the system and reduce its throughput, potentially causing timeliness requirements to be violated. Reliability techniques based on redundancy such as re-execution and replication also increase the variance in the system response time, which makes it more difficult to achieve the predictability required by real-time properties.

3.3 Unnecessary Attributes

Different distributed applications have different requirements for the abstractions they use. For example, consider building a distributed application using atomic ordered multicast. First, if the order in which the messages can be applied by the application is commutative—that is, processing messages in any order leads to the same result—the ordering property is not required. Second, if the application has no timeliness requirements, the time bound guarantee is not necessary. Finally, if the application can tolerate missing a message occasionally—as is often the case with audio and video—the atomicity and termination properties are not required either. Similar observations can be made for other abstractions such as the ACID attributes of the transaction abstraction. Unfortunately, a given atomic multicast implementation typically provides only a fixed set of guarantees, which may or may not be appropriate for the application.

One might argue that providing an implementation that satisfies all the possible attributes would also satisfy all possible applications that require this abstraction. However, this approach is not viable for two reasons. The first is the execution cost associated with each attribute. Implementing an attribute typically requires some combination of processor time, extra messages, and synchronization time, thereby slowing down the progress of the application. This cost can be large, even orders of magnitude. As an example, consider a token-based total-ordered multicast in a distributed system consisting of N computers connected by an Ethernet. Provided that the network is not congested, an unordered multicast takes $O(1)$ time, whereas an ordered multicast may take up to $O(N)$ time since the sending site has to wait for the token. As a result, if a distributed application that does not require ordering has to use this service, its response time can be severely affected.

The second reason is the tradeoff between attributes. Sometimes, particularly in the presence of failures, it may be impossible to guarantee all of an abstraction's attributes simultaneously. For example, with transactions operating on distributed replicated data in a partitioned network, it is impossible to guarantee simultaneously the progress of transactions on all sites and the consistency of the data. Furthermore, sometimes guaranteeing one property has a negative impact on another. For example, the implementation of a timeliness property typically requires anticipating the worst case and therefore, often introduces extra waiting, affecting properties such as response time. Both of these cases again illustrate the fundamental difficulties in attempting to enforce all attributes with a single all-encompassing implementation.

In addition to *which* attributes are provided by the abstraction implementation, *what level* of assurance is provided affects the suitability of an abstraction implementation for an application. For example, the reliability and availability of a service can be increased arbitrarily by increasing the level of replication. However, the higher the degree of replication, the larger the resource cost and the larger the performance overhead. Similarly, security attributes can often be made stronger by applying multiple authentication techniques or cryptographic techniques [23]. For real-time attributes, the level of assurance can be often increased by being more conservative in resource allocation decisions. All of these improvements of the dependability attribute occur at the cost of more resources and runtime overhead.

3.4 Mechanisms-Oriented Design

The development of distributed computing, in particular the networking aspects of distributed computing, has always been focused on protocols rather than the services or abstractions provided by the protocols. Protocols specify in detail the messages exchanged by communicating parties, including the types of messages and the bit-layout of the messages. The purpose of such specification is naturally to enable independent implementations of the protocol to interoperate. The details of how the service provided by the protocol is presented to the higher levels is often irrelevant and left as a local decision. Good examples are the traditional transport protocols UDP and TCP, as well as the new web services protocols including HTTP, SOAP, and other XML-based protocols.

While protocol-oriented design is not bad in and of itself, we argue that it often results in the abstraction provided by the service being ignored. A good case in point is SOAP (Simple Object Access Protocol), which was initially envisioned as an RPC-type abstraction for XML-based web service access. However, it was subsequently decided that SOAP should be a more general messaging service. The acronym for the protocol was retained, but it no longer stands for "Simple Object Access Protocol" [24]. However, it can be argued that in practice SOAP is primarily used as a remote method invocation mechanism for web services that act as distributed objects [25].

Another area in dependable distributed computing lacking good abstractions is survivability and intrusion tolerance. While some work in this area has focused on providing useful system abstractions such as the Saturne failure and intrusion tolerant storage [26], much of it focuses on mechanisms. These include, for instance, intrusion detection systems and firewalls, which do not provide explicit system abstractions on which applications or higher-level abstractions can be built. Moreover, other efforts in survivability are devoted to adopting fault-tolerance abstractions such as the Byzantine failure model and algorithms designed for this failure model to survivability. The fundamental problem here is that intrusions are not the same as failures, in particular, the common assumption of failure independence does not apply to intrusions.

4 Possible Solutions

The issues outlined above are all significant technical challenges and cannot be solved with a single all-encompassing idea or approach. Here, however, we give several ideas that we believe have the potential to address some of these issues and are examples of the type of research we believe is needed in this area.

4.1 Translucent Abstractions

A *translucent abstraction* is an abstraction that explicitly exposes useful information about the internal operation of the service implementing the abstraction. An example that illustrates the need for such functionality is when TCP is used over wireless links. On a wireless network, messages may be lost for a variety of reasons, including radio interference, message collisions, and congestion. However, TCP always interprets message loss as congestion and as a result, slows down message transmission. If the underlying MAC layer provided information about the reason for the message loss—i.e., was translucent—the TCP layer could operate more efficiently.

An example of a translucent abstraction related to dependability is an *accrual failure detector* [27]. A typical failure detector provides only binary information, that is, it just gives an indication of whether a node has failed or is operational. However, in any realistic distributed system, failure detection is unreliable and failure detectors are bound to give incorrect information at times in the form of false positives and false negatives.[1] To address this issue, an accrual failure detector does not provide binary information, but rather provides its estimate of the probability that the node has failed. For instance, at some point in time the accrual failure detector might report that node X has failed with probability 0.05, and thus, is operational with probability 0.95. While the abstraction provided by an accrual failure detector is weaker than that of a perfect failure detector with binary output, it gives different applications more flexibility in deciding when to react and how.

---

[1] Note that this problem has lead to a whole research area that characterizes failure detectors based on the properties required to solve consensus [28].

4.2 Customizable Abstractions

A *customizable abstraction* allows the attributes and their levels of assurance to be customized based on application requirements and on the characteristics of the underlying execution platform. As such, they make it possible to eliminate the problems introduced by unnecessary abstraction attributes, and also help alleviate some of the problems associated with compositionality. A customizable abstraction can be implemented using a number of approaches. A straightforward approach is to provide a family of implementations, each of which implements a different variant of the abstraction. However, implementing these variants can be very labor intensive if there are large numbers of different possible attribute combinations.

A configurable service implementation provides a solution to this problem. A configurable service is one that can be configured to provide different combinations of the service attributes without modifying the service code. A number of approaches have been proposed for constructing configurable services and protocols, including approaches based on linear (stack) composition (e.g., System V Streams [29]), class subtyping (e.g., Arjuna [30]), and protocol-specific backplanes (e.g., Adaptive [31]). Our own approach, realized in the Cactus system [32], is a two-level composition model. In this approach, a system is composed of layers of services (abstractions), where each service is internally constructed of *micro-protocols* that interact using a flexible event-driven execution model. This approach has been used to implement dependable services with customizable security [23], real-time [33], and reliability attributes [34], as well as combinations of such attributes [35].

4.3 New Abstractions for Survivability

As indicated above, we believe that survivability is an area that would benefit from the introduction of abstractions to simplify the construction of more secure and intrusion-tolerant distributed systems. Constructing systems of this type by simply combining different techniques such as firewalls, intrusion detection systems, honeypots, cryptography, and replication such as done currently typically results in a complex system that is hard to understand and with no guarantees on the level of survivability.

As an example of such an survivability abstraction, consider an *intrusion-stop process*. In a manner analogous to fail-stop processors, such a process is one that stops executing and issues a notification if it becomes compromised, e.g., through a buffer-overflow attack. This abstraction could then be used as a building block for survivable systems similarly to the use of fail-stop processors for fault-tolerant systems.

An intrusion-stop process can be implemented using system call monitoring, as described in [36]. This approach is based on, first, using compiler techniques to analyze an application executable and, second, using binary rewriting to authenticate system calls in the executable by adding a cryptographic MAC (message authentication code) to each system call that authenticates the system call number, system call location, and system call arguments, when known. The operating system then checks the MAC of each system call at runtime, enabling it to detect any attempt by a compromised program to deviate from the program's normal behavior. Note that this basic technique implements the abstraction subject to the assumption that a compromised process deviates from the normal system call behavior. While this technique provides a good starting point for implementing intrusion-stop processes, further extensions are needed to relax the assumptions about the possible attack behaviors.

5 Conclusions

Good system abstractions make it easier to architect a dependable distributed system by providing a logical hierarchy of functionality on which to build applications or other services. While the importance of such abstractions has long been known, the focus in dependability research increasingly seems to be on techniques, mechanisms, and protocols rather than on such fundamental concepts as designing elegant and efficient abstractions. Here, we outlined some issues that arise with the use of abstractions in dependable computing and proposed a number of solutions. These include translucent abstractions, which provide controlled visibility into the internal operation of the abstraction's implementation, and customizable abstractions, which allow the abstraction's attributes to be configured to match the specific requirements of the application and execution environment. We also argued that survivability is an area that generally lacks good system abstractions and proposed a new one, intrusion-stop processes.

References

1. Dijkstra, E.W.: The structure of the THE multiprogramming system. Communications of the ACM **11** (1968) 341–346
2. Day, J., Zimmermann, H.: The OSI reference model. In: Proceedings of the IEEE. Volume 71. (1983) 1334–1340
3. Schlichting, R., Schneider, F.: Fail-stop processors: An approach to designing fault tolerant computing systems. ACM Transactions on Computer Systems **1** (1983) 222–238
4. Schneider, F.: Byzantine generals in action: Implementing fail-stop processors. ACM Transactions on Computer Systems **2** (1984) 145–154
5. Birman, K., Joseph, T.: Exploiting virtual synchrony in distributed systems. In: Proceedings of the 11th ACM Symposium on Operating System Principles, Austin, TX (1987) 123–138
6. Chang, J., Maxemchuk, N.: Reliable broadcast protocols. ACM Transactions on Computer Systems **2** (1984) 251–273
7. Cheriton, D., Zwaenepoel, W.: Distributed process groups in the V kernel. ACM Transactions on Computer Systems **2** (1985) 77–107
8. Cristian, F., Aghili, H., Strong, R., Dolev, D.: Atomic broadcast: From simple message diffusion to Byzantine agreement. In: Proceedings of the 15th Symposium on Fault-Tolerant Computing, Ann Arbor, MI (1985) 200–206
9. Lamport, L.: Time, clocks, and the ordering of events in a distributed system. Communications of ACM **21** (1978) 558–565

10. Kopetz, H., Ochsenreiter, W.: Clock synchronization in distributed, real-time systems. IEEE Transactions on Computers **C-36** (1987) 933–940
11. Lampson, B.: Atomic transactions. In: Distributed Systems—Architecture and Implementation. Springer-Verlag, Berlin (1981) 246–265
12. Liskov, B.: The Argus language and system. In Paul, M., Siegert, H., eds.: Distributed Systems: Methods and Tools for Specification, Lecture Notes in Computer Science, Volume 190. Springer-Verlag, Berlin (1985) 343–430
13. Schneider, F.: Implementing fault-tolerant services using the state machine approach: A tutorial. ACM Computing Surveys **22** (1990) 299–319
14. Alsberg, P., Day, J.: A principle for resilient sharing of distributed resources. In: Proceedings of the 2nd International Conference on Software Engineering. (1976) 562–570
15. Gray, J.: An approach to decentralized computer systems. IEEE Transactions on Software Engineering **SE-12** (1986) 684–692
16. Wheater, S.: Constructing Reliable Distributed Applications using Actions and Objects. PhD thesis, The University of Newcastle upon Tyne Computing Laboratory, Newcastle upon Tyne, England (1989)
17. Haerder, T., Reuter, A.: Principles of transaction-oriented database recovery. ACM Computing Surveys **15** (1983) 287–317
18. Batory, D., Barnett, J., Garza, J., Smith, K., Tsukuda, K., Twichell, B., Wise, T.: GENESIS: An extensible database management system. IEEE Transactions on Software Engineering **SE-14** (1988) 1711–1729
19. Satyanarayanan, M., Mashburn, H., Kumar, P., Steere, D., Kistler, J.: Lightweight recoverable virtual memory. ACM Transactions on Computer Systems **12** (1994) 33–57
20. Fischer, M., Lynch, N., Paterson, M.: Impossibility of distributed consensus with one faulty process. Journal of the ACM **32** (1985) 374–382
21. Powell, D.: Failure mode assumptions and assumption coverage. In: Proceedings of the 22nd IEEE Symposium on Fault-Tolerant Computing. (1992) 386–395
22. Spolsky, J.: Joel on Software. Apress (2004)
23. Hiltunen, M., Schlichting, R., Ugarte, C.: Building survivable services using redundancy and adaptation. IEEE Transactions on Computers **52** (2003) 181–194
24. Vogels, W.: Web services are not distributed objects. IEEE Internet Computing **7** (2003) 59–66
25. Birman, K.: Like it or not, web services are distributed objects. Communications of the ACM **47** (2004) 60–62
26. Deswarte, Y., Fabre, J.C., Fray, J.M., Powell, D., Ranea, P.G.: Saturne: A distributed computing system which tolerates faults and intrusions. In: Proceedings of the Workshop on Future Trends of Distributed Computing Systems in the 1990's, Hong Kong (1988) 329–338
27. Hayashibara, N., Defago, X., Yared, R., Katayama, T.: The φ accrual failure detector. In: Proceedings of the 23rd IEEE International Symposium on Reliable Distributed Systems. (2004) 66–78
28. Chandra, T., Toueg, S.: Unreliable failure detectors for reliable distributed systems. Journal of the ACM **43** (1996) 225–267
29. Ritchie, D.M.: A stream input-output system. AT&T Bell Laboratories Technical Journal **63** (1984) 311–324
30. Shrivastava, S., Dixon, G., Parrington, G.: An overview of the Arjuna distributed programming system. IEEE Software **8** (1991) 66–73

31. Schmidt, D., Box, D., Suda, T.: ADAPTIVE: A dynamically assembled protocol transformation, integration, and evaluation environment. Concurrency: Practice and Experience **5** (1993) 269–286
32. Schlichting, R., Hiltunen, M.: The Cactus project. http://www.cs.arizona.edu/cactus/ (1999)
33. Das, R., Hiltunen, M., Schlichting, R.: Supporting configurability and real time in RTD channels. Software: Practice and Experience **31** (2001) 1183–1209
34. Hiltunen, M., Immanuel, V., Schlichting, R.: Supporting customized failure models for distributed software. Distributed Systems Engineering **6** (1999) 103–111
35. He, J., Hiltunen, M., Schlichting, R.: Customizing dependability attributes for mobile service platforms. In: Proceedings of the 2004 International Conference on Dependable Systems and Networks. (2004) 617–626
36. Rajagopalan, M., Hiltunen, M., Jim, T., Schlichting, R.: Authenticated system calls. In: Proceedings of the 2005 International Conference on Dependable Computing and Communication. (2005)

Author Index

Beckman, Nels 173

Cheng, Betty H.C. 194
Crnkovic, Ivica 257

de Lemos, Rogério 69
Dias, Marcio S. 122
Dumitraş, Tudor 212

Gaudel, Marie-Claude 59
Georgantas, Nikolaos 1
Gorbenko, Anatoliy 92
Grassi, Vincenzo 279

Hiltunen, Matti A. 331

Issarny, Valérie 1

Jackson, Michael 322

Kharchenko, Vyacheslav 92

Larsson, Magnus 257

Majzik, István 148
Malek, Sam 173
Martins, Eliane 300
McKinley, Philip K. 194

Medvidovic, Nenad 173
Mikic-Rakic, Marija 173
Mokhtar, Sonia Ben 1
Molina-Jimenez, Carlos 36
Moraes, Regina Lúcia de Oliveira 300

Narasimhan, Priya 212

Pintér, Gergely 148
Popov, Peter 92
Preiss, Otto 257
Pruyne, Jim 36

Richardson, Debra J. 122
Romanovsky, Alexander 92

Schlichting, Richard D. 331
Sowell, J.H. 232
Srivastava, Deepti 212
Stirewalt, R.E.K. 232

Tartanoglu, Ferda 1

van Moorsel, Aad 36

Yang, Zhenxiao 194

Zhang, Ji 194

Lecture Notes in Computer Science

For information about Vols. 1–3608

please contact your bookseller or Springer

Vol. 3728: V. Paliouras, J. Vounckx, D. Verkest (Eds.), Integrated Circuit and System Design. XV, 753 pages. 2005.

Vol. 3718: V.G. Ganzha, E.W. Mayr, E.V. Vorozhtsov (Eds.), Computer Algebra in Scientific Computing. XII, ? pages. 2005.

Vol. 3714: H. Obbink, K. Pohl (Eds.), Software Product Lines. XIII, 235 pages. 2005.

Vol. 3712: R. Reussner, J. Mayer, J.A. Stafford, S. Overhage, S. Becker, P.J. Schroeder (Eds.), Quality of Software Architectures and Software Quality. XIII, 289 pages. 2005.

Vol. 3711: F. Kishino, Y. Kitamura, H. Kato, N. Nagata (Eds.), Entertainment Computing - ICEC 2005. XXIV, ? pages. 2005.

Vol. 3710: M. Barni, I. Cox, T. Kalker, H.J. Kim (Eds.), Digital Watermarking. XII, 485 pages. 2005.

Vol. 3708: J. Blanc-Talon, W. Philips, D. Popescu, P. Scheunders (Eds.), Advanced Concepts for Intelligent Vision Systems. XXII, 725 pages. 2005.

Vol. 3703: F. Fages, S. Soliman (Eds.), Principles and Practice of Semantic Web Reasoning. VIII, 163 pages. 2005.

Vol. 3702: B. Beckert (Ed.), Automated Reasoning with Analytic Tableaux and Related Methods. XIII, 343 pages. 2005. (Subseries LNAI).

Vol. 3699: C.S. Calude, M.J. Dinneen, G. Paun, M.J. Pérez-Jiménez, G. Rozenberg (Eds.), Unconventional Computation. XI, 267 pages. 2005.

Vol. 3698: U. Furbach (Ed.), KI 2005: Advances in Artificial Intelligence. XIII, 409 pages. 2005. (Subseries LNAI).

Vol. 3697: W. Duch, J. Kacprzyk, E. Oja, S. Zadrożny (Eds.), Artificial Neural Networks: Formal Models and Their Applications – ICANN 2005, Part II. XXXII, 1045 pages. 2005.

Vol. 3696: W. Duch, J. Kacprzyk, E. Oja, S. Zadrożny (Eds.), Artificial Neural Networks: Biological Inspirations – ICANN 2005, Part I. XXXI, 703 pages. 2005.

Vol. 3693: A.G. Cohn, D.M. Mark (Eds.), Spatial Information Theory. XII, 493 pages. 2005.

Vol. 3691: A. Gagalowicz, W. Philips (Eds.), Computer Analysis of Images and Patterns. XIX, 865 pages. 2005.

Vol. 3690: M. Pěchouček, P. Petta, L.Z. Varga (Eds.), Multi-Agent Systems and Applications IV. XVII, 667 pages. 2005. (Subseries LNAI).

Vol. 3687: S. Singh, M. Singh, C. Apte, P. Perner (Eds.), Pattern Recognition and Image Analysis, Part II. XXV, ? pages. 2005.

Vol. 3686: S. Singh, M. Singh, C. Apte, P. Perner (Eds.), Pattern Recognition and Data Mining, Part I. XXVI, 689 pages. 2005.

Vol. 3684: R. Khosla, R.J. Howlett, L.C. Jain (Eds.), Knowledge-Based Intelligent Information and Engineering Systems, Part IV. LXXIX, 933 pages. 2005. (Subseries LNAI).

Vol. 3683: R. Khosla, R.J. Howlett, L.C. Jain (Eds.), Knowledge-Based Intelligent Information and Engineering Systems, Part III. LXXX, 1397 pages. 2005. (Subseries LNAI).

Vol. 3682: R. Khosla, R.J. Howlett, L.C. Jain (Eds.), Knowledge-Based Intelligent Information and Engineering Systems, Part II. LXXIX, 1371 pages. 2005. (Subseries LNAI).

Vol. 3681: R. Khosla, R.J. Howlett, L.C. Jain (Eds.), Knowledge-Based Intelligent Information and Engineering Systems, Part I. LXXX, 1319 pages. 2005. (Subseries LNAI).

Vol. 3679: S.d.C. di Vimercati, P. Syverson, D. Gollmann (Eds.), Computer Security – ESORICS 2005. XI, 509 pages. 2005.

Vol. 3678: A. McLysaght, D.H. Huson (Eds.), Comparative Genomics. VIII, 167 pages. 2005. (Subseries LNBI).

Vol. 3677: J. Dittmann, S. Katzenbeisser, A. Uhl (Eds.), Communications and Multimedia Security. XIII, 360 pages. 2005.

Vol. 3675: Y. Luo (Ed.), Cooperative Design, Visualization, and Engineering. XI, 264 pages. 2005.

Vol. 3674: W. Jonker, M. Petković (Eds.), Secure Data Management. X, 241 pages. 2005.

Vol. 3672: C. Hankin, I. Siveroni (Eds.), Static Analysis. X, 369 pages. 2005.

Vol. 3671: S. Bressan, S. Ceri, E. Hunt, Z.G. Ives, Z. Bellahsène, M. Rys, R. Unland (Eds.), Database and XML Technologies. X, 239 pages. 2005.

Vol. 3670: M. Bravetti, L. Kloul, G. Zavattaro (Eds.), Formal Techniques for Computer Systems and Business Processes. XIII, 349 pages. 2005.

Vol. 3666: B.D. Martino, D. Kranzlmüller, J. Dongarra (Eds.), Recent Advances in Parallel Virtual Machine and Message Passing Interface. XVII, 546 pages. 2005.

Vol. 3665: K. S. Candan, A. Celentano (Eds.), Advances in Multimedia Information Systems. X, 221 pages. 2005.

Vol. 3664: C. Türker, M. Agosti, H.-J. Schek (Eds.), Peer-to-Peer, Grid, and Service-Orientation in Digital Library Architectures. X, 261 pages. 2005.

Vol. 3663: W.G. Kropatsch, R. Sablatnig, A. Hanbury (Eds.), Pattern Recognition. XIV, 512 pages. 2005.

Vol. 3662: C. Baral, G. Greco, N. Leone, G. Terracina (Eds.), Logic Programming and Nonmonotonic Reasoning. XIII, 454 pages. 2005. (Subseries LNAI).

Vol. 3661: T. Panayiotopoulos, J. Gratch, R. Aylett, D. Ballin, P. Olivier, T. Rist (Eds.), Intelligent Virtual Agents. XIII, 506 pages. 2005. (Subseries LNAI).

Vol. 3660: M. Beigl, S. Intille, J. Rekimoto, H. Tokuda (Eds.), UbiComp 2005: Ubiquitous Computing. XVII, 394 pages. 2005.

Vol. 3659: J.R. Rao, B. Sunar (Eds.), Cryptographic Hardware and Embedded Systems – CHES 2005. XIV, 458 pages. 2005.

Vol. 3658: V. Matoušek, P. Mautner, T. Pavelka (Eds.), Text, Speech and Dialogue. XV, 460 pages. 2005. (Subseries LNAI).

Vol. 3655: A. Aldini, R. Gorrieri, F. Martinelli (Eds.), Foundations of Security Analysis and Design III. VII, 273 pages. 2005.

Vol. 3654: S. Jajodia, D. Wijesekera (Eds.), Data and Applications Security XIX. X, 353 pages. 2005.

Vol. 3653: M. Abadi, L. de Alfaro (Eds.), CONCUR 2005 – Concurrency Theory. XIV, 578 pages. 2005.

Vol. 3652: A. Rauber, S. Christodoulakis, A M. Tjoa (Eds.), Research and Advanced Technology for Digital Libraries. XVIII, 545 pages. 2005.

Vol. 3650: J. Zhou, J. Lopez, R.H. Deng, F. Bao (Eds.), Information Security. XII, 516 pages. 2005.

Vol. 3649: W.M. P. van der Aalst, B. Benatallah, F. Casati, F. Curbera (Eds.), Business Process Management. XII, 472 pages. 2005.

Vol. 3648: J.C. Cunha, P.D. Medeiros (Eds.), Euro-Par 2005 Parallel Processing. XXXVI, 1299 pages. 2005.

Vol. 3646: A. F. Famili, J.N. Kok, J.M. Peña, A. Siebes, A. Feelders (Eds.), Advances in Intelligent Data Analysis VI. XIV, 522 pages. 2005.

Vol. 3645: D.-S. Huang, X.-P. Zhang, G.-B. Huang (Eds.), Advances in Intelligent Computing, Part II. XIII, 1010 pages. 2005.

Vol. 3644: D.-S. Huang, X.-P. Zhang, G.-B. Huang (Eds.), Advances in Intelligent Computing, Part I. XXVII, 1101 pages. 2005.

Vol. 3642: D. Ślezak, J. Yao, J.F. Peters, W. Ziarko, X. Hu (Eds.), Rough Sets, Fuzzy Sets, Data Mining, and Granular Computing, Part II. XXIII, 738 pages. 2005. (Subseries LNAI).

Vol. 3641: D. Ślezak, G. Wang, M. Szczuka, I. Düntsch, Y. Yao (Eds.), Rough Sets, Fuzzy Sets, Data Mining, and Granular Computing, Part I. XXIV, 742 pages. 2005. (Subseries LNAI).

Vol. 3639: P. Godefroid (Ed.), Model Checking Software. XI, 289 pages. 2005.

Vol. 3638: A. Butz, B. Fisher, A. Krüger, P. Olivier (Eds.), Smart Graphics. XI, 269 pages. 2005.

Vol. 3637: J. M. Moreno, J. Madrenas, J. Cosp (Eds.), Evolvable Systems: From Biology to Hardware. XI, 227 pages. 2005.

Vol. 3636: M.J. Blesa, C. Blum, A. Roli, M. Sampels (Eds.), Hybrid Metaheuristics. XII, 155 pages. 2005.

Vol. 3634: L. Ong (Ed.), Computer Science Logic. XI, 567 pages. 2005.

Vol. 3633: C. Bauzer Medeiros, M. Egenhofer, E. Bertino (Eds.), Advances in Spatial and Temporal Databases. XIII, 433 pages. 2005.

Vol. 3632: R. Nieuwenhuis (Ed.), Automated Deduction – CADE-20. XIII, 459 pages. 2005. (Subseries LNAI).

Vol. 3631: J. Eder, H.-M. Haav, A. Kalja, J. Penjam (Eds.), Advances in Databases and Information Systems. XIII, 393 pages. 2005.

Vol. 3630: M.S. Capcarrere, A.A. Freitas, P.J. Bentley, C.G. Johnson, J. Timmis (Eds.), Advances in Artificial Life. XIX, 949 pages. 2005. (Subseries LNAI).

Vol. 3629: J.L. Fiadeiro, N. Harman, M. Roggenbach, J. Rutten (Eds.), Algebra and Coalgebra in Computer Science. XI, 457 pages. 2005.

Vol. 3628: T. Gschwind, U. Aßmann, O. Nierstrasz (Eds.), Software Composition. X, 199 pages. 2005.

Vol. 3627: C. Jacob, M.L. Pilat, P.J. Bentley, J. Timmis (Eds.), Artificial Immune Systems. XII, 500 pages. 2005.

Vol. 3626: B. Ganter, G. Stumme, R. Wille (Eds.), Formal Concept Analysis. X, 349 pages. 2005. (Subseries LNAI).

Vol. 3625: S. Kramer, B. Pfahringer (Eds.), Inductive Logic Programming. XIII, 427 pages. 2005. (Subseries LNAI).

Vol. 3624: C. Chekuri, K. Jansen, J.D. P. Rolim, L. Trevisan (Eds.), Approximation, Randomization and Combinatorial Optimization. XI, 495 pages. 2005.

Vol. 3623: M. Liśkiewicz, R. Reischuk (Eds.), Fundamentals of Computation Theory. XV, 576 pages. 2005.

Vol. 3622: V. Vene, T. Uustalu (Eds.), Advanced Functional Programming. IX, 359 pages. 2005.

Vol. 3621: V. Shoup (Ed.), Advances in Cryptology – CRYPTO 2005. XI, 568 pages. 2005.

Vol. 3620: H. Muñoz-Avila, F. Ricci (Eds.), Case-Based Reasoning Research and Development. XV, 654 pages. 2005. (Subseries LNAI).

Vol. 3619: X. Lu, W. Zhao (Eds.), Networking and Mobile Computing. XXIV, 1299 pages. 2005.

Vol. 3618: J. Jedrzejowicz, A. Szepietowski (Eds.), Mathematical Foundations of Computer Science 2005. XVI, 814 pages. 2005.

Vol. 3617: F. Roli, S. Vitulano (Eds.), Image Analysis and Processing – ICIAP 2005. XXIV, 1219 pages. 2005.

Vol. 3615: B. Ludäscher, L. Raschid (Eds.), Data Integration in the Life Sciences. XII, 344 pages. 2005. (Subseries LNBI).

Vol. 3614: L. Wang, Y. Jin (Eds.), Fuzzy Systems and Knowledge Discovery, Part II. XLI, 1314 pages. 2005. (Subseries LNAI).

Vol. 3613: L. Wang, Y. Jin (Eds.), Fuzzy Systems and Knowledge Discovery, Part I. XLI, 1334 pages. 2005. (Subseries LNAI).

Vol. 3612: L. Wang, K. Chen, Y. S. Ong (Eds.), Advances in Natural Computation, Part III. LXI, 1326 pages. 2005.

Vol. 3611: L. Wang, K. Chen, Y. S. Ong (Eds.), Advances in Natural Computation, Part II. LXI, 1292 pages. 2005.

Vol. 3610: L. Wang, K. Chen, Y. S. Ong (Eds.), Advances in Natural Computation, Part I. LXI, 1302 pages. 2005.